Institution of Railway Operators
Operators' Handbook

IRO Operators' Handbook

Published by
Institution of Railway Operators
The Moat House
133 Newport Road
Stafford
ST16 2EZ
United Kingdom

www.railwayoperators.co.uk

First printed 2013
Second edition printed 2014
ISBN 978-1-291-73510-9
Second Edition

© Copyright Institution of Railway Operators 2014

All rights reserved. No part of this publication may be reproduced, stored in a retrieval system, or transmitted in any form or by any means, electronic, mechanical, photocopying, recording or otherwise, without the prior written permission of the publisher.

Legal status/health and safety responsibilities
While this document reflects the authors' understanding of the law at the date of publication, it is a guide to operational practice, not a legal text book. Any operator, at any level, using the document must satisfy himself from other sources that he has complied with the duties placed on him by the law.

Contents

Introduction

Message from David Franks, IRO. vii
Acknowledgements. viii
About this Handbook ix
How to use this Book. x

Section 1: UK Heavy Rail – an introduction

1.1   Role of the Operator 2
1.2   Railway Industry Structure 3
1.3   Railway Geography and Infrastructure Configuration 11
1.4   TOC/FOC and Network Rail Interface. 13

Section 2: Personal behaviours

2.1   Attributes and Behaviours. 19
2.2   Competence. 21
2.3   Personal Presentation and Values. 25
2.4   Time Management 26

Section 3: Leadership

3.1   Safe Performance 29
3.2   Leadership. 30
3.3   Ownership of Delivery. 35
3.4   Winning. 36
3.5   Managing and Motivating a Team 37
3.6   Management by Walking About 40
3.7   Decision Making and Escalation 43
3.8   Delegation. 47
3.9   Empowerment 50
3.10 Professional Judgement 51

Section 4: **Train planning**

4.1	Train Planning	56
4.2	Timetable Planning Rules, Engineering Access and Network Change	63
4.3	Timetable Development and Validation	69
4.4	Timetables - Working and Public	72
4.5	Capacity and Reliability	74
4.6	Engineering Allowances	81

Section 5: **Other longer term planning**

5.1	Organisational Design and Capability	84
5.2	Resource Planning	87
5.3	Train Crew Links and Rosters	91
5.4	Signaller Conditions and Rosters	104
5.5	Performance Planning with Industry Partners	107
5.6	Contingency Plans	110
5.7	Engineering Work Planning Management	114
5.8	Seasonal Planning and Reviewing	120
5.9	Train Connectional Policies	126

Section 6: **Running a railway**

6.1	Passenger Perspective	130
6.2	Freight Perspective	134
6.3	Role of the Operator	146
6.4	Out of Hours Visits	147
6.5	Performance Management Real Time	148
6.6	Safety Management	152
6.7	Passenger Information	156
6.8	Train Service Delivery Systems & Processes – Overview	159
6.9	Control Office; Issues and Management	165
6.10	Logs – Using Control and other Logs	174
6.11	Delay Attribution	177
6.12	Simplifiers	182
6.13	Role of First Line Operations Staff	183
6.14	Fleet and Operations Interface	189
6.15	Train Characteristics	195
6.16	Infrastructure and Operations Interface	204
6.17	Track Issues	208

6.18	Temporary Speed Restrictions and Emergency Speed Restrictions	212
6.19	Level Crossing Characteristics	215
6.20	Electrification Systems	225
6.21	Signal Engineering Issues	237
6.22	Signalling Operations	248
6.23	Train Regulation	254
6.24	Signaller Management	257
6.25	Signalbox Visits	261
6.26	Train Driving Operations	263
6.27	Train Crew Management	271
6.28	Cab Rides	274
6.29	TOC Short Term Planning	276
6.30	Station Operations	279
6.31	Train Despatch	285
6.32	Energy Management on Heavy Rail	289
6.33	Risk Management	292
6.34	Security Issues	295
6.35	Trespass, Vandalism and Disorder	299
6.36	Signals Passed At Danger	302
6.37	Cable Theft	309

Section 7: **Running a railway during disruption**

7.1	Disruption Management	321
7.2	Prioritised Planning	323
7.3	Estimates for Resuming Normal Working	332
7.4	Restricted Track Access	337
7.5	Service Recovery	339
7.6	Passenger Information During Disruption (PIDD)	345
7.7	Major Incident and Accident Management	352
7.8	Working in Degraded Mode - including Single Line Working/ Pilot Working/Temporary Block Working	354
7.9	Possession Overruns	361
7.10	Failed Trains	363
7.11	Major Track and Civil Engineering Issues - including Bridge Strikes	366
7.12	Major Signalling Failures	376
7.13	Fatalities	379
7.14	Operational Irregularities	383

Contents

Section 8: **Reviewing**

8.1	Identifying and Adopting Good Practice	392
8.2	Plan-Do -Review and Continuous Improvement	393
8.3	Targets & KPIs	394
8.4	Improvement Tools & Techniques	396
8.5	Meetings Management	397
8.6	Remits and Terms of Reference	400
8.7	Audits and Auditing	401
8.8	Processes	407
8.9	Incident and Accident Investigation	409
8.10	Root Cause Determination	414

Section 9: **Change management**

9.1	Operating Standards Management	420
9.2	Change Management	422
9.3	Managing a Small Project	426
9.4	Managing the Interface with Major Projects	428

Industry Abbreviations 435

Index 441

Introduction

Message from David Franks, IRO. vii
Acknowledgements. viii
About this Handbook ix
How to use this Book. x

Introduction

Message from David Franks

Dear Colleague

This Handbook has been written to help Operators at all levels develop and hone their skills in train operations management. It contains good practice guidance and tips for professional rail operators, primarily based on heavy rail train operations in Great Britain. As such it covers the operational issues managed by Network Rail and Train & Freight Operating Companies. Technical knowledge is not explicitly covered by this Handbook, it is assumed that users have, or are acquiring, the necessary technical skills relevant to their responsibilities.

This handbook provides an over-arching description of how to manage a wide range of operational issues. However, it does not simply establish minimum competence levels, it describes what first class operational professionalism looks like and aims to push the boundaries of expertise within railway operations. The advice in this Handbook will help you improve your knowledge of the 'art' of Operations so you can focus on the right issues. This is crucial in the drive for continuous improvement in all aspects of train service delivery.

I believe that excellent train service results will be delivered through good people who:-
- Are well trained and knowledgeable.
- Set themselves high standards and demanding goals.
- Develop and deploy robust processes that deliver a consistent approach.
- Constantly assess the results and refine the approach being taken.
- Recognise the need to work with industry partners and build relationships at all levels with them.

This Handbook will help provide you with much of the knowledge you will need to achieve these aims. However, it is not a substitute for the Rule Book and associated publications - it is a guide and thought provoker to take you, and your profession, forward.

David Franks

Institution of Railway Operators

Acknowledgements

The IRO is indebted to the wide range of original authors and subsequent reviewers who have given freely of their wide operations experience. In particular all those who have provided, reviewed or updated the vast bulk of the contents for this expanded and revised IRO edition.

Tim Balance, Trevor Banks, Danny Barrett, Leo Beyers, Andy Bottom, Mathew Bourne, Derek Brown, Martin Duff, John Dwerryhouse, David Franks, Phil Heath, Mike Hogg, Neil Kirkwood, David Langton, Tim Leighton, Terry Oliver, Richard Phillips, Ben Rule, Jonathan Scott, Tim Shoveller, David Simpson, Joe Warr, Keith Winder.

Cover photograph: Gerard Noonan – The Cumbrian Coast Line near Bransty.

Note: Every effort has been made to trace and acknowledge ownership of copyright. The publishers will be glad to hear from any copyright holders whom it has not been possible to contact.

Introduction

About this Handbook

BACKGROUND

This document was originally written as a TOC based document during 2005 by Winder Phillips Associates with extensive input from senior operators within National Express - Trains. Previously titled the Operators Manual, it was revised during 2008 and re-issued as the National Express Operators' Handbook.

In late 2010 National Express kindly ceded copyright and future upkeep of the handbook to the Institution of Railway Operators in order that it could inform a wider audience. It has since been extensively revised and expanded by a small panel of experts to also cover FOC and Network Rail perspectives and is now being made available to members of the IRO.

Further complementary modules may be issued in due course covering other discrete operations, such as London Underground and Light Rail, but IRO members will find most of the current contents universally relevant.

The Handbook provides information and advice on how to best manage railway operations. Each Section also contains practical tips that will be useful in ensuring that all aspects of train service delivery are managed in a thoroughly professional way. Where relevant each Section also references other useful documents.

AIMS

Whilst the handbook originated from the train operators in Great Britain, it now covers all aspects of heavy rail operations including Network Rail and freight activities. One of the IRO's main aims is to improve understanding of the 'whole railway', an understanding that has been substantially lost since privatisation in 1994. This Handbook is central to promoting that aim.

In everything an operator does, as critically important as it is, they need to keep in mind that it is a means to an end – the provision of a top class reliable service to the customer – be it a passenger or freight customer. When things go wrong, and they will, this need to keep customers as the end focus becomes even more critical. Whilst most customers are usually passengers, the needs of the freight customer are just as important. Section 6 includes a specific Section on freight but readers should consider the freight context of the information in all Sections.

How to use this Book

THE STYLE

The IRO intends this book to be useful to all levels of railway operator from new starters through to old hands, from those not in supervisor or managerial positions to those running railway operation businesses.

It has been created by many authors each with a different viewpoints and styles. Some have written about technical fact and others about their role as they experience it.

Therefore some sections of the book are written as if you, the reader, is sharing with the author in a one to one discussion. It may be of a process, an issue, a contingency or a detailed aspect of operations but you will in any cases sense the voice of experience of the issue!

This is a useful presumption as any one reader is quite unlikely to occupy all of the roles in one career and yet these authors' insights can still be shared.

THE STRUCTURE

This Handbook is organised by activity Sections that contain chapters dealing with specific subjects.

Where appropriate, certain Sections contain the relevant information divided by two levels. These levels usually represent the following broad job requirements:-

Level	Target Group
1	Managers who interface with Operations and/or require an awareness of key aspects
2	Operations professionals who are directly responsible for managing train service delivery

Readers should always use the cross-referenced index to ensure relevant information on related issues is also considered.

Legal status/health and safety responsibilities
While this document reflects the authors' understanding of the law at the date of publication, it is a guide to operational practice, not a legal text book. Any operator, at any level, using the document must satisfy himself from other sources that he has complied with the duties placed on him by the law.

Introduction

Where appropriate the information is also broadly separated into the three classic PDR phases:-

This division is intended to help Operators adopt a structured, systematic approach.

GETTING INVOLVED WITH THE HANDBOOK

If you disagree with any of the comments in the book or would like to see improved or further coverage on a particular section please get in touch with us at handbook@railwayoperators.co.uk.

ABBREVIATION INDEX

Found at the back of the book, this index provides a useful quick reference for those dipping in and out of the book. It will tell you what the abbreviation stands for and at least one page reference for where it is used. The following Network Rail website can also be a useful resource - www.safety.networkrail.co.uk/Services/Jargon-Buster

Section 1: **UK Heavy Rail – an introduction**

1.1   Role of the Operator 2
1.2   Railway Industry Structure 3
1.3   Railway Geography and Infrastructure Configuration 11
1.4   TOC/FOC and Network Rail Interface. 13

UK Heavy Rail – an introduction

1.1 Role of the Operator

BACKGROUND

Operators are responsible for the railway on a number of levels starting with the commercial existence of the businesses which run it, ensuring the satisfaction of their passengers and the procedural safety and efficiency of the organisation. The role of the Operator is essentially similar on any railway in the world. Regardless of the organisational structure, Operators make sure that the railway runs and that it runs safely and efficiently. Operators are responsible for ensuring that all the necessary aspects of the service come together in the best possible way.

As such, an Operator can be likened to the conductor of an orchestra – organising, leading, coordinating, encouraging and ensuring everyone involved is playing the same tune!

The aim of the Operator must be to produce a safe, efficient, punctual train service that meets customer expectations.

A good operator will lead from the front with passionate enthusiasm and be focused on delivering the published plan (timetable).

ISSUES

A simple, completely reliable railway would be relatively easy to operate. However, railway systems are rarely simple and completely reliable. Railways are usually affected by infrastructure limitations. These might include sub-optimal equipment reliability, a complex mix of customer requirements and a mix of service types such as express passenger, metro services and freight. In these circumstances high levels of performance are very dependent on the skill of Operators and the ability of Operators at all levels in all companies to work together as teams with common aims and objectives.

In Great Britain many routes are operated close to capacity, usually with a diverse mix of traffic. This, combined with the number of separate organisations involved in delivery, emphasises even further the need for skilled operators. Other railways may have different challenges but the pivotal role of the operators remains central to good delivery.

Remember that the railway primarily exists to meet the needs of its customers and stakeholders by running the timetabled service. As such the railway belongs to the Operator.

Own the railway and all aspects that influence performance

1.2 Railway Industry Structure

BACKGROUND

Railways in Great Britain have been structured and organised in many different ways. The current privatised structure introduced from 1994 replaced the former British Rail and re-introduced private companies into railway operation.

In May 2011, the McNulty report was published which is likely to lead to further changes in the industry's structure. At the time of writing, the degree and type of change is unknown but as structures and organisations change, the role of the operator, across these boundaries remains constant. This Section has not attempted to incorporate changes that arise from the McNulty report.

Following privatisation in 1994, British Rail (BR) was divided into a number of principal parts. The national rail network comprising track, signalling, bridges, tunnels, stations and depots became the responsibility of Railtrack, now Network Rail. Passenger train operations were grouped geographically and let as fixed term franchises known as Train Operating Companies (TOCs). Freight was broken up and sold to private companies known as Freight Operating Companies (FOCs). Rolling Stock was sold to three Rolling Stock Leasing companies (ROSCOs) who subsequently compete for any new rolling stock procurement.

Strategic oversight of the industry has remained with the Department for Transport (DfT) whilst regulation - including Safety - is the responsibility of the Office of Rail Regulation (ORR). Safety investigations are undertaken by the Rail Accident Investigation Branch (RAIB). In 2005 responsibility for strategic oversight of the rail industry in Scotland was devolved to the Scottish Government, with Transport Scotland (TS) undertaking the equivalent role of DfT for the Scottish railway network.

The UK rail industry has always been subject to frequent organisational changes and it is essential that operators understand the roles and responsibilities of all those companies and organisations that are crucial to both sort and long term planning and delivery.

This Section sets out the responsibilities of the key organisations and lists the main agreements/documents that provide the legal framework.

UK Heavy Rail – an introduction

NETWORK RAIL

Network Rail (NR) operates as a company limited by guarantee. This means it is effectively a private company but does not have shareholders. The governing body comprises of 'Members' drawn from the industry and the public. Network Rail is funded through a series of 5 year "Control Periods" in which outputs are set by government. Network Rail prices the delivery of these outputs and this assessment is reviewed by the Office of Rail Regulation to set an agreed cost for delivery. It is accountable to its customers and is funded through contracts with them and centrally through government. It operates under a licence issued by the Secretary of State for Transport.

Network Rail is effectively the main supplier of infrastructure to TOCs and FOCs. It:
- Maintains, operates and renews the rail network.
- Plans the future use and development of the network.
- Enhances the network in such a way that meets the reasonable requirements of its customers and funders.
- Manages performance.
- Directs service recovery.
- Co-ordinates and publishes timetables.
- Allocates capacity.
- Leads industry planning.
- Operates the major London terminal stations and certain other managed stations such as Manchester Piccadilly, Leeds and Edinburgh Waverley.

The ORR regulates Network Rail's delivery of these activities.

TRAIN OPERATING COMPANIES

The majority of passenger services in Great Britain are operated by franchised Train Operating Companies (TOCs). Private companies submit bids to the Department for Transport (Transport Scotland in Scotland) to operate passenger train franchises which have lasted typically between seven and ten years though the trend now is towards longer franchises of fifteen to twenty years.

Note: There are some subtle variations to this e.g. Transport for London and LOROL.

1.2 Railway Industry Structure

Successful bidders require a licence to operate these services. This is granted by the ORR along with the access agreements with Network Rail that are necessary to operate services on the national rail network.

There are a small number of key companies that operate most of the franchises, e.g. Stagecoach, Govia etc. These are termed "Owning Groups" within the industry. There are also a small number of open access operators who operate services that are not specified by the Department for Transport. Like franchised operators, these companies require a licence to operate from the ORR.

Rolling stock vehicles for passenger services and some freight vehicles are leased from Rolling Stock Leasing Companies (ROSCOs). A few TOCs own some of their own rolling stock but this is the exception. With the exception of most major stations, passenger stations and depots are leased by TOCs from Network Rail. TOC responsibilities include:-

- Provision of the service specified in the franchise agreement with the DfT.
- Delivery of the service to a high level of safety, performance, customer satisfaction and financial efficiency.
- Identifying opportunities for development of the service to meet customer and stakeholder aspirations.

Additionally as private companies they have a corporate responsibility to maximise return on investment for shareholders.

FREIGHT OPERATING COMPANIES

Freight Operating Companies (FOCs) are private companies which compete for business against other forms of freight transport such as road hauliers. They require a licence to operate but they are not responsible for delivering a "franchise" or government-set specification. Essentially, freight customers provide the market place in which FOCs operate.

Some freight operations are long-term and consistent in nature, for example, where there is a demand for regular paths from intermodal ports, but FOCs also need to be able to respond quickly to new short term opportunities or changing and variable demand patterns: e.g. construction materials for the Olympic Park. FOCs also play a key role in maintaining the railway infrastructure. Network Rail contracts with FOCs for delivery of materials to worksites and operation of certain types of plant e.g. railhead treatment trains.

FOCs have lease agreements for wagons, owned vehicles and very commonly, customer-owned wagons. Freight facilities are customer owned, part owned or on hundred year 'peppercorn' leases from Network Rail.

UK Heavy Rail – an introduction

FOC responsibilities include:-
- Provision of those services the customer has contracted to a clear specification and high levels of safety, performance and customer satisfaction.
- Development of traffic levels in the identified market subject to these being financially worthwhile.
- Co-ordination with other transport modes such as road and shipping to provide as slick an interface as possible for customers' traffic.
- High degree of collaboration with the rest of the rail industry in order to retain or enhance freight's place on the network, including improvements in the efficiency of the freight transit.

ROLLING STOCK COMPANIES

There are currently three main ROSCOs that lease rolling stock to TOCs and Freight companies. By rolling stock we mean here locomotives, coaches, Diesel Multiple Units, Electric Multiple Units and some freight wagons.

At privatisation each ROSCO started with a broadly similar asset base but this has now changed according to the business each has pursued. They are now owned by private equity consortia, having been sold by BR through third parties initially to the major banks before being sold on again in the last few years.

In simple terms, ROSCOs purchase rolling stock and lease this to TOCs – usually on terms that are coterminous with franchise operating periods. However, because rolling stock assets have a longer life (usually 30 years plus), the DfT does have a significant role in planning rolling stock cascades and major procurement programmes, e.g. the Mk1 replacement on the former Southern Region a few years ago and the current High Speed Train (HST) replacement programme.

The three main ROSCOs are currently trading as:
- Angel Trains.
- Porterbrook Leasing.
- Eversholt Leasing.

DEPARTMENT FOR TRANSPORT

The Department for Transport (DfT) is responsible for setting the strategy for the railways including the level of public expenditure and key outputs to be delivered including safety and performance targets. The devolved government in Wales, and regional and local funders, including Transport for London

(TfL) and Passenger Transport Executives (PTEs) also have a role in specifying and funding services in conjunction with the DfT. Transport Scotland (TS) performs the DfT role in terms of specification and funding for the Scottish rail network

OFFICE OF RAIL REGULATION

The Office of Rail Regulation is the independent safety and economic regulator for Britain's railways. The ORR Board is appointed by the Secretary of State for Transport, and has a range of legal statutory functions, vested by Parliament, and statutory duties to perform.

In particular, the ORR is the economic regulator for Network Rail, and is responsible for:-

- Determining NR's budget and work programme for each Control Period (a defined period of 5 years).
- Exercising due diligence over NR processes and procedures.
- Maintaining a current overview of NR business performance across a range of regulated activities.

The ORR also fulfils an arbitration role in inter-company disputes which cannot be resolved by the industry's own internal dispute resolution processes.

The ORR undertakes safety regulation for the whole industry. In this role it has a range of powers:

- Informal liaison.
- Improvement Notices.
- Prohibition Notices: under which an activity must be stopped until specific health or safety matters are resolved.
- Prosecution under Health and Safety legislation.

RAIL ACCIDENT INVESTIGATION BRANCH

The Rail Accident Investigation Branch (RAIB) is the independent railway accident investigation organisation for the UK. It is a branch of the DfT. It carries out investigations into accidents and incidents without apportioning blame or liability with the aim of learning lessons from what has happened. Unless a deliberate criminal act has taken place, the RAIB leads the investigation into all serious accidents. The investigations are entirely independent and focused solely on safety improvement.

UK Heavy Rail – an introduction

RAIB makes recommendations to ORR which has the role of the National Safety Authority for the rail industry in Great Britain. ORR considers the recommendations and passes them to duty holders to consider and act on as appropriate. A duty holder is generally defined as an infrastructure manager or railway undertaking, e.g. Network Rail and TOCs/FOCs.

RAIL SAFETY & STANDARDS BOARD

The Rail Safety & Standards Board (RSSB) is funded by the industry and grants from the DfT. It manages key industry standards known as Group Standards which includes the Rule Book. It collates safety management information and commissions network-wide studies and research into topical safety issues. The support and facilitation provided by the RSSB is primarily achieved through cross-industry working groups and committees.

BRITISH TRANSPORT POLICE

The British Transport Police (BTP) is the national police force for the railways. It provides a security presence throughout the network, particularly at major stations and responds to all levels of criminal activity like fare evasion, theft, and trespass and is involved in preventative actions such as Operation Drum which is aimed at tackling cable theft. Following serious accidents, BTP, ORR and the RAIB will all be involved in the investigation.

Whilst the ORR has exclusive responsibility for investigating health & safety offences on the railway, only the police can investigate other crime.

ATOC

The Association of Train Operating Companies (ATOC) is effectively a trade association of TOCs and other train operators. It was set up after privatisation in 1993 and brings together all train companies with the stated aim of "preserving and enhancing the benefits for passengers of Britain's National Rail network".

The ATOC mission is to work for passenger rail operators in serving customers and supporting a prosperous railway.

Apart from providing a collective public voice for Train Operators, ATOC also has a number of discrete activities undertaken on behalf of TOCs. These are:-

- Rail Settlement Plan

This provides a range of common; largely computer based services that enable train operators to operate a network wide ticketing retail service.

- National Rail Enquiries (NRE)

This is a main source of rail information in Britain.

NRE operates the National Rail Communication Centre at Doncaster (NRCC) and provides information via its website and dedicated contact centres. NRE services include TrainTracker and Live Departure Boards.

- Commercial Activities

These include Analysis and Planning, Distribution, Marketing, Disability and Inclusion, Fares & Retail, London & South East and Integrated Transport.

- Policy, Operations and Engineering

ATOC provides a common TOC view on key policy issues and operates two schemes Operations and Engineering that seek to address ways of improving the performance of the railway.

- Rail Staff Travel

RST looks after Rail Staff Travel on a national basis.

PASSENGER FOCUS

Passenger Focus is the independent national rail consumer watchdog, set up to protect and promote the interests of rail passengers. London TravelWatch is the official watchdog organisation representing the interests of transport users in and around the capital.

UK Heavy Rail – an introduction

KEY AGREEMENTS/DOCUMENTS

Most of the key contracts are regulated by the ORR so the parties have little freedom, if any, to negotiate the terms.

Key agreements are:-
- Franchise Agreement (between DfT or Transport Scotland and TOC).
- Track Access Agreement (between NR and TOC).
- Station Access Agreement (between NR and TOC).
- Depot Access Agreement (between NR and TOC).

Note: Separate contractual agreements exist between TOCs for use of depot and station facilities.
- Safety Certificate and Authorisation documents (developed by the TOC).
- Rolling Stock Leases/Maintenance and Operating Lease Agreement (MOLA).
- Network Code and Railway Operational Code.
- Contracts for freight carriage with customers. This includes contracts with Network Rail for carriage of engineering materials.
- Private Siding Agreements/Connectional Agreements relating to freight connections with the Network Rail railway.

Those involved in multi-party work must challenge poor delivery by suppliers or partners. Contractual provisions provide clear escalation routes in certain circumstances.

Knowledge of the key contract provisions will help operations professionals head-off sometimes erroneous or implausible excuses for non-delivery.

Understand how the key players can work together - the industry arrangements are generally aimed at incentivising and encouraging good performance.

1.3 Railway Geography and Infrastructure Configuration

BACKGROUND

Having a thorough knowledge of your patch is absolutely essential. The importance of this cannot be overstated. You need to become familiar with the rail network and gain an appreciation of time and distance. Working from diagrams and plans is fine but being able to mentally picture the area in question and relate the plans to the actual layout and geography is a crucial part of sound knowledge.

A good example of the principle involved is the relationship between the London Underground map and the actual geography of London. Understanding the network is one thing, knowing how it relates to the real world gives a different perspective.

Knowing the broad configuration of the railway in your patch will assist the formulation of appropriate strategies and plans during serious non-routine perturbation. Examples of relevant configurations are signalbox signalling systems and boundaries of control, sites of Overhead Line Equipment (OHLE) feeder stations and a general knowledge of gradients. The more hands on a job is, the more knowledge will be needed daily, but good senior managers must have an excellent knowledge too – they need this to provide proper support. Incident recovery can be slowed down by suggestions or insistence on something that just cannot be done with the infrastructure available.

ISSUES

Acquiring a working knowledge of the following features is essential. Managers often have a wider span of on-call responsibility than their day job and it is therefore vital that the relevant railway geography and configuration is sufficiently understood to enable advice to be given to others key people e.g. controllers for the full range of possible incidents or events.

Essential areas of knowledge are:
- Line layout including key junctions.
- Signalling type/system and capabilities (e.g. bi-directional, existence of facing point locks, settable routes).
- Permissible speeds.
- Gauge and weight restrictions.
- Gradients, tunnels, level crossings and major bridges.

Institution of Railway Operators

UK Heavy Rail – an introduction

- Electrification type and main feeder points/neutral sections. AC/DC changeover points.
- Station specific issues (e.g. platform lengths, train despatch arrangements).
- Contingency working options (single line working, diversionary routes etc).
- Significant lineside features (including locally named sites).
- Loops and reversing facilities.
- Maintenance Depots and tanking facilities.
- NR maintenance areas and boundaries.
- Methods of working.
- Rolling stock characteristics and capability, e.g. coupling / multiple working.
- Local instructions.

Knowledge of the above aspects is an essential component of operating rules competence.

It is vital to learn your patch as soon as you have been appointed to a role or are given even intermittent "on-call" responsibilities. Do so before you are called upon to put it into practice with a significant incident. Try to undertake as much route learning as possible during your first two or three weeks in a new job.

Cab riding is often the best way to appreciate geography and track configuration, route learning videos are useful but they are rather tunnel-visioned and can be quickly out of date. Make sure you watch gradients and curves carefully - transitions are usually very gentle therefore it is often difficult to get a proper appreciation of these features, even from a cab.

Having a good set of maps for your on call area can be invaluable even in the age of satellite navigation equipment.

Do not worry about asking people to explain things you have not seen before. A little humility is a good thing where as pretending you know it all may well lead you to get caught out. Railway people will generally be very happy to explain operational aspects to you and seek your help in making things run better.

Other relevant/useful documents:-
- Sectional Appendices.
- Route Maps (as provided to Drivers).
- 'Baker' Atlas.
- 'Quail' maps.
- Signalling plans.
- Google maps.
- Aerial views from websites.
- Ordnance Survey maps.

1.4 TOC/FOC and Network Rail Interface

BACKGROUND

Collectively the TOCs/FOCs and Network Rail control all the critical activities necessary to operate and maintain a railway. As the split between the two was determined at privatisation and driven by contractual and political considerations, it is not necessarily logical in operating terms.

The Railways Act 2005 clarified certain responsibilities between TOCs and NR but this has not changed the overwhelming and fundamental business imperative to integrate effectively, and work together collaboratively and cooperatively. These issues have been further examined by the 2011 McNulty Review into railway structure and costs.

This section covers three main areas:
- General Principles
- Operating Interfaces
- Silos

TOC/FOC and NR operations managers at all levels should have a good working knowledge of all relevant activities and practices of the organisations they interface with.

UK Heavy Rail – an introduction

GENERAL PRINCIPLES

NR is currently responsible for reporting performance results to the Secretary of State at the DfT. Conformance with their licence conditions is policed by the Office for Rail Regulation (ORR).

TOCs are also responsible to the Secretary of State through the DfT for their aspects of performance, largely through the requirements of the Franchise Agreement. TOCs are also responsible to passengers and passenger representative and pressure groups for overall delivery. The role of PTEs varies, and ranges from concession authority, for example, Merseytravel/Merseyrail to a service specifier for a TOC/ DfT franchise, for example, Centro West Midlands/ London Midland. Ask for an explanation of the current local position if you operate in a PTE area. The relationship between TOCs and Transport for London (TfL) is still evolving. A concession TOC – London Overground Rail Operations Limited – LOROL operates on a different contractual basis to the franchise agreement used elsewhere on the railway.

FOCs are the truest manifestation of the privatised railway. Apart from some grants in the field of intermodal movement their revenue comes purely from customers. If the customer does not wish to use rail then the train does not run. This is an important distinction. A TOC offers a timetable and passengers elect whether to travel – the train will run whether they do or not. There is no franchising within railfreight companies are owned outright. They have contracts with their suppliers, for example, fuel, maintenance and with NR for track access (see section 6.2 titled Freight Perspective).

The contractual framework will not naturally or automatically provide for good working arrangements, they must be developed and nurtured. The key foundations for this should be based on day-to-day delivery requirements, development and delivery of performances plans, for example, Joint Performance Improvement Plans (JPIP) and the supporting review arrangements, for example, Joint Performance Review.

TOC/NR interaction is currently centred on the NR Route organisations. While some TOCs have good alignment on a TOC or Route basis, others have to deal with a patchwork of interfaces (e.g. Cross Country and freight).

FOC/NR interaction is complex. Individual freight flows very commonly operate across more than one route and handovers in planning and in day to day running must be seamless. In any type of operation where one part is geographically based (in this case NR) and one is based on flows (FOCs) there will be multiple interfaces at route/local level. The skill for the Operator is to not allow these to load in cost or reduce quality of service.

1.4 TOC/FOC and Network Rail Interface

Network Rail has been criticised for wide variation in operation amongst its Routes. It has worked to adopt a more consistent approach, removing unnecessary variance. However, local customer requirements can suffer if this is pushed too far and Network Rail Route operations teams are key in reacting responsively to these needs. Central functions remain where a national perspective is required this is critical for freight).

Accordingly, the following sections are centred on the current NR Route organisations, and, where appropriate, the Route Managing Directors or General Managers who support them.

OPERATING INTERFACES

All companies obviously have the right to determine their own organisational shape but it is necessary for Operations managers to understand the structure of interfacing organisations in order to identify any inherent weaknesses and develop ideas to address any barriers to delivery.

Without good delivery from your key interface organisation you will not deliver optimal performance. Therefore involving your opposite number and his/her team in all aspects of train service delivery is not optional, it is a pre-requisite.

There is a statutory duty for Operators to cooperate (ROGs: Railways and other Guided Transport Systems Regulations), but it is manifestly sensible to forge good relationships with those who you rely on to deliver good performance.

Consequently the best delivering areas are a product of excellent personal co-operation and understanding of targets and outputs between operators in Network Rail and TOCs/FOCs. How these operators work together to manage their interface with other Network Rail and TOC departments is vitally important. The impact of organisational boundaries on delivery must be minimised.

Exact generic mapping is not possible but clear working relationships and routine 'one-to-one' arrangements must be formed between the key people and documented. There is some overlap between 'levels' and the correct contact will be driven by the issues involved. Most of the critical meeting based interfaces will be codified in the performance meeting remits contained in the relevant JPIP arrangements. However, avoid duplication. Nothing will frustrate your colleagues more than multiple approaches from within your organisation.

Operations Managers frequently provide the most immediate interface between NR and TOCs/FOCs and act as a conduit into the respective organisations. This is illustrated in the following schematic diagram.

UK Heavy Rail – an introduction

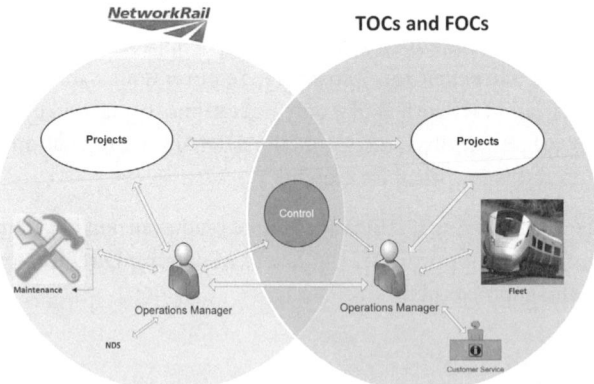

The primary focal point for day-to-day liaison and inter-working is the Control activity. Controls vary in their level of integration and a simple hierarchy is:
- Fully integrated controls. Single control manager supervising all TOC and NR staff on duty. Normally known as the Route Control Manager, in a fully integrated control this person is a clear controlling mind for the Control. At the time of writing the Anglia Integrated Control also has a single Control Manager who works jointly for NR and TOC.
- Co-located controls. TOCs and NR staff work together in the control, but with separate lines of command. There will be a senior NR Controller and a senior TOC Controller on shift.
- Separate control offices. TOC control separated from NR Route Control often by a considerable distance.

Whilst co-location is the most common current arrangement :-
- It will not be best for every operator.
- It is not essential.
- It is not always practical (multiple routes).
- It does not bring integration organically.
- It does not automatically remove duplication.

Operations Managers and their teams must ensure that whatever the location of Control the working arrangements and processes are properly co-ordinated. This will require co-ordinated and documented procedures that are incorporated into the competence requirements for the respective Control Office personnel. Duplication of effort and "man-marking" should be eliminated where possible to aid efficiency.

Operators must build a good working relationship with their opposite numbers responsible for delivery, structured around the Control arrangements and the performance management systems and processes enshrined in the JPIP.

1.4 TOC/FOC and Network Rail Interface

SILOS

Functional and departmental boundaries are key interfaces to manage, both in Network Rail and in TOCs/FOCs. Whilst they are useful in terms of managing different work disciplines they can create difficulty in communications in a broader, whole industry perspective. The term 'silo' refers to this negative consequence of functional organisations.

The separation between maintenance and operations in Network Rail caused problems which were addressed by a reorganisation in 2011 to introduce Route Managing Directors (RMDs) but there are similar difficult interfaces within TOCs, for example between operations and customer service which can cause problems with responsibility for passenger information and the use of station staff on operational duties.

Engineers work in separate departments or functions whether they are Network Rail track or signal engineers or TOC fleet engineers.

Support your opposite number and his/her team but manage their delivery in a firm professional manner.

At relevant joint meetings (e.g. JPIP reviews) insist that other key players such as infrastructure maintenance managers and fleet engineers attend.

Make sure that interfaces are clear and duplication is avoided.

Undertake joint visits and cab rides with your opposite number whenever possible.

If it goes wrong, phone your contact. If the response is not adequate or the problem is persistent formalise the concern in writing. If the issue is not resolved then escalate it.

Similarly, if flaws in your key interface organisation cause issues, gather factual evidence and escalate it within your own organisation.

Be firm, fair and professional but do not tolerate poor delivery or mediocre performance; you would not in your own organisation so you cannot from your suppliers or industry partners.

Personal Behaviours

Section 2: **Personal Behaviours**

2.1	Attributes and Behaviours.	19
2.2	Competence.	21
2.3	Personal Presentation and Values.	25
2.4	Time Management.	26

2.1 Attributes and Behaviours

BACKGROUND

An Operator must be technically proficient in the Rules & Regulations and other procedures that are relevant to their position and role. However an encyclopaedic knowledge of these does not necessarily make an individual a first class competent Operator. This requires individuals at all levels to also possess certain personal attributes and exhibit certain behaviours.

ATTRIBUTES OF A GOOD OPERATOR

A good Operator is:-
- A professional who understands the principles of safe operating.
- Passionate about delivering the service.
- Someone who lives and breathes their patch.
- Able to apply their detailed knowledge.
- Not just 'nine to five'.
- Prepared and able to lead from the front.
- Is visible on a daily basis and engages with the other people who run the railway.
- Not prepared to accept mediocrity.
- Observant with an eye for detail.
- Confident and capable when dealing with people at all levels.
- Able to make judgements and not see everything as black and white.
- Good at making decisions.
- Firm but fair.
- A sceptic who challenges fait accompli and seemingly intractable problems.
- Capable of working cross-functionally.
- Someone who understands the challenge of balancing commercial, operational, safety and financial issues in railway operating.
- Able to prioritise – good at managing time.
- Can learn from a wide variety of sources not just their own experience.

Personal Behaviours

A good Operator does not:-
- Ignore a problem/issue or something that is not quite right.
- Sit in front of a computer and manage by email.
- Ignore people or fail to challenge shortcomings at the time.
- Use the structure of the industry as an excuse for poor delivery.
- Lose sight of key aims and objectives.
- Ignore things because they happen outside office hours.

BEHAVIOURS

A good Operator will:-

- **Manage time effectively.**

All Operators have problems with this aspect of their job, but Operators need to be better disciplined than most. How can we demand punctual delivery if we cannot organise our own time well?

The need for effective meetings with clear remits is addressed in the Section covering Reviewing.

- **Probe and Enquire**

Nothing is ever quite as it seems and people can sometimes tell you what they think you want to hear, or what they would like the position to be, or what they think will get you off their back.

e.g. "The delays are minimal".

Wishing this to be the position will not make it happen.

Learn the skill of testing what has been said by replaying the issue – using different wording back to your informant.

e.g. "So what you are saying is that no trains are being delayed more than five minutes?"

Poor information is frequently the root cause of bad decisions and subsequent actions. Always try to take two points of reference and if all else fails go and look for yourself. Use your previous experience to check that information passes the common sense test.

- **Be a Pareto Expert**

According to Pareto 80% of the problems are caused by 20% of the issues.

Operators can use this almost universal fact to become sufficiently knowledgeable in all the key engineering activities and other areas that are crucial to good train service delivery.

Fleet, Track, Signalling and Electrification are the critical engineering activities (see relevant sections in this Handbook) and here too the Pareto principle is the basis of much of the advice in this Handbook.

Absolute precision is rarely required for most tactical decisions so remember – It is better to be roughly right than precisely wrong

Be proficient in Rules and Regulations and other procedures.

Get out and about to find things out.

Try to learn from your own mistakes and those of others.

Know your purpose and manage your time accordingly.

Other relevant/useful documents:-

"– I Tried To Run A Railway." G F Fiennes. Ian Allan 1967. An excellent discourse on keeping in touch with the sharp end whilst making excellent strategic decisions. Ignore the publication date of the book – it is still relevant. (The author's final post was as General Manager, BR Eastern Region.

– Fiennes on Rails. G F Fiennes. David & Charles 1986. Gerry Fiennes' autobiography which, whilst full of amusing stories, gives some valuable practical insights into man management and the trials and tribulations of railway operations generally. It has some sound advice on timetable and performance issues.

2.2 Competence

BACKGROUND

This Section provides guidance to help individual members of the IRO in this crucial aspect of their career.

Competence is a term used to denote the level of skill, knowledge and practical understanding that an individual has acquired. The fundamental point is that an individual is only competent if they have the knowledge and skill required and they are able to put their knowledge and skill into practice in the real world. Accordingly assessment measures used to assess competence are increasingly

Personal Behaviours

also testing the confidence an individual has in using this expertise.

Whilst all organisations may have slightly differing arrangements for acquiring, maintaining and demonstrating competence, all professional operators in the rail industry need to develop and manage their own competence and the competence of the people that work for them. It is important to remember that this includes general business skills and customer service skills as well as others specific to the operations role and function.

ROLE OF THE IRO

The IRO is committed to the underpinning of strong operations competence with excellent cross-industry knowledge and understanding. Rules competence (in the Rule Book, associated operating publications, and certain Group Standards) is but one part of the overall competence requirement for Operations professionals of all levels within the railway community.

The better and wider the grounding is, the more effective decision making will be. This is why this Operators' Handbook has been developed as a further resource for broadening knowledge and understanding of the key issues involved in running a safe, punctual railway. It is also why the Professional Operators Development tool was created. Read on for more detail.

CONTINUING PROFESSIONAL DEVELOPMENT

As a professional, you should ensure your skills and knowledge are up to date and relevant to your career needs. You should also be able to demonstrate continuing professional development to your employer or prospective employer and should have the ability to develop your team by promoting the same Continuous Professional Development (CPD) approach.

CPD is essentially an investment that you make in yourself. It helps you keep your skills up to date, and prepares you for greater responsibilities. CPD also includes maintaining an important evidence portfolio that demonstrates your proactive efforts to develop yourself that the IRO can certify. This will give both current and prospective employers confidence of your development.

The IRO can guide you through the basics of CPD and provide you with mentoring and networking opportunities to supplement the core requirements. It can also provide certificates of attendance for IRO events to prove that attendees are making steps to increase their professional standing through their participation.

The IRO with its industry partners has developed a competency map for railway operators called Professional Operators Development (POD).

2.2 Competence

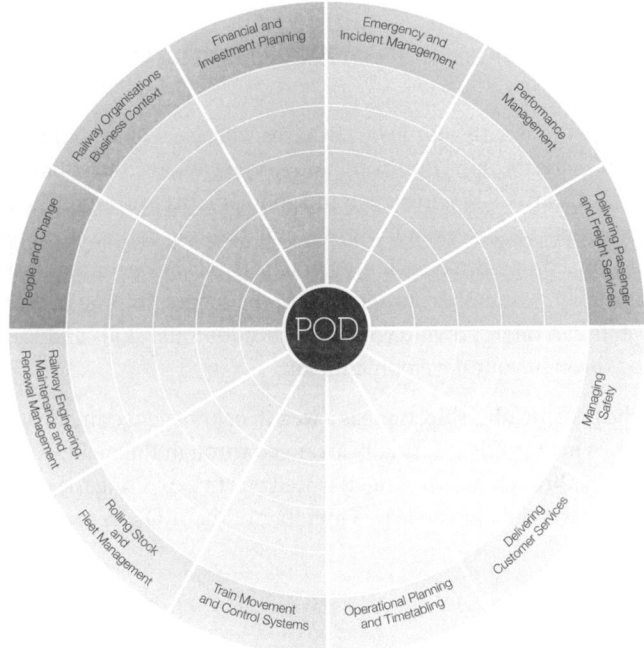

POD profiles - as at Dec 2012.

The competence map covers railway operations from the different perspectives of a business, a customer service, a safety process and a user of engineering solutions.

It is a professional competency model which is derived by operators for operators and which can add value to recruitment and development situations equally.

It is freely available to all IRO members as an online resource on www.railwayoperators.co.uk complete with a personal record of continuing professional competence which can be used both for planning and recording purposes.

IRO RESOURCES

The IRO has a network of Area Councils that hold regular meetings on subjects closely associated with the day to day operation and development of the railway. The subjects are also closely mapped to the learning outcomes of the IRO's educational modules that form the basis of accredited Certificate, Diploma and Degree programmes through Glasgow Caledonian University. Attending

Personal Behaviours

these Area Council meetings and visits will provide a useful and interesting way to progress your CPD.

Becoming involved with your local IRO area will also widen your networking circle and provide the opportunity for you to meet fellow professionals who are willing and eager to share knowledge and good practice with you. The IRO also runs occasional study weekends and specific training courses to supplement the educational programme, including practical railway operating sessions and open days to allow members to see behind the scenes. Joining in with one of these events can often provide you with the additional skills and knowledge identified through your development plan.

Within the IRO membership, there is a wealth of knowledge and experience to be shared. Whether this is formally arranged through the mentoring process or informally through networking, it is well worth exploiting the competence related benefits that being an active member of the IRO can bring.

Go to www.railwayoperators.co.uk to join the IRO. Membership is very affordable and even free at certain levels to employees of over 30 organisations including TOCs/FOCs and Network Rail.

Use the POD and our Area meeting calendars to immediately target and plan some broadening development activities.

Being competent means having the confidence to apply the knowledge and skills you have acquired.

If you take part in the CPD or mentoring events inside or outside work retain inside or outside work certificates of attendance and take brief minutes of your mentoring meeting and include it in your CPD online portfolio.

Use the IRO area events and training programmes to help in your own development and the development of your team.

The IRO is your professional organisation - use it to help develop your competence and the competence of those who work for you.

2.3 Personal Presentation and Values

PRESENTATION

Personal presentation should accord with accepted standards of appearance. You should take care to have a good personal appearance, looking professional and smart.

VALUES

These vary from company to company but typically an operational company will reflect the sort of themes bullet pointed below. Whatever the values of your employer don't see them as just a set of words on a wall or on a handbook – employees and managers will have taken care in their construction. They should be a positive thread in daily activity, a statement of purpose.

- Safe – Everywhere, Everyday, Everyone.
- Caring – For each other and our customers.
- Positive – We find solutions and deliver what we say we will.
- Responsible – We do the right things for our community and our environment.
- Connected – Working together to achieve more.

SETTING AN EXAMPLE

Good operators:
- Role model the company values to their peers and staff.
- Become actively involved in improvement activities.
- Stimulate and encourage collaboration across company and functional boundaries.

Tips

Practice what you preach, be open, honest and fair. Integrity is probably the key attribute for anyone - in a manager it is essential.

Think how you want to be thought of and present yourself accordingly.

Personal Behaviours

2.4 Time Management

BACKGROUND

Time is always in short supply and pressures on managers are always increasing. Being too busy to do what is important is a frequent problem. Time management is therefore very important.

ISSUES

There is no magic solution but there are a number of basic principles that can ease routine tasks and enable managers to make the best use of available time. This advice is not operations specific and can be applied to any line management position in the industry.

Making more effective use of time can be achieved by using proven tips and techniques. Some of these will require training. Key points are:-

- Plan your day in advance.
- Manage meetings well against clear remits (see Meetings Management, Remits & Terms of Reference).
- Learn to speed read.
- Pick up each piece of paper once (and when you do – do something with it).
- Tackle two things each day from the 'difficult' part of your 'To Do' list.
- Balance an open door policy with periods of closed door – to get on with some work.
- Allocate dedicated time slots for dealing with emails.
- Turn off your mobile for short periods when not on call.
- Make good use of your team and the wider organisation.
- Take your holidays (and don't take your Blackberry).

Remember regularly being the first to arrive and last to leave does not make you a good manager.

2.4 Time Management

Tips

There is no quick fix for improving your time management

Plan and be organised.

Follow the advice in this Handbook and recognise the need for secluded periods. Most jobs are about making improvements in addition to managing the day-to-day.

Remember - when you are continually fighting the crocodiles - the real task is to drain the swamp.

Section 3: **Leadership**

3.1	Safe Performance	29
3.2	Leadership	30
3.3	Ownership of Delivery	35
3.4	Winning	36
3.5	Managing and Motivating a Team	37
3.6	Management by Walking About	40
3.7	Decision Making and Escalation	43
3.8	Delegation	47
3.9	Empowerment	50
3.10	Professional Judgement	51

3.1 Safe Performance

BACKGROUND

A punctual railway is always safer than an un-punctual railway. There is a view that in certain circumstances passenger or freight performance and safety objectives can conflict: experience suggests this is rarely true.

The operator's objective is to deliver a punctual railway and achieving that safely is an underpinning requirement.

ISSUES

There are no circumstances in which safety requirements should be short-cut – for any reason whatever. However, if you choose the right time there is every reason to challenge potentially inappropriate or overbearing safety requirements that are not felt to be fit for purpose. Any manager can do this, and all companies have processes and mechanisms to handle such challenges. Remember that running the railway is what operators are here for. It has to be done safely, but safety is a means to an end and is not the end itself.

When mounting a challenge prepare your case well and test the proposal on a colleague – this will help you think it through and improve your presentation of the proposal.

Overall customer requirements must always be served by established operations rules and procedures. That is why we run a railway.

Individual passenger needs may not always be met, for example, during disruption - but sub-optimal situations must be managed in order to provide the best solution for the largest number of passengers. Similarly, it is obvious that some passengers will be seriously affected during contingency operation or service recovery. That is why all TOCs must have robust well thought through customer service arrangements incorporated in their service recovery plans.

Generally, if objectives conflict some of them will be found to be inappropriate and should be revised. At the heart of an operator's skill should be his/her ability to make such judgements and take the necessary corrective action.

Leadership

Tips

Safety and performance are two sides of the same coin. The best performing railways in the world are also the safest. The disciplines that produce good performance are the same as those that provide good safety standards.

Conversely, poor safety performance will generally impact adversely on operating performance, and higher levels of "Signals Passed at Danger" (SPADs), indiscipline by operating staff, safety critical fleet failures etc., are wholly incompatible with a punctual and reliable railway.

Never allow the notion of safety and performance objectives being in conflict or being incompatible to take root amongst the team you work in. If people are seeing a specific, apparent conflict in objectives organise a review.

3.2 Leadership

BACKGROUND

The success of an organisation or company will very much reflect the quality of the leadership at the top. Countries enjoy pre-eminence and can achieve major strategic change by the work of great political leaders. Unions can achieve significant advances for their membership by the efforts of good leadership such as Lew Adams for ASLEF in raising the headline salaries for drivers. Companies can increase their profitability and customer satisfaction by the leadership provided by successful chief executives.

WHAT IS LEADERSHIP?

Successful leaders increase the productive output of an organisation by getting the most from all the individuals involved, working with them to maximize their contribution to achieve a common purpose, in a consistent way. Leaders exist throughout an organisation, often managing small groups or teams.

The European Foundation for Quality Management (EFQM) definition of good leadership is also helpful. The description is as follows:

"Excellent leaders develop and facilitate the achievement of the mission and vision. They develop organisational values and systems required for sustainable success and implement these through their actions and behaviours. During periods of change they retain a constancy of purpose. Where required, such leaders are able to change the direction of the organisation and inspire others to follow."

For more on leadership choices see section 3.8 and 3.9.

VISION AND PURPOSE

Most organisations periodically spend time defining their possible future state or vision. This can be for many reasons including: to review competition and reshape their response, to take advantage of new strategic opportunities or to ensure maximum benefits are derived from forthcoming technologoical/environmental or investment possibilities. Vision statements are therefore written in a future tense and are not usually intended as anything more than inspiring 'compass' for the shareholders and the employees. This said, they can influence a company's purpose and so they are often communicated at the same time.

A purpose or mission, tend to be scaled for the immediate and mid term horizons and are created as statements in order to encourage their delivery. Organisations are often multi dimensional and are actually unlikely to have a single purpose. However, for the purposes of focusing on specific objectives and communicating them a single purpose is often developed.

Vision and purpose rely on organisations and individuals core competences in the organisation to deliver them. Just as importantly purpose requires people's commitment and capable processes to succeed.

As a team member knowing how your individual objectives relate to the purpose of your company is really important and will help in your decision making and time management as well as easing difficulties with those who seem to work for a different purpose.

As a manager scoping the purpose of a particular project or policy ensure you distil your objective with absolute clarity so that everyone can understand it.

Regularly communicate the objective and review how your purpose is effecting people in their work. Pre-exisiting job descriptions or decision making precedents will need to be dismantled or remodelled to help people adopt the new way forward.

Leadership

COMMUNICATION

A core attribute of an effective leader is being a highly effective communicator. A leader must communicate the mission or aim of the organisation or operation and how it will be achieved. The communication devices available are many and varied. Politicians use key note addresses, speeches and announcements, chief executives will use press briefings, web cam presentations, voice conference calls and local level leaders may use team briefing and conversations.

The most impressive of all methods is by role modelling.

With the wide range of media available it is easy to think that communicating within an organisation is simple. In fact it can be quite difficult to ensure that a message is clearly understood in large organisations. It is important to remember the following:

- The message must not be too complex and it needs to be written in a style which the recipient will find comfortable. Writing in tabloid style paragraphs with punchy headings might at first seem unsuited for business communications, but newspapers chose that style for a reason!

- Sending messages through a wide range of different media will strengthen the message. For maximum effect use face to face communication, emails, videos, posters etc in combination.

- When you are planning any internal communication ensure you have considered the following steps:
  - Define Communications Objectives.
  - Develop a Comprehensive Communications Strategy.
  - Establish a Communications Team.
  - Encourage Two-Way Flow of Information.
  - Identify Audiences - frequency and interval of reaching them.
  - Identify Issues and Develop Key Messages.
     (how will you create listening to your messages?)
     Phase I: What is going to happen to me individually?
     Phase II: What is going to happen to management?
     Phase III: How will the changes take place?
  - Establish Change Communications Methods and Channels (deliverers and media).

PROFESSIONAL DEVELOPMENT

Part of a leader's duty is to be mindful of the professional development of others in the short and long term. It is important to encourage employees to establish developmental goals for themselves which are supported by you with feedback and review. Equally it is a leader's duty to be honest with staff when their performance is not acceptable and needs to be improved.

The annual review is a good time to help employees identify their unique strengths and weaknesses in light of their aspirations. However, do not leave it until the following year to offer instructions and feedback. When feeding back to people on their observable use of strengths and demonstrable consequences of their weaknesses, try to keep the feedback as close to the time you observed it as possible. In some instances you might consider trading off immediate standards of performance for long term development reasons.

If the skills or knowledge under discussion is technical rather than behavioural then make use of the IRO's POD tool in discussions your team members/manager.

Look behind the person's job title. There are countless people whose current role does not reflect their career history - excellent engineers, now general managers, clerical support people who used to be supervisors or managers, before, perhaps, a career break, train drivers who would make excellent managers. Many people have ambitions which are fully in line with your needs but you cannot see this just from the role they currently occupy.

MAKING IT HAPPEN

- Identify talent in the organisation and make sure it is being used to best advantage.
- Coach and develop people to become more successful.
- Empower people, and encourage questions and a willingness to listen.
- Communicate confidence in what is achieved and challenge people to achieve more.
- Remain absolutely focused on the mission or aim but do not ignore present realities.
- Avoid the pitfalls of poor leadership by being overbearing or ruthless – identify your own leadership style and recognize the different styles and requirements of others.
- Lead from the front by building trust and respect – demonstrate good work habits and value the contribution made by your staff.

Leadership

- Be clear about unacceptable performance and require clear plans for improvement.

CONCLUSIONS

Identify the key elements of the organisation, who they serve and their core strengths.

Establish what needs to be done today to move everyone forward. This will be achieved through a combination of detailed processes and symbolic actions.

Be optimistic, confident and decisive - above all be **CLEAR**.

Tips

Conditions for success in carrying out your organisations purpose are:

- To have competence at organisation and individual levels which are relevant and underpin the purpose.
- Have capable processes to deliver consistency.
- Ensure people are well communicated with and have an appropriate amount of discussive opportunities when introducing or re-wakening the corporate purpose.

Identify a suitable role model and try to model your behaviours on traits that you admire.

Get feedback on your own personal style and make it safe for people to give you feedback. Sometimes traits you do not recognise or resent could be the negatives you should be working on so it is useful to.

When communicating purpose in an organisation make sure you plan every aspect from audience to frequency.

Get out frequently and provide active support when things go wrong.

Identify and develop people who have good potential.

Be open and take time to listen to views. Provide a real lead and practise what you preach.

3.3 Ownership of Delivery

INTRODUCTION

As stated in the introduction of this Handbook and further developed in the element covering Attributes and Behaviours – a good operator owns delivery.

ISSUES

There are many functions that contribute to the effective delivery of a train service but ultimately accountability rests with the operator.

On any one day problems such as the failure to put enough trains into service or the failure to adequately maintain track assets can have a significant impact on the service.

It will be the responsibility of operators to achieve the best outcome through:-

- Deployment of effective contingency plans to mitigate the impact.

- Rapid deployment of rescue & recovery resources to the site of any incident in order to minimise the duration of the event.

- Deployment of effective service recovery plans to restore normal working as quickly as possible.

- Close liaison with other operators to agree the optimal response.

- Encouraging other departments and suppliers to raise their game and provide what is necessary to deliver the plan.

- Ensuring that information to staff and customers is effective and timely.

- Subsequent post-incident investigation aimed at determining the root cause and solving and preventing its recurrence.

- Dealings with other functions, suppliers and partners – helping them to reach correct root cause for failures and appropriate corrective action for incidents that are their responsibility.

Each of these steps is a primary operations responsibility.

There is no place in the operators lexicon for poor performance being the suppliers' fault – the operator is responsible for service delivery performance and must take the lead in providing the best service under all circumstances.

Leadership

Tips

Leadership is a complex concept but owning delivery is the key component.

Own your service with a passion - grasp it, shake and shape it - make sure you get the best out of it at all times.

Never hold back - you will always be able to make a difference.

Lead from the front in your own job. It will be the best thing you ever do. It will also help deliver good performance.

3.4 Winning

BACKGROUND

Meeting your purpose or aims and objectives are management speak for what constitutes 'winning'. For frontline staff at all levels it is essential for them to know how their performance will be assessed and therefore what is important. The relevant aspects must be codified as objectives backed up by measures – this will define 'winning'.

ISSUES

Ensure the company aims and objectives are properly cascaded. Make sure that staff are aware of the importance of delivering the company aims and objectives and do not get distracted by other issues. Most staff will have performance targets; make sure these are complemented by departmental and individual objectives.

Check that all key operations activities are defined, measured and reviewed. This applies to all groups of staff regardless of the owning department. Examples are:-

- Measuring train despatch punctuality. At intermediate stations compare arrival and departure times. Winning is a higher percentage of on time departures than on-time arrivals.
- Departures from fleet depots and carriage sidings.

- If it is your responsibility to brief staff on the company's objectives and targets – it is important that you portray, and concentrate on, the 'winning' aspects rather than the consequences of failure. It drives positivity.

Ensure all operations pulse points have measures and the people involved know what winning is. This is a win-win approach. You will get what you want and the people involved will get a higher level of job satisfaction.

Tips

Make sure that simple clear objectives are in place, and that these are positively portrayed.

You do not need masses of KPIs/metrics, but you do need to measure the pulse points.

For frontline staff, one or two key definitions of winning should be adequate.

Define winning - unless you do, you never win.

3.5 Managing and Motivating a Team

BACKGROUND

Building and being part of a good team can be one of the positive joys of railway operating. It is also a well-known truism that effective teams generally produce the best results.

There is nothing particularly unique about operations teams or the team dynamics, but being responsible round the clock for train service delivery does introduce a certain 'A Team' camaraderie.

Operators will frequently need to manage teams who are remote from each other – e.g. signallers, drivers etc. who by definition work alone and (in the case of the former) often do not meet other colleagues or managers frequently. The dispersed nature of operations staff is a key challenge as it is not practical to get a whole 'team' in a room together, for example to deliver a brief. Accordingly operators will need to work hard to engender a team spirit amongst such groups.

Leadership

ISSUES

Managing is generally a question of personal style and preference. Similarly, different things motivate different people. Each individual will require a slightly different approach, a different emphasis, a different need, and will expect a degree of personal attention adapted to their needs.

Your ability to respond to those needs will, to a large extent, determine how well your team is motivated and how effective they are in delivering objectives. Time and energy devoted in this area will often pay back many times over, will avoid much rework, and will avoid fire fighting downstream.

Providing visible leadership and reinforcing the team through the meetings structure and away days etc. will help provide motivation.

When considering the overall health of your team it is worthwhile considering these items in turn. The following eight areas of team working are proven to give business advantage when working well. The questions are aimed at promoting the correct approach to this important aspect of management.

1. Goals, Objectives and Measures

Effective Teams know what they have to do, how they will do it and how they will measure their progress. There is no substitute for having a clear and simple plan that the team are all committed to delivering. Providing each team member with clear written extracts of their individual responsibilities is a good way of reinforcing this. Questions to think about:-

- Does the team see the importance of achieving its goals and objectives?
- Does the team know what will happen if it fails to achieve?
- Are the team informed about progress against objectives?

2. Capable Processes

Effective teams have processes which work and deliver quality every time. Questions to think about:-

- Does all of the team work to its processes?
- Does the team regularly review its processes?

3. Flexibility
In effective teams every team member is willing to be as flexible as the team requires in order to achieve its tasks. Questions to think about:-
- Is the team willing to make/accept changes?
- Are team members willing to do tasks outside of their normal roles?

4. Skills, Competence and Training
Effective teams have the skills and competence to reach their goals. Questions to think about:-
- Is the team able to develop the skills it requires?
- Do individuals share their learning with other members of their team?

5. Involvement, Contribution & Recognition
In effective teams every team member has the chance to take part in the team's successes and be valued. Questions to think about are:-
- Are individual views heard and respected by all?
- Do team members generally speak well of one another and assume the best?

6. Communication
In effective teams, all team members must know what is going on in the team and in the Company. Questions to think about:
- Does the team receive and give feedback to its members?
- Where shifts are worked is there a process for communication between them?

7. Environment
An effective team's working environment supports the needs of the team. Questions to think about:-
- Does the team have a sense of pride in its work?
- Does the team make its environment a better place to work?

8. Effective Leadership
In effective teams the role of the leader is defined and supports the needs of the team and in turn is supported by the team. Questions to think about:-
- Does the leader show that he/she values a job well done?
- Does the team support the leader when difficult circumstances arise?

Leadership

Tips

You could usefully use the eight point structure in a team meeting to find out what the team think of themselves. Ask them to rank themselves from 1-10 and discuss any areas requiring improvement.

Developing a strong team is very much about getting a balance of skills, knowledge, experience, styles and capabilities.

Occasionally take time out from running the railway to work with the team on the team's dynamics, challenges and issues. Engage a specialist resource to assist at times if this will help.

3.6 Management by Walking About

BACKGROUND

This is a colloquial description of visible leadership and describes the vital need to get out and about and talk to staff at all levels in all functions. This could include other organisation's staff such as signallers, fleet maintenance or station staff at stations managed by other operators. Make sure that you really look, see and listen – this is an invaluable part of this activity.

Managers will never obtain the best possible results if they are invisible to the staff. Some situations are more stressful than others when putting in an appearance as the boss, but as with most techniques, it gets easier with practice.

Always remember you are the boss but you are also part of a team.

ISSUES

Avoid "pigeon holes" for your walkouts – even a Safety Tour should address all the issues you alight upon. Set yourself a target to cover your entire patch (once a quarter, once a year etc).

Do not just organise your visits 9 to 5 – the railway is a 24/7 operation. It looks different at night, and it will behave differently at night. Research before you go and highlight relevant issues:-
- Worst performing trains.
- Key safety issues/risks.

3.6 Management by Walking About

- Recent customer/supplier issues.
- Audit results at that location.

Always greet staff you meet. This may sound obvious but has not always been the case. Not remembering or knowing names is an inevitable problem but "Hi there" or "How are you?" usually overcomes any problem and such an approach is infinitely better than using the wrong name. A quick talk through the shift roster with the location's boss may well be of use.

Take an interest in what people are doing and ask them about issues that are topical – you will often get a useful perspective on familiar problems/issues.

Try to get the balance between talking and listening right, you should always do more of the latter.

If you encounter a seemingly hostile atmosphere in some locations then stay longer to find out what is causing the strong feelings. When people feel passionate about something it shows they care about something. Even if it is a passionate dislike, knowing the causes will be useful.

Hold your ground on important issues if you need to even if your position is unpopular, but do empathise and show absolute willingness to engage. Do consider why something may be so unpopular.

Body language is important in this environment and in your management generally – remember that most of what people get from a conversation is not in the words themselves, but in the tone and manner in which they are spoken and your physical stance in delivering them, and then listening. Write key points down that you intend to action – doing so demonstrates that you are listening and that something may come of your involvement. Be clear about what items you will action and make sure you deliver. When staff see that you take an action and something happens as a result they will respond positively.

You will find that the time you spend out will be useful to both front line staff and yourself and the fact that you habitually make the time to do so will be widely noted and appreciated.

Use safety tours, etc. to provide a structured means of getting out. Record what you see/hear. Make sure unsatisfactory features are dealt with currently, and reported to the responsible manager.

Cab ride whenever possible and appropriate. This is a good use of travelling time. The natural situation will be a useful discussion covering a wide spectrum of issues. Remember that you are in a safety critical environment and steer clear of anything contentious. Your company will have laid down cab etiquette rule. Follow these to the letter, for instance ceasing the conversation when adverse

Leadership

signals are being encountered or when braking for a station stop.

Do not neglect the Conductor or Train Manager – a walk through the train with him or her, checking tickets and dealing with customer queries is an equally valuable and rewarding experience. Make sure that discussion about 'the job' does not get in the way of commercial duties!

Never ever stand back from a problem when out on the patch e.g. an altercation between a member of staff and a passenger/customer. Provide support and step in as necessary without undermining the natural authority of the employee.

If you commit to doing something such as resolving a problem, answering a question etc, always respond to the member of staff or customer promptly and personally, even if you have not been able to resolve the problem. Always challenge if someone is doing something wrong or incorrectly. If you are able to take the individual aside, do so.

Diary time out of the office - there is always a good reason not to go but make management by walking about part of your routine. Ensure your managers do likewise as part of their daily/weekly routine.

Tips

KPIs are useful but they will never tell you the whole story - get out there!

Learn and practice the art of listening. You have two ears and one mouth, and they should be used in those proportions.

If you do not live on the patch you will need to do more managing by walking about.

Beware of advances in technology - as useful as they are many have further squeezed the time spent on managing by walking about. If you do not get out you will lose touch.

You cannot operate a railway from behind a PC.

Other relevant/useful documents

Changing Trains V. Stewart and V. Chadwick. David and Charles 1987.

3.7 Decision Making and Escalation

BACKGROUND

Routine train service delivery decisions are normally straightforward - choices are frequently limited and invariably constrained by resources.

It is usually during major disruption or serious incidents that decision-making becomes more challenging. This can often lead to a lack of decisions, which invariably exacerbates the delays.

Decision making happens very quickly. If it were to be slowed down and watched in slow motion the following steps could nearly always be observed:
1. The problem becomes known.
2. Limiting factors to a solution are identified.
3. Potential alternatives exist and are identified.
4. These alternatives are analysed.
5. An alternative is selected.
6. A decision is implemented.
7. An evaluation system is put around that decision.

In control room situations this all needs to happen, however, it is entirely possible that Step 1 is still on going on one part of the railway whilst in a different location Step 6 is being carried out as a result of earlier problem definition.

So Control Room planning can be interactive as it can be elsewhere on the railway. Operation decision making is rarely done in an ideal environment with all the correct information at your fingertips and time to spare. So the skill is in making the best decision possible with the information, resources and time available. For example:

- Deciding on feasibility of a solution.
- Getting a fix on when you might know the extent of the problem and from where.
- Using prior experience/knowledge to determine which alternatives you have with the highest probability of success.
- Assign probability to different aspects of a solution before you commit to it. How many action steps does it rely on and how available and reliable are the communication means/processes/resources required for the step?

You will have your own style of decision making and you will also have your own level of experience or competence to bring to bear. If you are highly intuitive you will be making decisions based on years of management practice and

Leadership

experience. This is greatly helpful when command and control is required as a decisive start on an incident or other break in procedure can help everyone engage in the solution quickly and clearly. However, also be aware that as you do not do your thinking out loud (as you do not have to) there are people around you who will not be sure that you have considered options that have occurred to them and additionally you are not helping others develop their thinking (leaving your skills behind) for the day you might not be there.

If you have a "predisposed" style then you are likely to decide on a solution and not really search out all possible alternatives.

Maybe a situation seems similar enough to something else you ran successfully once and so you opt to run the same solution. Again, this is useful for those around you in the sense that they can now all get on with sorting things out. Be aware though that you may not have the best solution for the most people on the railway and afterwards it may be useful to review the alternatives you had so you can add new solutions to your list for the next time.

ISSUES

Decision-making rests on a number of key considerations:-

Have I got the authority to make the decision?
This is black and white, you either have or have not. If you do not then escalate it by talking to the person who does.

Do I understand the implications that flow from such a decision?
If you do not understand the implications, you should not make the decision but seek more data until you can.

Have I got sufficient information on which to base the decision?
You will never have all the information but what constitutes "sufficient" is a matter of judgement. You might consider how recent, comprehensive or practical your "information" is.

Have I involved the correct people in a structured decision making process?
Who needs to be involved both to agree that a course of action is correct and that it has been made using the correct information

The key advice is do not stall. You either make the decision, seek guidance or escalate the task. Getting a quick second opinion often helps, but do not use this or escalation just to avoid making a difficult decision. Sometimes another perspective will help to identify implications that you had not thought of but time spent consulting is also time delay in decision making.

3.7 Decision Making and Escalation

Operations is a structured framework and provided you operate within that framework, decisions carry less risk. Decision-making also becomes easier with practice – but you will make some wrong calls – do not be put off.

Delays can be longer than necessary if no one takes charge or is decisive enough at the appropriate time.

The following guidance is aimed at helping you make decisions in a structured way.

ALL LEVELS

Plan
- Know your authority levels and those of your people.
- Wherever possible provide frameworks within which people can make decisions.
- Ensure all your staff understand their responsibilities and have the confidence to make related decisions.
- Ensure everyone understands when it is necessary to escalate decision making and how this should be done.
- Personally commit to making decisions when they are needed - practice will increase confidence.

Do
- Make decisions according to the facts.
- Make decisions when they are required.
- Try and be consistent when making decisions.
- Involve the correct people in a structured decision making process.
- Clearly communicate your decisions and ensure they are understood.
- Ensure you record the decisions you have made (a handwritten note is fine).
- Once a decision is made stick to it but…
- …if a decision or a plan really has to be changed, do so in a considered manner. Avoid impulse.
- Escalate issues that are beyond your capabilities or authority.

Review
- Consider decision making as part of post-incident reviews.
- If you are in a management position personally review individual's performance in 1 to 1.
- Seek feedback own performance from colleagues
- Identify what decision making support can be provided (this may range from printed flow charts to decision support IT).
- If a decision was wrong, confront it and admit it.
- If a decision really had to be changed, review why the wrong one was initially made.

Leadership

Note

The Operator will frequently be the person where the buck stops. Having a trusted deputy will enable difficult decisions to be discussed and determined in a structured way. Similarly, using a colleague in another TOC or in NR as a sounding board also has benefits. A useful aspect of operations is that there are few commercial confidentialities and your peers in other companies will be only too happy to discuss issues with you. You can genuinely learn from experience (and repay this through doing the same for others).

Tips

The two main enemies of effective disruption management are poor estimates for resumption of normal working and an inability or reluctance to make clear timely decisions.

Know when decisions are needed and make them logically, carefully but expeditiously. You will get some wrong but when dealing with perturbation management that will still probably produce a better outcome than the consequences of no decision at all.

The key points are:-
- Always make decisions - not guesses.
- Involve the correct people in a structured process.
- Do not avoid making a decision just because it is difficult.
- If you are clearly unable to make a necessary decision then escalate it.
- When you have decided on a plan, stick to it.
- If circumstances change such that the plan needs to change, do so in a considered manner - if possible, avoid 'ad hocery' as this is difficult to communicate quickly and to all those who need to know
- If the decisions were wrong, be brave enough to admit it. Humility is an undervalued trait that will earn huge respect in the workplace.

Proactive learning from error is far better than blame.

3.8 Delegation

BACKGROUND

Delegation is the cornerstone of all management activity. Without delegation organisations would collapse under the weight of the supervisory/managerial task.

However, Delegation is different to Empowerment. Delegation is the structured transfer of responsibility to another person(s) – always remembering that the responsibility for the task can be delegated but the accountability rarely can.

ISSUES

Delegation must be structured and preferably be instigated by written instructions that contain details of the task being delegated and the boundaries of the delegated responsibility (i.e. a documented framework). Written remits are an invaluable means of incorporating precision into specific delegated tasks/projects.

Knowing what to delegate is important too. Sometimes you will delegate in order to get something done and at other times in order to grow the competence of another. Manage these differently and in the latter case remember it's about the person.

A key aspect of delegation is the follow up to determine that the task has been completed and the outcome/finished article is the one required.

Delegation is not difficult but delegation that gets a good result requires real effort up front. Be specific, and precise, and provide sufficient information. Ensure the delegate is aware of your continuing interest and commitment and take the informal opportunities to ask them how it is going.

Once you have delegated something do not constantly interfere with it. Delegating a project that is half way to completion is particularly difficult: it may be very difficult to disengage from something you have been heavily involved with.

Always know how you yourself are doing as a delegator. Know what your own blocks are in terms of what you will give away and what you won't and challenge yourself on this. Also ask previous delegates how you did. Did you ensure they had the skills, that they understood the task, that they were appropriately supported and not too "interfered".

Make sure that the person is capable of being delegated to in the first place. By

Leadership

definition delegation requires the delegate to be in a position to run the work so choose the appropriate level of delegation according to the diagram shown.

Levels of delegation

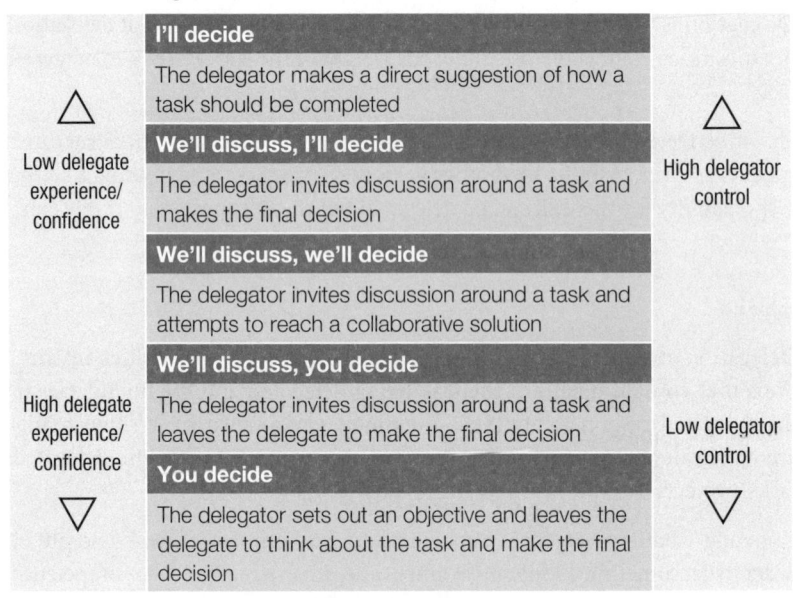

△ Low delegate experience/ confidence ▽ High delegate experience/ confidence	**I'll decide** The delegator makes a direct suggestion of how a task should be completed **We'll discuss, I'll decide** The delegator invites discussion around a task and makes the final decision **We'll discuss, we'll decide** The delegator invites discussion around a task and attempts to reach a collaborative solution **We'll discuss, you decide** The delegator invites discussion around a task and leaves the delegate to make the final decision **You decide** The delegator sets out an objective and leaves the delegate to think about the task and make the final decision	△ High delegator control ▽ Low delegator control

Have regard for people's capabilities. Some people thrive on new challenges. Others visibly wilt so assess your team members' capabilities early on. Establish the check and review arrangements for your delegate and allow there to be two-way interactions to track progress. If the delegate is struggling, make sure that you give help and support. If he/she is thriving, thank and encourage.

3.8 Delegation

ALL LEVELS

Plan
- Ensure delegated responsibilities are clearly sent out.
- Permanent in Job Descriptions.
- Temporary in Remits.
- Make sure delegation is appropriate.
- Check the managers to whom tasks are delegated are properly trained, competent and confident.

Do
- Manage in a way that supports the delegated responsibilities/tasks.
- Do not interfere.
- Encourage and support.

Review
- Keep an eye on manager's progress.
- Review regularly and frequently.
- Revise delegation as necessary.
- Recognise differing capabilities and skills.

Tips

Delegation is about getting the results you want through those that work for you.

Delegate, do not abdicate.

A good manager can delegate routinely in order to deliver the required results and develop his/her people

Leadership

3.9 Empowerment

BACKGROUND

In appropriate situations your people should be encouraged to take the initiative, own problems and deliver solutions through the use of judgement. However, staff acting purely on their own initiative can be a liability to delivery of a good, consistent train service and therefore it is vital that clear boundaries are established through structured delegation. Operators must not be in any doubt over where they can exercise initiative and when they have to follow the rules.

Empowerment is also about being clear about what people are responsible for and making sure they have all they need to discharge that responsibility. This will ensure that:-

- They do not keep coming to you for decisions on what is theirs to manage.
- They do not overstep the mark.
- You do not keep interfering in their area of responsibility.

ISSUES

Control & Command, conformance to procedures and processes, and a consistent response will produce high levels of safety and the best punctuality and reliability. Empowerment within this consistent and safe structure will give great reward to managers, job holders and outcomes alike.

Unfettered empowerment is rarely seen in large companies particularly ones which rely on consistency of output or high safety levels. Sometimes unrestricted empowerment can be used as a phase in an organisation, or in a project, to assist with the identification and challenge of barriers or patterns restricting growth or customer satisfaction or procedural efficiency.

However, these instances do not need to run in real time and come with significant risks and great stresses for the workforce.

Empowering competent employees who are clear about their terms of reference, have distinct, well defined spheres of influence and know to act within the permitted levels of discretion is the end goal.

When considering empowerment issues it is essential to read the advice contained in the Sections dealing with:-
- Ownership of Delivery.
- Delegation.
- Decision Making and Escalation.
- Professional Judgement and Legislative Considerations.

Good operating requires disciplined and consistent application of rules and procedures, and therefore the extent of freedom of action (empowerment) is necessarily limited.

Tips

Where freedom of application does exist, this should be clearly defined and the extent of authority documented, agreed and closely monitored.

Exercising such freedom of application will require the careful use of judgement.

Always use your experience and professional judgement when taking the initiative.

3.10 Professional Judgement and Legislative Considerations

BACKGROUND

Operators need to be committed focused individuals but they must be aware that the social climate is increasingly litigious and the prevailing mood often fuelled by the media is for blame to be apportioned and for individuals to be punished, almost regardless of the circumstances of an accident.

Accordingly this more difficult environment must now be carefully considered when making critical decisions. Risks must be considered by exercising professional judgement in a structured way. Good professional judgement will be based on competence and knowledge gained through training, development and experience.

Leadership

ISSUES

The main protection for Operators is to act in accordance with the published rules and regulations and ensure all key decisions are properly made, and recorded, using risk assessment procedures and ALARP principles.

If ever in doubt – seek advice from more experienced operators.

Prosecutions historically concentrated on front-line staff, such as drivers, signallers and crossing-keepers. Health and Safety law (and earlier legislation) did concentrate on employers, but it is only in recent years that attempts have been made to convict companies for corporate manslaughter. Until recently a company could only be convicted if a 'Directing Mind', that is someone senior enough to embody the company, was individually guilty of manslaughter. This would usually only happen in small companies, so various railway companies were accused of having escaped justice when no company was convicted of manslaughter after accidents such as Southall, Ladbroke Grove, Hatfield and Potters Bar.

The corporate manslaughter legislation now applying avoids this requirement, so a company can now be found guilty of manslaughter (or homicide in Scotland) without identifying a Directing Mind. Lower level failures can be aggregated to find that a company fell well below the standard required.

Corporate manslaughter is, however, only part of the picture. The record health and safety fine for a company is £7.5M in England & Wales (Balfour Beatty after Hatfield, reduced from £10M on appeal), but it is £15M in Scotland (Transco, formerly British Gas, after the Larkhall explosion). Individuals have been fined sums exceeding £100,000 (with the same again in costs) for health and safety offences, and now individuals can be imprisoned for most health and safety offences.

Individuals can still be charged with manslaughter offences, as happened to a signaller in 2010, and guard in 2012.

Whatever the prevailing legal position, operators will often be involved in making critical decisions and must therefore adopt a thoroughly professional approach to risk management.

Never be afraid to challenge poor working arrangements even if they are established custom and practice. As an example, the HST involved in the Southall accident was operating with AWS isolated, which was defined as a Category B failure (the train to be removed from service at the first available opportunity without causing delay or cancellation) in the BR Rule Book still applying at the time. Previous prosecutions both inside and outside the rail industry highlight the perils of allowing poor practices to continue unchallenged.

3.10 Professional Judgement

When faced with a difficult issue that has safety implications always play through how you would justify your actions in a police or ORR interview, in Court, an Inquiry or at an Inquest. If you cannot make a convincing case for your proposed course of action do not go down that route. How you decide is almost as important as what you decide.

Remember that in health and safety law there is a reverse burden of proof: once an employer is charged with most offences it has to prove that it did all that was reasonably practicable (discussed further below) to avoid the situation leading to the charges.

Keeping records of decisions and thought processes can be key to justifying your decision. Record all the outcomes of risk assessments and keep written notes of your thought processes.

If you need more comprehensive legal advice, ask for it. Seminars with legal advisors are often beneficial in clarifying some of the complex legal issues involved.

ALARP PRINCIPLES

ALARP is an acronym of As Low As Reasonably Practicable and is a term used to describe the management of risks in a structured way. (It is sometimes described as AFAIRP, 'as far as is reasonably practicable', but the two phrases mean the same).

Some health and safety duties are absolute; the employer must maintain equipment in a safe state, so it has no defence if equipment fails. But much health and safety law relies on the employer reducing risks to the health and safety of employees, visitors and others who might be affected by their undertaking to an ALARP level. This is the legal requirement.

Textbook definitions and guidance can be found in the Health & Safety at Work Act 1974, and associated publications from the ORR and the Health & Safety Executive, but the key essence is to ensure that risks are as low as reasonably practicable.

At a high level this sets the limits for spend on safety arrangements and/or infrastructure systems based on an amount per life saved (or Value of Preventing a Fatality - VPF). It is not considered to be reasonably practicable to expect companies to spend more than a specific amount per likely life saved and the current 2011 VPF values derived by RSSB from DfT data is £1.763m. This can, however, be a high burden, as the HSE's view is that expenditure to reduce a risk is required until it becomes grossly disproportionate; in other words

Leadership

disproportionate expenditure is required. This is not the sort of calculation than an individual operator will be asked to make, but on a dark, wet night you might be balancing more immediate risks, such as where and when to evacuate a train, which is why a basic understanding of these concepts is needed.

More details can be obtained from the RSSB and specifically the Railway Strategic Safety Plan 2009-2014.

At a more mundane working level the test will be:
- Have I/we taken all reasonable steps to minimise risks?
- Have I recorded the reasons for my decision – especially if I/we have decided that no change to existing practice is needed?

This will require knowledge, expertise and professional judgement, but as with all such concepts, applying the ALARP principles will become easier with experience.

More detailed information about managing risks in a structured way can be found in sections 6, 7 & 8.

Tips

No job is worth going to prison for.

However, do not use this issue as an excuse for maintaining the status quo when you have the appropriate skills and experience to challenge and change.

Use your professional judgement and experience but recognise the prevailing social climate and increasingly litigious environment.

Section 4: **Train Planning**

4.1	Train Planning	56
4.2	Timetable Planning Rules, Engineering Access and Network Change	63
4.3	Timetable Development and Validation	69
4.4	Timetables - Working and Public.	72
4.5	Capacity and Reliability	74
4.6	Engineering Allowances	81

4.1 Train Planning

BACKGROUND

Train planning is a vital activity because the train plan is fundamental to the commercial and operations activities of the infrastructure provider and train operators. Good train planning is essential for Network Rail because an efficient timetable makes best use of available capacity and provides an essential foundation for good punctuality and reliability. Good train planning is also essential for train operators as the timetable is at the heart of an operator's promise to its customers, specifying the available journey opportunities and their speed and frequency.

As infrastructure owner Network Rail controls access to the railway. In very simplistic terms passenger train operators bid for paths in accordance with the access rights held by virtue of their franchise (or open access) rights. Freight companies bid for paths that are required for their commercially negotiated contracts with end customers

Network Rail coordinate bids and reconcile conflicts using the Train Planning processes. In extreme cases where no acceptable solution can be found the Rail Regulator may be asked to make a binding determination.

PASSENGER OPERATORS

For passenger operators the timetable is the basis on which money is made by selling tickets. It also allows non-operator specific revenue to be divided on routes where there is more than one operator.

The timetable is a major determinant of costs because:
- It fixes (or is planned within) the resource base (DMUs, EMUs, locomotives, wagons).
- Train/unit mileage is largely set by the timetable and determines:
  - the amount of variable track access charges.
  - the amount of fuel needed.
  - the frequency of maintenance activity.
- The way resources cycle influences, and is influenced by, where and how fuelling and maintenance can be carried out.
- It heavily influences traincrew costs and efficiency.

The timetable is also the yardstick by which passenger train service franchise compliance is measured. The train service must comply with the Passenger Service Requirement (PSR) or Service Level Commitment (SLC), which are part of the operator's Franchise Agreement, normally with the Department for Transport (DfT).

FREIGHT OPERATORS

For the freight operator the dynamics that drive the plan are very different, though the above list of things that need to be considered by the planner are comparable. The Section entitled 'The Freight Perspective' in Section 6 covers the issues in some detail but the fundamental difference compared with passenger planning is that the train will only run if the customer wants the train to run and that there is a far higher level of change involved in the planning - again almost wholly driven by customer need. Unlike passenger operations the DfT has no locus as a service specifier.

TRAIN PLANNING CONSIDERATIONS

Train Planning activity and the timetable produced is fundamental to the operating railway. However, the relationships with SLC/PSR obligations and the impact on resources and costs make this a complex iterative process.

A clear commercial specification is vital at the start. Good train planning practice will ensure that the timetable is robust, but unless it meets customer expectations the timetable will not be a success. Nevertheless, every timetable is a compromise, commercially and operationally, and the implications of any compromises made must be fully understood by all concerned.

A timetable which looks good on paper but is routinely unworkable in practice is useless. Ability to recover from routine disruption is crucial. Arguably, a high level of asset reliability means that a tighter timetable is appropriate. This will increase the level of train service able to be offered from the resource base and therefore improve value for money for Train Operators. It will also potentially generate extra revenue for the Infrastructure provider.

Frequent services are generally more efficient to crew than infrequent ones. Faster journey times coupled with efficient turn-rounds also improve traincrew diagram productivity.

Long turn-rounds can help to provide timetable resilience but they can also be a lost commercial opportunity if retiming is possible and the resources can be more efficiently utilised.

Train Planning

What constitutes a 'good' timetable will also depend to some extent on the circumstances of the operator – how much cost is recouped in revenue, and the relative significance of specific arrival or departure times, journey times and repeating patterns.

Timetable Planning Rules are agreed between the operators and Network Rail. These often do not represent the absolute minimum that the railway can achieve, for example in headways or junction reoccupation margins, but include a sensible small additional allowance. It is crucial to the process that these Rules are fit for purpose, and are applied intelligently. Any non-compliance should be very much the exception and should be documented by Network Rail and the operator concerned.

It is of course possible to have a timetable which is completely Rules compliant, yet does not offer the required level of train service robustness and resilience. The art of the train planner is crucial here.

Planning activities should comply with industry processes and timescales. Late changes or too many STP (Short Term Planning) changes to plans carry risks and are to be avoided as far as possible.

Finally it is important to remember that implementation of the timetable is absolutely crucial. A potentially excellent train plan can fail if the myriad of processes, resources and associated systems are not fully integrated and deployed.

HOW CAN ALL THIS BE ACHIEVED?

Recent work by the industry and ORR has defined a model to ensure that major timetable changes are carried out consistently. The model involves the following steps.

Stages of the Consistency Framework	
Stage	**Output**
1 Rationale for change	High level problem statement
2 Option generation and filtering	Objectives & Statement of required outputs
3 Option selection	Single option
4 Single option development	Concept timetable
5 Detailed design	Rolling / Baseline timetable
6 Planned minor change	Applicable timetable
7 Operation	Train service
8 Review (short term and long term)	Recommendations

4.1 Train Planning

There are various different methods of achieving the best holistic results. One is that timetable development is steered by a, formally constituted cross-company forum (a Timetable Development Group),) chaired by a senior manager of either the TOC or NR (e.g. The West Coast Working Group for the December 2008 timetable). Such a group must also include representatives from the local operations and maintenance teams within Network Rail to ensure all good ideas are harnessed, all inputs are made, all issues are resolved and robust timetables developed.

Network Rail is now using Event Steering Groups to develop timetable principles around upcoming infrastructure enhancements. For smaller scale schemes, inter-disciplinary timetable development groups within an individual TOC may be appropriate, with occasional Network Rail involvement as necessary.

A robust, cooperative and professional relationship with industry counterparts is very important, as is preparation for, and participation in the necessary iteration meetings. However, a good timetable was never designed by a large committee and the best final results need all the necessary input and a guiding mind.

Having developed the timetable it is most important that planners observe its operation post-implementation and that they get feedback on how it is performing. Close relationships between train planners and the performance monitoring and control functions are essential in order to understand where timetable adjustments are needed, and where regulating and other late-running contingency arrangements can improve the performance from a timetable. In the first few days after a timetable is introduced there will normally need to be an intensive effort to ensure that train running is carefully monitored, problems identified and solutions implemented quickly. The long term success of a timetable can depend on the ability to iron out initial niggles quickly and effectively.

Therefore robust processes that conform to industry codes managed by professional Train Planning staff, both in the TOC and within NR, form the foundations for good train service delivery.

The following sections outline the industry train planning processes, highlight key interfaces and dependencies, and describe the key attributes of good train planning.

Train Planning

INDUSTRY PROCESSES

Industry train planning processes are contained in Access Condition Part D of the Network Code.

The arrangements specify key dates and timescales and link to both the Engineering Access arrangements and the Informed Traveller process – known as D 12 (trains or changes to train times to be in the timetable 12 weeks before they are due to run). These enforceable requirements form part of NR's license conditions and obligations and are included in the terms of each individual TOC's franchise agreement.

The Permanent Timetable has two change dates per year. The Principal period is December to May, the Subsidiary from May to December. While normally the more major timetable changes occur at the December change, significant changes can occur in May (for example the new East Coast Main Line timetable in May 2011), or at other times (for example the first West Coast Pendolino timetable in September 2004 and the Chiltern line rewrite in September 2011). It is also possible for operators to submit Timetable Variation requests (formerly known as Spot Bids) at any time.

Operators provide Network Rail with a Priority Date statement twice per year for each timetable change, at a date specified in the development process (generally between 8 and 9 months before the commencement date of the timetable). In it they specify the access rights they wish to exercise, the nature of the services, and any other information (such as balances and empty stock workings) which Network Rail needs to plan the services. For major changes earlier development work is needed.

Planning activity routinely starts more than a year out and Network Rail issue a Production Schedule for each year's timetable. The following example was for the 2013 timetable, which commenced on 9 December 2012. D- refers to the number of weeks before the commencement of the timetable (formerly termed as T- or TT-).

Most TOC Train Planning offices have a detailed timeline showing key activities and dates from D-67 through to the timetable change date. This is an important reminder to Train Operators' staff who have influence on the timetable of the timescales by which their part of the process needs to be delivered.

4.1 Train Planning

TIMETABLE DEVELOPMENT DATES 2013 TIMETABLE	Principal Change	Subsidiary Change
D-67 - Formal Notification of Process Dates	26.08.11	-
Revision of Timetable Planning Rules		
D-64 to D-60 – NR to Consult Proposed Changes to Rules	16.09.11	-
D-59 – Publish 'Draft Rules'	21.10.11	13.04.12 (D-57)*
D-54 – Operator Responses to 'Draft Rules'	25.11.11	18.05.12 (D-52)*
D-54 to D-44 – NR review Operator Responses		
D-44 – Publish 'Final Rules'	03.02.12	13.07.12
D-41 – End of Appeal Period 'Final Rules'	24.02.12	03.08.12
Initial Consultation Period		
D-64 – Publication of draft Calendar of Events	16.09.11	24.02.12
D-55 – Publication of Strategic Capacity Statement	18.11.11	27.04.12
D-55 – Notification by TT Participants of major TT changes	18.11.11	27.04.12
D-55 – Start of Initial Consultation Period	18.11.11	27.04.12
D-54 – Publication of Final Calendar of Events	25.11.11	04.05.12
D-45 – NR to provide copy of 'Prior Working Timetable'	27.01.12	06.07.12
Timetable Change Assessment Group (D-44)	03.02.12	13.07.12
D-48 – Notification of Provisional International Paths	06.01.12	-
D-40 – Priority Date for the 2013 timetable	02.03.12	10.08.12
Timetable Preparation Period		
D-40 – Start of Timetable Preparation Period	02.03.12	10.08.12
D-26 – NR Publish New Working TT	08.06.12	16.11.12
New WTT and associated system files available to ATOC	08.06.12	16.11.12
Operator responses to New WTT	22.06.12	30.11.12
D-22 – End of Appeal Period 'New Working Timetable'	06.07.12	14.12.12
Timetable Briefing process complete (D-15)	24.08.12	02.02.13
CIF Electronic Data available (D-14)	03.09.12	12.02.13
NRT Data sent to publishers (D-4)	09.11.12	19.04.13
Timetable Commencement Date	09.12.12	19.05.13
Timetable End Date	19.05.13	07.12.13

* Dates changed in line with industry consultation to increase the time between final Principal and draft Subsidiary versions. Previously dates were 16.03.12 and 27.04.12 respectively.

Institution of Railway Operators

Train Planning

SYSTEMS AND SYSTEM INTERFACES

Network Rail use ITPS (Integrated Train Planning System, sometimes known as TPS) for their train planning activities. TOCs and FOCs generally use Voyager Plan, with a minority using Trainplan or other systems. Bid and Offer information is transferred between the systems with bids from the operators to Network Rail and Offers from Network Rail to the operators. Generally, this is achieved by electronic data transfer, although for operators with smaller numbers of trains this is achieved by submitting paper bids.

The train plan ultimately drives or feeds through the myriad of operational IT systems (e.g. TRUST) and most Customer/Passenger Information Systems. More information, including the key interfaces and linkages, is contained in Network Rail's Performance Manual.

FINALLY

Without a robust train plan consistently good, cost-effective train service delivery is not possible. However, first class train planning outcomes will be destroyed unless all the necessary supporting resources, processes and systems are fully provided and properly integrated.

Tips

Steer train planning activities properly on a cross-functional/cross-company basis.

Remember that a flawed plan with a lot of non-compliances will not work in practice.

Train planning skills are a relatively scarce resource, and take a long while to "grow", so ensure you develop talent through the introduction of trainee train planner positions.

Without a good train plan, you will never consistently achieve good performance results.

4.2 Timetable Planning Rules, Engineering Access Statements and Network Change

BACKGROUND

In Great Britain the contractual details that govern the shape of individual timetables are set out in Access Condition D which forms part of the Network Code.

The two key working documents that underpin the train planning process are:
- The Timetable Planning Rules (formerly known as Rules of the Plan) are a compendium of all the essential information needed to create a timetable.
- The Engineering Access Statements (formerly termed as Rules of the Route), which must be agreed with the affected operators, detail Network Rail's engineering access requirements in terms of routine blocks (possessions) of specified lengths of route, one-off blocks, and longer blockades for major items.

Between them, these two documents, which are managed by Network Rail on behalf of the industry, define when, and under what rules, trains can operate.

TIMETABLE PLANNING RULES

Timetable Planning rules documents define all the train/infrastructure issues and the mathematical components for creating a timetable such as:-
- Mandatory timing points for each route.
- Route opening hours.
- Minimum headway between trains shown in minutes or sometimes shown as AB (Absolute Block) where only one train is allowed over a section of line between two signal boxes.
- Junction margins/allowances.
- Connectional allowances for passengers.
- Single line re-occupation times.
- Allowances: engineering (box time), and performance allowances (diamond time). Adjustment allowances (fast to slow line moves, approach control etc.) do not appear in working timetables but are shown in train planning systems in curly brackets. (see also the Section on Engineering Allowances).
- Station dwell times.
- Minimum turn round allowances for rolling stock.
- Allowances for other operational activity (e.g. coupling/uncoupling in service, crew relief etc.).

Train Planning

Additionally, the Timetable Planning Rules can contain enhancements to minimum requirements – usually inserted at the Operator's request. Examples of these are enhanced dwell times and longer turn round times at termini.

Alternatively operators may simply bid enhanced times as part of the normal timetable development process. NR will usually insist that specified minimum standards and allowances be fully observed and have the right to reject any timetable bid which is non-compliant. However if a train operator makes a case for a minor deviation (e.g. on the grounds of economy or practicability) such breaches can be permitted if the train operator also commits to mitigating the performance implications.

The aim of all these arrangements is to help produce resilient timetables, which makes the Timetable Planning Rules of critical importance. Regular reviews of their appropriateness and effectiveness are therefore essential. Ideally the accuracy of train planning rules should be tracked through time by regularly measuring timings in service. This minimizes the workload required when an update is required. Many train operators are now using real time monitoring software to keep a continuous track on the accuracy of train planning rules.

When a physical feature of the operational railway changes, this needs to be reflected, and in such circumstances a Network Change document will be produced by Network Rail and consulted with affected operators. More details about this process can be found later in this Section.

Identifying and reviewing all planning rules non-compliances as part of a formal timetable development process is essential. Well-meaning train planners and over enthusiastic commercial managers can undermine the resilience of a timetable. Such changes are often very subtle and may appear innocuous. Furthermore if they are not rejected at the bid stage by NR they will appear to have official sanction.

However there can be instances where flexing of specific rules is agreed between the relevant operator(s) and Network Rail. In these circumstances a proper record should be kept of the non-compliance. If the situation is likely to be permanent, a Rules amendment should be considered. Conversely if the deficiency occurs in error or without proper authority and cannot be rectified, an appropriate mitigation plan should be agreed by the train operators and Network Rail. This should be underpinned by an acceptance that the non-compliance will be eliminated at the earliest reasonable opportunity.

Train operators should always check an accepted timetable against the Timetable Planning Rules to ensure nothing gets lost or compromised during the NR process of blending the various TOC/FOC timetable plans.

4.2 Timetable Planning Rules, Engineering Access Statements and Network Change

Remember - an inaccurate or out of date Timetable Rules document can result in an unachievable or inappropriate timetable – a classic example of planning to fail.

ENGINEERING ACCESS STATEMENT

The Engineering Access Statement details Network Rail's engineering access requirements in terms of routine blocks (possessions) of specified lengths of route, one-off blocks, and longer blockades for major items. The remaining time periods are the times of day at which services may operate, provided of course the Timetable Planning Rules specify that the route is open.

The Engineering Access Statement is planned for a whole year and starts to be developed at circa 80 weeks before the timetable year starts – roughly May for the timetable starting in December the following year. This is the point at which the first draft of the work-bank is released by Network Rail.

The document is split into 7 sections:
- Sections 1 to 3 set out in detail the national process for negotiating and securing engineering access to the rail network (so should be read to give greater detail on what is outlined in following sections).
- Sections 4 to 7 form the bulk of the Engineering Access Statement document and contain route-specific details of Network Rail's engineering access opportunities and requirements.
- Section 4 contains 'Standard Possession Opportunities'; i.e. the times when routes would normally be available for engineering access.
- Section 5 describes the 'Possession Strategy' by line of route – in particular regular midweek possession opportunities that are available that may not lie entirely within the Standard Possession Opportunities. These possessions are disruptive and require trains to be retimed under short-term planning arrangements. This access provides for routine maintenance requirements and takes the form of cyclical midweek possessions, for example applying one week in 6, with an overall phasing of routes blocked to provide diversionary routes.
- Renewal or enhancement work may be proposed as a number of equal length blocks over a period of weeks, and in such circumstances will appear in section 5.
- Section 6 is not currently used.
- Section 7 contains the 'Register of Possessions'. These are identifiable major possessions likely to take place which it has not been possible to contain within Standard Possession Opportunities and are not reflected in the Permanent Timetable. These are Disruptive Possessions.

Train Planning

Any one project may include possessions that feature in Section 5, Section 7 or a combination of both, so it can be very useful to get a project-specific view of the access plan for major schemes, in conjunction with understanding the overall Engineering Access Statement. When a major project requires a program of possessions extending over more than one year, Network Rail will normally issue a Possession Strategy Notice which sets out the proposed method of implementation and the required possessions. However the blocks needed will still also appear in the relevant Engineering Access Statements.

The currently-agreed Timetable Planning Rules, Engineering Access Statements and scheduled dates of issue are available from Network Rail's website < www.networkrail.co.uk>.

A reasonably firm Engineering Access requirement should be available at circa TT-62 (62 weeks prior to timetable change) when the first version is published by NR. However the timescales for agreement are often such that firm details of engineering work may not be available at this stage.

Note. At the time of this 2012 revision both (TT –) and (D –) were in common use. These designations are interchangeable.

Access proposals in the Engineering Access Statement are consulted with affected operators, and NR is required to take into account any comments received from TOCs/FOCs. The document goes through successive iterations (version 1, version 2 etc.) between TT-61 and TT-44, when the 'decision' version is published. This includes the changes that Network Rail has agreed based upon the responses received from train and freight operators.

Subsequent versions are issued at regular intervals after this, until TT-23, in order to produce the Engineering Access Statement for the second half of the timetable year (May – December).

In recent years there have been 5 versions of the EAS:
- Version 0 Draft Rules.
- Version 1 Proposal document for the Principal Timetable.
- Version 2 the Decision document for the Principal Timetable.
- Version 3 the Proposal document for the Subsidiary Timetable.
- Version 4 the Decision document for the Subsidiary Timetable.

Between TT-44 and T-26 (26 weeks before the start date of the timetable), the 'Period Possession Plan' is built, documenting all possessions by route. The Draft Period Possession Plan is issued on a 4-weekly basis and after confirmatory meetings with operators the CPPP (Confirmed Period Possession Plan) is issued at T-26. On this basis weekly amended timetables in connection with engineering work are bid to Network Rail at T-18. Network Rail is required to reject bids that conflict with the published CPPP, at least initially pending any agreement to amend the published possessions. Changes at this stage are much more difficult to accommodate so the key is to use the long production timescales to establish and confirm the train plan as much as possible.

TOCs and FOCs may refer Network Rail's decisions on engineering access as issued in Version 2 or 4 (or at any other timescale, for example following a Late Disruptive request post-T-26) of the EAS to the Access Disputes Committee if they do not agree with Network Rail's decision and a compromise cannot be agreed.

NETWORK CHANGE

Network Change is a process contained within the Network Code. This requires Network Rail to consult on permanent changes to the railway infrastructure with all operators who have services on a section of railway, or who may aspire to have such services. It can also apply to proposed changes to certain critical processes e.g. TRUST Berthing offset times.

A Network Change Notice (NCN) is issued to each affected TOC/FOC outlining the proposed change and seeking comments plus specifically an acceptance or a rejection. NCNs may be issued for major schemes (a new junction layout for example), for making a Temporary Speed Restriction (TSR) into a Permanent Speed Restriction (PSR) or for a small change (upwards or downwards) in a PSR.

The TOCs/FOCs together with Network Rail representatives need to consider the ramifications of the proposed change. A reduction in line-speed of a route may be enough to necessitate a new timetable and may break unit diagrams whilst an improvement in speed or the provision of a new signalled route into a station may be of real value in performance, service offer or resource utilisation terms.

NCNs are not issued for 'like-for-like' changes – for example a replacement of a set of points without change to the speeds over them and sometimes this can be a lost opportunity. For example if the train operator has an upcoming service aspiration that would benefit from the points being slightly re-located or designed for a slightly higher speed. Such a TOC will not automatically be made aware of the like-for-like renewal and will need to rely on local intelligence.

Regional Investment Review Groups, chaired by NR with TOC and FOC participation, meet quarterly to review and discuss proposed infrastructure changes and to suggest possible enhancements. These can also be a good source of information.

Train Planning

Tips

Protect the agreed parameters codified in the Planning Rules but do not assume they are timeless. Regular good quality reviews are essential.

Ensure all non-compliances are logged and reviewed for formal approval or rejection.

Pay careful attention to Engineering Access Statements. Ensure the long development timescales are used - not ignored

Keep ahead of the proposed infrastructure changes on your routes. Network Change proposals should never be ignored. The implications of a missed change can be serious.

Engage in route planning meetings.

Train operators should establish a close rapport with NR colleagues – this will allow 'like for like' renewals to receive similar consideration to those submitted under Network Change.

Robust Timetable Planning Rules and Engineering Access arrangements are fundamental to good service delivery. The difference between appropriate and out of date timetable rules and arrangements can be several PPM percentage points.

4.3 Timetable Development and Validation

BACKGROUND

As the timetable is the foundation of good train service performance it is essential to have in place structured arrangements for timetable development and change validation. Validation must cover all aspects – those internal to the TOC and those that are the responsibility of Network Rail all of which must be signed off at the appropriate level.

The cost of getting a timetable (and the associated resource allocation) wrong can be immense. Inbuilt errors and inefficiencies will recur every day and furthermore take a long time to change. It is therefore a basic requirement to manage this key operations process in a systematic way.

ISSUES

The timetable development cycle follows strict timescales and internal review and validation processes should fit around the key milestones.

Within TOCs the establishment of a Timetable Delivery Group may be an appropriate way of providing the necessary focus. Such a group can probably meet eight-weekly but attendance by all the relevant senior managers/directors is essential. Such a group should have a dated forward program as at any point in time there will be at least two separate timetable cycles running in parallel and must ensure that any identified timetabling risks as properly assessed and documented.

For significant timetable changes it may be necessary to organise temporary sub-groups and for a fundamental re-write the appointment of a project manager and team is essential.

Within Network Rail the Timetable Change Risk Assessment Group (TCRAG) oversees timetable change and manages risks – the relevant TOCs and FOCs will generally be able to contribute positively to this process.

Many timetable planning decisions will be dependent on downstream implementation issues e.g. a timetable enhancement might be depend on the recruitment and training of additional drivers. This means that a high degree of iteration may often be necessary.

Train Planning

Key areas that should always be addressed by timetable groups are:-
- Does the proposed timetable fully meet the commercial specification and the reasonable needs of maintenance colleagues? Both the Infrastructure maintainers and train maintainers.
- What is the impact on the resource base (trains and crews – the former may include additional mileage based lease costs and increased maintenance)? There is a need to understand how these benefits are measured in both performance and financial terms?
- What are the non-compliances against the Timetable Planning Rules and what is the impact?
- What is the performance impact – can the timetable deliver the punctuality and reliability (e.g. PPM/CaSL Targets)?
- Will platforming arrangements benefit the customer?
- Has the timetable and its resource requirements been adequately validated?
- Is there an agreed joint timetabling briefing process to include all front line staff in advance of the implementation of the timetable (later stages)?
- Have necessary simplifiers been produced (later stages)?
- Have all relevant contingency plans been revised (later stages)?

Finally for major TOC changes it is sensible practice for each functional director to sign off their individual department's readiness to operate the new timetable.

Further relevant details can be found in the element covering the Timetable Planning Rules and Engineering Access Statements.

CASE STUDIES

There are a number of recent case studies that illustrate the skill required to get the balance right in timetables.

- The 2005 SWT timetable change which introduced realistic dwell and running times (albeit at the 'cost' of some overall journey times) delivered some impressive improvements in punctuality and resilience but some now view this as probably over cautious in the current climate. It grew from the post-Hatfield traumas, and longer journey times mean higher resource costs (or less use being made of them) which in the current context is a significant factor in relation to capacity and value for money.
- The December 2008 'VHF' West Coast timetable did produce some impressive performance delivery without the resource inefficiencies of the 2005 SWT timetable. However, some features of the 'Operation Princess' cross country timetable of 2002 rendered the overall timetable too tight, especially

4.3 Timetable Development and Validation

post-Hatfield. Some significant changes, especially in relation to turn-round times and the length of time stock was available for maintenance, were necessary to give an acceptable level of robustness.

OBLIGATIONS

It should be borne in mind that any alterations should also take into account the obligations set out in the SLC (Service Level Commitments) which is generally a DfT document in the case of franchised train operators.

This lists maximum journey times that are on routes, stopping patterns and intervals of service which must be complied with. Some franchises have more onerous SLCs than others. These are agreed between the TOCs and DfT but have no legal standing in the relationship with Network Rail which is covered through the Track Access Agreements

FINALLY

Delivering good performance is often difficult enough. Starting with a poor timetable is planning to fail. The best performing timetables have often been developed over a few years rather than those rushed in to achieve short term results.

Tips

The need for the timetable and the associated resource plans to be managed and validated at all stages cannot be over emphasised.

Make sure you have a common understanding of what constitutes winning. A very resource efficient timetable that creates performance problems is probably not a good idea.

For a major timetable change having a Timetable Delivery Group is vital.

To undertake a proper timetable rewrite all aspects of the timetable need looking at especially the underpinning Timetable Planning Rules which are the base rules on which any timetable is developed.

Remember you will never deliver consistent good performance if the timetable is sub-optimal

Train Planning

4.4 Timetables – Working and Public

BACKGROUND

The timetable is the visible output from the train planning process and has two main manifestations – the Working Time Table (WTT) and the various 'Public Timetable' versions issued by various organisations in hard copy and soft copy formats. It is important to note that the industry paper based National Rail Timetable (NRT) is no longer published by Network Rail.

There are differences in some of the times shown in these two types of timetables and it is important to understand the reasons for this.

The following section therefore highlights the relationship between the two main forms of timetable and also the main differences.

KEY ASPECTS

Working Timetables

Contain the details of each service (including freight and ECS) and the precise timings to the nearest half-minute.

These timings cover stations, junctions and other key points. They are generally at a much finer level of detail than TRUST reporting points.

The WTT reflects the base timings in the NR owned rail industry Integrated Train Planning System (ITPS) base data warehouse (previously called the Train Service Data Base – TSDB) and will be supplemented by short-term alterations that are published in various routine operating publications. As ITPS drives many primary systems, such as TRUST, ARS, and customer information systems, the importance of the WTT is very evident.

The WTT also explicitly shows the various allowances as follows:-
- Engineering – known and shown as Box time. The relevant number is contained in square brackets within the timetable column e.g. [1].
- Pathing – known and shown as Circle time e.g. (2).
- Performance – known and shown as Diamond time e.g. <1>.

Differences in timings between the WTT and public timetables are indicated in the WTT by use of a letter code in the relevant time e.g. 12w00 shows an arrival time of 1200 in the WTT which is shown as 1202 in the public timetable. The definitions of the letter codes are shown in the WTT.

4.4 Timetables – Working and Public

The WTT also shows the type of stock which the service is assumed to use. This affects the timings used.

The potential shortcomings with WTTs are:-

- Timings are rounded up or down. A station stop may be timed for 40 seconds, but reflected in the WTT as 30 seconds or 1 minute.
- Platforming information is not always included. This should be added at key locations where defined in the Timetable Planning Rules and can be added at other locations especially if this improves the quality of information given to the public through the CIS system at those locations.
- Whilst regular freight paths will be in the WTT, around a third of freight is run on a Short Term Planned bases to allow response to freight customer arising demands. Sometimes on-the-day customer demands require 'control specials' or VSTP (Very Short Term Planned) trains. On heavy freight routes suitable paths are generally secured for such flex. These may be referred to as 'Q paths'. Freight train speeds/sectional running times must be able to cope with such path parameters. See also Section 6 – Freight Perspective.
- General lack of traction information (some timings are based on generic traction types and notional load/weight data)

The use of formally produced WTTs now has a reduced value within the industry as most signalboxes and control offices use the electronic systems (TRUST etc.) to monitor and regulate services. Some locations draw up localised simplifiers that are kept up to date with the permanent plan and rely on TRUST for updates of the amended plan (see Simplifiers). Nevertheless having ready access to a copy of the WTT can be useful.

Public Timetable

Whilst directly derived from the WTT, details in the public timetable differ. Public timetables only show timings for stations where the service is booked to call and general details concerning train type (e.g. if first class/catering is provided or other TOC specific details), not generally the type of train or traction.

The main difference between the WTT timings and public timings is that WTT arrival timings at termini and key intermediate stations are sometimes earlier than those shown in the public timetables. This may be due to the inclusion of a performance allowance or can result from giving the train the ability to benefit from any unused intermediate engineering allowances which create a quasi-performance allowance.

Train Planning

Similarly at key intermediate stations the public timetable may show later arrival and earlier departure times than the WTT. Once again this allows a service to capitalise on any quasi- performance time picked up en route and depart a minute or two early if it is ready.

Because PPM is measured against public timings the addition of public timing allowances can be the subject of criticism. There may be some justification to this claim where the additional allowance is excessive, or where the termination point of the train (for example Aberdeen for a train from London) is not where the majority of passengers are travelling to (e.g. York, Newcastle, and Edinburgh). However, the reality is that reasonable performance allowances are a prudent approach. Compare this with the allowances in airline schedules which are often very sizeable.

Tips

Make sure you have access to a copy of the WTT. The extra information over that contained in public timetables can be useful.

Be aware of the performance opportunities that exist between WTT and public timings.

4.5 Capacity and Reliability

INTRODUCTION

The degree to which the capacity of a route or railway is utilised will be dictated by the timetable that is planned to operate. In very simple terms at higher levels of utilisation there will be less slack (sometimes termed "operators padding") to absorb delays.

Therefore both the quality of a timetable and the amount of capacity that is utilised will have a direct bearing on reliability.

The amount of capacity used by a timetable will usually influence performance to some degree. When a railway is heavily utilised, the less unused capacity there is, the less likely it is that delays will be absorbed. This is not an issue on lightly used lines but where demand exceeds sensible levels of use of line capacity – there are important trade-offs to be made.

The theoretical capacity of a route section is determined by the design of the signalling system, line speeds, train types and performance, train length and stopping patterns and terminal constraints. Capacity is usually expressed as trains per hour (tph), a figure that is derived from the headway of the route i.e. the minimum achievable time between trains. However capacity cannot just be viewed in this simplistic way and this Section highlights some of the main issues relevant to this complex but fundamental aspect of train planning.

CAPACITY AND UTILISATION

The capacity of a route or railway is the maximum number of trains that could be run. However capacity can be defined in a number of different ways. Examples include:-

- The number of trains that can be passed along a given line at full speed.
- The number of trains that can be incorporated into a timetable that is conflict free, commercially attractive (featuring, for instance, regular intervals at all stations but still including some fast trains amongst the stoppers) and compliant with regulatory requirements.
- The number of trains that can be incorporated into a timetable that is conflict free, commercially attractive, compliant with regulatory requirements, and can be operated within the laid-down performance targets in the face of prevailing levels of Primary delay.

The more sophisticated the definition – the less the capacity becomes! Also such definitions primarily relate to the number of trains that can pass and take no account of how many passengers or tonnes of freight can be conveyed.

In the 2007 Rail Technical Strategy published in the UK by the DfT this issue was addressed by adopting two specific definitions:-

- Network Capacity- the number of trains that can operate on a rail network in a given time period, reflecting factors such as junction interactions, terminal capabilities, the mix of train speeds and the number and order of trains of different speed capabilities and stopping patterns called for by commercial and regulatory requirements.
- System Capacity – the total capacity of the railway system to carry passengers or freight. This is the resultant of the passenger capacity of each vehicle of payload of each freight wagon, the number of vehicles on each train and the Network Capacity.

Train Planning

This helps link theoretical train capacity with actual passenger/freight capacity because ultimately it is System Capacity that is the most relevant to train operators. It also becomes apparent that issues such as service/stopping patterns, train types (and technical performance) and train lengths (passenger/freight tonnage capacities) are all crucial factors relevant to the real capacity of a railway.

MAXIMISING CAPACITY

Network Capacity

On routes where demand for train paths is high there are a number of recognised approaches that can be used to maximise the number of trains that could be run.

It is self-evident that a slower speed or stopping train will use more space on the train graph than a higher speed or non-stopping train but commercial or contractual requirements often dictate that a mix of train service types is required. On a two track railway the consequences can result in a drastic reduction in available Network Capacity.

To ameliorate this impact it is standard train planning practise to 'flight' trains or use 'skip-stop' patterns.

- Flighting – involves running one or more consecutive trains of a similar type. This minimises the space used by each group of trains and is used through the channel tunnel (by flighting groups of fast Eurostar trains followed by flights of slower car and lorry shuttles).
- Skip stop patterns – this involves using pairs or patterns of trains to cover all stations using semi-fast services with different stopping patterns. This avoids running slow all-stations services which use more capacity.

Ask your train planning experts for more details on these and other techniques for maximising the use of Network Capacity

System Capacity

Demand for train paths is directly related to the expected passenger demand or freight tonnage forecasts.

Train Operators will require paths in order to meet this demand using their available resources (trains, rolling stock and crews). Accordingly the amount of paths required will be heavily influenced by the commercial need to operate an efficient resource base.

Running longer trains is the obvious solution to provide the maximum System Capacity, whilst using the least Network Capacity, but such an approach will be entirely dependent on the spread of demand and the operator's resource base(s).

This can also be a contentious issue where two or more train operators compete for revenue on a route. Providing 'co-share' services similar to airlines is rarely an option as it stifles completion and removes customer choice. Where regulation is a feature as in Great Britain, this can be problematic.

Currently Network Rail's Route Utilisation Strategies (RUSs) include an assessment of useable capacity.

PUNCTUALITY AND RELIABILITY CONSIDERATIONS

Leaving some spare Network Capacity to assist delivery of the required levels of punctuality and reliability is a recognised approach.

If the timetable planning rules allowances and related timings are spot-on, and infrastructure and rolling stock are very reliable, then more capacity can be used on a congested route. However, a rule of thumb would say that if you use no more than 80% of the available capacity then the timetable can be a robust one with the ability to recover from incidents. Note: The international union of railways organisation (UIC) recommends a maximum level use of 85%.

If all trains start on time, no errors have been made in the planning rules or the resultant timetable, and no incidents are experienced on route, then all trains should run on time and end their journeys on time. In practise this rarely happens.

If trains are timed precisely to minimum Sectional Running Times and dwell times, any incident on route invariably leads to delay. Once a train is late it may then delay other trains particularly at junctions. Each train delayed in consequence may then further delay other trains so delays escalate in a chain reaction. The train planner can help minimise the potential for this reactionary delay risk by working to greater than minimum margins if the available Network Capacity allows.

Train Planning

The susceptibility of a timetable to this escalation of delays essentially depends on:-
- The complexity of the route or railway, which determines the number of opportunities for one train to delay another e.g. at junctions.
- The complexity of the train plan, which determines the possible interactions between trains arising from factors such as crew relief, one arrival forming 2 departures, splitting or joining on route etc.

Acting with these factors is the intensity of utilisation which determines the likelihood that that where an opportunity for one train to delay another exists, this will actually happen.

Infrastructure design such as grade separated junctions may improve performance and performance time may be allocated to allow some scope for recovery. However, too much performance time may encourage slack working, which will have the opposite effect to the one desired. So train planners should guard against both plans that are too slack and plans that are too tight.

The fundamental point is that a timetable must be able to deliver the required service performance targets. If this cannot be done then a railway cannot be said to have spare capacity. In such a situation the means of creating spare capacity my lie in reducing the frequency and/or impact of disruptive events or reducing potential conflicts due to the track layout. Solutions to track based constraints may range from the greater use of parallel moves to the construction of grade separated junctions.

Studies for Network Rail have identified clear relationships between the intensity of capacity utilisation and the escalation of delays. Above certain levels the escalation becomes severe. However introducing extensive performance allowances does further erode Network Capacity and whilst sensible performance margins are entirely appropriate they can be contentious on a route or railway where demand for paths is high.

A study on a UK main line showed that a minimum braking distance Line Capacity of 95 tph was reduced to approximately 10 tph once worst 'green to green' signal times, planning headways, traffic mix factors and reliability margins had been factored in!

As an example on the Fast Lines of the WCML a four aspect automatic signal will normally cycle from red (train just passed) to green (approaching train can run without signal-led speed restriction) in around 95 seconds. After taking account of the time needed by a driver to sight the signal on approach - another train could theoretically be planned two minutes behind the previous one. In practice the planning headway is almost double the signal cycle time at 180 seconds/ three minutes.

4.5 Capacity and Reliability

There is no rigidly laid down guidance and interpretation of the signalling values has traditionally been undertaken by the timetable planners.

ARRIVING AT THE BEST SOLUTION

On many routes train paths are extremely valuable and because of the complexities involved in railway systems, timetable proving is best undertaken using simulation tools. This can provide a low risk means of testing robustness, identifying conflicts and developing solutions. Correctly used some simulation tools can also forecast delivered punctuality results using actual historic delays and disruption data.

A number of proprietary modelling systems are now available but remember that modelling must be factored into timetable development and validation programmes. It is also best undertaken by experienced practitioners.

Post implementation analysis can also be undertaken using systems such as CCF/P2 and on-train data recording (OTDR) systems. This can be very useful for identifying minor recurring conflicts that can often be resolved through minor retiming etc.

For operators the ability of a given timetable to support the required levels of punctuality is essential. From a review of UK and worldwide best practise the following were suggested to be the maximum achievable practical capacities offered with a suburban stopping service:-

- Conventional heavy rail – 20 trains per hour.
- Heavy rail enhanced with ATO – 24 tph.
- Conventional metro – 26 tph.
- Metro with ATO – 30 tph.
- Metro with high technology signalling and control and dwell-time discipline - 40 tph.

Finally remember the goal – an efficient timetable that will provide the foundation for delivery of good train service results.

Train Planning

KEY POINTS

Plan
- Ensure that the Timetable Planning rules codify what proportion of theoretical capacity is to be used and how this will be measured.
- Check that the plan is not too slack.
- Ensure that modelling/simulation tools are used to assess the likely impact of a new timetable.

Notes
1. Design signalling headways and actual workable headways are often different.
2. Modelled performance and actual performance of rolling stock are often different.
3. Actual station dwell times often exceed planned dwell times.

Do
- Monitor train running on busy sections of route.
- Use common sense and live running to validate the modelling.
- Be alert to applications for paths that adversely erode capacity.

Review
- Regularly analyse results of monitoring to determine if congestion is becoming a source of lateness/delay at key points.
- Arrange a formal brief and review before and after timetable implementation.
- Formally review appropriateness of Rules allowances (e.g. dwell times, SRTs etc.) at defined intervals.
- Feedback to the Plan for consideration of options etc.

Note: Use of CCF/P2 and OTDR information to analyse section delays is a good starting point.

Tips

If 95% of services are running to plan on a congested route – using more paths will usually depress that figure.

Getting this balance wrong on congested routes can be disastrous for performance – ensure all changes are carefully evaluated and modelled using simulation tools.

Once a timetable has been implemented use live running data to analyse what actually happens over route sections.

Remember - it is possible to get too precise when planning timetables and that a performing timetable is better than a precise one. However a precise and performing timetable is the goal!

4.6 Engineering Allowances

BACKGROUND

Engineering allowances are a key component of timetable allowances that can have an unexpected impact on punctuality and reliability. They form part of the Train Planning Rules (see separate Section) and have always been included in the Working Timetable. This extra time allowance is shown and known as, box time.

Whilst the engineering allowance is exactly as it is described – an allowance for engineering work that will cause extended point-to-point journey times (usually by the imposition of TSRs), the impact of exceeding the allowances or increasing the quantum of engineering allowances that is actually used, can have damaging and far reaching consequences.

Accordingly, this aspect is of critical importance to operators.

ISSUES

Engineering allowances in the timetable are designed to allow minor delays from routine engineering activity – such as temporary speed restrictions – to occur without unduly impacting on performance. They are usually pitched at a level that absorbs "average" delays and must be consistently applied to all trains that are to run in accordance with the agreed Train Planning rules.

Engineering allowances are inserted in WTTs and can be documented in two ways:
- By the showing a box time in the timetable e.g. [2].
- Inflating the point to point timings by 5% which is currently the practice in Network Rail Wessex, Kent and Sussex Routes (the former Southern Region).

Unused allowances provide train operators with a quasi-performance allowance that will absorb delays of any type and provide additional resilience within the timetable.

Train Planning

However, when allowances are actually used by the engineer for the purpose they are intended – routine delays that were previously absorbed can appear and are often misinterpreted as new delays. The reality is that they were hidden from view within the engineering allowance.

Train operators have no contractual claim to use engineering allowances as a performance cushion but any material changes in maintenance arrangements can suddenly inject several minutes extra delay per train – with significant repercussions for PPM. Train operators must therefore understand what engineering allowances are in their route sections, the consequences of the routine use of such allowances changing and the impact this could have on punctuality and reliability.

It is important to regularly review all timetable allowances to ensure the details in the train planning rules are fit for purpose. In order to do this effectively train operators must understand the fundamental maintenance regime arrangements that apply and any planned changes to working practises.

Similarly it is important that engineering work is planned so that engineering allowances are not exceeded - too many TSRs on a route (especially in close proximity on a high speed route) can cause PPM to collapse. Check the actual effect of TSRs on a sample of trains of all types. Is the actual level of delay within the Timetable Planning Rules? Carefully managing TSRs/ESRs is essential if the take-up of engineering allowances is to be kept within the agreed levels.

Tips

Engineering allowances are wonderful absorbers of low-level delay – of any kind. Encouraging infrastructure maintainers not to use the allowances and not to treat them as an entitlement can produce huge performance benefits for train operators but this carries a substantial risk. The allowances are not performance allowances and can disappear in a moment.

Improvements in engineering techniques (for example faster hand-back speeds) should help enable a long term reduction in the quantum of engineering allowances.

Infrastructure maintainers such as NR should not be planning for any engineering allowances to be exceeded. Train operators should carefully monitor TSRs and intervene if needed.

Engineering allowances are a double-edged sword. Make sure they are fit for purpose and understand the dynamics.

Section 5: **Other Longer Term Planning**

5.1	Organisational Design and Capability	84
5.2	Resource Planning	87
5.3	Train Crew Links and Rosters	91
5.4	Signaller Conditions and Rosters	104
5.5	Performance Planning with Industry Partners	107
5.6	Contingency Plans	110
5.7	Engineering Work Planning Management	114
5.8	Seasonal Planning and Reviewing	120
5.9	Train Connectional Policies	126

Other Longer Term Planning

5.1 Organisational Design and Capability

BACKGROUND

All organisations must be fit for purpose and because of the number of interfaces within the area of operational management and supervision. This is particularly true on the railways.

Regardless of the structure of the rail industry the task of delivering good train service punctuality and reliability is relatively timeless and requires all the constituent elements to be constantly under proper managerial control.

The following section addresses the key requirements and the necessity for well integrated arrangements within individual organisations in order to ensure that collectively Network Rail, TOCs and FOCs have all key aspects properly addressed.

It is important that the capabilities and competence of all organisations are routinely reviewed as part of a structured process in order to ensure that the actual arrangements are fit for purpose and form a coherent whole. Many of the areas shown are covered by formal Self-Assessment or Audit & Check processes but you should regularly review other aspects of your responsibilities as well as the 'collective sum of the parts'.

5.1 Organisational Design and Capability

KEY ISSUES

The key components of good train service delivery are illustrated in the following diagram.

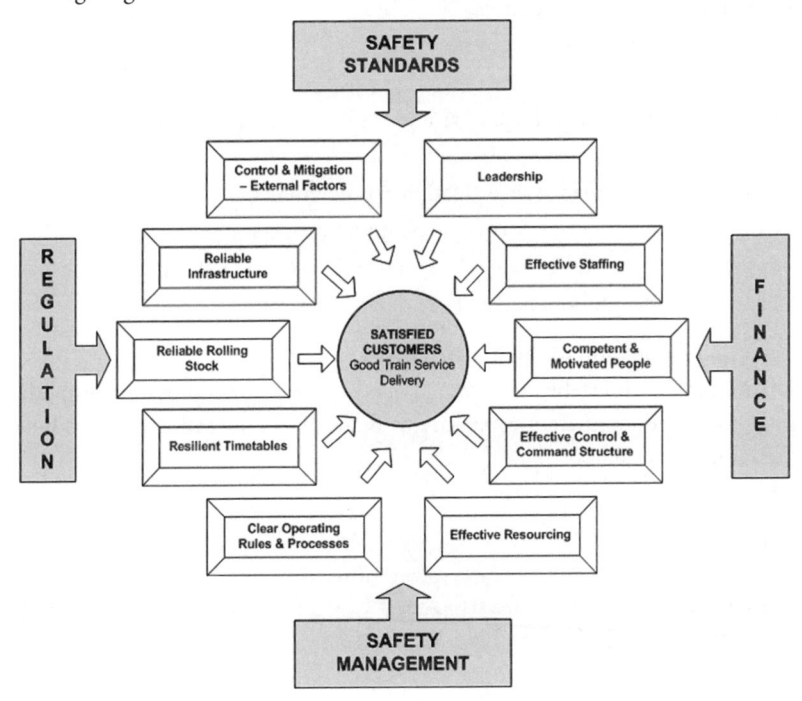

```
                      SAFETY
                    STANDARDS
                         ↓

        Control & Mitigation          Leadership
        - External Factors

  R     Reliable                        Effective Staffing      F
  E     Infrastructure                                          I
  G                                                             N
  U                    SATISFIED                                A
  L     Reliable       CUSTOMERS       Competent &              N
  A     Rolling Stock  Good Train      Motivated People         C
  T                    Service Delivery                         E
  I
  O     Resilient Timetables           Effective Control &
  N                                    Command Structure

        Clear Operating                Effective Resourcing
        Rules & Processes

                         ↑
                      SAFETY
                    MANAGEMENT
```

These activities are frequently undertaken by a variety of departments within individual companies and by a number of companies acting together. It is because of the critical nature of interfaces that organisation design and capability is so important.

Organisations must be regularly reviewed at all levels to ensure they remain fit for purpose.

It should also be obvious that organisations must be reviewed each time circumstances change. This will include whenever a key partner's organisation changes for whatever reason.

The aim is to make sure that the collective arrangements – people, plant and processes – can provide an integrated competent resource that is capable of managing the key components and producing the required results.

Other Longer Term Planning

In the area of Operations, the critical interfaces are primarily between the TOC/FOC and NR. All aspects are critical but Control & Command is particularly dependent on robust well integrated arrangements. Areas to consider are:-
- Common Control procedures.
- Contingency & Service Recovery Plans.
- Integrated incident response.
- Complementary on-call response and escalation arrangements.
- Integrated communication arrangements.
- Integrated performance investigation arrangements.
- Common/integrated performance planning processes.
- Sufficient competent operators (within companies and between companies).
- Passenger Information, particularly during disruption.

The crucial question for all activities is:-
Do the sum of the established arrangements and resources provide a properly integrated and competent capability to manage the operation and produce the required results?

Tips

Historically there have been lots of gaps in some areas of operation responsibility. Look hard at interfaces and the current level of integration.

Sitting people from different companies side by side does not automatically produce integration. This is delivered through processes and procedures that are either common or interlocked.

Reducing duplication will reduce costs and improve efficiency BUT make sure you retain an appropriate degree of control over aspects that are critical to delivery of your business requirements.

Organisational design should avoid over-dependency on a few superstars and should provide adequate support in all relevant areas.

5.2 Resource Planning

BACKGROUND

Manpower planning is usually associated with critical groups that require high levels of training and development e.g. Drivers, Fleet Technical staff and Signallers. However, there are many specialist skills involved in running an effective railway and less obvious groups such as Train Planners, Performance Managers and Performance Analysts should also be covered by a structured manpower planning process. The key aim is to always have the right level of resources to deliver the timetable.

Inadequate or poor manpower planning can have a huge impact on our ability to deliver the timetable. It is therefore essential to plan sufficiently in advance and hold regular resource plan reviews. Conversely too large a resource-base will incur unnecessary operating expenditure that could either be spent on other things or used to improve profitability.

History suggests that companies repeatedly get caught out on this routine task and the consequences have often been very damaging and very public.

Succession planning for Supervisors and first line Managers is also a key responsibility. The role of such personnel in the modern industry is often underestimated and undervalued, yet they are the first line of defence in the delivery of a safe and efficient train service.

Developing the right individuals – those with obvious talent and those with potential – to manage staff and activities of which they may currently be part, often requires patience and a high degree of personal attention.

ISSUES

A manpower planning process can be a very simple forecast that includes:
- Actuals.
- Forecast future requirements.
- Natural leavers (i.e. retirements, resignations, dismissals etc.).
- Natural joiners (qualified staff).

However, a more sophisticated manpower plan which recognises staffing by crew and fleet depots, yards, stations and signal centres/boxes etc., will be necessary to capture the resource reductions and increases at different locations resulting from timetable change.

Other Longer Term Planning

For roles such as Drivers or Guards where numbers are closely tied to train service timetables, the tracking and monitoring of these planned changes 12 – 18 months in advance of timetable change is essential and should be done at least monthly.

Other groups such as signallers are less likely to be tied to timetable change, although this can have an impact: for example earlier train on a branch line requiring new opening hours. Staff establishments may be heavily impacted by re-signalling or enhancement projects and the impacts will need to be identified early so that plans can be established in sufficient time to be managed effectively.

Adequate review processes will enable gaps to be quantified and fed into the recruitment, training and development process in a timely way.

Uncertain business plans and long lead times for recruiting and training are amongst the reasons for manpower planning being less effective than it should be.

Timetable and resource plans, especially allocation of work to depots, need to be firm 18-24 months ahead of implementation. This is because the lead time between identifying a need, and providing a fully trained individual – can be up to two years for Drivers and 12 months for a signaller.

Understanding the key linkage between timetable and manpower requirements is very important. Unfortunately, the nature of the timetable planning process can mean that Driver numbers are the last thing calculated accurately. For significant changes it may be worth investing in modelling work to predict the approximate manpower increase in advance so that early assumptions can be made around recruitment. Poor or late manpower planning can also lead to inefficient and wasteful deployment of people, through inefficient diagrams, rosters and work schedules. This will reflect in budgeted cost overruns, or budgeted efficiency savings not being achieved. (See Train Planning section for further guidance on iterative timetable planning).

Dealing with a reduction in manpower requirements brings it own problems of reallocation of resources or redundancy.

Shorter timescale reorganisations need to consider manpower planning issues and implications at an early stage, and not as often occurs, only at the end of the process.

As with all critical activities the recruitment, training and development will require routine formal monitoring. Similarly manpower plans must be regularly reviewed and updated.

Make sure you understand the various Promotion, Transfer & Redundancy (PT&R) arrangements within your company, and how they affect your freedom to move manpower between depots and locations, and how they might affect the scale and extent of retirements and resignations. Be aware of the scale and complexity of training requirements – having a qualified driver with limited route knowledge is not much use, neither is a signaller with limited panel knowledge. Similarly many 'technically' qualified staff will require a period of experience under supervision before they can actually undertake the full requirements of the job.

Make full use of your company's professional HR and personnel resources to interpret PT&R arrangements and maximise training and development opportunities for your people. Establish monitoring, review and feedback routines to check the progress of individuals and groups. Be alert to slippage in training programmes that may impact on sequential modules, or future training slots, or indeed the dates when staff will become available for work. Again these are particularly important when they relate to new timetable plans.

MYTHS

Small establishments do not obviate the need for manpower plans. Small complements are even more at risk from unexpected shortfalls.

Stability is not a good reason for not planning. Look at the age profiles small sub-groups may have personal intentions to retire at the same time.

Consider whether your company or location is an historic training location for certain grade groups, which have a tendency to migrate elsewhere after training. If so, consider the options available to you for improving retention rates. For TOCs and FOCs this may mean adjusting driver terms and employment conditions – which can be both a blunt, and expensive, instrument – but this issue may be partially (and possibly more effectively) addressed through improving working conditions. A 'feel good' factor in the workplace is difficult to value, but should not be underestimated as a positive contributor to staff retention rates. Where such adjustments may not be possible, you may need to increase establishment size and must keep a closer eye on recruitment cycles and vacancy gaps. Communicating with your staff to understand what plans they have will also help you plan for the future.

Be aware that pay deals and other changes for example new train introduction in other companies, can alter the traditional flow of staff.

Also changes to terms and conditions for example shorter working days, restrictions on driving time etc. can alter the size of required establishments – often radically.

Other Longer Term Planning

Be particularly careful of changes to train crew conditions or requirements which change the time taken to do things such as increased walking time, preparation and disposal times, additional booking on/booking off allowances etc. These can have a substantial impact on diagrams and rosters, and may well force changes in establishment numbers.

Within Network Rail, terms and conditions and rates of pay are negotiated centrally, so in some ways there is less room for local manoeuvring. However there are areas which are agreed locally which will have a significant impact. Be aware of the impact of your local agreements, such as roster patterns, how many staff can take leave at any time, use of spare turns and how flexi-staff are utilised.

Running such issues to earth as early as possible is key to not getting caught out later on.

Tips

Resource planning for critical groups cannot be ignored.

Ensure there is a robust process that incorporates regular reviews.

Do not underestimate the importance of good intelligence. Internal information regarding who may leave and why is vital. Similarly, in TOCs/FOCs information regarding what other TOCs/FOCs are up to is crucial.

Do not abdicate responsibility for manpower planning. The HR department may well undertake many of the activities but the planning has to remain the direct responsibility of the operations team.

5.3 Train Crew Links and Rosters

BACKGROUND

Efficient links and rosters are a clear indication that a train crew depot is under management control. A poorly constructed roster and an inefficient link structure (or poor linking within a link structure) will:-

- Generate unnecessary costs.
- Waste resources.
- Create artificial shortages.
- Generate unnecessary road learning/refreshing and/or traction refreshing.
- Create unmanageable backlogs of accrued leave and training.
- Generate unnecessary overtime and rest day working.
- Cause cancellations and delays.

Planning and management of traincrew links and rosters requires care. Attention to detail can be critical and careful analysis can identify significant performance and financial benefits. For many years staff representatives have applied pressure to take control of the process. This might seem like a welcome escape from the pressure of short timescales and interminable detail. However, the risk of significant losses and waste are too great to leave this process to chance. Over the past few years TOCs have started to re-learn the importance of controlling the process of linking and rostering. The creep of concessions on terms and conditions has also slowed to some extent.

Traincrew costs will be one of your largest areas of expenditure. Do not leave this part of your role as an Operator to chance. Use the plan, do, review cycle.

The following terms are used throughout the text and definitions are provided here:

Depot – A location where traincrew are based. This can include a number of different links.

Link – A link is a sub-set of the total depot structure. All drivers in a link need to know all routes and traction for that link's allocated work. Other links may sign other routes or types of traction and may have different allocated work. The logic of such depot sub-division is to ensure that route learning costs are contained and that drivers can remain competent through driving regularly enough over each route. Linking by its nature has the effect of reducing the flexibility of the depot but this downside is outweighed by the upsides, particularly in route retention compliance. A typical depot with around a hundred drivers may have three mainline links and maybe a small 'pilot' or 'starter' link. At a

Other Longer Term Planning

small depot there may only be one link.

Roster – The pattern of shifts worked by a link within a depot.

Diagram – A plan of work for an individual driver or conductor on a specific day. Long term diagrams are associated with the long term timetable and form the basis for the base roster. Short term diagrams are produced in response to short term timetable changes.

Spare – A member of traincrew who is not rostered to a specific diagram but is left available to cover sickness, leave etc. This is not the same as standby.

Standby or cover – A member of traincrew who is working a diagram which is created specifically to provide emergency cover at a particular location. Standby turns are diagrammed, spare turns are drivers over the number required to cover the diagrams at the depot.

Turn – The particular activity that an individual is carrying out on that day. This can be a rostered diagram, standby turn or spare turn.

Establishment – The total number of staff required at a depot to cover all the booked work. It is often calculated using an agreed formula and multiplier.

Instance of work – A diagram that must be covered at a depot.

A&U return – Availability and Utilisation Return. A record of the way in which traincrew at a depot are used and the activities they carry out. It is used to monitor the efficiency of the roster and links.

Shift – A term that refers to the broad time of day when a turn occurs e.g. early shift (morning), late shift (afternoon), night shift. Can be used interchangeably with 'turn'. Rosters are usually arranged so that staff work a particular shift each week.

Rest Day – A day within the roster when the member of staff is booked to have a day off. This excludes annual leave and usually excludes Sunday. In a five day week there is one rest day. In a four day week there are two.

Rest Day Working – Where a member of staff works on their rest day.

Average turn length – The average length of all the turns in a roster. Used for calculating establishments and the numbers of rest days required.

Unproductive work – Work that is not directly related to the running of trains e.g. medicals, training, union release.

5.3 Train Crew Links and Rosters

PLAN

Changes to links and rosters must be planned in advance even where the timetable is not changing significantly. Work to a clear project plan and allow sufficient time to complete the process. Production of traincrew diagrams is one of the final stages of the planning process and can often be left to the last minute. This is not desirable. Roster negotiations carried out under time pressure can lead to costly concessions to meet the required deadline for implementation. Having a clear idea of what the objectives are for each timetable change is the start of the process.

The longest planning timescale involves major timetable changes. The effect of these on manpower requirements and link structures must be understood well in advance to enable recruitment and training to have taken place in sufficient time to implement the timetable. The structure of the timetable will also influence the optimum roster for example through changing the balance of shifts, increasing diagrams on particular days and altering the requirement for standby turns at particular times of day. Take managerial control of the process in advance of timetable change, and use whatever administrative and managerial resources are available to you, to establish a workable, viable managerial link structure and roster at each Depot, for each grade group.

Even where the timetable is remaining largely unchanged it is important to plan carefully for any roster change. If the costs and weaknesses of previous link structures and rosters are understood then targeted areas for improvement will be obvious. Analysis of A&U returns (see below) will inform these decisions.

A fundamental question is whether the establishment is sufficient to cover the timetabled work and the current levels of productivity at the depot. Establishments are commonly calculated based on the instances of work at a depot using the following formula:

Establishment = (total instances of work per week / days worked per week) x establishment multiplier

It is difficult for this formula to be applied precisely because the calculations involved can be circular - for example unless the number of days worked per week is fixed through terms and conditions it will depend on the final roster.

Establishment multipliers are often agreed formally with staff representatives. In other cases the establishment figures are just agreed for each timetable change without reference to a formula. In any case however, the size of the establishment needs to be sufficient to cover the expected unproductive work at the depot without placing undue reliance on rest day working and overtime.

Once establishments have been calculated the number of drivers per diagram

Other Longer Term Planning

can be checked and this KPI is often used to compare depot efficiency. As a guideline you might expect to have between 1.5 and 2.2 drivers per diagram. Depots at the higher end of this range will probably have efficiency issues to be resolved. Depots at the lower end may well be efficiently run but they could be a source of significant overtime working or traincrew cancellations. A figure of 1.8 may be a reasonable benchmark.

Some key issues to consider when planning are:

- Are there the correct number of hours in the roster? Surprisingly this is a common mistake which simply results in staff being paid for not working. Just add up all the hours across the roster and make sure it gives the right numbers of hours per week.
- Are the spare turns set correctly? Are they the correct length? Are all diagrams covered by a spare? Is each spare positioned to be able to cover the maximum number of diagrams? Are there the right number of spares in the roster? The exact detail will depend on the terms and conditions that apply to the depot. However, every effort should be made to maximise the effectiveness of spares.
- Are the links set up efficiently? Links with larger route and traction knowledge must have sufficient qualified spare cover: it may not be possible to cover these jobs with spares from other links. Making the link larger may make it more robust, but may be expensive to carry out the required training. A worked example is shown at the end of the Section.
- Are there the correct numbers of rest days in the roster? Where there is a reduction in the average turn length this may result in a reduction in rest days over the roster.
- Consider whether standby cover is required in a roster to avoid last minute cancellations. Standby turns are not the same as spare cover and if they are really needed should not be left uncovered.
- If there is any slack time in the diagrams could this be used more effectively? For example can a diagram be saved by using a number of diagrams with slack time to cover shunting and washing activities?
- How will leave be rostered? Usually this is through a separate leave roster which identifies groups of staff who take leave at the same time. Care is needed here. For example if the leave roster plans for several staff on the same shift to go on leave at the same time then it can be difficult to cover the vacant turns.

Work openly and honestly with staff representatives over rosters and links. Diagram content is a consultation item and you should be firm in resisting proposals for change that do not add benefit. Rosters are more commonly negotiated, but even so management should always propose the first version of the roster in any negotiation.

5.3 Train Crew Links and Rosters

You should be prepared to impose a management roster if reasonable consultation fails to achieve the required result. This can take the form of the previous roster but with staff reverting to spare at their booked times (known as supplementary rostering). This can be an unattractive option for staff and can be an effective deterrent during roster negotiations. Nevertheless the consequences of such action need to be carefully thought through.

The benefits of diagram and roster optimisation tools should not be overlooked. Although they are unlikely to be able to produce a polished final product when used intelligently they can identify significant efficiencies. They can also help to provide a good estimate of the establishment requirement well in advance of the final timetable being produced.

Although the comments above relate to annual timetable changes short term planning is also relevant. In certain locations 8 week cycles of train planning changes can drive roster changes for traincrew. These changes can have a disproportionate impact on traincrew efficiency within the depot but tend to be low profile, and a low management priority.

DO

Rostering

Achieving an efficient and effective roster is vitally important to ensure financial efficiency and good performance. However, unless the application of the roster is continuously monitored over the year there will be significant scope for waste and erosion of certain principles. It is important that practices which build up around working the roster maintain fairness and equality in the workplace. Key things to consider are:

- Keep watch for the unofficial depot practices – being around the depot, and with the individuals at their work will often alert you (largely unwittingly) to any unauthorised, or condoned practices which manipulate the roster – unofficial changeovers, working through a booked break to get another individual off early, unauthorised booking on/off arrangements etc. Some of them will have safety implications others may appear to favour some staff over others.
- Speak regularly to your Train Crew Supervisors or Controllers; it is likely they will have identified, or at the very least have heard of, some of the 'fiddles' to be found in diagrams and rosters.
- Monitor efficiency of the links and rosters, and insist upon basic weekly returns from each Depot covering at least basic information about availability and utilisation of staff, sickness/absenteeism, off-roster staff and overtime/RD time worked.

Other Longer Term Planning

- Managers should also maintain a close watch through a range of KPIs covering the efficiency of diagrams, rosters and link structures. For instance;
  - Proportion of train working to diagram time.
  - Ratio of staff to base diagrams.
  - Rostered average weekly hours.
  - Average hours worked as a percentage of paid time and available time.
  - Balances of the above between the links at the depot.
  - What spare cover is being used for.
- Take a clear line on release for staff representatives. This should be positively authorised for agreed events only.
- Make sure you track the outstanding route and traction training required in each link. Links populated by Drivers who do not have full competency will generate cancellations and additional costs. Saving on the training costs is often a false economy. Where there are many links and wide variations in route and traction knowledge care is needed to understand the implications of promotions between links.
- Consider whether diversionary route knowledge is providing net benefit. Although being able to divert in a crisis or for engineering work is useful, retaining the route knowledge can be difficult and expensive especially where there is no booked work over that portion of line.
- Take an interest in the progress and development of trainees, those on coaching plans, and those who are temporarily restricted off roster. This will help to ensure they are restored to normal working as quickly as possible.
- Ensure an accurate list of Terms & Conditions and local agreements exists and is kept up to date. Make sure supervisors and managers know how to get the most out of the agreements and when they can insist on flexibility from staff. You should be getting the most out of your agreements.
- Never rely on driver rest day working (RDW) – reduce reliance to as close to nil as possible. It can easily become institutionalised and can allow staff to take disruptive action (refusal to work rest days) without the need to go through a ballot on a particular union grievance such as pay. The ability of unions to use this as a lever to exert pressure on management should not be underestimated.
- Try to ensure Sunday and Bank Holiday working is either in the working week or there is a contractual commitment to work rostered Sundays. Unions are able to apply considerable pressure by refusing to work where they have no obligation to do so.
- Make sure your roster team and your train planning team are speaking about engineering work planning. Where additional diagrams need to be issued which would be the best depot to diagram the work to? Certain depots may have more spare resources at the weekend than others. Are the diagrams

and roster optimised together? There is no point in generating very efficient diagrams that cause inefficiency in rostering!
- Where Bank Holiday working and Sundays fall at the same time (every so often around the Christmas period) ensure that your resource plan is robust and set the parameters before the Unions set them for you. You do not want to be in a position whereby extra pay is offered for what should be a 'normal' day, once set, precedents are very hard to "unset".

Managing For Attendance (MFA)

Minimising staff absence is a key part of getting the most out of Traincrew rosters. As part of your continuous monitoring you should consider the following:
- Ensure your staff attendance records are up to date and accurate, and that both your formal and informal arrangements for monitoring attendance are carefully documented – you will need these if you ever have to face an Employment Tribunal for attendance related dismissal.
- Take a close interest in staff that are off sick or absent – implement your company's Managing for Attendance arrangements strictly. Make a point of speaking with those who have time off, but stay below the MFA thresholds. Letting staff know that you know is itself a powerful disincentive to unauthorised absence.
- Ensure you offer all support you can to ensure that your absence levels are kept to a minimum. Your staff will appreciate it.
- Make time to support staff that are seriously ill. The trade unions are often good at this. As the employer you need to be even better. A supportive approach will often bring staff back to work sooner.
- Look for trends in staff attendance – absence on particular shifts or days of the week, those which coincide with other extraneous events (Arsenal home matches, golf outings etc.).
- It is general good practice that a 'return to work' interview is carried out to ensure that:

  a) The reason for absence is satisfactory, and

  b) There are not any other welfare issues you need to be aware that sickness leave is being used to cover for.
- Make the most of your Occupational Health provider. Seek their advice when necessary, but always provide a detailed referral so that the doctor understands the issues. If you do not do this then the direction of the consultation may be directed by the patient's aspirations.

Other Longer Term Planning

REVIEW

Your ability to review Traincrew links and rosters will depend on the quality of your records. Maintaining a good A&U return is the starting point. You also need a set of KPIs to monitor your efficiency over time (see above).

When reviewing A&U data consider the following questions:

- Are there days or shifts when there are spare resources unused?
- What are the spare resources being used for?
- Are there days or shifts when rest day working is high or there are leave requests being refused? It can be difficult to get staff to agree to sufficient spares on Saturdays, but this is when most of the leave requests are received.
- Are there certain links with high rest day working? Why is this?
- Is rest day working variable throughout the year? Why? Are the annual leave rosters affecting this?
- Is the unproductive work within the amount agreed within the establishment calculator? If not then what are the main causes? Can these be reduced or should the calculator be increased to ensure it is robust?

A LINK STRUCTURE CASE STUDY

This worked example shows how links are used to organise the work at a depot. It highlights the issues involved in getting the links set up correctly and demonstrates that there is normally no perfect answer.

The example depot covers a number of routes with 3 different traction types. Details of the depot are as follows:

- There are 100 drivers at the depot covering 50 diagrams per day 6 days per week.
- Drivers start as depot drivers and are only qualified to work in the depot on a lower rate of pay.
- Depot drivers are promoted to be mainline drivers when vacancies become available.
- Depot drivers are able to work all traction types, but only in the depot.
- The depot is at A.
- There are routes to locations B, C, D and E.
- There are two main traction types. Class 100 trains are used to B, C, D and E. Class 200 trains are used to B and C only.

5.3 Train Crew Links and Rosters

- There is also a rescue locomotive at the depot. There is only one diagram on the rescue locomotive each day, but the rescue locomotive must be able to work on all routes.
- There are frequent services to B, D and E.
- The service to C is very limited: there are only 2 diagrams per day that go to C.
- The training standard specifies that new mainline drivers will initially only learn the route to D. They can only extend their route knowledge after about 6 months of driving. New mainline drivers also train only on class 100 units.
- To retain their route and traction knowledge each driver must work each route and traction type at least every 28 days.
- Normally the two most experienced depot drivers are qualified to drive on the mainline and receive higher grade duty on days when they do so, although for the first 6 months they are only allowed to drive on the route to D. Allowing depot drivers to be qualified to drive on the mainline makes manpower planning easier because there is a ready qualified pool of mainline drivers.

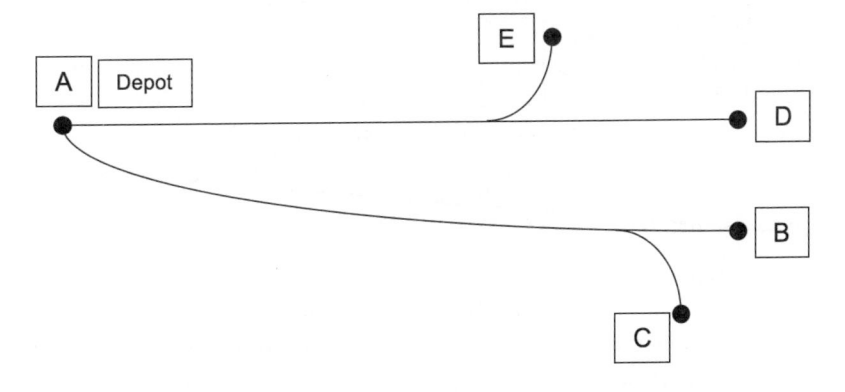

How might the depot be organised into links to cover the routes and traction in the most efficient way?

Work within the depot can be covered more cheaply by using depot drivers rather than mainline drivers. It is therefore sensible to have a separate link of depot drivers. This link needs to contain the spare cover for the depot drivers.

It could be possible to put all of the remaining work into a single link. However, there are awkward consequences of doing this.

- New drivers only know the route to D. They would be unable to work any diagrams needing other route knowledge for the first six months. This would result in other drivers having to cover the diagrams. This could incur additional rest day working costs.
- New mainline drivers only learn class 100 trains. Initially they would be unable

Other Longer Term Planning

to work any diagram including class 200 trains or the rescue locomotive.
- There will be a significant training requirement since all the drivers will have to be trained to work all of the traction types and all of the routes.
- There are only two diagrams per day to C and only one diagram on the rescue locomotive. It is unlikely that drivers in a single large mainline link would be able to retain their knowledge of the route to C or the rescue locomotive without unproductive refresher days in the roster. There might also be concerns about expecting newer drivers to carry out the full range of duties in the roster before they have had time to consolidate their initial training experience.

A more efficient way of organising the depot might be to have the following link structure:

Link Name	Routes	Traction	Diagrams	Drivers
Depot	Depot only	Class 100 Class 200 Rescue loco	5	10
Starter	D, E	Class 100	25	50
Main	B, C, D, E	Class 100 Class 200	15	30
Rescue	B, C, D, E	Class 100 Class 200 Rescue loco	5	10

In this example the links are progressive, meaning that the links are organised in a hierarchy and vacancies in a higher link are filled using the most senior driver from the lower link. In this case the depot driver link is the lowest and the rescue link is the highest.

This structure resolves many of the problems of the single link structure described above. However, some problems remain, and the multi-link structure may create some new problems.
- There could still be some new drivers in the starter link who do not have the required route knowledge to drive to E. However, it is likely that if some depot drivers are trained to mainline standard then this will be overcome while they are working in the depot. Even so, on days when they are covering mainline work they will be unable to drive to E. A further refinement might be to have a small link of mainline qualified depot drivers containing a mix of depot work and diagrams that only involve journeys to D.
- The issue of route knowledge retention for the route to C has been largely resolved. Each member of the main link should visit C every 15 days on average, although there will still be problems if a driver misses a diagram

5.3 Train Crew Links and Rosters

due to sickness or annual leave since the gap will then be 30 days. Some arrangement for refreshing may be required.
- The members of the rescue link are required to know the route to C, but have no booked work there. This could be resolved by allocating a refresher diagram to the link. It might be possible to include a refresher journey to an existing diagram. Alternatively drivers could be expected to drive the rescue locomotive to C when on duty to retain their competence.
- The rescue link is very small and has two items of specialist knowledge: the route to C and the rescue locomotive. Shortage of cover for sickness etc. is more likely in a small link such as this and this is likely to increase rest day working. Even though the link should officially contain enough spare cover it may be sensible to have a number of members of the main link trained additionally to cover the rescue locomotive if required.
- Spare coverage is shared equally amongst the links (the ratio between diagrams and drivers is the same for each link). It may be desirable to have more spare cover in the main link because a spare driver in this link could also cover work in the starter link. It might be possible to do this without causing further problems with retaining route knowledge to C.

It can be seen that there is not necessarily an ideal solution to the arrangement of the depot into links. In fact possible solutions may come from changing the nature of the work at the depot. For example:
- Could the rescue locomotive work be contracted out to another company e.g. a nearby freight depot with wider route and traction knowledge? Could the rescue locomotive be done away with without unacceptable performance risk?
- Could the work to C be given to another depot where journeys to C are made more frequently?
- Is it possible to change the standards to allow a new driver to learn routes to D and E and possibly B as well? Could new drivers learn both types of traction?
- Could the standards on route knowledge be changed to allow a longer retention period?

There can also be significant consequences of having a progressive link structure. A vacancy in a higher link can cause a cascade of training requirements as drivers move up from each of the lower links. In the example above the implications of this are not severe: the route and traction of the lower links is generally included in the higher link so the accumulated knowledge is not lost and the changes are small. However, progressive link structures with the following characteristics can cause major problems:
- Large numbers of progressive links.
- Significant differences in route and traction knowledge between links.

Other Longer Term Planning

- Higher links do not contain the route and traction knowledge from lower links.

Progressive links are generally favoured by staff representatives. This is partly to allow more desirable work to be retained for more senior staff. It also reflects a general union preference for promotion by seniority although the fact that progressive links generate a larger training requirement may also be relevant. If it is possible to overcome staff side objections moving to non-progressive links where vacancies in any link (or at least groups of links) are filled by new recruitment can result in significant savings.

Tips

Train crew resources are usually the largest single group of staff in a TOC - and generally the most expensive. Therefore efficient management is a critical obligation, which must start with the linking systems and rosters at the Depot.

Do not get this issue wrong - at best it will damage your bottom line; at worst it will have severe Industrial Relations implications.

5.4 Signaller Conditions and Rosters

Availability and Utilisation

DEPOT:						PERIOD:				
	Drivers Main Form of Utilisation	Sun	Mon	Tue	Wed	Thu	Fri	Sat	Total
Productive Drivers	Rostered Diagrams	160	247	247	247	247	247	225	1620
	Drivers on rostered work	160	247	247	247	247	247	225	1620
	Specials or Additionals	0	5	5	5	5	5	0	25
	Drivers covering other Depot Diagrams	0	0	0	0	0	0	0	0
	Total Part A	160	252	252	252	252	252	225	1645
Non Productive Drivers	'As Required' Drivers Not Utilised	0	25	30	44	35	28	13	175
	L.D.C & H&S	0	2	6	5	8	4	0	25
	Route Learning / Route Refreshing	0	1	1	2	4	1	1	10
	Training / Briefing	0	5	7	19	4	1	0	36
	Medical including Counselling	0	1	0	2	0	1	0	4
	Miscellaneous (specify #)	0	7	10	7	11	6	2	44
	Total Part B	0	41	54	79	62	41	16	294
Drivers Not At Work	Sickness Long Term	0	0	0	0	0	0	0	0
	Sickness Short Term	17	18	16	16	17	17	20	121
	Annual Leave	0	49	49	49	49	49	49	294
	Lieu Leave	0	6	6	6	5	11	31	65
	Other Leave (specify #)	0	2	4	2	3	5	3	19
	Absent	0	0	0	0	0	0	0	0
	Rest Day/'Free Day' Off	259	68	55	32	48	61	92	615
	Establishment Vacancies	0	0	0	0	0	0	0	0
	Total Part C	276	143	130	105	122	143	195	1114
Must Balance	Establishment	436	436	436	436	436	436	436	3052
	Total A+B+C	436	436	436	436	436	436	436	3052
	Total Hours Of Overtime								
	Rest Days Worked Total	0	6	7	5	7	8	8	41

\# Notes:

Other Longer Term Planning

5.4 Signaller Conditions and Rosters

INTRODUCTION

Efficient rosters are a clear indication that an activity is under managerial control. A poorly constructed signaller roster, inefficient use of flexi-staff and panel cover in Signal Centres will:-
- Generate unnecessary costs.
- Waste resources.
- Create artificial shortages.
- Create unmanageable backlogs of accrued leave and training.
- Generate unnecessary overtime and rest day working.

It is therefore vital to give this important aspect adequate managerial attention before problems occur and bad practises become embedded.

ISSUES

Signaller pay & conditions are largely agreed at a national level so local staff representatives will always apply some pressure to take control of the rostering process. For many years this proved a welcome managerial escape because of inadequate managerial resources and insufficiently skilled/competent managers. In certain areas staff representatives may even have been given responsibility for creating the base rosters.

It is vital that managers recognise the need to take control of rostering, manage complements effectively, and stop the creep of concessions on terms and conditions.

Mobilising those staff who understand rosters (e.g. roster clerks, resource managers and local managers with particular skills) to construct the management proposition in sufficient time for consultation with staff representatives, subsequent iteration and comprehensive managerial review, is absolutely crucial. Signaller costs will always be a very significant cost driver so it is no good managing your supplies of pens and paper whilst avoiding dealing with this vital issue.

Setting down some achievable but demanding targets when creating and reviewing rosters is a good discipline. Examples include a reduced numbers of spare turns, reduction in flexi-premiums paid etc.

5.4 Signaller Conditions and Rosters

GOOD PRACTICE

The essentials of good practice are:-

- Take managerial control of the process and use whatever administrative and managerial resources are available to you, to establish a workable, viable roster.
- Consult openly and honestly with staff representatives but make clear the principles on which the rosters are based.
- Negotiation means that both sides must agree, not that if a large enough majority of Signallers want something you must let them have it. Be clear about which aspects are non-negotiable and why.
- Be prepared to impose a managerial roster if reasonable consultation fails to achieve the required result and plan how the consequences of that will be managed.
- Monitor efficiency of the rosters. Insist on weekly returns covering at least basic information about availability and utilisation of staff, sickness/absenteeism, off-roster staff and overtime/RD time worked.
- Managers should also maintain a close monitor through a range of KPIs covering the efficiency of rosters and link structures. For instance;
  - Ratio of resident to flexi staff.
  - Flexi premiums paid.
  - Inefficient placing of free days.
  - Minimisation of spare turns.
- Keep watch for the unofficial practices. Spending time out and about, and with individuals at their work will often alert you (largely unwittingly) to any unauthorised, or condoned practices, which manipulate the roster e.g. unofficial changeovers, letting the meal-break signaller leave early. Some of them will have safety implications.
- Take a close interest in staff that are off sick or absent – strictly implement your company's Managing for Attendance (MFA) arrangements, and make a point of speaking with those who have time off, but just stay below the MFA thresholds. Letting staff know that you know is itself a powerful disincentive to unauthorised absence.
- Ensure you offer all support you can to ensure that your absence levels are kept to a minimum. Your staff will appreciate it.
- Make time to support any staff that are seriously ill. The Trade Unions are often good at this. As the employer you need to be even better.
- Look for trends in staff attendance – absence on particular shifts or days of the week, those which coincide with other extraneous events (football home matches, golf outings etc).
- Ensure your staff attendance records are up to date and accurate, and that both your formal and informal arrangements for monitoring attendance

Other Longer Term Planning

are carefully documented. You will need these if you ever have to face an Industrial Tribunal for attendance related dismissal.
- Ensure any conversations regarding staff attendance records and reasons for absence are recorded and placed on file, whether or not the member of staff breaches the attendance criteria or not. This allows you to build a picture of irregular attendance and evidence to challenge the member of staff with.
- It is general good practice that a 'return to work' interview is carried out to ensure that:-
  a) The reason for absence is satisfactory, and
  b) There are no other welfare issues you need to be aware that sickness leave is being used to cover for.
- Make sure that training plans specify training timescales and monitor trainees' progress against these timescales. It is very easy to loose sight of how long trainees are taking to achieve competence and this may mask underlying issues.
- Take an interest in the progress and development of trainees, those on coaching plans, and those who are temporarily restricted off roster – this will help to ensure they are restored to normal working as quickly as possible.
- Ensure an accurate list of Terms & Conditions and local agreements exists and is kept up to date. Review local agreements when you first take up a new role.
- Never over-rely on free day working (FDW) – there is a fine balance between adequate levels of resource with a small vacancy gap and being overstretched. A small vacancy gap with a reasonable amount of overtime can be more financially efficient than a full complement but it is easy to let this develop too far unless a very close watch is kept on resource levels.
- Know the terms for Sunday and Bank Holiday working (including lieu leave entitlements for the latter).

Tips

Signaller resources are usually the largest single group of staff for certain operations manager - and generally the most expensive. Therefore efficient management is a critical obligation, which must start with the rosters at local management level.

Do not get this issue wrong - at best it will damage your bottom line, at worst it will have severe Industrial Relations implications.

5.5 Joint Performance Planning with Industry Partners

BACKGROUND

With the development of the JPIP (Joint Performance Improvement Plan) there has been a move towards joint performance planning between TOC/FOCs and Network Rail rather than the more historical single plans which were not usually linked, shared or monitored.

Train Operators and Network Rail need to have a clear understanding of the performance improvement plans within their business and that of each other in order to improve the train service performance.

Performance plans should contain targets and plans for PPM, CaSL, delay minute, cancellation and significant lateness measures. Joint performance plans should reflect the priorities of the TOC/FOC and Network Rail Route and may therefore include other relevant targets and plans.

KEY ISSUES

The joint planning process must begin with a clear understanding of the business priorities over the following 18 months (this will extend to an outline plan for the following five years). This must be understood in the context of longer term performance plans. This analysis will help identify the most appropriate targets.

PPM targets will form the core of the document for most passenger operators, although increasingly there is a focus on right time statistics both as a customer expectation and as a way of driving improvement in PPM. The required target in PPM and CaSL for the time period in question need to be identified (usually the 12 month JPIP period but this is now extended to incorporate a five year look forward as a Long Term Performance Plan). The JPIP must be agreed and understood by all parties from the Managing Directors down.

Appropriate analysis must be undertaken to understand the delay minute and cancellation levels which will deliver this PPM trajectory. Correlation between PPM and delay minutes can easily be calculated based on historical performance levels. The gearing between each will vary with the type of operation and may also change with the implementation of a new timetable.

Analysis will also be required to identify actions necessary to achieve the CaSL targets. It may be helpful to consider CaSL as two separate targets for cancellations and significant lateness. The significance of each part will differ depending

Other Longer Term Planning

on nature of the operation (long distance will have a higher proportion of SL, Metro operations will have more Ca).

When considering PPM, delay or cancellation trajectories it is also important to consider factors which may depress the level of delivery. Large programmes of engineering work, introduction of new trains, and passenger growth may all cause reductions in performance if not managed. Performance plans should recognise the magnitude of any potential problem and ensure that adequate plans are in place to mitigate the effect.

Both Network Rail and the train operator must then challenge relevant areas of the business to provide details of how they will improve the performance in their area of management. Periodic performance reporting and the use of performance measurement/management systems should already be in place to assist Responsible Managers within the business to decide on their action plans.

Freight operators have their own Freight Performance Measure which is monitored by them and by Network Rail. Actual performance against this measure is published four weekly and reflects not just the effect poor freight performance can have on passenger TOCs but also the increasing freight-customer need for good timekeeping performance, especially on intermodal flows and those which form part of the 'just in time' production line of industrial customers.

Each and every plan must have the following characteristics to be accepted:-
- **Specific** – (Clear in their outcome and improvement).
- **Measurable** – (Clear understanding of performance benefit).
- **Achievable** – (Within the manager's realm of responsibility).
- **Realistic** – (Driven by a business case or properly financed).
- **Time based** – (Clear milestones for delivery of the plan with clear ownership).

The acronym phrase SMART provides neat shorthand here.

Both Network Rail and the Operating Company must come to a clear agreement as to the ongoing management of the improvement plans. Best practice is a single, joint document that forms an appendix to the signed JPIP. This document should contain all the performance improvement plans as well as a clear management structure designed to keep the plans updated and relevant. A single person should be tasked with keeping the plan updated and distributed.

Note: Because JPIPs are contractual there can be a temptation to hold separate 'reserve' or stretch plans. This is never helpful but it is unfortunately quite common.

Network Rail is responsible for the management of TOC on TOC plans. This does not just include other Train Operators plans to reduce their own delays

5.6 Contingency Plans

(and therefore a reduced knock on to your services) but also clear Network Rail actions regarding regulation, and service recovery.

The cumulative savings indicated by the plans must be seen to be great enough to deliver the joint PPM targets previously agreed

As delivery of the joint plan progresses all parties should remain aware of the risks to delivery and be prepared to act to mitigate the effects of emerging issues. An up to date risk register will anticipate potential problems and provide agreed mitigations.

JPIPs started off a few years ago as new exercise and were novel. They should now be 'day job' in planning for future performance improvements.

Tips

A good joint performance planning process takes a considerable number of management hours to create and maintain. Use the meeting structure already in place to manage updates to the plans - this can also be used to manage risk as well.

Given the effect on performance of train reliability on most TOCs, Fleet must be an integral part of the planning process and should both be fully engaged and also feel itself to be fully engaged in the Operations-led JPIP.

When a Network Rail Route contains a number of depots then their performance plans should be individually reviewed to ensure all depots have plans to address all relevant KPIs.

Going public on the broad content of the JPIP is now seen as industry best practice.

Close collaboration on performance planning and management is essential if good performance results are to be consistently delivered.

Other Longer Term Planning

5.6 Contingency Plans

BACKGROUND

Contingency plans should be in place for a range of identified operational scenarios. The purpose is to contain risk and manage predictable events in a structured and consistent way. They should be agreed by NR, and all affected Operators and form part of the suite of Control Office reference documents.

There is no section in this handbook on fire fighting. Contingency plans and the other relevant arrangements should remove the need for this in all but the most extreme circumstances. Even the difficult initial phases of a serious incident can be planned for in advance.

Although contingency plans cannot be prepared to cover all circumstances, development of an appropriate suite of plans will help provide guidance in most situations. Some plans will require high levels of detail (e.g. Restricted Access plans should be developed on a junction to junction or core route section basis) whilst others will only need to contain core principles.

However remember that the existence of contingency plans will never completely remove the need for the decisive management of incidents and good decision making processes.

ISSUES

Some contingency plans would be more correctly described as contingency strategies – they describe the principles to be adopted in managing a deviation from normal operation. They should embrace the range of foreseeable circumstances, events or incidents and should, where possible, be tested periodically – tabletop exercises if properly planned and executed can be a very useful, and thought provoking, way of achieving this.

Other more detailed contingency plans should be in place for the following key areas:-
- Restricted Access (these are prepared by Network Rail, but each TOC/FOC should have its own document listing the detailed train service implications).
- Shortage of Rolling Stock – this should include reference to key business trains.
- Shortages of traincrew and other critical staff.
- Loss of key TOC facilities e.g. fuelling points, depot inlet/outlet roads, stabling points.
- Loss of key NR facilities e.g. power boxes.

5.6 Contingency Plans

- Weather plans – for all seasons, Summer, Autumn, Winter and all weather types – hot, cold, wet and windy.
- Consequence of other critical incidents (e.g. a fleet depot not being available).
- Bespoke plans for large scale and high risk engineering works. Likely overrun scenarios should be considered with Network Rail and both engineers and operators should understand their actions to minimise disruption.
- Specific Event Plans (e.g. Festivals, sports events etc).

Ensure low level but frequent events get appropriate consideration.

It is essential that customer requirements and commercial considerations are carefully evaluated when developing contingency plans.

When creating contingency plans make sure that you consider the actions to be taken in the first hour of the incident as well as the expected steady state. Having a clear plan for the first stages of an incident can make managing the recovery much easier.

The introduction of the Integrated Train Planning System within Network Rail has provided the ability to store contingency timetables ready for implementation with 24 hours notice. Serious consideration should be given to holding contingency timetables in this format since implementing them will mean that downstream systems such as TRUST and CIS will show the correct amended timetable. Even where this facility is being used some issues will remain such as:

- Are the contingency plans for different TOCs compatible over the same route?
- Are all operators on the route implementing their contingency plan?
- Will the timetable reach automatic route setting systems (ARS) within 24 hours?

INTEGRATION

The key to all plans is the need for sensible integration. Ensure that routine business strategies support the contents of contingency plans. For example:

- Does the TOC diversionary route knowledge strategy fit the Restricted Access contingency plan?
- Do station disruption plans link in with and support the overall contingency plan?
- Does the staff resource level support the Winter Key Route Strategy?
- Do different operators' plans fit together? What happens if one operator on a route implements their plan and the other doesn't?
- What passenger communication activities will be required? If you issue a plan late in the day will all the critical systems have the revised information?

Other Longer Term Planning

Remember the best plan in the world is not much use if passengers do not know what you are running.

Contingency plans require wide consultation – in some cases, agreement – in order to ensure the plans are relevant, appropriate and cover all the issues. Consultation also gets 'buy-in' from the staff that will be expected to operate the plan in real time and engagement generally ensures a more disciplined and consistent application when it is most needed.

They must be reviewed after use. Were they successful, could they be improved?

PLAN OWNERS RESPONSIBILITIES

Plan
- Periodically, and at least at every timetable change, check the relevance of plans and update as required.
- Ensure all relevant scenarios are covered.
- Ensure that plans are reviewed post incident.
- Ensure that suppliers are included in the preparation and content of the plans.

Do
- Check the application of plans through the regular review of logs and reviews of the recommendations from post-incident analysis.
- Make any difficult real time decisions regarding deviations from the plans.
- Promote the use of sensible structured contingency plans throughout the organisation.

Review
- Check the suite of contingency plans is appropriate at specified frequencies (at least an annual review).
- Ensure the outcomes from post-event reviews are acted upon.
- Identify any significant gaps and weaknesses through the various review processes.
- Identify and consider emerging good practice elsewhere in the industry.

PLAN USERS RESPONSIBILITIES

There are a number of important considerations:-
- Achieving the right balance between sufficient detail and clear strategy. Ensuring that the plan is not too complex to be implemented is important too.
- Creating plans is important but there must be joint commitment to actually

5.7 Engineering Work Planning Management

using them in action: all too often, good documents remain on the shelf gathering dust.
- Timescales. Decisions on implementing a contingency plan or emergency time table need to be made early. It can be tempting to delay in case a situation changes but early communication to end customers requires early decision making.

Plan
- Ensure all contingency plans are available and in date.
- Check that any revisions are compatible with current business practices and arrangements.
- Ensure that the relevant staff are aware of the contents of plans and understand their role in discharging the plans.

Do
- Implement contingency plans as necessary.
- Make real time decisions regarding deviations from the plan in a controlled way.
- Ensure plans are properly communicated to staff and customers.

Review
- Post-event review the continuing relevance of plans.
- Notify any issues and suggested amendments/changes.

Finally – once a contingency plan is implemented remember to establish how the transition back to normal working will be achieved – this can be a neglected phase.

Tips

The need for contingency plans should not be in doubt - the trick is producing an appropriate level of detail for each plan area.

Make sure that the plan contains clear instructions on the immediate actions to be taken to get control of the situation. A common mistake is only to plan for the steady state which is only reached after several hours of disruption management. Having a plan for the first critical hour can dramatically improve the management of the incident.

Use contingency plans to codify a framework and agreed principles - particularly if the plans cover contractual areas e.g. restricted access. It is better to have disagreements at the planning stage - not during an incident.

Other Longer Term Planning

5.7 Engineering Work Planning Management

BACKGROUND

Network Rail is responsible for managing the railway infrastructure; this includes maintenance, renewals and enhancements. Other outside parties may also need to undertake work affecting the network, such as County Councils and local developers.

Plans for works which will disrupt normal train services are developed annually, and the timetable year (TTY) runs from December to December. The year is split into broadly two halves; a principal TTY, December to May, and a subsidiary TTY, June to December. Although negotiated separately, generally the year is constructed as a single plan. Disruptive possessions are those which require the TOC or FOC to bid an amended train plan against the base Working Timetable.

At circa TT-80; 80 weeks from the commencement of that particular timetable year, the Network Rail planning teams will receive all the requests for disruptive access from Network Rail engineering disciplines and outside parties. Where practical, work will be undertaken in the no train period (white space) but sometimes this is insufficiently long. In such circumstances engineering access may be required during the train running period. The challenge is to develop a plan that enables all the requests from the engineering disciplines but also meets with approval from of all the operators, some of whom may have conflicting preferences.

Note: At the time this Section was reviewed T- XX was the common term used. However the Access Conditions now use D- XX.

KEY PRINCIPLES

Compliance with the Network Code part D and Network Rail line standards is essential in building the plan. It is a requirement of NR's license agreement that it agrees a plan with its customers to allow them to manage their business, whilst minimising the amount of engineering access required. Plans must be constructed and declared against laid down timescales.

To maximise passenger opportunities, key national routes are classified under Route Categorisation (RC) as Category A routes. On these key routes, bus substitution is a last resort with disruptive possessions requiring supporting evidence and high level sign-off, diversions are acceptable providing journey times are not extended by more than 25%.

5.7 Engineering Work Planning Management

PROCESS COMMENTARY

The process is complex and must be managed at both a strategic level (director/ executive) and a detailed nuts and bolts level (train planning and routes). The quality of the engineering plan and delivery of alternative plans will be a reflection of the effort and commitment to the consultation process by all parties. Getting this right is very important as it will affect both train operator profitability and train service performance.

The process starts at approximately D-90 when work deliverers submit their disruptive weekend and weeknight requirements to the NR planning teams, these will form Section 5 (Midweek Possession Strategy) & Section 7 (Register of Disruptive Possessions) of the Engineering Access statement (EAS - formerly Rules of the Route). Between D-90 and D-65, the NR planning teams will look to build the access plan whilst adhering to Route Categorisation principals and also known planning rules. These rules are ever growing and are critical for a successful plan. A few prime examples are:–

- No 'double bussing' unless absolutely essential or a customer request.
- One through route always to be available between London and Scotland
- No summer possessions on routes to the coast
- Care with dating possessions to avoid festivals and events (e.g. Six Nations Rugby, Southend Air Show, Notting Hill Carnival etc.)

Diversionary routes are also a key component of the plan, particularly for freight. These can be particularly complex in key urban areas, but it is perhaps surprising that a possession in the Camden area can affect routes in Scotland, or a possession in the Sheffield area can affect routes in Bristol or Norwich. As freight moves closer to a 7 day business, and the volume of work on the network grows, such planning rules become harder to adhere to.

Resources must be considered with as much importance as access, this includes NR resources; locomotives, trains, wagons, contractor resources including manpower and scarce or critical resources; testing and commissioning engineers, Kirov cranes etc. Routing of engineering trains must also be taken into account, ensuring that a route from the Logistics Delivery Centre (LDC) to and from the site is available. This can be quite a task given the location of some LDCs and the volume of non-disruptive possessions that will be applied for much later on in the process after these routes have been identified.

Version 0 is a non-contractual snapshot of the plan produced at D-65, responses from the operators are welcomed but not mandatory although providing a guiding response is seen as best practice. Further detailed work on the plan is on-going post v0 and would include any responses received for v0.

Other Longer Term Planning

Version 1 (V1) is the formal proposal for the principal TTY and is issued at D-59, although the plan would include details for the whole year. Responses from the operators are sought within 5 weeks, although minor time alterations are inevitable, any disagreement should only reflect major issues or points of principle. Following an assessment of issues raised by operators, version 2 (V2) is issued at D-44, which is the decision document for the principal DY. V3 and V4 replicate the process for V1 and V2 but refer to the subsidiary TTY. Post V1 and V3, the mechanism for NR generated change is tightened up which highlights the need to engage in extensive early discussion to ensure the plan is robust and accurately represented at all key stages in the its development. This will also assist the planning teams closer to delivery who will not want to be dealing with surprises just weeks or days away from the actual possession.

Change is a major frustration to all parties, whether it is the result of budgetary issues, late awarding of contracts, general specification changes or just insufficient detail at plan conception. Plans can be so tightly interwoven, that any type or level of change whether additional or cancelled possessions, can have a major effect on the plan, with much good work and time wasted. This particularly applies to routes that pass through 2 or more NR areas of responsibility where access strategies are carefully crafted to avoid multiple disruption to operators.

If on-going discussions fail to resolve any particular issue after V2 or V4 (depending on the TT period), then the operator has 3 weeks after the issue of the respective decision document to escalate it to the secretary of the Access Dispute Committee, highlighting how, in their opinion NR's proposal is contrary to the conditions set out in part D of the Network Code. This requires Network Rail to balance the needs of all within the industry. This can be quite a task as some operators prefer all day Sunday possessions, some prefer Sat PM/Sun AM whilst others may prefer a blockade than a series of weekends etc. The role of the planning teams is to balance the wishes of each customer whilst ensuring the work can be delivered. As with all industry processes an operator is deemed to have accepted the Engineering Access Statement unless an objection is made.

Compensation to the operators is payable under Schedule 4 and is based on the duration of the possession and missed monitoring points / stations. Possessions that can be declared in V1 / V3 will receive a greater discount than those declared further down the process. Freight compensation is not covered within this mechanism, but via a separate arrangement that compensates according to the level of disruption and whether it is prior to or post T-12. Possessions that require a moderate increase in journey time will not incur the same level of compensation as that of a diversion of a gauge restricted route that requires diesel instead of electric haulage.

Planning then moves from a yearly cycle to a 4 weekly cycle with the next

5.7 Engineering Work Planning Management

major stage being the issuing of the Draft Period Possession Plan (DPPP) to operators at T-30.

Once the revised train service is confirmed and the engineering detail firmed up, the Confirmed Period Possession Plan (CPPP) is issued at T-26. This acts as formal notification to the operators who start the bid and offer process for train services, otherwise known as the Informed Traveller process, a key part of the NR licensing agreement, which ensures that the amended train plan is finalised and uploaded to all systems at T-12. Finally, planning moves to a weekly cycle with the Weekly Operating Notice confirmation of all planned work, disruptive and non-disruptive. A final check should be made by operators against the final document e.g. checking details of ECS (Empty Coaching Stock) workings and line codes.

A small amount of additional access to deal with short term engineering problems will probably be needed after the CPPP. Each of these requests will need to be assessed against the risk to train service performance and the operators business of not doing the work against effect on the business of disrupting customers by doing the work. Most likely reasons are a removal of a speed restriction, late delivery of an enhancement or perhaps an incomplete renewal site.

ISSUES

The engineering plan proposed by Network Rail in the EAS process will need to be assessed by Train Operators for the effect on the business. The items that negotiators consider are:-
- Minimising risk to passenger revenue, by avoiding disruption to high value business such as weekdays on mainlines. Many operators now work with NR to move intrusive engineering access to Sundays but this day, particularly late afternoon and evening has grown in recent decades from being relatively quiet to being very busy on some routes (for CrossCountry it is the second busiest day of the week - after Fridays).
- The time of year and the pattern of the disruption are also important, with January to March being the months of lowest revenue. Continuous runs of engineering work that can be planned into period blocks are encouraged as it can be published in the working timetable; a repeating train plan gives a consistent message to the travelling public.
- Certain routes lend themselves to blockades, with work being delivered in a single hit rather than continuous weekend disruption.
- Maximising the use of single line working to access key locations, a reduced service over a single line is encouraged ahead of bus replacement. Surveys

Other Longer Term Planning

show that keeping passengers on a train, even if journey times are lengthened, has a very high value – they dislike changing to a bus. We are moving as an industry to re-use operating techniques that fell out of favour in the 1990s. Operators have to use the available rules (such as Single Line Working and Temporary Block Working) to keep the railway running where-ever possible, around or past, engineering possessions. Like minded TOC/FOC and NR managers working together will allow innovative approaches to be applied.

- Freight customers often do not even have this choice – they cannot deliver the quantities of coal expected at a power station by the use of road transport. Possessions on Sunday generally find favour with freight operators, but as freight expands, particularly the Intermodal service, opinions may change.
- Practicality of train and bus plans needs to be considered. Can trains be terminated at locations efficiently? Can enough buses be procured? Can buses use the station forecourt and is the interchange practical – narrow or steep stairways, congestion on platforms etc.? Consideration of fleet maintenance, fuel range and shut down and start-up of services is also needed. Can the alternative service be manned? What are the safety implications? (Should we be increasing passenger risk through crowding at low capacity stations that are not usually subject to large numbers of passengers and their luggage or by their joining/alighting from/travelling on road coaches?).
- Compensation needs to be considered; revenue loss for TOCs is via a formula in Schedule 4 of the Track Access Contract. Since April 2009, most rail replacement bus operations are also compensated by Network Rail. This is based on a bus and train mileage formula with a fixed payment rate regardless of how many buses are required to operate the service. TOCs can now only claim actual costs for longer duration possessions and only when costs exceed a difference of more than £10,000 after all Schedule 4 compensation received has been taken into account (Part G of the Network Code).

Be careful – think, test, consider. Ensure that full input has been made to your decision making by liaising with your commercial colleagues. The main aim must always be a workable temporary timetable that will deliver the best service for our customers. Compensation for TOCs is important but it should not be the key driver.

5.7 Engineering Work Planning Management

Tips

The effect of engineering work has potential to significantly impact on your operational and financial performance.

Good practice is to use the engineering plan to inform the budget process and ensure that the effect engineering work is reflected in the business plan.

Understand any risks and the potential impact of any changes to the plan.

Actual work must be managed to minimise deviation from any assumptions made in the planning phase.

Remember, the main aim of the engineering planning process should be to minimise disruption to the fare-paying public whilst making sure that we get all the necessary work done as efficiently as possible – follow the process!

Other Longer Term Planning

5.8 Seasonal Planning and Review

BACKGROUND

This activity is also known as weather preparedness and covers the systematic, cyclic approach to mitigating the impact of severe weather of all types. Autumn is important but seasonal planning must cover all year. Accordingly, seasonal planning should cover hot/cold, wet/dry, wind and flooding; it should also include specific threats such as snow, lightning and coastal flooding.

This is an area where sometimes we are good, sometimes we are not. But when we mess up it is all very public.

It is really important that we avoid complacency.

ISSUES

Seasonal planning and preparedness requires a number of simple components:-
- A weather calendar that describes all tasks (TOC and NR) that must be undertaken/checked and when, in order to maximise readiness. An example extract is shown at the end of this Section.
- A cross-company group that reviews the plans in detail on a monthly basis – ideally reporting to a more senior cross-company performance improvement group.
- Clear remits, accountabilities, reporting lines and escalation arrangements (see relevant sections of this manual).
- An agreed audit programme that checks critical activities at pre-determined times of the year e.g. point heaters, readiness of MPVs and Sandite/water jetting trains, stocks of Killfrost (or equivalent).
- A clear review process that draws out lessons learnt from each season.

In addition to these arrangements there must be a clear recognition that weather patterns are changing and accordingly preparedness must be dynamic and flexible. Using a daily telephone conference to decide on actions 24 hours in advance is a good practice.

Senior Managers must ensure that weather preparedness features as a regular agenda item on all appropriate performance meeting agendas. The very strong lead now shown by NR to all aspects of seasonal preparedness should be embraced and strongly supported as this is very much a joint activity.

Strong integrated seasonal preparedness should be a key routine activity. It must

5.8 Seasonal Planning and Review

never be seen as anything other than a key element of the day job, even when a succession of benign seasons reduces the priority of weather preparedness. Recent winters have shown the continued weakness of the industry in dealing with snow and ice.

Accordingly, make sure that the following areas are covered (this list is not meant to be exhaustive):-

Hot Weather
- Air conditioning in passenger accommodation on trains.
- Air conditioning in mess rooms, cabs of locos/units and signalling relay rooms checked – are spares and expertise in place.
- Rails de-stressed and known problem sites contained to the shortest possible distance (confirmation required from NR).
- NR to share list of known problem spots with TOC.
- Are adequate ballast shoulders in place (if they are they'll do much to hold rails against potential to buckle).
- Ready availability of boards for any necessary ESRs.
- Supplies of water available for staff/passenger use in extreme conditions.
- A sensible policy on employee uniform is in place.

Cold Weather
- Units/trains winterised in accordance with the VMIs (Vehicle Maintenance Instructions).
- Depot track/points precautions in place.
- Stations ready with de-icer, grit for walking routes and platforms etc.
- Priority routes and arrangements agreed with NR.
- Point heaters individually checked and confirmed as working.
- Point heater fuses to hand with maintenance/faulting staff.
- De-icing/proving trains available during severe frosts.
- 3rd rail heaters (where fitted) checked and working.
- Drivers fault finding reminders briefed.
- Resource Plan during winter timetable to include provision of night ferry drivers to run 'ghost trains' to ensure network stays open.
- Consider provision of snow ploughs or equivalents germane to your TOC and key locations.
- Walking routes on depot and at stations etc checked and a process with clearly defined resources to clear/treat them as appropriate.
- Circumstances defined where DMU/diesel locos will be left running to avoid failures to start in the morning.
- Driver reminders for winter driving conditions briefed/available.

Institution of Railway Operators

Other Longer Term Planning

- Arrangements for getting key staff to work – particularly in remote locations.

Wet Weather
- Culverts, drains and ditches kept clear.
- Tunnel pumps serviced and available including spares.
- High risk flood sites prepared for mitigation.
- Bridge scour sites policed/patrolled with plans in place for permanent pier protection.

Dry Weather
- High risk fire locations identified.
- Cable routes and troughs cleared of rubbish/detritus.
- Tamping increased on vulnerable "heave" embankments.

Windy Weather
- High risk OHLE locations identified.
- Wooded areas identified – special attention to tress encroaching on OHLE.
- High risk areas for lineside rubbish checked and cleared.
- Large advertising hoardings at stations checked for security.
- Temporary scaffolding checked by contractors.
- MOM overhead line competencies and equipment in date.

Autumn
- Effect of possessions on railhead treatment circuits identified and mitigated against.
- Process in place for checking and filling sand boxes on trains.
- Driver reminders for autumn driving conditions briefed/available.
- Additional actions for high risk days identified and communicated to staff.
- Leaf-fall timetable (if there is one for the TOC) checked and briefed.
- Daily review of problem locations. Re-allocate hand sanding resources and railhead treatment trains accordingly.
- Ensure NR run the Railhead Treatment Trains (RHTT) as per plan, and identify a contingency should the RHTT train not run its circuit as per plan.

5.8 Seasonal Planning and Review

Tips

British weather is no respecter of the seasons - we must always be prepared for adverse weather.

Weather management is not just about planning for autumn - as important as that activity is.

With current UK weather patterns heat related problems and flooding are likely to be just as disruptive and potentially more damaging to PPM. Weather patterns mean that the issue can only grow in importance in coming years.

Weather management is now probably the single most important determinant of good train service delivery.

Other relevant/useful documents:-

– Network Rail Seasons Management Team Website (http://www.smtweather.co.uk/). Your NR colleagues will give you the current login and password.

Other Longer Term Planning

One - Autumn Preparedness Matrix (Extract)
Autumn 2007

Legend: **N** - No Progress | **P** - Progressing | **C** - Complete | **A** - Awaiting update

	Task	TOC/NR/BOTH	One Owner	JAN	FEB	MAR	APR	MAY	JUN	JUL	AUG	SEP	OCT	NOV	DEC	% complete	Notes
5	**Vegetation**																
a	Identification of sites where Tree Felling is required (prioritised)	BOTH	Performance Managers with WU					C								100	Complete for 2007, but ongoing
b	Additional checks on vegetation growth prior to autumn season	TOC	Performance Managers								P	A	A			30	Routes cab riding and reporting direct to NR when required
6	**High Risk Sites and Special Working Arrangements**																
a	Does the Sectional Appendix reflect the high risk sites?	BOTH	Performance Managers with WU							C						100	
9	**Static Sanders**																
a	Identification of new sites	BOTH	Performance Managers with WU	P	P	P	P	P	P	P	C					100	Lakenham UM, Palgrave UM, Diss UM, Manningtree UM, Brentwood DM, Forest Gate U+DE, Bury St Edmunds UM, Hockley DM
12	**Production of Local Autumn Working Arrangements**																
a	Autumn Plan 2006 reviewed	BOTH	KP with WU	C												100	
b	Agreement of special working arrangements	BOTH	Stewart Player with WU							P	P	A				20	
13	**Freight issues**																
a	Brentwood bank issues	NR	KP with WU								P	P				n/a	Discussed at August JPR. Needs final check that trains are booked down main
b	Freight train loccs. Ask NR to confirm arrangements for checking freight trains not overloaded during autumn.	NR	KP with WU								P	A				0	
14	**Drivers**																
a	Driver Training e.g. Skid Pan / simulator	TOC	Justin Willett + Ops and Traincrew Managers						P	P	P	P				50	PGA and high risk drivers will use simulator. Mainline also running skid pan training on Mid Norfolk. Comparison of methods being organised by Justin Willett. Simulator programme includes anticipating LA, reaction to LA, response following LA (reporting etc) and controlled test stop.
b	Review driver instructions for different units.	TOC	Stewart Player					P	C							100	
c	Driver briefing	TOC	Keith Palmer							P	P	A				60	Keith Palmer collating company wide and route based content for briefing leaflet. To be produced by Jill Caswell
d	Driver Managers to travel with first services on red and black days	TOC	Ops and Traincrew Managers										A	A		0	
e	Whiteboards to be used at depots for rapid feedback of driving conditions	TOC	Ops and Traincrew Managers										A	A		0	
f	No newly qualified drivers on the route during red and black days	TOC	Ops and Traincrew Managers										A	A		0	
15	**Timetables**																
a	Emergency timetables ready for use during autumn.	TOC	B. Rule		P	P	P	P	P	P	P	C				100	Unable to reach agreement on a public differential emergency timetable in advance of the autumn season. Requests will be put to control on a case by case basis.

5.8 Seasonal Planning and Review

	Task	TOC/NR/BOTH	One Owner	JAN	FEB	MAR	APR	MAY	JUNE	JULY	AUG	SEPT	OCT	NOV	DEC	% complete	Notes
b	Planned timetable alterations for autumn	TOC	B. Rule					P	P	P	P	A				80	2 minutes differential agreed with DfT on rural services. 5 up and 4 down Norwich services to have additional 5 minutes. Publicity for customers and severed connections only outstanding issues.
c	Will units be strengthened to increase braking capabilities during Autumn? (e.g. 4 to 8 cars)	TOC	Matt Dickerson							P	P	A				30	See 7d
16	**Fleet**			JAN	FEB	MAR	APR	MAY	JUN	JUL	AUG	SEP	OCT	NOV	DEC		
a	Do wheel profiles comply fully with standards in readiness for Autumn? What records are kept?	TOC	Steve Mitchell						P	C						100	
b	Are all trains sander fitted? - If not what services are at risk of poor rail adhesion?	TOC	Steve Mitchell			P	C									100	Only 153s not fitted. Complete but see action ai below on 153 units
c	NCP Review fleet maintenance arrangements eg tyre turning	TOC	Steve Mitchell							P	P					90	Reviews but need to finalise whether further slots will be booked on the lathe.
d	Ensure locos remain on 4 motors	TOC	GJ							P	P	A	A	A	A	30	Locos with only 3 motors to be used on load 9 only. Need to ensure this is recorded as a restriction in Datastream
e	NCP Ensure adequate sand is available	TOC	BW							P	P	A	A	A	A	80	Delivered
f	NCP Ensure suitable dry storage facilities	TOC	BW								C					100	
g	NCP Generate spec for sanding equipment	TOC	TT						P	C						100	
h	NCP Inspection of sanding equipment	TOC	GJ									A				0	
i	NCP Review "checking and topping up" strategy	TOC	MeW							P	C					100	
j	NCP Ensure Bombardier are "ready"	TOC	MW							P	C					100	
k	NCP Additional Brake block supply	TOC	BW												A	0	
l	NCP Isolate Rheo on Red and Black days	TOC	MeW									A	A	A	A	0	

Section 5

Other Longer Term Planning

5.9 Train Connectional Policies

BACKGROUND

Connectional Policies will specify the way in which the following requirements are balanced.
- The expectations of passengers that connections will be made (especially if shown in timetable publications).
- The need to prevent delays spreading across the network due to connections being held.
- Whether delays due to connections can be attributed an original causal incident.

Connectional Policy is one of those issues in a TOC where, if you do not have a clear, enforced and documented arrangement, then one – or more likely, several – will emerge by default.

Policies must be consulted with Network Rail and other relevant TOCs to ensure that Signallers, Controllers and station staff carry out the agreed plan. In addition, delays caused by connections being held will only be attributed to the original incident if Network Rail and any affected TOC are in agreement. Obtaining Network Rail agreement may be difficult as there is no obligation in the Network Code for Network Rail to agree.

ISSUES

Protecting overall performance and preventing the cancerous spread of late running is an enormously important consideration. However, a blanket 'no hold' policy is rarely tenable. The need to maintain good punctuality will need to be balanced with the needs of passengers and the financial ramifications of triggering 'Delay Repay' compensation schemes.

As a minimum, a connectional policy will need to address:-
- A review of the arrangements at each Timetable change date.
- Connections which are shown in the National Rail Timetable.
- Connectional margins documented in the National Rail Timetable.
- Connections with last services – not necessarily only the last train to a range of destinations, but also those feeding into last trains further down the line.
- Minimum levels of demand required to justify holding a service. Where demand is very low then alternative transport might be more appropriate.
- A connection that just fails – to address the issue of a connection pulling

5.9 Train Connectional Policies

out of the platform as aspiring customers disembark from their late running service. Often known as 'tail end connections'.
- How customers with specific train seat reservations are to be dealt with when a connection is missed.
- The thresholds beyond which customers who have been denied their connection will be provided with alternative transport.
- Services which will not be held under any circumstances, and the alternative arrangements proposed for customers intending to connect.
- Principal connectional arrangements with adjacent TOCs.
- Engineering work connections between buses and trains. A key issue is providing stations with information on the location of the bus so that sensible decisions can be made.
- Ad hoc connections – what might be considered and how authority is obtained.

Policies should also outline the range of general alternatives for customers, which may include different routeings, or alternative transport modes. The Policy is best contained within, and re-issued with the TOC Contingency Plans at timetable change.

Briefing is important – all affected staff should be aware of what the Policy says, and equally importantly, why.

Authority to vary the policy should be vested in a senior post in the Control, to which any requests should be directed.

Beware of false connections which can be created when incoming trains regularly arrive early. This can generate a belief amongst customers that a connection is possible with the outgoing service. The underlying cause may be that the timing of the incoming train is slack, but connections should not be held in this case and ideally the situation should be avoided through careful planning.

Tips

TOCs Connectional Policies should be highly visible and understood by all relevant staff - station staff, conductors, controllers etc.

The interface between a TOC's Policy and those of adjacent TOCs should be seamless.

Prior agreement with NR is essential.

Other Longer Term Planning

Adherence to the Policy must be mandatory, and non-compliance should not be tolerated. However, Control Staff should be encouraged to be sensitive to requests for dispensation to vary the Policy guidelines, even if such dispensation is given sparingly.

Connectional Policies are difficult to formulate but a clear position will minimise customer dissatisfaction and provide staff with clear guidance.

Section 6: **Running a Railway**

6.1	Passenger Perspective	130
6.2	Freight Perspective	134
6.3	Role of the Operator	146
6.4	Out of Hours Visits	147
6.5	Performance Management Real Time	148
6.6	Safety Management	152
6.7	Passenger Information	156
6.8	Train Service Delivery Systems & Processes – Overview	159
6.9	Control Office; Issues and Management	165
6.10	Logs – Using Control and other Logs	174
6.11	Delay Attribution	177
6.12	Simplifiers	182
6.13	Role of First Line Operations Staff	183
6.14	Fleet and Operations Interface	189
6.15	Train Characteristics	195
6.16	Infrastructure and Operations Interface	204
6.17	Track Issues	208
6.18	Temporary Speed Restrictions and Emergency Speed Restrictions	212
6.19	Level Crossing Characteristics	215
6.20	Electrification Systems	225
6.21	Signal Engineering Issues	237
6.22	Signalling Operations	248
6.23	Train Regulation	254
6.24	Signaller Management	257
6.25	Signalbox Visits	261
6.26	Train Driving Operations	263
6.27	Train Crew Management	271
6.28	Cab Rides	274
6.29	TOC Short Term Planning	276
6.30	Station Operations	279
6.31	Train Despatch	285
6.32	Energy Management on Heavy Rail	289
6.33	Risk Management	292
6.34	Security Issues	295
6.35	Trespass, Vandalism and Disorder	299
6.36	Signals Passed At Danger	302
6.37	Cable Theft	309

Running a Railway

6.1 Passenger Perspective

BACKGROUND

In everything the Operator does, whatever part of the industry they work for, the customer perspective is vital and all operational decisions should be focused on achieving the best outcome for the largest number of passengers and freight customers.

Operating rules and procedures are aimed at delivering the safe, punctual service that meets customers' expectations. When the railway is disrupted or recovering from disruption, it is important to adopt the best overall solution considering the actual impact on passengers and freight customers. You are unlikely to delight all your customers in a disruption situation but they do expect disruption at times and will be appreciative if it is handled professionally and they are kept well informed.

Details of the freight perspective are contained in 6.2.

National Passenger Surveys (NPS) are an important way of checking how our passenger railway customers rate our ability to deliver a good service and the results from these surveys can shape future initiatives.

KEY ISSUES

The key issues that passengers tell us are important include:-
- Good punctuality.
- Avoidance of cancellations or short formations.
- Good information – particularly during disruption.
- Honest advice regarding alternative travel choices.

All the advice in this Handbook is aimed at helping to deliver these essential customer needs and all operational decisions must explicitly consider these needs. All operational staff, whether frontline or not, must ensure this passenger perspective is always maintained.

You will obviously need to think about delay minutes, PPM impact, CaSL, Schedule 8 payments and so on, but focusing on KPIs can result in perverse decision making. Remember that these are indicators of performance and what really matters is keeping our customers as satisfied as possible.

Cancellations, particularly en route, are very disruptive and must be managed carefully. It is very easy to see the operational benefit of terminating a

6.1 Passenger Perspective

train short in order to get the return working back to plan, but it is essential that sufficient consideration is given to the customer service consequences, especially the length of time for the next service to the missed stops of the cancelled train. Be mindful of who your passengers are, the time of day and if seat reservations are involved. Special care should be taken of minors, the elderly or other needy passengers.

It is important to address these aspects in service recovery contingency plans and ensure that operations contingency plans take account of passenger flows and cancellations, particularly those that will generate disproportionate problems regarding alternative travel.

Remember that many railway staff involved in managing disruption do not really get a good feel for the impact on individual customers. Examples are Signallers and Controllers, who may rarely use rail transport, and are not necessarily able to look out of a window to see a heaving station concourse.

Ensure that controllers consider the passenger perspective. Understanding the problems that arise when tipping 800 people off a train is something that controllers should routinely consider when managing perturbation and service recovery. Exposing controllers to these issues during out of office days is desirable but difficult to stage manage. The 'unit of currency' should be the passenger, not just the train – i.e. 'we had fifteen hundred people disrupted this morning through the track circuit failure' rather than just the more traditional 'three trains were delayed by the track circuit failure'.

The principle of taking action for the greater good is a sound one, but the effectiveness of the company's response to disruption is best measured by the way it deals with customers caught in the 'eye of the storm'; those most severely affected - those on the cancelled train, those stranded at stations for long periods, those who have missed important connections, appointments, or last trains.

Having a company policy on such matters is a good start. This might state:-
- Thresholds beyond which alternative transport is invoked.
- Circumstances when hotel accommodation may be provided.
- Storage and provision of refreshment (on train, on station or elsewhere).
- Special arrangements for customers on trains terminating short of destination.
- Special arrangements for customers experiencing multiple or sequential bad experiences on their journey.

Running a Railway

Even if it is not possible to meet the needs of every customer on each occasion (as many will not even be known to you or the organisation at the time), striving to enact the policy on all such occasions will establish a good practice for all staff to follow. Make sure you use any feedback you get from staff or customers to assess the effectiveness of the policy and your application of it. Reading the customer complaints (and the rarer plaudits) from previous incidents can be extremely illuminating and should be shared with the Control staff. Build the customer perspective into any post-incident review which is commissioned.

Some useful tips when dealing with disrupted, frustrated, sometimes angry passengers:-

- Encourage supervisors and managers to deal face to face, it is easier than people think and usually defuses the most difficult situations. Be aware some customers will be more vocal than others and no matter what you say to them they will not be satisfied!
- Use your on call staff to attend unstaffed or single staffed stations to provide support or assist the duty staff at the bigger stations, it shows the company cares, and ensures passengers needs are met sooner than they otherwise be.
- Be wary of the odd customer who knows how to play the system and is effective at drawing away attention, resources and solutions from those who most need them. These may be passengers who are not late but are travelling on a very late service which happened to arrive for them to join at their planned time – their issue may be a 'missing' seat reservation. It may not, actually, be the lateness others on the train are experiencing.
- The 'savvy' passenger, especially on TOCs with a high commuter base, will normally be understanding of one-offs and will very often know an awful lot about the operation, gained from years or even decades on the same route, knowing all the work-rounds that you, previous TOCs and British Rail used. If you are level and straight with them you'll be fine and they may be strong supporters in a public environment.
- Do not promise things you cannot deliver. Customers will be livid at being 'fobbed off'. "Catch this train to X where you'll be able to get a connection/bus etc" is a classic in the railway, and should only be used if you are absolutely sure it is true. Do not pass the buck to a colleague down the line.
- Be aware of the limits of authority of you and your team. If you need to extend this in particular circumstances, know who to ask and how to secure it.
- Do not be hidebound by bureaucratic rules such as "the company does not compensate for disruption outside its control".
- Your response to customers' needs must be proportionate. Take the initiative. If you do not feel that you have the authority to make decisions on the front line; for instance hiring of taxis; raise this within the company. You or your

staff may be the only face of the company at times of high emotion. Nothing angers customers more than a 'jobsworth' and a delay in the middle of disruption whilst permission is sought will only serve to detract from their satisfaction if you are eventually able to meet their request!
- Conversely, a customer whose expectations are exceeded by the service he/she receives during disruption can often be more satisfied, more loyal and more likely to return than if the incident had never occurred.
- Read the six monthly National Passenger Survey results for your TOC. Identify the trends, especially those that you as an operator can directly influence. Engage your team, in driving the NPS numbers up.

Tips

It is helpful if the staff involved in perturbation management - such as controllers - can regularly spend some time on the front line, face to face with passengers.

A spell on the barrier/platform/concourse at a major station during disruption is a very illuminating experience. Ensure that you and your team get this experience.

You should ensure that staff know what the company policies of compensation are, so what they tell the customers is correct. This avoids the other classic 'fob off' of telling a customer "Send in a complaints form and you might get your money back"; this may well just inflame an already delicate situation.

The aim is to get controllers and operational staff to make balanced decisions that consider the impact on passengers and freight customers as an integral part of the decision making process.

6.2 Freight Perspective

BACKGROUND

The majority of the elements of the Handbook apply to freight as much as to passenger operations but there are certain issues that are bespoke to freight. Concern about the likely future shortage of good operators was one of the drivers for establishing the IRO in 2000. The UK rail-freight operation is far smaller than the passenger operation and there are even fewer people with freight operating competence. It is therefore quite a specialist area of expertise but one that all Operators need to understand even if they are not directly employed in managing freight operations.

This Section of the Handbook briefly outlines the issues that are dealt with by the freight operator where they differ from the more generic operating task. As a minimum, this Section aims to promote a greater understanding of positions taken when freight needs its time on the network.

This Section covers the following aspects:-
- A Brief Recent History.
- Railfreight Business Issues.
- Railfreight Operating Issues.
- Summary.

A BRIEF RECENT HISTORY

At privatisation British Rail's freight operation was split into six sections. Three geographically split bulk haulage companies, the 'wagonload' business, the national Royal Mail rail business and the container business. In 1996 a small railway from mid-western USA, Wisconsin Central, bought the first five parts and the latter part was bought by the ex-BR managers who were running the container business. This was generically known as freightliner operation and eventually became entitled Freightliner Intermodal. The large Wisconsin Central operation was given the name EWS (English, Welsh and Scottish Railway).

Wisconsin was bought out by Canadian National after a few years and the EWS operation was then bought, in 2007, by the German state railway Deutsche Bahn (DB) and renamed DB Schenker. Freightliner moved additionally into bulk freight with Freightliner Heavyhaul and is now under Middle Eastern ownership. Several new entrants appeared; GB Railfreight and Direct Rail

6.2 Freight Perspective

Services being the two that have been around for the longest period of time. The former is now owned by Eurotunnel and the latter by the nuclear agency; its origins having been in the specialised transport of nuclear flasks.

The supply of trains to support the major infrastructure maintenance business for Railtrack and then Network Rail passed at privatisation to EWS but the other companies now also successfully compete for such work. As with the rest of the freight portfolio, this is real competition in action, a characteristic which, for many reasons, has not been nearly so evident in the passenger railway.

Freight grew quickly during the ten years from 1996 with massive efficiencies in staffing, increase in train size and significant modernisation and re-equipping. The rise in traffic has been around 50% though recession has since slowed and in some cases reversed growth.

RAILFREIGHT BUSINESS ISSUES

General

Critically – and this is what really drives rail freight operators - you only win the traffic if you can use the asset base efficiently. Costs have to be tightly controlled to get your rate per tonne quotes down below other players. Customers are also increasingly demanding over issues such as arrival punctuality.

The profit is often genuinely 'all in the last wagon' so if you short-form a train you're probably hauling it for no reward or making a loss or if you have empty spaces on a container train you likewise may lose money. Time slots at ports and power stations are often measured at +/-15 minutes on arrival (similar to the passenger railway's Passenger Performance Measure (PPM) requirements, but note that very early arrival can also be unacceptable).

It is for these reasons that freight has to address operational efficiency and ensure it gets its place on an increasingly busy network. It has had to punch above its weight within the industry. So, what drives freight operations? What are the key operational parameters?

Customer Requirements

Trains are run because a customer needs the product. With the exception of a minority of intermodal contracts (where the train runs anyway and the space on it is sold on the day to container shippers), and the small number of remaining 'wagon-load' services, if the customer doesn't need the product at that time or on that day, then the train simply doesn't run.

Note:- Wagonload services are the traditional freight train which runs to a fixed timetable and which takes whatever traffic is offered on a 'wagonload' rather than

Running a Railway

'whole train' basis. These have been massively reduced, almost to extinction, by the high costs of tripping these wagons to a central yard to be made up into a decent length train and then distributing the wagons to the customers at the other end of the trunk movement. Wagonload had a final reduced-network flourish in the late 1990s but has again succumbed to the flexibility of road.

It follows that if a customer decides that he permanently doesn't need a train, the service ceases. There is no service level commitment as in the passenger railway that ensures that the advertised trains run through the timetable or life of the TOC.

More positively a customer may need a new flow to start 'tomorrow'. The FOC that is fleetest of foot and which provides the best price and service package will get the contract. In a passenger world, conditioned to T-80 timetable planning and the provision of a fixed train plan many months out, this is sometimes a difficult concept to grasp.

The customer may also need flexibility. Unlike the passenger who has to turn up for the train that is on offer, the freight customer needs his suppliers to be able to flex with his production process. A power station may for instance suffer a broken conveyer belt and have to cancel off an afternoon's coal train arrivals, making up the week's tonnage on, say, a Saturday afternoon. If a FOC cannot rise to such a challenge, the next FOC will (and the power station may be tempted to go to the other FOC next time the base contract is up for grabs).

Paths and Access Rights

Railfreight access rights are thus a constant issue. The FOC may wish to keep 'As Required' paths (termed 'Q' paths) in the timetable for eventualities or for when a customer's production cycle needs the flex – an aggregates supplier, for instance, may run a train a day from the quarry to its market but needs a second daily Q path in the trainplan for the fairly regular occasions when he has to further top up supplies at his customer's depot.

The passenger operator, perhaps wishing to use this extra Q path for a daily passenger train, will understandably ask why he cannot use it. The trade off is then between the FOC not being able to grant its customer the flexibility and the TOC not being able to meet its objectives.

The clever operational answer may be to persuade the aggregates customer that he will get the same product to market but it will be hauled at night and still be at the local stone sidings for the morning. The passenger operator would then get their path. Neat, but there are other factors to consider; is the aggregates customer as happy with the solution; can the FOC resource the night-shift path; has NR applied to have engineering access to the route on nights, thus scuppering the plan?

6.2 Freight Perspective

Industry Cooperation

In reality there is much excellent co-operation between the FOCs and NR, and between FOCs and TOCs. For instance there is a significant reduction in freight around London during the morning and evening passenger peaks. A stone train that has travelled up from the Mendips overnight and is heading for Crawley in Sussex, for example, will not be allowed past a particular signal on the freight route at Battersea if it arrives at that signal after 0630 hrs. It will sit there until 0900 hrs so as to not get in the way of the scores of heavily loaded EMUs using the busy Brighton Mainline. The customer gets his stone three hours later than planned and the locomotive and wagons are now well behind their time for getting back to the quarry.

Such is the daily challenge for freight a challenge that can be mitigated by a good trainplan with a bit of flex in it. Requiring consideration by the freight train planner are the particular characteristics of freight trains and their 'fit' with the Network Rail railway. Several of the characteristics have a direct influence on the routing the train can take.

RAILFREIGHT OPERATING ISSUES

Route Availability

The heavy rail network in Great Britain is classified from Route Availability (RA) RA1 to RA10, the latter being the most heavily engineered railway. The vast majority of the Network is at RA8 or above, allowing heavy loads on each axle. The absolute limit in the UK is 25½ tonnes over each axle (RA10) and for this reason modern-build wagons are generally built to gross out at 51 tonnes for a two axle wagon and 102 tonnes for a four axle one. Most locomotives, with six axles spreading the load, have a lower RA (usually RA6 or sometimes RA7) and thus have the authority to be on the Network without an axle-load problem. Should the route over which a wagon, or more rarely, a locomotive, need to pass be below the RA of the heaviest vehicle on the train, there are two choices –

- To 'download' the wagon – in other words to load less in it. This will obviously bring the axle weight down. Putting twelve tonnes less in may bring the individual axle weight on a four axle wagon down by 3 tonnes, and thus bring the wagon into the RA8 band so as to be able to work over an RA8 route, but it takes away significant profit from the train and will cause the customer to be asked to pay a higher rate per tonne. (The weight of the product is aptly termed the 'payload'. The weight of the empty wagon is its 'tare' weight).

- The solution usually sought is to use an extremely useful concept known as

Running a Railway

the RT3973 process. This is based on the fact that the RA of a route will usually be driven by under-track structure capabilities. One weak underbridge on a stretch of line will cause that whole stretch to have a lower RA than the track and other structures could support. If the structures engineer can agree to it, he may say that a wagon or train with a higher RA than the route can go over the structure at a lower speed and still keep within the dynamic force limits the structure has. This authority is given to the driver as a form RT3973. More specifically RT3973HAW (Heavy Axle Weight). It is the driver's authority to run over the lower RA route and it is the specifier of the speed over each restricted structure. Almost unknown outside the freight world the RT3973 has been the saviour of many freight flows but it has its difficulties. For example a loaded coal train routed from Ayrshire via central Scotland and Berwick down to Yorkshire power stations, will have an RT3973 provided which shows more than thirty speed restrictions. For a driver to be able to identify UB [Underbridge] 234 at mp [milepost] 77½ on a dark rainy night so as to be able to reduce speed from 60 mph to, say, 30 mph, is a real test of route knowledge (but one that becomes second nature to freight drivers).

It is important to note that the speed restrictions used in RT3973s are never indicated with a sign out on the track and that, until the last few years, have not been adequately accounted for in Working Time Tables (WTTs). A heavy freight train will have to slow down and then accelerate at the restriction site. NR is now addressing the timing issues.

Finally, under Route Availability, is the issue of train dimensions. When introduced in 1965 all shipping containers were 8 feet high. Now the majority of those being shipped in and out of the UK are 9'0", 9'3" or even 9'6" high. (Metrication has never formally supplanted the Imperial sizes given to containers). With the Victorian legacy of a small infrastructure, particularly bridge and tunnel dimensions, the UK has had real difficulties with handling the 'hi-cube' boxes. Small wheeled/low floor wagons are one solution but they have various technical disadvantages. Lowering of tracks and raising of bridges is expensive but allows standard kit to convey the containers.

This whole area is the second main area of Route Availability. It is covered by an RT3973CON (Container) authority form. This lists the routes that a train carrying containers can travel. As a form, like its axle-weight equivalent, it can be many pages long, listing several combinations of authorised routes. In a few cases there may be an authority on a RT3973CON to go over a route with a tight bridge clearance subject to a severe speed limit under the bridge (so as to reduce the risk of wagon 'suspension bounce' through the bridge hole) but this is relatively rare.

As is the case with route sections with specific RA categorisation, each route section will have a designated loading gauge. The coding used is a 'W' code and the routes in Great Britain with the tightest bridge holes / tunnels are shown as W6. The most generously proportioned routes are classed W12. The dimension designation also includes the area under the wagon floor and its interface with platforms and other lower level structures.

'High-cube' boxes (a rapidly growing percentage of containers that are now being transported) generally need a W10 route profile and much effort is currently being expended in achieving this. As with the RA process a train will generate, through its wagon size or container size, combined with wagon floor height, a W categorisation and TOPS will generate a Warning Message on the train list that the train cannot proceed without an RT3973CON form. A W10 train needs a W10 or better route from origin to destination. If any section of the route is, say W8 then the train may be allowed to proceed with perhaps a speed restriction through a specified bridge or tunnel. It will be prohibited from such a route if such a form has not been authorised. Currently there are significant parts of Great Britain without a high W code route for example - there are no east / west W10 routes north of the North London line until you get to Scotland! The current Felixstowe to Nuneaton route clearance scheme is aimed at addressing this and trans-Pennine electrification will free up the very restricted mainline between Manchester and Yorkshire.

An alternative to route clearance, but with downsides in terms of wagon cost and wheel maintenance is the low-floor wagon. This of course carries the container lower down. 'Pocket wagons' are used by one FOC and contain a 40' container in a low-slung area between conventional bogies.

It is worth remembering that Signallers are often not aware of the restrictions which need to be applied and the onus is very much on the driver to manage the restrictions applied.

The RT3973 process is complex, but greater understanding and awareness of it is a real advantage for all Operators.

Train speed

Compared to the complexity of RT3973 forms, this is relatively straightforward. The maximum speed of the slowest wagon is the maximum speed of the train. However, unlike passenger trains, there will often be differences between speeds in loaded or empty status – bulk coal bogie wagons can run at 75 mph empty ('in tare condition') but only at 60 mph loaded. In general loaded trains in the bulk sector (aggregates, coal, steel, petrochemicals) run at a maximum of 60 mph.

The intermodal container railway runs at 75 mph. Almost all mainline locomotives are capable of hauling at 75 mph (There is an exception to this in the

Running a Railway

shape of two small classes of locomotives that can only haul at 60/65 mph but have the advantage of a greater haulage ability through using relatively low speed gearing).

However always be aware of the issue of acceleration. If you have never travelled on the footplate of a heavily loaded freight train ask one of the FOCs if you can do so – it will transform your understanding of the dynamics of freight train operation, in particular the significant issue of gradients and the time it takes to wind up a slowed or stopped train to its maximum speed.

Train length

This is measured in feet and in 'SLUs'. Another quirk of freight operation is the formal measuring of freight train length in 21 foot units called Standard Length Units. The SLU was the length of a traditional British four wheel freight wagon and the term's continued existence is due to it having been built into the base UK-equivalent software of the TOPS computer system that BR bought from the Southern Pacific railway and introduced to its operations in 1975. (TOPS is referred to again later in this Section).

A train may be shown as 115 SLUs long ('115 in length' in freight operator language). Newer infrastructure schemes refer to meters. The TOPS trainlists, Sectional Appendices, project plans etc that the railway uses continue to exist in an uneasy mix of length measurement units that bamboozle non-UK companies, of which there have been many, who have interests in the UK railfreight industry. There are no real safety issues connected with this issue but plenty of potential pitfalls for the unwary in planning and performance areas.

Brake Force

Each wagon and locomotive will have a set brake force (i.e. the force that its brake gear and air pressure systems can apply). A freight train is the same as any other train, it can only be driven at a speed that the driver will be able to stop from in order to conform to the 'braking curve' to signals and speed restrictions.

The TOPS system will calculate the Brake Force that the complete freight train can provide and from this calculate the maximum speed that the train can run at. In the past trains ran with some unbraked wagons (and the guard riding in a brake van at the back) but now with a railway in which all wagons are fitted with brakes it is almost always the case that there is enough brake force to cope with the planned speed. Where there is not – for instance some wagons have their brakes isolated because of defects – then TOPS will show a speed restriction for the train below the normal maximum speed.

Dangerous Goods

Some freight trains will convey dangerous goods. These range from petroleum products, through chemicals and military explosives to nuclear loads. Each has specific actions to be taken to secure the safety of the cargo and ways to react if there is any mishap. The whole issue is covered by the freight operators' other bible– the Working Manual for Rail Staff (the generic Rule Book being the first one).

The 'Pink Pages' section of the Working Manual list cargos that are deemed Dangerous Goods and the arrangements for their transit and for the response by emergency services should there be a mishap. Be aware too that a notionally empty tank wagon that has been conveying petroleum or other Dangerous Goods is not in fact empty when on the railway. It is treated by the railway as 'Discharged' – the remaining vapours can make it just as dangerous a wagon as when it was loaded with 70 tonnes of petroleum.

Load Securing

One of the highest risks that a FOC has to mitigate against is an insecure load moving during transit so it is outside the permitted loading gauge (becoming 'out of gauge') and thus potentially striking another train or a structure. Obviously some loads are higher risk than others and it is in the carriage of steel products that the greatest risk lies.

Specific arrangements are made for securing of steel. Usually it is secured on an own-weight basis plus strapping, using strong nylon straps, and the provision of vertical stanchions to limit any movement that may take place. A heavy steel slab may be very slightly curved ('banana slab' in the freight vernacular) and thus can move should it be loaded with the lowest point centrally. It should be loaded with its lowest points at the end so as to anchor the load through its weight. You can imagine the challenge a steelworks would have in turning over a 25 tonne slab to comply and to satisfy the FOC's loads inspector. Not something that the TOC operations manager has to face in his day job!

'Comparative Load Trials' are carried out to ensure that a load has not moved on route – the place on the wagon deck of a load is chalked and photographed and any movement against the chalk is checked at the other end. The introduction of digital photography has allowed the transmission by e-mail of the pre-trip loading images to a colleague at the destination point, significantly simplifying the process.

Timing Loads

Planners have to bear in mind that the trailing weight behind particular types of locomotive will heavily influence the pathing of a freight train. A 2000 tonne train behind a diesel locomotive will have very different characteristics from an 800 tonne train behind an electric locomotive over the same route. Freight trains are thus given 'timing loads' in the planning calculations which are a close

Running a Railway

as possible proxy for power/weight calculations. Relatively easy when the flow from a customer's yard is always fifteen 100 tonne loaded wagons hauled by a class 66 diesel. More difficult when the train is a contracted wagon-load one with various different numbers and types of wagon on different days. The prudent signaller will run a TOPS enquiry to see the weight of a train, and confirm the locomotive type, when making regulating decisions for wagonload trains.

Short Term Planning and Very Short Term Planning

As well as the management of his train's place in the 'permanent' WTT, the freight train planner has to deal with a far higher level of short term planning. Much of this as we have seen is driven by the needs of his customers, but the rest is the work needed to respond to requests for intrusive possessions of routes outside of the normal ROTR. Whilst NR's planners are now more in tune with freight's needs for paths and punctuality than was once the case, there remains a huge workload to produce and agree shorter term plans.

A customer simply does not care that a route is closed – he just expects his train at the normal time and a Short Term Plan (STP) path that means that this time is changed needs iteration by the FOC not just with NR but with the customer. The planner is at the centre of a complex web of needs and only the best planners in the business, with an encyclopaedic knowledge of railway geography and capabilities will make the grade as a competent freight train planner.

A lot of freight runs on STP conditions where track access has been agreed but the short-term arrangements need to be advised out to all concerned. They also need to be reflected in staff diagrams and rosters and seen as workable in terms of wagon and locomotive cycles. Finally, and crucially, the FOC has to continue to make a profit on the new timings.

Very Short Term Planning (VSTP). It essentially consists of trains retimed by the FOC's control in association with NR's Control Office. VSTP timings are not validated against other traffic and effectively freight 'takes its chance' to get a path. In practice VSTP paths will not be sanctioned through a very busy passenger railway unless this is the only possible way to get the freight through and a judgement has been made that it can be done without real risk to passenger operation. When this judgement is wrong – and it certainly can be – then TOCs will be quick to criticise.

TOPS

The unsung hero at the heart of all of the above freight operations issues is the Total Operations Processing System (or TOPS) which has been in front line use, through massive change in the industry and within an IT environment that has changed beyond recognition, since it was first introduced by British Rail in 1975 and based even then on 1960s US railroad technology.

6.2 Freight Perspective

TOPS was introduced to make freight operations more efficient and cost effective, but it is crucial to both freight and passenger operations. Dependence on TOPS is now a concern as countless other rail industry systems have their origin in the TOPS system architecture and are linked to it. TRUST is one of the more important but there are many commercial feeds too with track access accounts and customer billing being directly based on the information on train movement that has been captured by TOPS-based sub-systems. Rolling stock and locomotive maintenance is often based on 'TOPS Hours' and mileage run statistics supplied by TOPS.

The system's longevity is partly based on this myriad of complex links; the cost of upgrade is very high and several 'son-of-TOPS' projects have been scoped over the years and not proceeded with. The risks of not producing a more modern system to underpin the industry are however increasingly apparent. Only a handful of people (many now retired) really know their way round the technical core of TOPS.

Within the freight operation, the way TOPS is accessed has changed completely. When originally set up the country had scores of TOPS offices where shifts of clerks processed information for the adjacent yard or for an area. The yard sent hand-written lists of the wagons on a train, these were typed into a basic computer terminal, the trainlist was validated using the RA, speed, brake force etc criteria described earlier. It was then sent back to the yard through an early form of fax or by hand. A 'fag-break' for the clerk could, and did, result in late departures.

The run-down of wagonload started the closure of the TOPS offices and in 1999 the breakthrough came with TOPS Direct whereby the yard staff themselves were trained to use a PC connected to the TOPS system. The 'green-screen' information display was then paralleled by clear mapping so that the position and status of all wagons and locomotives in a location could be seen. Shunts could then be reflected by dragging wagons or strings of wagons by the click of a mouse from siding to siding. Simple highlighting of a train on the yard map would allow the running of a validated trainlist, printed off in the yard for checking, signing as valid and handing to the driver. Incoming trains could be seen on TRUST and a click-through gave the inward train formation, allowing the upcoming shunts to be planned. TOPS Direct was massively popular with yard staff for obvious reasons, despite the loss of jobs elsewhere.

An important subsequent further improvement (the 'J6-1' process) has allowed the schedule for that train that day (which may be running under STP conditions and/or from a range of Q paths) to be printed at the foot of the trainlist, therefore allowing the freight driver to know exactly what timings are in the system today and to drive to them. Until this enhancement, almost unbelievably,

Running a Railway

freight drivers had no information on their intermediate timings apart from the crude 'depart from' and 'arrive at' times printed on the personal diagram for the day. Such detailed timing information is still unfortunately a far from universal part of the driver's information provision. It should obviously be.

Note: Traditionally there was a freight WTT but this was withdrawn as a document some years ago. By definition STP trains were not in the WTT and providing the driver with timings for such trains had always been a bit hit and miss. Often printed STP documents did not reach the yard until long after the train had departed.

Since 2000 the FOCs have made significant strides with harnessing the capabilities of Global Positioning Systems on their locomotives, responding to the fact that much activity and almost all loading and unloading activity is away from the signalled railway. Precise location and status information is now available in the freight railway. The strides forward have been truly impressive and there are aspects that have transferability to the TOC environment.

SUMMARY

This Section of the Handbook can only briefly outline the key differences between the freight and the passenger operations. Freight remains a very 'hands on' task for the operator with a lot more time spent dealing with trains shunting, loading, checking, retiming etc. The operations manager will be very flexible and extremely customer focussed. Many freight managers spend large amounts of their time with a specific customer or group of customers and are seen as a key part of the customer's production process. Similarly many customers are extremely knowledgeable about the wider railway (even if they do not accept the wider railways issues as valid excuse for poor performance by the FOC it deals with).

Freight operations also contain unique safety risks as well as particularly challenging train planning issues. Much of the rest of it though has themes common to railway operations in the TOCs and almost all the managerial attitudes, processes and requirements are common to both.

TOC Operators could usefully schedule the odd day with their FOC colleagues (and of course vice versa); mutual understanding has real value in today's fragmented railway operation.

6.2 Freight Perspective

Tips

Freight is an integral part of the railways in Great Britain - it is vital to understand the issues involved.

The challenges of running a mixed traffic railway, especially when fast passenger trains are involved, are often difficult.

It is up to the operators to reach an optimal balance between the needs of freight and passenger operations.

Find out what your TOC/FOC colleagues do - it will help you improve overall performance.

Sources:

Railfreight Operation – Paul Shannon. Publisher: Ian Allan 1999

Freightmaster: the Complete Guide to British Railfreight Operations – Mark Rawlinson. Publisher: Freightmaster. Annually re-issued.

Note:
A useful website showing the characteristics of UK rail wagons, sorted by TOPS types, can be found at www.garethbayer.co.uk

Running a Railway

6.3 Role of the Operator

INTRODUCTION

Whilst this Handbook describes the different facets of operations and seeks to provide advice based on experience, it is easy to get overwhelmed with the breadth and complexity of train service delivery.

The aim of this Section is to strip the operator's role down to the fundamental parts and provide a simple guide to maintaining a clear focus.

Whilst engineers want to mend or modify things, operators frequently have to find ways of delivering a good service when things are broken!

ISSUES

Operators will usually have a range of supervisory and managerial responsibilities that will compete for their precious time. So what does a good day look like?

The Good Day checklist
Because of my actions:-
- I have made a difference to the train performance we have achieved.
- I have enhanced the safety of the railway system.
- More customers will be satisfied because of the actions my team has taken.
- My people and those they work with are more skilled than they were yesterday.
- Our approach will be more structured tomorrow than it was yesterday.
- My trains will routinely be more punctual and cleaner in the future.
- The information we provide to customers during disruption will be better.
- Our reputations have been enhanced.
- We have learnt lessons and are able to avoid repeating mistakes or problems.

Tips

Use the guidance in the Handbook to develop your expertise and confidence.

Make sure you own your train service.

Make a difference - even bad days can be improved by positive action based on the advice in this Handbook.

6.4 Out of Hours Visits

BACKGROUND

The railway is a 24/7 operation and it's good practice to visit key locations. If you only see the railway during office hours then you will never fully understand the operation.

For NR this applies to Signalboxes, manned level crossings, Electrical Control Rooms, Control Offices and similar locations.

For TOCs this applies to all manned locations and activities e.g. Train crew, Depots, Controls, Stations, and Fleet Depots etc.

NR and TOC/FOC managers might consider undertaking occasional joint out of hours visits – particularly to fleet depots, signal boxes and possession sites.

ISSUES

Managers should recognise the value of routine, visible attendance during weekends and evenings. Not only does this provide support and encouragement for staff at times when managerial cover is usually limited (or non-existent), it also helps avoid the inevitable slippage in standards that often occurs during these times.

Remember that most train maintenance depots are far busier at night. This can also apply to freight facilities.

Routine attendance during special events at key times especially at weekends, also does wonders for morale when staff are at their most stretched.

When undertaking visits have an agenda of things to check but mainly observe and listen. Your antennae should pick up what is wrong – who is missing etc.

Vary your routine – if visiting stations or signalboxes on a line of route, visit out of sequence. Vary the interval of your visits. If you have concerns about locations, or the performance of particular groups of staff or individuals, devote your out of hours efforts to rooting it out.

Obviously visits will need to be strengthened under certain circumstances (i.e. during disputes or prolonged adverse operating circumstances e.g. line closures with train diversions).

Remember to document and retain details of all visits including any action taken.

Running a Railway

Tips

Unauthorised working practices are more likely to arise out of hours. If you undertake out of hours visits you will curtail these (and earn some respect), but be ready to challenge the behaviour when you first identify it.

Some activities are relatively harmless (e.g. full Sunday dinners in Control Offices) others (e.g. unauthorised swapping of turns) are potentially much more damaging and should be stopped.

You will find that some practices are long standing and will have become institutionalised.

Tread a firm, fair but realistic line.

6.5 Performance Management Real Time

BACKGROUND

The primary focus for real time management is in Control Offices. Controllers are not a self contained agency but the agents and coordinators of the companies they work for.

Accordingly operations managers and their teams need to regularly and routinely work closely with the Controllers in order to provide direction and support at appropriate times.

KEY CONSIDERATIONS

Make sure the actions and processes of the Control Office are as fully integrated as possible with the wider operations, fleet and maintenance organisations within both NR and the TOCs/FOCs.

Lay down clear requirements for management information provision and differentiate between messages that are provided for information purposes and those that are sent as part of the escalation process.

The Control teams need to know what response managers expect for defined incidents and scenarios. It is essential to define what constitutes Major Service Disruption, Customer Service Level 2 (CSL2) – 'Code Yellow' and 'Code Red'

6.5 Performance Management Real Time

type escalation. See the Section on Passenger Information During Disruption for more details.

Provide advice and guidance at an early stage of any serious perturbation. All too often hindsight is applied to current operations management when what is required is support and intervention during the problem. Make sure that you know the structured escalation and management involvement processes and can help to continuously improve them. Unstructured and informal managerial interference is usually unhelpful and likely to hinder good train service management.

Beware innocuous incidents that become major disruptive events. Failed trains often have this potential, and electrification incidents almost always seem to). Always be mindful of the passage of time. Do not become so immersed that you lose track of time.

Ensure operations and fleet managers support the Control Office as escalation will inevitably involve line managers.

Develop a positive culture within the Control Office and get both NR and TOC personnel to own performance in a pro-active manner. Monitoring is important but intervention and remedial action are the most important Control responsibilities. When the service is running well a targeted intervention, for example a regulation decision, can prevent the service deteriorating or improve running even further. When things do go wrong rapid and decisive action can prevent a collapse of the service. In some places such action is often too little, too late.

Establish a set of easy performance recovery tactics that can be used on a regular basis. These will include such things as:-

- Agreed priorities for cancellations and skipped or additional stops for service recovery purposes.

- Broader Service Recovery protocols between TOC and NR, and other TOCs.

- HST on one power car/DMU and EMUs with engines or motors isolated – codify if lightly used stops or those on adverse gradients can be omitted to help maintain end to end journey times, or whether such sets can be re-deployed to more suitable diagrams.

- Diversionary routes for which crew knowledge is maintained within the link structure.

- Passengers taken ill on trains – know the TOC policy for dealing with trains that are stopped because a passenger has become ill along your route. Notices on trains advising that assistance can be best provided at stations are good practice. A main aim must always be to get someone with authority to site,

Running a Railway

particularly if the emergency services become involved. Detraining a passenger at a staffed station which is easily accessible, if need be, by ambulance is always best if the person's illness/injury can allow without danger. The train can then proceed without further delay.

- Coasting through unpowered or damaged OLE sections. A train can travel for miles on level or falling gradients as long as no stops are needed within the isolated section. Watch for specific rolling stock quirks such as certain dual voltage EMUs which search for a 3rd Rail power source if the OLE power is lost and come to a stand under the dead OLE if they do not find it.

- Using rolling stock and crews "by stepping them up" (i.e. to a previous train to the one diagrammed to be worked) or "stepping them down" (i.e. to a train later than the one diagrammed to be worked).

- Tactical deployment of unplanned spare resources when they are available such as rolling stock, locos, crew.

- Closer control of traincrew at terminus stations and depot locations during disruption with access to using a manager or supervisor in order to manage effective contingency use of available staff.

- Re-location or deployment of 'Thunderbird' (standby) locomotives.

- Adequate and clear plans for alternative working arrangements such as Temporary Block Working, Single Line Working and Pilot working. Pre-prepare where possible by making the most of derogations that can be applied (Modified Working on Single Lines for example).

Ensure all individual TOC/Network Rail strategies for regaining right time running are clearly understood (e.g. use of Special Stop Orders/Not to Call Orders etc.) and that they balance the needs of customers with the need to restore timetabled running.

INFORMATION

Ultimately, real time management of the train service, and the decision making which supports it, particularly in Signalling Centres and Control Offices, relies heavily on the flow of information from site or from those most closely involved in the disruption or plan deviation. Simplifying the flows of information, ensuring the information is accurate and timely, and reducing duplication and wasted effort within these arrangements, are essential to good and prompt decision making, and critical for the effective deployment of contingency plans. Above all, make sure that there is a plan for communications, good information flow does not just happen.

6.5 Performance Management Real Time

The UK rail industry has been notoriously poor at giving good, timely, accurate information to customers during times of disruption, and this problem often results from poor information and dissemination to and from Control Offices. Ensure your company has devised and implemented a suite of management protocols and processes to address these issues. These must address all the links in the communication chain within both NR and the TOC right through from site to customer. See Section 7.6 on Passenger Information During Disruption for more information.

Customer communication is often mistakenly regarded as Retail or Customer Service responsibility. In practice, most of the key information which eventually ends up passing to the customer originates from, or flows through, operations staff. It is these links and flows which are vital to the dissemination of accurate and timely information to staff and customers. Consequently, making sure that your arrangements cover all relevant activities; from site through to customer, are up to date and working, and that this aspect of operations responsibility is accorded high priority, is very important indeed.

Similarly disruption is often poorly managed because an incident has not been split into the separate manageable components. Doing this enables appropriate priorities to be established, and scarce resources to be used to best advantage. Remember that NR priorities may be different from the TOC's and it is essential that a customer focused approach is taken to overcome these differences. See Section 7.2 on Prioritised Planning for more information.

Tips

Getting ownership within Control Offices and getting NR and TOC/FOC people to work closely together is not always easy but it is vitally important.

It is equally important to ensure that relevant NR and TOC/FOC line managers are plugged into Control and clearly understand their role in all escalation requirements.

Take a positive interest in your industry partners' key real time activities - signallers and controllers, fleet and maintenance. Visits to Signalling Centres and depots will be educational, and will be rewarded with a positive attitude towards you and your company.

Work with and through your Control Offices - they cannot manage train service delivery in isolation.

Running a Railway

6.6 Safety Management

BACKGROUND

The health and safety of our employees and others affected by the operation of the railway is assured through the effective design, construction, maintenance and operation of the network. Safety management is a key element of the Operators task and as such it must inform every action that we take.

Operations Managers must manage their particular areas of responsibility with due regard to safety; it must be integral to everything that an Operator does. Classic "pure" safety management is covered elsewhere in individual NR and TOC/FOC safety manuals, therefore this element deals with Operational Safety.

To enable safety management to be effective there needs to be strong safety leadership throughout the organisation and particularly by those who have a line management responsibility. Operations Managers must never forget that the activity that they are running is part of a system and they must recognise that any changes they make could have an adverse effect on another part of the operational railway. Because of this there must be co-operation between all parties responsible for the safe operation of the railway.

ISSUES

The main aim is to safely deliver a punctual railway that is as close as possible to the planned timetable.

Without adequate controls operating the railway could be very dangerous. Basic physics will tell you that fast moving, heavy objects have significant destructive capability.

Traditionally railway safety has been achieved by engineered controls and compliance with detailed and extensive rules and regulations. Effective rules have been achieved at the cost of many accidents, deaths and injuries over many years of railway operations. An informed reader of the Rule Book will be able to identify the accidents that introduced specific rules.

Relatively few accidents are now caused by failures of infrastructure and equipment; it is usually non-conformance that causes a process or task to become unsafe. Increasingly accidents are caused by failure of the human element in the system and often this involves failure to comply with rules and regulations.

Human failings can be classified as deliberate acts or omissions (violations), or unconscious errors. The latter can be broken down again into slips (right intention but wrong action), lapses (failure to carry out an action due to distraction or memory failure), skill based mistakes (inadequate skill or ability) or rules based mistakes (misunderstanding the right action to take in a given situation).

Accordingly, while Operators need to have an impeccable working knowledge of the rules and regulations, increasingly it is the ability to manage human behaviour which will deliver the best safety results.

Safety management processes must pay sufficient attention to the behaviour of staff. Too often only processes are covered. Given that most safety non-compliances are caused by human factor related errors or violations, it is essential that checks include the observation of actual practices in order to identify unacceptable behaviours. Observation, Safety Tours, and Managing by Walking About are classic examples of this type of check.

To help reduce reoccurrence all errors and violations all should be investigated and the use of a human factors tool is recommended in order to more readily identify the underlying causes. Further information regarding human factors can be found on the RSSB website http://www.hse.gov.uk/humanfactors/

Where unacceptable or sloppy behaviours are identified these should be challenged with the member of staff at the time. This applies to all areas of the company and not only the operational aspects or specific areas of responsibility. This reinforces the message that poor safety practices will not be tolerated.

Safety management also needs to strike a balance between encouraging good behaviour through training and development, and incentivising good behaviour through identifying what is unacceptable and having clear consequences of failure to comply.

Sustainable safety improvement involves more than just identifying and correcting non compliances. Organisations must have a positive safety culture.

Safety culture can be defined as the way in which members of an organisation act collectively in order to achieve safe operation. Take the following example:-

- In the UK when a car driver is approaching a cyclist on a country road the driver may sound his horn at the cyclist. In many cases this might be a sign of aggression and frustration. The cyclist may respond with a suitable hand signal! The car driver, having sped past might also respond with an appropriate hand signal.
- In France the approach is different. Cycling is a more established part of the culture. A car driver approaching a cyclist will also sound his horn, but this is intended as a gentle warning to the cyclist who interprets it in the same way. The cyclist may give a handsignal to the driver, although in this case it

Running a Railway

is an indication that the cyclist is ready for the car to pass. Once safely past the car driver will acknowledge the cyclist with a friendly wave.

Same actions, but the French case illustrates a positive safety culture where the parties work together to achieve a common goal.

Theoretically when a safety culture is well developed it will become less important for rules and regulations to be minutely defined. A high level of awareness of safety issues and the determination to avoid them can replace strict compliance with rules and regulations. However, a mature safety culture is not achieved overnight. In fact it is questionable whether any aspect of the British railway system has reached this point yet.

Finally, many rail companies use a Human Errors model to provide guidance for line Managers on this issue. A current TOC version, which is derived from a Health & Safety Executive (HSE) model, is shown on the following page.

Tips

Consider how you act in your home life. Can you think of instances when you have cut corners and narrowly avoided a serious accident? If that is how you act at home is there a chance that you may bring that behaviour with you to work? What about those you manage?

A key risk is to believe that safety directors and managers 'look after safety' on your behalf - they do not. Safety directors and managers are a rich source of professional advice and support as well as establishing company standards and managing the Safety Certificate & Authorisation documentation.

The people responsible for delivering a safe railway are the line managers and self-evidently they are therefore the primary custodians of safety.

Good safety management should be part of a professional approach to everything we do as operators.

6.6 Safety Management

Error & Violation Guidance Table

Start at the bottom of the table and track the decision process by clicking on the boxes for the path you have decided and changing the box colour to Red. Please keep this table on a single page.

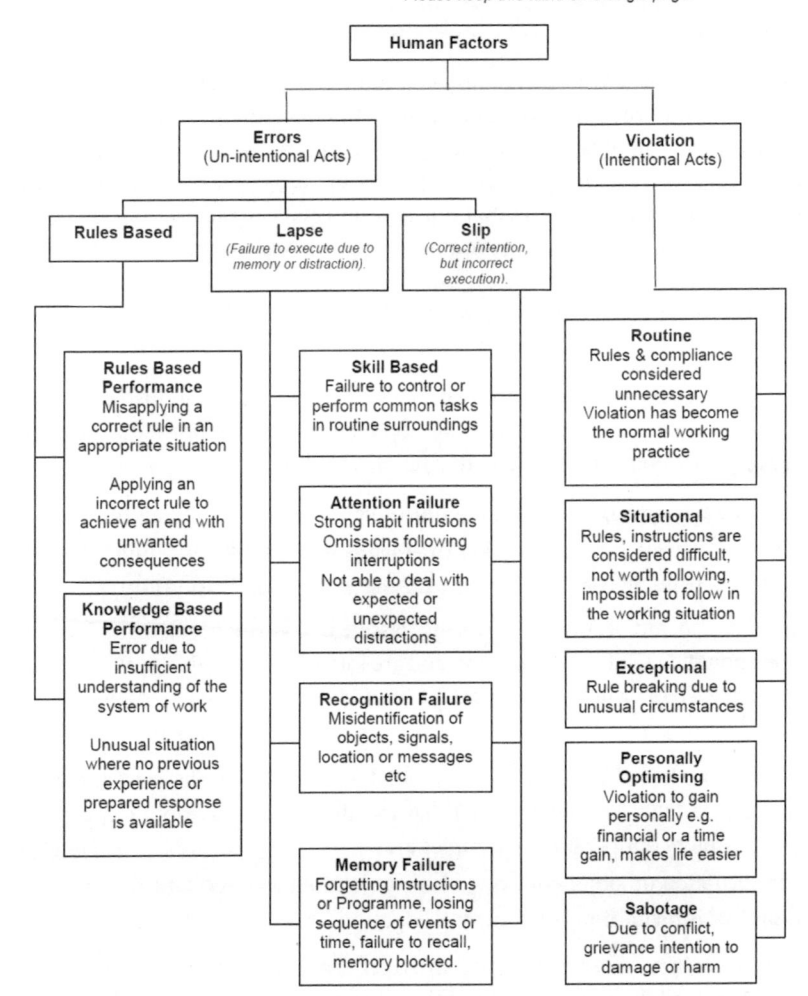

Human Factors

- **Errors** (Un-intentional Acts)
  - **Rules Based**
  - **Lapse** *(Failure to execute due to memory or distraction)*
  - **Slip** *(Correct intention, but incorrect execution)*
- **Violation** (Intentional Acts)

Rules Based Performance
Misapplying a correct rule in an appropriate situation

Applying an incorrect rule to achieve an end with unwanted consequences

Knowledge Based Performance
Error due to insufficient understanding of the system of work

Unusual situation where no previous experience or prepared response is available

Skill Based
Failure to control or perform common tasks in routine surroundings

Attention Failure
Strong habit intrusions
Omissions following interruptions
Not able to deal with expected or unexpected distractions

Recognition Failure
Misidentification of objects, signals, location or messages etc

Memory Failure
Forgetting instructions or Programme, losing sequence of events or time, failure to recall, memory blocked.

Routine
Rules & compliance considered unnecessary
Violation has become the normal working practice

Situational
Rules, instructions are considered difficult, not worth following, impossible to follow in the working situation

Exceptional
Rule breaking due to unusual circumstances

Personally Optimising
Violation to gain personally e.g. financial or a time gain, makes life easier

Sabotage
Due to conflict, grievance intention to damage or harm

Institution of Railway Operators

Running a Railway

6.7 Passenger Information

INTRODUCTION

Passenger information has often been seen as a by-product of operational processes or as the preserve of other departments but it now ranks with performance in importance to those who use our trains. Delivering a reliable and punctual train service is the surest way to keep customers happy but the quality of information provided during disruption is the element that they most commonly cite as being unsatisfactory. This added emphasis has mainly been driven by the worldwide explosion of information availability - primarily internet web based, and the increasing use of mobile phone and Blackberry type devices.

It is against this more demanding background, that the rail industry in Great Britain has struggled to provide an acceptable level of information to passengers/customers, particularly during serious disruption.

The foundations for providing good information are briefly highlighted in Section 6.8 Train Service Delivery Systems and Processes, but a more detailed outline is listed here.

This Section and Section 7.6 covering Passenger Information During Disruption should be read in conjunction and are intended to provide some essential guidance. Further information can be found in the relevant Codes of Practice issued by ATOC.

Note – The term 'passenger information' is also used to describe information aspects that are not train service specific. These may not be the direct responsibility of operators. Examples are:-
- Information on other connected transport providers' services.
- Station information, including navigation around the station and other signage.
- Commercial information about ticketing and ticket types and so on.
- Local area information relating to specific stations.

The provision of good, timely passenger information is totally dependent on defined integrated arrangements that cover all aspects of delivery and include both NR and TOCs.

At the time of this 2013 edition, the ORR is taking an increasing interest in the quality of the information provided which underlines the importance of the issues for all operators.

6.7 Passenger Information

ISSUES

Passenger information has historically been a by-product of mainstream operational processes or at best a secondary consideration. However, good, timely information provision involves key activities throughout NR and TOCs. Accordingly it will only meet the needs of passengers/customers if all the requirements are codified, well integrated and delivered by well trained, competent people.

The key points to remember are:-

- Passenger information covers the information provided to passenger facing staff as well as passengers who are travelling (on-train or on-station) plus intending passengers and meeters/greeters. It also covers advance engineering information.
- Passenger information provision must be considered a key operational requirement.
- TOCs must own the totality of information provision even though NR and National Rail Enquiries have critical roles. Note: National Rail Enquiries (NRE) is part of ATOC and therefore effectively owned by the TOCs.
- Regardless of the organisational shape within a TOC, there must be a clear, end to end owner of Passenger Information (and ideally accountability should be vested in a single nominated Director).

Key aspects to consider when reviewing the adequacy of established Passenger Information arrangements are:-

- Ensure all passenger information flows are mapped from start to finish (origin to passenger). Do this right through NR, the TOC and NRE. This will enable you to codify your information flow and identify the critical communication activities and important transmission links.
- Identify critical staff groups e.g. Information Controllers, Station Announcers, Guards and other on-train staff. Do not forget that some less obvious staff will also have critical roles (e.g. Rail Incident Officers (RIO) at the site of an incident).
- Write down what is expected from such staff and train accordingly. This is an area where competence assessment and certification should be strongly considered.
- Regularly review the effectiveness of arrangements. Whilst the bi-annual National Passenger Survey (NPS) undertaken by Passenger Focus is the main measure on heavy rail systems, it is also important to undertake regular "mystery shopper" type checks and post incident reviews. Regular checks on public facing websites (both your own company and NRE) are good ways of checking what your customers are being told.

Running a Railway

- Consider whether you have sufficient emphasis on proactive communication. New social media such as Twitter give the opportunity to get more control on the messages being received by customers when things are running well and when there is disruption. A regular message to say that a full service is planned for the morning peak and a good service is running can really influence passengers' perception of the railway.
- There is likely to be an element of culture change required to maximise performance in this area; customer service has not always come naturally to the rail industry.

Make sure your arrangements for Passenger Information during Disruption follow the guidance in Section 7.6 of this handbook. Routine information provision is generally well established but the industry track record on information during disruption generally falls well short of what is now deemed acceptable by users and the ORR.

Getting this aspect of operational delivery right is a major challenge and it will only by achieved by relentless attention to detail and a resolve to afford information provision the high importance it deserves.

Tips

Ensure Passenger Information provision is clearly owned – both responsibility and accountability.

Make sure all the arrangements are properly integrated, codified and trained.

Regularly look at what the passenger is seeing rather than what your people input.

Review regularly and critically.

Providing good information day after day will invariably need a culture change

Passenger Information provision is making more headlines than performance as a critical industry issue - treat it accordingly.

6.8 Train Service Delivery Systems & Processes - Overview

INTRODUCTION

Your company will have a suite of operational systems and processes that are aimed at producing efficiency and consistency in key aspects of operational approach. This Section provides a general overview whilst more detailed information can be found in the relevant applicable sections.

Key operational systems and processes will include:-
- Performance Management and Improvement Plans (PMIP) – the management of train service delivery performance.
- TOC Train Care and Presentation Policy – a systematic approach to train cleaning and maintenance of the on-board passenger environment.
- Customer/Passenger Information Arrangements – an integrated approach to Customer/ Passenger Information, with an emphasis on Major Service Disruption.
- Notification of Engineering Works, Amended Train Services and Infrastructure Alterations to Staff – through the use of notices (e.g. Weekly Operating Notice and circulars for example).
- TOC Engineering Work Communications – a structured approach to the provision of planned train service alterations to staff and customers as a result of engineering work.
- Infrastructure Maintenance Regimes by Asset Type – covering inspection frequencies and specific tasks to be undertaken.
- Infrastructure Fault Management Processes – including what to do in the event that no fault is found and use of Remote Condition Monitoring.
- Signal Box Special Instructions and Local Instructions.
- Train Regulation Policy – describing general principles as well as important priorities at key locations.

Expanded details on each of these systems/processes and the tools they use are contained in the following sections.

Performance Management and Improvement Plans
Core arrangements should include/cover:-
- Performance calendars.
- Delay attribution.
- Punctuality & reliability statistics.

Running a Railway

- Performance investigation requirements.
- Routine reports.
- Action plans.
- Annual performance assessments.

Assessment & Review arrangements should cover:-
- Meeting structures & remits.
- Periodic reviews (at least quarterly).
- Escalation arrangements.
- Audit & check requirements (including independent oversight).

The objective is to provide clear consistent processes for performance management within a specified framework in order that managers can focus the maximum effort on delivering performance budgets and meeting or beating forecasts.

TOC Train Cleaning & Presentation policy

The objective is to put in place a set of standard arrangements that ensure high standards of delivery, and continuous improvement in train cleaning, and the maintenance of passenger amenities and facilities on board. Challenging targets should be set for and variation from these targets must be justified and approved.

Train Cleaning & Presentation must:-
- Have appropriate priority for managerial attention and action.
- Be allocated adequate resources.
- Be properly planned at timetable, depot operations and activity level.
- Be properly managed and supervised during execution, it will be mainly done at night making high quality supervision even more important.
- Be given appropriate priority in the event of service disruption, vandalism or non-availability of key customer facilities.

Functional responsibility for train cleaning and presentation is usually vested with the Fleet/ Engineering Director in each TOC.

Compliance should be routinely measured by audit.

Quality should be reviewed each period against target and the Engineering/ Fleet director should meet his cleaning manager and review performance, compliance and future plans every quarter if standards are improving and more often if they are not.

The Operator has a vital task in ensuring that trains arrive at the cleaning point as planned and that any special arrangements (e.g. set X needs a heavy clean) are known of and acted upon in the Control Office to ensure that set swaps during the day do not deliver the wrong set to the cleaning team.

Customer/Passenger Information Arrangements

Whilst this is often seen as a TOC responsibility all organisations must ensure that their arrangements meet industry and customer requirements and are deliverable. It is important that the following critical aspects are properly linked and integrated:-

- Information flow architecture – what the communication structure looks like.
- Communication activities.
- Information transmission links – how the information transfer takes place.
- Key staff groups' responsibilities (e.g. at stations, on-train).
- Dependencies on other organisations.
- Training and competence.

Typically a set of TOC processes will also set out codified arrangements for:-

- Receiving and Passing on Information.
- Announcement Scripts for stations and on-train.
- Managing Service Disruption including Passenger Information During Disruption (PIDD).
- On Call.
- Advance Customer advice of Service Disruption.
- 'Do Not Travel' Policy.
- Retrospective Apology Messages & Posters.

Notification of Engineering Works, Amended Train Services and Infrastructure Alterations to Staff

Organisations must ensure that their staff are aware of engineering works (and associated protection arrangements) that are being undertaken, including any associated alterations to the train service. Engineering works are advised in Part B of the Weekly Operating Notices (WON) which provides the level of detail required for operations staff such as signallers to make the arrangements required.

The WON also includes details of temporary speed restriction (Part A), infrastructure changes (Part C) and amendments to operating publications (Part D).

It is important that staff are aware of the changes in Sections C and D as they could impact on the way they undertake their work. Make sure that your briefing arrangements are robust, receiving a document and not opening it can become habit forming.

Staff must also be made aware of weekly and daily amendments to train services. These may occur to accommodate engineering work but may also be due to

Running a Railway

special events, or especially in the case of freight services due to short notice changes in demand.

Make sure that your staff receive the information that they require to carry out their responsibilities effectively. In particular make sure that changes to the norm are understood and have been acted upon. For example, in the case of new working arrangements at a level crossing put in as a result of a renewal or engineering work that requires Single Line Working, you would need to check that resources had been correctly allocated.

TOC Engineering Work Communications

A TOC Engineering Communications process should describe how information about train service alterations caused by planned Network Rail engineering work will be communicated to Retail and Customer Services Staff who interface with customers.

It should also describe how such information will be provided to customers, either directly or indirectly. This must include information on websites and information provided via NRE, the media and other third parties.

It should cover both advance information and day of travel information.

The key aim is to make sure that amended train service information is readily available and accessible to front line staff and customers.

This should be provided in such a way that:-
- Details of the arrangements (train and bus if appropriate) are clear and readily available and accessible.
- Sufficient details are available within the specified timescales. Tell customers what is being done and don't hide behind the phrase 'essential engineering work'.
- The impact of Engineering work is kept in proportion. It should be clear which services and routes are affected.
- Customers can get consistent, jargon-free information on demand from all available sources.

Infrastructure Maintenance Regimes by Asset type

There are detailed arrangements for maintenance frequencies and component replacement in Maintenance and Asset standards. Much of this is the concern of Fleet engineering but:-
- Will concern others if repeat problems occur. Why are the standard arrangements failing or are set processes not being followed accurately?
- Some processes will be undertaken and can have a significant impact on operational safety and performance;

6.8 Train Service Delivery Systems & Processes - Overview

- Track Patrolling Possessions during traffic hours.
- Facing Point Lock Testing and other maintenance activities which are often done during day time.
- Arrangements for granting line blockages in traffic hours (how many, frequency etc).
- Red zone working prohibited areas
- There may be areas where your Mobile Operations Managers (MOMs) may be able to assist. For example, calling a member of maintenance staff out to act as an attendant at a Level Crossing during a failure may mean that that individual is not able to work their booked shift at night and a job may be cancelled as a result.
- The proactive management of heat and other weather related mitigation is critical. For example, know your heat mitigations, speeds that might be imposed and trigger temperatures.

Infrastructure Fault Management Processes

These consist of specific working arrangements between the Control and maintenance staff. They should include:

- How events are to be recorded in the Fault Management System (FMS) - including categorisation of risk and management of safety related failures.
- Liaison and communication between teams for types of asset.
- Access arrangements for fault teams. For example a '10 minute rule' for allowing a quick, disruptive line blockage to establish facts or quick fix.
- Escalation processes.
- Asset Recovery Manager (ARM) processes.

Since Operations Controls have been integrated with Infrastructure Fault Controls, the Network Rail route-based Control Offices have both operations and maintenance 'customers'. It is vitally important that clearly defined arrangements are put in place with maintenance staff so that expectations and requirements are clearly understood.

Signal Box Special Instructions and Local Instructions

These documents explain the detailed working arrangements and amplify Rule Book requirements as applied at specific locations. Certain methods of working explicitly referenced in the Rule Book must be specifically authorised in Signal Box Special Instructions (e.g. modified working on single lines).

- Isolation instructions are provided to Electrical Control to detail the actions they must take when isolating specific sections or sub-sections of overhead line or third rail and Signallers have equivalent instructions detailing protection signals and other arrangements for providing blockages to electric traction.

Running a Railway

- Bridge Strike Appendices are produced covering each bridge and whether any form of derogation has been applied enabling trains to run prior to the attendance of a Bridge Strike Nominee or Examiner.

Train Regulation Policy

A Train Regulation Policy will contain the following elements:-

- A Train Regulation Policy Statement that sets out the overall policy.
- Arrangements for the management of trains operating over several operational boundaries (cross-route trains).
- Arrangements for the management of trains that run early.

The intention of regulating guidance is to achieve the best balance between:-

- The most efficient use of the infrastructure available to the signaller.
- Minimisation of delay to the trains concerned.
- Minimisation of delay to passengers or freight conveyed on the trains concerned.
- Maintaining connections between passenger services where these have been agreed.
- Priorities or other requirements determined from time to time by Control.
- Avoiding undue discrimination between Train Operators.

Where detailed specific guidance is provided to Signallers (around specific junctions or even individual trains for example) this must be agreed with all train operators and it is important to carefully balance their needs. Bear in mind that the more detailed the statements are, the more difficult it can be for signallers to retain and implement the requirements, and this is particularly important in areas with Automatic Route Setting.

You should review Regulating Statements on a regular basis (at least at every timetable change) and make sure that signallers are familiar with the requirements within their areas of responsibility.

Tips

Use documented arrangements - they will help you take a more structured approach. If they are not documented cause this to happen quickly in conjunction with all relevant parties

Always make sure that front line/customer facing staff know what they need to do and have the means to deliver it.

Remember these systems are tools to help deliver what our customers expect - punctual, clean trains and good information.

6.9 Control Office; Issues and Management

BACKGROUND

Control Offices are the 24/7 focal point for train service delivery. Whether the Network Rail and TOC Control functions are separate, co-located or integrated, the collective Control Office resources are responsible for minute by minute delivery of the train service. This is a key operations function with huge commercial and passenger and freight customer responsibilities. Specific tasks of a control office can be broken down further as follows:-

- Management of the train service over a geographical area including out of course running, train service perturbation and effective train service recovery.
- Management of incidents and accidents involving trains, stations and the infrastructure.
- Management of the infrastructure in the case of faults and failures.
- Management of short-notice access to the infrastructure for engineers and for train services.
- Management of traction and rolling stock in the case of faults and failures, reallocation in times of train service perturbation and possibly allocation of trains for the start of service.
- Management of rolling stock allocation and maintenance scheduling.
- Management of train crew and other on-train staff in delivery of the base plan.
- Management of the relationship with interfacing organisations, suppliers and customers (other transport networks for example).
- Communication of all changes to the booked train plan to those who need to know (rail staff and passengers).
- Recording what has occurred so that further management action can be taken (includes logging of events, wrong side failure reporting and delay attribution for example).
- Call out and liaison with response staff and on call/senior managers.
- Focal Point for the provision of information to front-line staff and customers (particularly during disruption).

However Control is not where the buck stops. The final accountability for good delivery lies with the Network Rail Route and TOC Managing Directors. Whilst passengers invariably complain to the TOC, delivery of a good service is clearly the joint responsibility of the Train Operator & Infrastructure provider.

Accordingly Operations teams across all organisations have a clear responsibility to plan, deliver and review the train service jointly. A key part of this is

Running a Railway

managing the Control Office function and ensuring that all delivery activities are correctly interfaced with the Controls and that TOC and NR Controls are properly communicating whether integrated or not.

Similarly Control Offices require direction and support from TOC and NR Line and On Call Managers appropriate to the prevailing operating position. This element of the manual is primarily focused on that requirement.

ATTRIBUTES

It is difficult to describe the ideal Control Office in terms of the building blocks, but the following is a brief list of what 'good' looks like.

A good Control:-
- Has a good atmosphere when you walk in.
- Works to common objectives.
- Is pro-active not reactive.
- Is structured in approach.
- Has clearly defined role responsibilities.
- Routinely evaluates its performance .
- Is resourced to do its job with :-
  - Properly trained people who are competent and confident.
  - Appropriate IT systems which provide real time information and decision support capability.
  - Accurate and easily available sources of information e.g. simplifiers.
  - Up to date and relevant contingency and emergency plans.
  - Reliable communication tools.
  - Easily accessed manuals, plans and procedures.

DIRECTION AND SUPPORT

Control Office managers have a wide remit to direct and influence the deployment of the resources to deliver the most effective train service possible in any given set of circumstances, in almost all cases remote from the scene of the action.

Many managers involved in train service delivery will only know Controllers by the sound of their voices over a telephone, and such conversations are often conducted in stressful circumstances and may therefore be abrupt, very directive and sometimes confrontational. This can be made worse when the Control Office plan, which will be seeking to protect 'the greater good' appears at odds with local and sometimes parochial concerns and aspirations.

6.9 Control Office; Issues and Management

Consequently you should:-
- Get to know the role of each post and its key interfaces.
- Understand the plans and imperatives which underpin controller decision making.
- Ensure the Controllers understand your part of the organisation and how it works.
- Communicate clearly what you and your people expect to be consulted on, and at what stage.
- Communicate clearly what you want to know and when.
- Establish a working mode which encourages the Control to seek the advice of you and your people, and welcomes your input, and guidance and direction when services are disrupted.
- Get into the habit of popping into control regularly and to get to know all controllers. At operations director level it is highly appropriate to call the shift leader in control first thing in the morning and pre-evening peak for an update.
- Encourage Controllers to think worst-case scenario and quickly implement plans for those incidents which, from experience, are likely to be very disruptive. Calling out and mobilising too many responders, or too much rescue and recovery resource is always preferable to too little, and these resources can be stood down if and when appropriate. Make sure you back up your controllers if this results in complaints about over reaction.
- Always be healthily sceptical of predicted or forecast outcomes. Dissect them to understand how they have been arrived at and then add your own common sense to the others. Prepare for the worst, it is easy to have an optimism bias.
- Ensure Controllers continue to learn, develop and gain knowledge and not get set in their ways. Ensure that they are always in date for specified competencies.
- Harness readily available technology. Make sure that your staff are able to use the available tools and maximise their understanding of functionality. E-mailed photographs, for instance from a derailment, a broken rail or lineside fire, are of real assistance in the control. Websites such as 'wagonsontheweb' show photographs of all types of wagon running on the UK railway. Google Earth or streetmap.com can be used to provide an aerial view of a site, albeit not current, allowing real understanding of access points and roads, width of formation, yards etc.
- Challenge the status quo and do not accept complacency or second best – remember the passengers on the receiving end of Control Office decisions.

Running a Railway

CO-LOCATION AND INTEGRATION

Network Rail and TOC Control Offices are becoming increasingly co-located or integrated, where lines of route, areas of operation, or boundaries are common or shared.

'Co-location' describes a situation where the two offices are housed in the same accommodation, with unchanged roles and responsibilities of the respective offices and personnel within them.

'Integration' describes a location where company boundaries are set aside in the structure and ethos of the control. Tasks are assigned to controllers according to need and duplication is removed. This arrangement usually involves a single manager in charge of all staff on each shift.

After a decade of separating NR and TOC Control Offices after privatisation, it is now generally accepted that, where NR and TOC have common routes or boundaries, co-location is the right thing to do.

There is no 'one size fits all' especially as some TOCs are organised by lines of route that are not coterminous with Network Rail Route boundaries. TOCs and FOCs with a national focus have controls located to optimise their company requirements and need to deal with many NR control offices to ensure that their trains have their service delivery needs satisfied.

When considering where best to locate a control office account has been taken of the relative benefits of TOC/NR co-location or integration, co-location with other front line staff such as signallers and co-location with other functions such as train planning or performance. It has not usually been possible to achieve all of these benefits in one location but some have a few of these.

INFRASTRUCTURE AND MAINTENANCE CONTROL

At privatisation, infrastructure companies set up their own Infrastructure Fault Control offices (IFCs) to manage the interface with response staff and the relevant Network Rail Control(s). Since the maintenance activity has returned to Network Rail these IFCs have been integrated with Network Rail Operations Controls.

There are two main control posts involved in infrastructure activity:-
- Incident Controllers who manage the response to any event which impacts upon railway operations. They are responsible for response resource allocation and site liaison. They co-ordinate the plan to return to normal working. Their focus is on the response to the event itself rather than the railway which is operating around it.

6.9 Control Office; Issues and Management

- Incident Support Controllers provide assistance and manage input into Network Rail's Fault Management System (FMS) which is a highly structured logging tool used to analyse asset performance and reliability.

Note: Responsibility for rescheduling routine maintenance that has been cancelled or postponed as a result of an incident will usually be undertaken by the relevant depot planning team.

FLEET SUPPORT

In the same way that NR has been incorporating infrastructure fault management in its Control Offices, almost all TOC Controls now have fleet management representation, to encourage rapid fault finding on defective trains, to provide a 'one stop shop' for advice to Drivers about fleet issues whilst out on the road, and to provide the authority for operational decisions during disruption – such as "Cut & Run", terminate short, one journey only etc.

It is interesting to note that ten years ago fleet control was in some cases physically separate from 'operations' or train running control.

Fleet management in Control has been an almost universal resounding success, giving Drivers confidence to tackle problems, providing rapid advice and expertise in time critical situations, and shortening dramatically the lines of communication and decision making. Very often, the flow of information to depots and communication to maintenance or repair staff is dramatically improved. (See also Fleet/Operations Interface). Where fleet management/ fault finding is co-located in the Control Office you fully own the disruption inside the Control Office, and can plan accordingly, rather than wait for a decision from elsewhere whilst trains queue behind the failure!

CONTROL ROLES

All control offices will have some core jobs with broadly similar roles. Additionally all controls will have other control responsibilities according to the needs of the TOC/NR operation.

Core roles often include:-
- Duty Control Manager

Overall responsibility for real time train service delivery within the geographic area of control. This includes management of incidents/accidents.

- Train Service Controller

Overview management of train regulation, adjustment to train services

Running a Railway

including reduction of train services to match available track capacity, terminating trains short of destination and or omitting booked stops to regain lost time. Plans service recovery to stabilise services during disruption and then return to the base plan.

- Incident Controller

Direct management of the response to any event which impacts upon railway operations which can cover NR and/or TOC activities). Responsible for the allocation of response resources and site liaison. Also responsible for the co-ordination of plans to return to normal working. The focus is on the response to the event itself rather than the railway which is operating around it.

- Train Crew Controller

Adjustments to all train crew and other on board staff in the light of late running, failures, cancellations and other non planned events to maintain booked train services as far as possible. Train service recovery as necessary.

- Fleet Controller

Adjustments to fleet in the light of late running, failures, cancellations and other unplanned events to maintain booked train services as far as possible. Supports train service recovery through re-diagramming of the fleet to support contingency plans. This may include allocation of units to diagrams at the start of service and maintenance allocation.

- Information Controller

Current and continuous update of advice to members of rail staff, passengers and public including changes to advertised train services in the event of late running, altered stopping patterns and or train cancellations. This will include co-ordinating the services of third parties, such as advice to other transport networks, management of rail-replacement bus services and so on. The role is also responsible for providing core messages during service disruption.

Note:- There are a variety of permutations of these roles. For example some TOCs combine TOC Incident management & train running.

Support activities may include:-

- VSTP Controller

Creation of very short term planning schedules in TSDB / Train Running System TOPS (TRUST) for unplanned movements required to run on the network.

- Trust Delay Attribution

Creation of Delay Incidents in TRUST including Delay Causation and Responsible Manager codes. This post will need to work closely with other controllers

6.9 Control Office; Issues and Management

on shift with respect to acceptance or dispute of individual incidents.

- Information Operators

Management of information provided to passengers at stations through visual display and audible announcements using Customer Information Systems (CIS) and Public Address (PA) equipment.

- CCTV Operator

Operation of station CCTV equipment, including evidence management procedures and profiling.

- Fleet Support

Often provided as the 'phone a friend' helpline for train drivers to contact a fitter for real-time train fault management advice.

- Infrastructure Technician

Technical specialist to support field technicians in managing infrastructure, often through interpretation of Remote Conditioning Equipment.

Running a Railway

RESPONSIBILITIES - Level 1

(e.g. Local Manager, charged with area line management and delivery)

Plan
- Ensure that the Control function forms an integral part of routine management arrangements.
- Ensure that liaison arrangements with Control are clearly briefed and understood.
- Ensure limits of authority and escalation requirements are clearly briefed and understood.
- Understand the plans that Control use and the way in which such plans underpin decision making.
- Ensure all controllers understand your organisation and how it works.

Do
- Work with the Control function to deliver optimum performance.
- Ensure that defined processes are followed – particularly decision making authorities and escalation.
- Ensure all appropriate Control personnel are engaged during the recovery from perturbation.
- Visit and call Control Offices regularly.
- Ensure that relevant members of your team regularly update Control during incidents in line with the agreed Communications Plans.

Review
- Involve Control personnel in post-event reviews.
- Provide feedback to Control Office personnel.
- Use agreed measures to review incidents and audit the effectiveness of decisions made. P2/CCF are useful tools to support such reviews but remember that they will show you the effect of actions taken, but not why and how it was done.
- Use speech recording equipment to check the standard of verbal communication. This includes quality of information as well as adherence to communications protocols.

P2 is a map based system which provides train running information to station staff.

CCF – Control Centre of the Future is a Network Rail system similar to P2 which shows precise movements of trains over the track layout in power signalling controlled areas. As well as showing real time running, it can play back earlier train movements.

6.9 Control Office; Issues and Management

RESPONSIBILITIES - Level 2

(e.g. Senior Manager responsible for the Control function - usually at HQ level)

Plan
- Define the authority levels of Control Offices and how decision making fits with the wider organisation – including the decision escalation processes.
- Arrange for key procedures to be documented as Standing Orders or Protocols and maintained as controlled documents.
- Ensure that Control arrangements are properly integrated with all other relevant activities – regardless of owning company.
- Establish KPIs/analysis that enables the effectiveness of the Control function to be monitored and assessed.
- Ensure training and development arrangements are robust and include meaningful competence assessment and re-assessment.

Do
- Visit the Control Office very regularly.
- Manage the Control activities according to the specified arrangements.
- Use protocols defining how you will provide support and leadership during disruption. Lead rather than interfere).
- Take charge of large incidents or intervene when smaller incidents are not brought under adequate control.
- Make sure that Control Office staff understand company targets and the importance of customer service.

Review
- Periodically review the effectiveness of the Control function. This should be undertaken jointly by NR and the TOCs/FOCs at intervals not exceeding 12 months.
- Identify and review industry good practice from other comparable operations.
- Consider alternative methods for controlling train service delivery.

Tips

Control teams are crucial to the delivery of good performance. They have the ability to maximise or minimise punctuality results in any given situation.

Operations Managers should form a very close working arrangement with the relevant Control Office whether they are Integrated, Co-located, or separate.

Running a Railway

Regular contact between key operations personnel and control throughout the day is very important

Remember low-level routine disruption is often more damaging for your Public Performance Measures' Moving Annual Average (PPM MAA) than one-off large incidents - make sure your Controllers know how and when to intervene.

6.10 Logs – Using Control and other Logs

BACKGROUND

Ensuring that logs contain a full record of events and appropriate business critical information and that the information is acted on is a key operations priority.

As a minimum logs should record rolling stock and network infrastructure availability for the day.

All logs should also summarise incidents, including time, locations, people involved, action taken as it unfolds and the impact on train service. Ideally logs should be recorded in real time and kept in a database to aid search and analysis.

Most importantly the information in logs should be used in a positive way. This can normally start with a structured conference.

NR/TOC/FOC

Control, and other critical logs, should form the backbone of first level performance review arrangements. Similarly it is essential to ensure control log information flows through the relevant performance management activities in a structured systematic way.

The Network Rail FMS logs are a key source of information about infrastructure faults, failures and events. They are also a valuable source of information on infrastructure trends and important in the management of infrastructure Wrong Side Failures.

WRITING GOOD LOGS

It is critical that logs should be produced according to a specification concerning content, timescales and distribution. They should also contain essential core information:-

- Every delay causing incident.
- Timeline of events.
- Both incident management, train service recovery and customer service activities.
- Actions taken.
- CCIL – NR's Control Centre Incident Log.
- TOC Log – Completed by TOC Controllers.
- FMS – Fault.

Other important considerations are the value of recommendations to prevent recurrence and the need to avoid duplication – we often have at least four versions of the same event! (CCIL/TOC Log/FMS/TDA).

USING LOGS

Get the logs early preferably as soon as they are published and follow up issues before the day gets going. Make sure your people know you are passionate about this and the need for good follow up.

Visit Control regularly, let Controllers know you use their work to improve the railway.

The review process should be a structured conference based set of arrangements that formally link to the performance investigation/analysis processes within the performance arrangements. A Network Rail conference should include a review of infrastructure issues, regulating and timetabling issues. A TOC conference should include Fleet and train operations. It is good practice to undertake conferences jointly.

Daily conferences should also contain a look ahead for important issues such as forthcoming engineering work, expected weather impact and mitigations and so on. You may adopt a weekly schedule of different issues for each day as well as the review of the performance of the previous day.

A periodic objective review of control log contents and usage is essential.

Control logs must always contain facts – recommendations should be welcomed but personal opinions have no place in logs and should be actively discouraged. Names of customers (for instance any customer injured) should not appear

Running a Railway

but should be readily available from the control. Staff names should likewise be protected. Names of responding managers should of course appear to allow for follow up in reports and on the Conference.

Information in control logs is only as good as that passed to the Control, and should not be assumed to be complete, or necessarily wholly accurate, until an incident has been properly investigated. Links can be added to a log to access photographs and voice tapes relating to a particular incident. These can be invaluable. Pictures, using the cliché, are worth a thousand words.

Logs should form the basis of current performance review and the Chairman of the daily conference should ensure key items are discussed and corrective action formulated. Actions agreed on the conference should be recorded for future follow up.

Senior operators should review the logs and chair the daily conference without fail. Routine involvement by senior managers (including in TOCs the Operations Director) works wonders for commitment to the process of managing current performance. The conference should be high profile and sharp. If an organisation is going through a particularly poor run of performance it may be prudent to hold a conference seven days a week with the weekends on call staff calling in to the senior on call director or equivalent.

The discipline of following up is key to a good outcome. Instigating a process that requires answers preferably to the chairman of the conference by a specified time is good practice and ensures the arrangements stay meaningful. It is vital to record actions and follow-up to make sure that they are completed. Do not action too many items each day or the volume will become unmanageable

TOC Operations Managers should also review the Fleet log detailing availability, stopped units, etc. Challenge the Fleet Director on issues such as repeat failures and units awaiting material, check these have not become "Christmas Trees" (a colloquial term used to describe units/trains that have parts taken to repair other units/trains – available spares = presents on a Christmas tree). Make sure that the process is simple and does not bog conference participants down.

Network Rail Operations Managers must involve infrastructure maintenance managers in their conference arrangements. Without them you will cover less than half the story.

TOC managers should read the NR logs and vice versa. It is important to look at issues from all perspectives and challenge your opposite number when appropriate.

Tips

It is essential that all involved know that senior managers read and act upon the logs.

Senior Operations Managers should review the logs and chair the conference without fail. Pick some items - not necessarily the biggest or highest profile - and drive hard to find root causes. Test particularly those incidents in which functional or inter-company interfaces are highlighted.

Do not tolerate poor preparation by those participating in such conferences. The response 'I'll come back to you' as a cover for not knowing is not acceptable preparation in all but a minority of cases. Demand prompt responses and prompt action from both your own managers and those in your industry partners' organisations.

Keep it businesslike and tight. It is always worth putting a specific time limit on the conference.

Use the logs and associated conferences to demonstrate a strong personal commitment to current performance management.

6.11 Delay Attribution

BACKGROUND

The delay attribution process was under review at the time of this latest revision (December 2011), therefore readers should double check the current status of the arrangements in place.

The processes surrounding delay attribution were developed as part of the 1994 railways privatisation.

Prior to that time the attribution of delay was limited and in some places non-existent. For example, the former Southern Region did not have access to the TRUST system until railway privatisation.

Whilst the attribution processes were designed to support the various incentive regimes. (Schedule 8 between TOCs and Network Rail, and Schedule 7 between TOCs and the former Strategic Rail Authority), the real performance benefit

Running a Railway

was a step change in the quality and quantity of management information.

Increasingly the industry has recognised that the current attribution process is focused on attributing blame rather than determining root cause. However, the attribution process only exists in its well-resourced form because of the sums of money that have been involved in the incentive regimes, primarily Schedule 8. There is an intrinsic tension in the arrangements between establishing root cause and minimising financial risk.

However in TOCs the greater use of Bugle (a performance data handling system/tool) by a wide range of staff has usefully moved the investigation of incidents away from the performance teams to the managers responsible throughout the TOC. Therefore greater accuracy of attribution on Day 1 is critical to the success of Bugle.

The current challenge for the industry is to move to more effective and accurate determination of root cause without losing the imperatives within the current arrangements that have historically been driven by the large sums of money involved. It is vital that Delay Attribution processes are robust and use all the available tools.

However, the value gained must be worth the effort expended – obtaining On Train Monitoring and Recording (OTMR) information or signalling downloads through management action is a very costly way of establishing the root cause of a 3 minute delay. 100% accuracy is not necessary; settling for the appropriate level to tackle the issues that are causing problems should be the aim. In particular, shuffling delays around internal departments of the same company will have zero impact on the bottom line.

PROCESSES

The various contractual regimes are specified in the TOC's Franchise Agreement, Network Rail's Licence Obligations, the Track Access Agreements and the Network Code. Further supporting details are codified in the Railway Operations Code and Delay Attribution Guide.

Details of the Level 1, 2 and 3 layers of attribution are codified in the NR Business Process Manual and TOC equivalents.

Details of TRUST attribution codes and attribution precedents are contained in the Delay Attribution Guide (the 'DAG'). This document and the responsibility for developing attribution arrangements is vested in the Delay Attribution Board, an independently chaired group with nominated cross-industry members that also now arbitrates in attribution disputes and points of principle.

6.11 Delay Attribution

NORMAL ARRANGEMENTS

Delay incidents are attributed by Network Rail to the appropriate root cause. Those incidents attributed to TOC causes may be accepted or rejected on shift in the TOC Control, or within 7 days by the TOC Data Quality Manager. The Attribute-Dispute model is based on an adversarial approach but some delay attribution teams will try to foster an approach where accuracy first time around is the aim.

Most TOCs aim to resolve over 90% of attribution on shift or via the nominated Level 1 manager (e.g. Data Quality Manager), with the balance being referred to Level 2 and few if any instances going to Level 3.

Dispute resolution between NR and TOCs at Level 3 whilst rare, does usually involve large incidents and resolution through a commercial deal can often resolve the money but not the attribution of the minutes. Such deals can, and have, frequently distorted published data. Level 3 resolution can be used when a number of similar issues come to light whereby a greater understanding of the cause is required. It may also need management intervention to resolve inherent problems, such as system berthing errors and signaller actions.

An incident reaching Level 3 can be a sign of lack of ownership and lack of confident, robust investigation at an earlier stage. However this can also arise if senior managers do not encourage ownership at local level.

Performance Managers and their teams should liaise with their Level 1 teams to ensure all issues are understood. Level 1 should be fully able to work to the guidelines for creating accurate delay incidents and incidents should be reviewed to establish whether the delay attributed is accurately recorded. If this is not the case, this should be raised for reallocation to be made and if this is not acceptable to both parties, the incident can be 'disputed' for resolution at a higher level.

Difficulties in determining responsibility can occur regularly with certain types of incident, including security alerts, suspicious behaviour, train striking objects (including unexplained air losses), bird strikes and all unexplained loss in running. Detailed guidance is usually drawn up for these types of incident, sometimes after a ruling by the Delay Attribution Board.

Some TOCs have policies setting out levels of delay above which any incident must be disputed so they can be checked by an attribution expert. Such policies should be shared with Network Rail colleagues so there can be a clear understanding of processes.

Running a Railway

ISSUES

Attribution is a tedious but important job and there are numerous perverse incentives on staff to not attribute correctly. NR must carry out an adequate investigation of their own before attributing to the TOC and TOCs must use reasonable endeavours to help NR establish cause. Unattributed delay is the responsibility of NR, not the TOC.

If you want to tackle root cause of delay you should place accuracy above commercial gain, but that is easier said than done!

It is important that there are efficient processes for obtaining the information to confirm or reject attributed delay. In many instances the incident involved will be forgotten unless reports are obtained quickly. It can then be very difficult to construct a clear case to reject a delay and get it attributed to the right place. Some TOCs have telephone reporting lines for traincrew and others to report delays in real time. Controllers should also attempt to gain information from staff on shift if at all possible.

The DAG contains instructions on how to deal with all normal issues and test cases have established precedents. Do not enter into local commercial agreements, they only cause long term problems and undermine the contracts.

Key points are:-
- Give guidance to attribution checkers and encourage your team to do likewise. Staff may otherwise do what they think is right based on custom and practice.
- Delay Attributors are usually the most junior members of the control team but as such they are an ideal recruitment ground for Control positions – it is worth spending time developing their skill and knowledge.
- Establish actual root cause and ownership. Insist that owners reduce their delays and give practical assistance and support where required in order for them to do so.
- Attributed delay provides a rich source of management information. The scope, depth and quality of this data is probably better than any other railway in the world.
- Attribution behaviours and practices have changed over time – beware of this when analysing data and determining trends.
- Watch how reactionary delay (Y coded) is attributed. Primary and reactionary delays require different solutions and much more can be done to understand this aspect.

Note – Most of the post-Hatfield increase in delay was due to a rise in reactionary delay. This can be thought of as a measure of our collective efficiency/effectiveness in dealing with incidents/perturbation.

6.11 Delay Attribution

- Monitoring, check and audit, with structured feedback to attributers is essential.
- Engagement of Control duty managers and sign off of attributed delay on a shift basis is a good practice.
- Regularly review attribution effectiveness with senior colleagues at NR.

Tips

Challenge and dispute all the way if you consider attribution is incorrect.

Make sure your processes for collecting delay reports are efficient.

Some delay codes are intended as "holding codes" until full information becomes available. Make sure that these are properly investigated and amended when the cause is established. For example: AZ (Terminal other); TO, FO (TOC/FOC Unexplained); OI (Joint Inquiry).

Have an occasional blitz on certain codes that are used as dustbins (i.e. TO/FO, Y and P codes).

Establish audit, spot check, and feedback mechanisms for attribution staff - do not allow them to get too cosy - correct attribution is the goal.

Internal departmental attribution squabbles are a threat to corrective action. A possible rule of thumb is that you should not discuss a delay incident for more than the number of minutes involved. If you do you are probably wasting precious time!

Delay attribution is a subject worth devoting time to, and staff responsible for this tedious task will appreciate your interest.

Other relevant/useful documents:-
– Delay Attribution Guide (DAG)

6.12 Simplifiers

BACKGROUND

Many routine operating tasks benefit from what have been termed as Simplifiers. Modern database train planning systems have gradually reduced the need for crew diagram simplifiers but many signal boxes, and the larger, more complex stations, still compile box and station platforming simplifiers at the start of each new timetable because such aids do make the job easier.

ISSUES

Most simplifiers exist because they are a proven way of identifying the key requirements at important locations without cluttering with superfluous detail. Have a look at any simplifiers that you come across e.g. Station Working books which are in some locations called 'dockers'. They help provide an insight into the important activities in control offices, signal boxes etc.

Historically, the biggest problem with any simplifier has been the size of the production task. They have been almost always prepared manually, by personnel who are interested and good at the task, often on overtime, and always very late in the timetable implementation process. As a result, the simplifier can be susceptible to error – particularly when amendments are made to the plan after its creation; e.g. Short Term Plan services.

Some TOCs have made significant headway in automating the task. Recent advances in train planning systems are allowing further improvements in this area.

Know who is responsible for creating simplifiers at your locations and what additional payments they get as a result. All too often Simplifiers just appear with little or no management involvement at all.

When tackling a delegated task or identified problem in a specific area, simplifiers can sometimes help boil complex information down to a manageable size.

Tips

Simplifiers are developed, often with considerable effort, to fulfil a need not met by "normal" systems. They do therefore provide an insight into what is important at the coalface.

A lot of effort is required to produce simplifiers. Using IT to reduce this burden is a key challenge.

6.13 Role of First Line Operations Staff

INTRODUCTION

Responsibility for train service delivery on mainline railways in Great Britain is split between a number of different organisations, primarily Network Rail, TOCs and FOCs. It is essential that Operators understand who does what.

When the railways were privatised in 1994 some key groups of first-line staff had their operational duties reduced in scope because of the responsibilities of the organisation they were now charted to.

Key examples of this were:-
- MOMs - who went from being general first-line operational responders (including attending failed trains) to being infrastructure failure focused - working for NR.
- Station Staff - who had traditional operational duties such as the manual operation of points during a failure or the emergency level crossing attendant etc. removed as these became Network Rail responsibilities and the majority of station staff now worked for TOCs.

Whilst some of these anomalies have now been eased, it is still a fact that:-
- NR own the only real first-line response staff.
- TOCs vary but first-line response staff, if there are any, are usually Train Crew Supervisors and Managers of some description. This means that the majority of such staff have a train crew focus.

The problem is compounded as few operators move between NR and Operating Companies during their careers so 'whole railway' experience is diminishing over time.

This is why it is vital for operators to understand the roles and responsibilities of all first-line staff within their areas of operation, regardless of which company such individuals are employed by.

Running a Railway

TOCs

Train Operating Companies all have slightly different approaches to train service delivery and widely varying attitudes to the provision of first-line operations staff. Remember that this will include roles in departments other than operations

- Station staff may or may not be within the operations department but they have a key role to play in the management of disruption.
- Fleet Fitters may be required to attend rolling stock faults and failures and may well travel on certain key services or be strategically placed at important locations.

Consequently, TOC operations managers must clearly establish the capabilities available within the TOC and ensure there is a clear collective understanding with Network Rail colleagues - who may be dealing with a number of TOCs with different structures.

Similarly, Network Rail operators must understand the TOC position and plan incident response arrangements accordingly.

No assumptions should be made. Even designated emergency TOC roles such as TOLO and SIO are not consistently used by all TOCs.

Note:
TOLO = Train Operations Liaison Officer - A person appointed to lead for a Train Operator during a serious incident.
SIO = Station Incident Officer - A person appointed to lead for a station operator during a serious incident.

NETWORK RAIL

NR has a much more clearly defined and standardised first-line operations structure and there are generally a number of standardised roles in every NR local organisation. The prime groups are:-
- Shift Signaller Managers.
- Mobile Operations Managers (MOMs).
- Local Operations Managers and Operations Managers (LOMs and OMs).
- Current Operations Managers.

Personnel in these positions will usually be the first point of contact for TOC Operations staff, particularly during perturbation, incident or accident.

6.13 Role of First Line Operations Staff

ISSUES

Operations managers at all levels should devote considerable time and energy to the interface and relationship with counterparts in other companies - in Control, in depots, in Signalling Centres, and with outdoor staff such as Mobile Operations Managers.

Take time to understand issues from another perspective. Where possible, building relationships with Engineering staff such as Maintenance Managers, Possessions Managers, or fleet technicians, will also generate benefits. These benefits may be difficult to quantify and often be extended longer term and will more than compensate for time invested. Visiting a station and understanding normal operations or disruption from the station control room or platform staff perspective will be invaluable in understanding how decisions can impact upon end-users

Similarly including NR front line staff into TOC training, briefing/debriefing, investigation and routine walkouts/visits and vice versa, will have a particularly positive effect on the overall approach and response to the TOC/NR interface.

The benefits will be two-way; Operations Managers will have a much better understanding of how each other respond and why in any given set of circumstances, and how to broker the best outcome,. The response of front line operational managers can and does, make the difference between an effectively managed incident and one that will be memorably bad for everyone involved.

The roles and responsibilities of the first-line NR staff described above are covered in the following sections.

SHIFT SIGNALLER MANAGERS (SSMs)

In the large signalling centres Signallers are continuously supervised by one or more Shift Signaller Managers. SSMs are responsible for managing the team of Signallers on duty and also act as a hub for communication with other operating teams such as Operations Control and Electrical Control Rooms.

Where necessary the SSM will direct Signallers actions within the constraints of rules and regulations. This includes regulating decisions as well as key decisions when managing an incident. SSMs are almost always competent to operate all of the panels or workstations that they supervise and can be a valuable source of information about the operation of the Signalling Centre.

Although they supervise teams in real time Signallers and SSMs report to the relevant Local Operations Manager.

Running a Railway

LOCAL OPERATIONS MANAGERS (LOMs) AND OPERATIONS MANAGERS (OMs)

Local Operations Managers are the first-line managers of the staff involved in signalling trains. Depending on the type of signalling system in use and the density/complexity of traffic, the LOM may be responsible for a number of signal boxes on a line of route or a single, large Signalling Centre.

LOMs have five generic responsibilities:-

- Management of a group of Signallers and/or Mobile Operations Managers– for their welfare, working needs, development and ongoing competence.
- Signaller/MOM compliance with Rules, regulations and instructions in the signalling of trains – primarily, but not wholly, in respect of safe working.
- Accommodation standards, health, safety and welfare issues in relation to signalling centre and signal boxes, and access routes.
- Managing the performance of the staff in their area.
- Managing the budget for their group of staff.

Engaging with, and motivating LOMs can be a force for good in the management of train service delivery, as this may tap into a rich vein of knowledge, support and activity that would otherwise be dormant and lost under the weight of other responsibilities.

Many LOMs have little day to day contact with TOC Managers and therefore little appreciation of TOC plans, priorities and performance profile. Most LOMs will really relish the opportunity that closer contact will bring.

Previously the LOM role had been heavily focused on compliance and competence management; sometimes been to the detriment of focus on real time performance. However this has recently improved and LOMs are now providing a real focus on performance in signalling centres.

CURRENT OPERATIONS MANAGER

Within each Network Rail Route the Current Operations Manager is responsible for managing the Control function and therefore leads real-time operation of the network. However the Current Operations Manager does not have direct line management responsibility for Signallers and MOMs and this can lead to tension between Control and Signaller in respect of actions taken during incident response and recovery. Accordingly there are plenty of examples (and anecdotes) where Signallers have been requested by Control to undertake an action which has not then happened.

But remember that these issues occur in the heat of the moment and there are varied reasons for them happening, such as:
- Not reaching a clear understanding over exactly what is required.
- Requesting something to be done which rules and regulations do not permit.
- Independent decision making in the Signalbox/centre without reference to the Control.
- Lack of understanding of the importance of a particular action in the overall strategy.
- Suggesting unrealistic plans which are difficult to deliver.

This aspect can be improved by:-
- Being clear about levels of accountability and responsibility.
- Devising clear and jointly agreed plans (Control, Technician and Shift Signaller Manager Conference call to agree a plan for example).
- Excellence in communication skills (including listening and documenting agreements reached).
- Swift involvement of on-call Local Operations Managers to help devise efficient methods of working when rules are used as a reason for not doing something.
- Joint training, briefing and team building exercises.
- Post-event hot debrief involving the staff involved.

MOBILE OPERATIONS MANAGERS

Mobile Operations Managers (MOMs) are Network Rail's first response resource to any incident or accident on, or affecting, the operational infrastructure.

MOMs have a number of other responsibilities, including routine checks on lineside security, lineside equipment, level crossing installations, possessions, access routes, and signage. However their primary responsibility is to provide response, when required, to incident, accident, blockage or damage to the infrastructure, however caused.

As a result, MOMs provide a level of coverage which reflects the operational hours of the route(s) – 24/7 in some cases – with an office base reflecting the response requirements of the busiest, most vulnerable sections of route.

MOMs are directed by the NR Control and will have a range of competencies for dealing with the operational implications of points, signals, track circuit and electrification failures, as well as bridge strikes by road vehicles, fatalities on the line, and line obstructions.

Running a Railway

These competencies include Rail Incident Officer certification – a broad based range of responsibilities, which allows the MOM to take charge of an incident or accident site as the lead rail industry presence on site. This will include assuming responsibilities of 'Silver Command' in the Command hierarchy established by NR and the emergency services.

The MOM will often be the first railway manager on site during a TOC-caused incident such as a train failure. Whilst he/she will be proficient in protecting the blockage, setting up single line working and securing the safety of staff such as driver or any fitter sent to examine the train, the MOM is likely to be less well versed in TOC issues.

Examples of these are - coupler incompatibilities between the failed train and the rescue 'loco', emergency coupling arrangements, 'cut and run' policies, supervision of emergency propelling moves, carrying out of brake continuity tests after freight train divisions, train evacuation requirements and degraded modes of operation for stock, including design life for onboard auxiliary power when traction current is isolated or diesel engines are switched off.

Inclusion of MOMs in TOC briefings and training opportunities is an effective way of equipping individuals with all the necessary knowledge to manage a TOC incident competently without the need for a physical TOC presence. Briefings should include:

- TOC policy, plans and performance.
- Rolling stock characteristics, or rolling stock new to a route.
- Distribution of driver briefing material.

Additionally it is good practice to engage actively with MOMs during routine and pre-planned walkabouts, or pre-planned inspections of possessions etc.

Whilst appointing a TOLO (a Train Operator Liaison Officer) is an ideal arrangement, very often the remoteness of TOC resources will prevent this. In such circumstances, a MOM with appropriate technical understanding or appreciation will be a most valuable resource.

Key issues for MOMs are:-

- Are they based in the correct locations?
- Do they have current competencies relevant to location/role?
- Do they have competency in critical TOC issues (e.g. for dealing with train failures)?
- Is their productivity level improved through taking on other ancillary duties?
- Where there is a limited MOM resource what alternative arrangements can be made to cover the gap?

Tips

A strong TOC/NR relationship at each level of management is the best long term protection against the natural emotions of distrust, and suspicion, and the inevitable bad mouthing, verbal abuse, contractual disputes and delay attribution disagreements which can plague a poor TOC/NR relationship.

Nurture the relationship - take a day every now and then to shadow your opposite number.

You may also want to organise some social time. Buy them a coffee or a pint now and then or go for a team curry.

6.14 Fleet and Operations Interface

BACKGROUND

This Section has been written from the perspective of a TOC that directly undertakes its own light maintenance (Level 1 to 4) but most of the advice is just as applicable when such maintenance is undertaken by a different TOC or separate maintenance company (e.g. Alstom, Bombardier, Siemens etc.). Regardless of structure, how well the Fleet and TOC/FOC Operations departments interface and interact will be crucial to the effectiveness of train service delivery.

Close working at all levels, from the Fleet or Engineering and Operations Directors to the shop floor, is essential.

In some TOCs the two roles of Operations and Fleet or Engineering Director are combined into a Production Director's role, especially those that contract out their train maintenance. If such a role is filled by an operations-background professional, then there will be a qualified engineering manager within the team as Professional Head of Engineering, and vice versa. This will be a requirement of safety validation.

Close working between the two functions must apply to all aspects of train service delivery – from train and fleet planning to real time delivery. It is essential that these good relationships are established and maintained between Fleet and Operations at all levels. Shared objectives and common processes are also vital.

Running a Railway

Similarly Operations and Fleet should not have different performance management arrangements. They must be identical and integrated.

Fleet delay minutes are generally the largest component of TOC-on-Self delay and many of the root causes are not technical, they are process, people or interface based.

ISSUES

Fleet/Operations interfaces start with good planning and lead through to close cooperation on real time delivery.

Planning

Fleet/Operations interface arrangements should cover the following areas. Many should be contained in the Rules of the Depot (ROTD) document, which will codify a series of critical factors relating to interfaces. These are:

- Depot Parameters – e.g. stabling capacity and other physical features, where the depot departure point is (normally a departure signal), minimum time between arrivals/departures, equipment access points, maintenance capabilities, etc. Also any depot constraints e.g. curvature restrictions etc.
- Maintenance Plan Requirements – e.g. What units are required when in order to deliver planned availability at all times. Minimum turn round times for given types of examinations.
- Train Plan Requirements – e.g. What is required when and at what point in order to operate the planned timetable.
- Critical Facilities and Alternatives – e.g. Details of alternative stabling, tanking, toilet emptying, fuelling, carriage washing.
- Critical Staffing (ROTD) – e.g. Details of depot signalling arrangements, shunt driver requirements and key depot staff.

Other interface arrangements listed elsewhere are:

- Contingent Train Diagrams – e.g. Details of out and back diagrams, diagrams suitable for alternative stock substitution, short formation or cancellation etc.
- Depot Logistics – e.g. Order of stock movement around the depot, special access requirements to depot facilities, depot safety/ protection system, time taken to isolation and re-energise OHLE/3rd Rail etc.
- Depot Method of Working – e.g. How train movements are safely controlled within the depot as well as arriving and departing the depot.

6.14 Fleet and Operations Interface

Real Time Delivery

It is essential that availability is closely monitored and that the operation of depots and stabling sidings are seen as an integral part of the train service delivery operation.

Most fleet organisations have integrated fleet management and maintenance IT systems. Operations managers are encouraged to be aware of what the system can do and what information it can provide, to engender a 'no surprises' culture. Where the fleet systems and train position systems such as CCF/P2, can be integrated, or at least have integrated aspects, this also is to be encouraged.

Close integration is particularly important in Control Offices where Fleet management should be given equal focus to infrastructure management. Control must ensure that units go onto depots on time in order to meet exam requirements. Right Time in – Right Time out.

Key points are:-
- Work closely with the Fleet Director and Depot Managers, and ensure this relationship is visible to your teams, especially train planners, Train Crew Managers, and local Operations Managers.
- Engender a spirit of cooperation at all levels. Good relationships must run from the Operations and Fleet Directors right through to the Drivers and Fitters.
- There should be routine liaison between the people who use the fleet (mostly Drivers) and those people who maintain the fleet. Effective exchange of information between these people will identify causes of failures, opportunities to avoid failures and opportunities to recover more quickly from failures.
- Take a close interest in the fleet maintenance staff working in Control. These are the Fleet Director's real time service management resource. They are important in the management of defective or failed trains in service, and are the key contact for Drivers needing advice (See also Performance Management Real Time). You must make sure they understand operational requirements – it's easy for fleet maintainers to be more concerned about fixing a problem than getting the railway running again.
- Understand and work to the Rules of the Depot document.
- Ensure that the depot Method of Working is both safe and effective. Review it regularly, particularly when traffic flows change.
- Ensure shunt drivers are adequately resourced and properly supervised.
- Understand the 'pinch points' at the depot – critical resources, critical time periods, servicing last trains on/ first trains off the depot etc.

Running a Railway

- Monitor arrivals and departures – once you have established what point departures are measured from.
  - Is it arrival at outlet signal?
  - Time outlet signal is cleared?
  - Time off stabling point?
- Monitor day to day delivery. Look at trains stopped by number of days. Watch out for "Christmas Trees" (trains that are cannibalised for spares).
- Routinely monitor the level of repeat failures – this is a good underlying measure of reliability
- Ensure Control know how trains that enter service with restrictions can be utilised (e.g. isolated engines/traction motors) and identify suitable diagrams, for example branch line work. Challenge the Fleet department if the numbers of such restrictions exceed targeted levels.
- Make sure that the control document covering the entry into service of trains with defective equipment is always up to date and applied. This is a key safety responsibility of an operations controller. Watch that in an effort to get a train off the depot, you don't take a train into traffic with a defect not allowed for in the document.
- Operations and Fleet should jointly produce a fault matrix based on the rule book requirements and any other company specific objectives or restrictions. This allows timely and appropriate advice to be given to frontline operations staff and depot.
- Ensure you have a robust system for recording faults or restrictions on rolling stock which is updated in 'real time' from both Control and the Maintenance Depot. This should be used in conjunction with your fault matrix.
- Where a fleet is covered by real time monitoring equipment make sure that maximum benefit is obtained from the information both in real time and as a source of information for performance improvement. Examples include identifying locations of wheelslip, correct train preparation etc.
- Take some time to have a good look at the rolling stock that you depend on. With a member of the fleet team, climb under, round and through the trains and take on board the key maintenance issues or troublesome components that the engineer will point out to you.
- With your Fleet colleagues, visit other companies' depots with excellent delivery records or look out for the depot visits you can attend with the IRO.

6.14 Fleet and Operations Interface

RESPONSIBILITIES - Level 1 – Local Operations Manager

Plan
- Ensure all interface tasks are well integrated, robustly resourced and properly supervised.
- Ensure that routine performance meetings and daily performance conferences are cross-functional and that the tactical objectives remain fully aligned.
- Organise regular and routine liaison with opposite numbers in Fleet/Operations.

Do
- Ensure arrangements work well and support real time Train Service Delivery.
- Check daily availability and non-availability and follow through underlying issues.
- Identify areas that require improvement.
- Spend an appropriate amount of time on interface issues – even if it is outside your comfort zone.
- Ensure that follow-up actions are a two way process between Operations and Fleet.

Review
- Monitor KPIs and follow up feedback from Control Logs.
- Follow up service delivery or service quality failures and solve or escalate as necessary.
- Ensure that arrangements remain fit for purpose by promoting and amendments to the plans and ROTD.

Running a Railway

RESPONSIBILITIES - Level 2 – Operations Manager/Director responsible for delivery

Plan
- Identify where the interfaces are, instigate regular liaison at all appropriate levels and ensure adequate KPIs/metrics are in place.
- Ensure that plans - in particular the Rules of the Depot and Depot Contingency Plans – are comprehensive and reflect current operating requirements.
- To review the plans at each timetable change or when circumstances change for whatever reason.
- To work closely with Fleet/Operations colleagues to ensure all interface activities are managed appropriately.
- Consider the provision of spare sets/hot standbys.
- Ensure adequate train deployment contingency plans are in place.

Do
- Monitor KPI/metrics and logs to identify issues.
- Carefully review availability on a daily basis and follow through key issues e.g. waiting materials etc.
- Routinely check the level of repeat failures.
- Ensure post incident reviews always consider interface issues.
- Promote close working between Fleet/Operations and provide visible leadership.
- Engender team working - not blame culture.

Review
- Check that the ROTD and other arrangements remain relevant.
- Identify any gaps and weaknesses through the various routine review processes.
- Initiate joint investigation of incidents and root cause analysis with Fleet counterpart.
- Identify and consider emerging good practice elsewhere in the industry.

Tips

The Fleet/Operations interface is often not given adequate management focus.

Fleet is a key supplier to operations, just as NR is. Manage the interface accordingly.

Fleet is not all about widgets - good operations/fleet integration is worth several PPM percentage points and will repay close attention.

Good relations with the wider Fleet Director's team are important - Depot Managers, Fleet Engineers and Fleet Planners. Good personal chemistry works wonders.

Regular conferences during fleet shortages will allow a meaningful plan to be produced so the fleet can be deployed most usefully.

Check that 0600 availability is meaningful and not just for that minute!

Keep an eye on the level of repeat failures.

Watch for the emergence of functional silos and barriers - break them down.

Ensure processes are owned - particularly at interfaces. Do not allow the buck to be passed backwards and forwards under any circumstances.

6.15 Train Characteristics

BACKGROUND

This element looks at the key features of each generic traction type from an operator's perspective. Technical details can be obtained from the Fleet department and the advice given in the following section should be supplemented by class and sub-class specific tips that Operating teams will probably have gained from experience but not necessarily have written down.

GENERAL

There is a huge amount of variation in type and capability dependent on age and the purpose that the train was designed for. Key differentiations are:-
- Route availability (RA) is a code between 1 and 10 given to every vehicle and route, or part of a route, giving details of their maximum permissible axle loading. A train can only travel on a route which has an equivalent or higher number. RA is generally not an issue with passenger operators as most equipment is at the lower end of the categorisation, but is a fundamental with bulk commodity freight where the higher the number of tonnes you can convey in one vehicle, the more money you can make. (also see Section

Running a Railway

6.2 titled Freight Perspective).
- Route clearance – this is self-explanatory and is usually determined by the varying vehicle gauge (profile) of any particular train and the gauge of the infrastructure that the train will pass through. Again a big issue with freight particularly with intermodal containers which are increasingly of the 'hi-cube' 9'6" high variety. Bridges, tunnels and station canopies are often the restrictive elements to increasing gauge. (also see Section titled Freight Perspective).
- Frequently modern trains have profiles that break the standard gauge profile (e.g. passenger steps) and this is one of the reasons why route clearance is usually class specific. Each new variant of rolling stock must be assessed on its design against the route characteristics over which it must travel. Older rolling stock which was in use at the time of privatisation 'inherited' the right to run over that part of the network that it was used on at the time.
- Coupler types – the rail industry in Great Britain missed an opportunity to simplify operational complexity by not choosing a standard coupler type for new trains on the network. As a consequence there are a number of different types. Current coupler types in service include:-
  - Traditional screw coupling (generally only between locomotives and trains and between non-passenger carrying vehicles).
  - Instanter – freight vehicles only.
  - HST bar.
  - Tightlock.
  - Buckeye.
  - Dellner.
  - BSI.
  - Scharfenberg.

Make sure this aspect is considered when dealing with train failures, and ensure the issue is covered in contingency plans. One look in the Technical Manual for most new trains will convince you that assistance using an adaptor is a very long job (and usually requires a PhD in engineering plus the strength of ten men!). It is vital that such adaptor couplings are managed correctly – where are they kept, how are they maintained and how will they be deployed are all critical issues. Network Rail has a coupler compatibility matrix which is used to decide whether assistance is feasible using the vehicle in rear. Note - A failed train with an incompatible train in the rear is often best dealt with by bringing a compatible train onto the front using a wrong direction move.
- Traction types. Diesel traction can nearly go anywhere subject to some minor route availability and clearance restrictions, whilst electric traction is restricted to routes with an appropriate supply system.
- Electrification characteristics. Some trains can work on either 25kv OHL or 650/750V DC (e.g. Class 319 EMUs) whilst Eurostar services can cope with

three power systems (one British, one French and one Belgian. They also used to be able to operate on the Southern 3rd Rail system). Extreme care needs to be taken when working these types of train in degraded mode or in other than regular operation. For example, what are the implications for staff working on an isolated third rail?

- Speed profile. The permissible speed of a particular type of train is determined by a complex series of issues. Just because a type of traction is an electrical multiple unit does not mean that it can be guaranteed to be permitted to run at speeds signed for EMU! This is a classic infrastructure to train interface issue. Further detail is provided in the remainder of this Section.
- Braking Characteristics. Different trains have differing systems and braking characteristics. Whilst all trains will conform to certain essential network requirements this aspect forms a crucial element of driver training and practical competence.

It is worth noting that many new DC trains are also fitted with AC equipment. Conversion is often a case of fitting the collection equipment such as the pantograph.

Although traction training should cover the faults and failures that a Driver will normally experience, it is useful for the Driver to have a source of help with fault finding and clearance of the line. Fleet support helplines can therefore be a crucial aide during failures and should be an integral part of the control arrangements. There should be regular liaison between fleet support staff, Control and Drivers to establish best processes when failures occur. Drivers should then be encouraged to phone the helpline for assistance in all but the most routine failures. All parties should understand and strictly apply cut and run policies.

Diesel Multiple Unit (DMUs)

Diesel Multiple Units started out as relatively lightweight vehicles fitted with commercial diesel engines distributed over a number of the vehicles that make up the unit. As these trains have become more technically complex, and have additional equipment on board such as air conditioning, toilet retention tanks etc, they have become significantly heavier. Compare a 1980s Class 158 Super Sprinter vehicle at 11.5 tonnes axle weight with a recent Class 185 Desiro vehicle at 17.5 tonnes.

The diesel engine is the source of traction power which is either transmitted to the driving wheels via a gearbox and drive shaft or used to create electrical energy which powers electric traction motors (Diesel Electric Multiple Unit

Running a Railway

– DEMU). Transmission shafts are often a weak point because of the degree of 'play' required. The engine is solebar mounted, the wheels are bogie mounted.

One of the most significant advantages of distributed power multiple units is the level of redundancy which several underfloor engines gives you. Failure of a single engine, for instance, will not be a show stopper.

As a result, the biggest critical failure modes on DMUs are not related to engines although loss of power, low coolant, or underpower are significant features of delay causation. In general, door systems and their associated traction interlock; brake systems, air system/compression and transmission are the problems most likely to cause complete failure. Batteries are also a very vulnerable area, especially if the unit has its engines shutdown whilst auxiliaries are still powered up, or the unit has not been properly immobilised by the Driver.

DMU reliability usually ranges from 7,000 to 20,000 mpc (miles per delay causing casualty). Information on train reliability is published monthly. Your fleet colleagues will have access to this.

Electric Multiple Units (EMUs)

Whatever the traction supply Electric Multiple Units are very similar. Trains that operate on the 3rd Rail system usually just have additional inverters (in simple terms a transformer for converting DC to AC) to provide a suitable supply for the traction motors. The traction motors and associated electrical equipment is usually termed the traction package. The bogie mounted traction motors are the direct source of traction power.

EMUs are usually very reliable ranging from 20,000 to 60,000 mpc. As before, information on train reliability is published monthly. Your fleet colleagues will have access to this.

Complete failure of EMUs is rare, but when they do occur, the reasons are generally associated with:-
- Power doors and their associated traction interlock because they are a relatively complex sub system with lots of components in series.
- Traction package – purely because this delay category describes all the electrical equipment together.
- Power supply and collection such as the pantographs or shoes.

As with DMUs, air systems, brakes, and batteries can be the root cause of complete failure, though generally less so.

6.15 Train Characteristics

High Speed Trains (HSTs)

The ubiquitous High Speed Train formation of two power cars at opposite ends of a rake of seven, eight or nine Mk 3 trailers has been in service in Britain for 35 years and still provides the backbone of InterCity services on many routes. All but one sub-fleet have recently received new MTU (made by German Diesel manufacturer Motoren-und-Turbinen-Union) engines (and the sub-fleet's engines have also been replaced with modern 'VP185' units).

There is probably no better understood train in the country, but the combination of high mileage usage, age, binary driving style, and the limitations of diesel engine technology in this application mean that reliability is at best modest. Power car failures still occur although total failure of a set, because there are two power cars, is much rarer. Reliability ranges between 8,000 and 15,000 mpc.

Traction failures do, therefore, dominate HST failure modes, notably
- Low power.
- Overheating/ reversion to idle/ low coolant/ cooler group.

With a preponderance of summer events when ambient air temperatures are higher despite a great deal of investment over the years in technological solutions and modern technology.

Individual TOCs have different policies on HST operation with one power car shut down, but Operators should be sceptical of routine operation in such a condition, especially if trains enter service on one power car, or are expected to finish their daily diagram with one power car disabled. Network Rail also imposes restrictions on where and when HSTs can operate One Engine Only (OEO). These are detailed in the relevant Sectional Appendices to the Working Timetable which prevent, for example, operation on the steeply graded routes to and from Inverness and the southwest of England.

If you really have to operate an HST with only one functioning power car and if there are good adequate alternative trains for passengers, consider taking low-usage stops out wherever possible, particularly if they are on significant gradients. Details of the options should be included in the relevant contingency plans.

LOCO HAULED

Most loco hauled trains now run in permanently coupled formations with a locomotive at one end and a DVT (Driving Van Trailer) at the other. This is also known as push-pull working for obvious reasons. Because of this configuration driving control instructions from the DVT to the locomotive have

Running a Railway

to be transmitted electrically and this is normally routed through the jumper cables using a Time Division Multiplexer (TDM). This can be a problem area – particularly when sets are split and reformed for whatever reasons.

Beware of the mismatch between stock and locomotive, especially if the loco is hired in at short notice. Lack of Electric Train Supply capability on the substitute loco will prevent Mk2 or Mk3 coaches from being heated and once the batteries are drained from being lit.

If this is the only option for running the train during the winter months, then service cancellation will almost always be a better option.

The most common faults on a loco hauled train usually relate to the locomotive itself:
- Engine failure/ low power/ loss of power.
- Low coolant.
- Air system/ compression.
- Brake system (often related to air supply).
- TDM failures.

Work hard to prevent sets being split because this impacts on maintenance, cleaning and reliability (e.g. TDM failures).

It is difficult to generalise with Loco Hauled reliability statistics. Ask your Fleet colleagues for details.

DIFFERENTIAL SPEEDS

The principle behind differential speed restrictions is that the infrastructure can support different speed limits for different types of train. Differential freight train and passenger train speed limits have applied for many years but differentials between different types of passenger train increased significantly with the arrival of lightweight Sprinter DMUs, and now exist for a wide range of different trains. The number of differential speeds which can apply at any one location is limited to 3, to avoid excessive and potentially confusing signing. The lineside signing convention is for the lowest speed differential to be highest up the sign post, descending down the post in ascending speed order.

Permissible speed is determined by a number of factors:
- Minimum braking performance curve to meet signal sighting requirements.
- Maximum design service cant deficiency.
- Maximum axle load.
- Dynamic vertical track forces.
- Dynamic lateral track forces.

6.15 Train Characteristics

Each new class or sub-class of rolling stock must be assessed against these criteria in order to determine its permissible speed.

The approved list is currently contained in Module SP of the Rule Book but will soon be moved to the Sectional Appendix.

ENHANCED PERMISSIBLE SPEED (EPS)

EPS is a particular kind of differential speed, and only applies to tilting trains, with tilt activated by track-based transponders. Currently in the UK (2011), the only tilting trains operating are on the West Coast route - Cl. 390 'Pendolino' electric units, and Cl. 221 'Super Voyager' diesel units - and therefore the only route signed for EPS is the West Coast. EPS is designated by special lineside speed signs - black numerals on a reflective yellow background for enhanced visibility, rather than the usual 'motorway' style black numerals on a white reflective background.

TILTING TRAINS

The concept of tilting trains was first introduced into the UK with the prototype Advanced Passenger Train (APT), developed by BR in the 1970's as the next generation of train for the long distance West Coast Services. Although APT was subsequently abandoned by BR when further development funding was declined by government, much of the innovative technology developed at the time was subsequently incorporated into the designs of the Alstom Cl. 390 Pendolino. The Bombardier Cl. 221 Super Voyager tilting trains, also ordered by the Virgin Rail franchises in 1998, used independently developed tilting mechanisms.

The rationale for tilting trains is that 'active' tilt - which is generated by a computer controlled power mechanism (initiated by track-based equipment), as distinct from 'passive' tilt which responds to gravitational forces - will allow trains to take corners at higher speeds, and achieve journey time reductions which could not be achieved by conventional trains. On the Pendolino tilt is initiated by the first vehicle in the train sensing the forces of the curve. The computer then tilts the carriages as the train continues round the curve. Tilt can be inhibited by the Tilt and Speed Supervision system (TASS) which turns off tilt where there is insufficient clearance e.g. in certain tunnels. TASS also ensures that the train does not overspeed on severe corners. TASS uses balises on the track to confirm whether tilt is allowed. The higher speed that tilting trains can operate at is called Enhanced Permissible Speed (EPS), and is signed at the lineside with special signs. In the event of failure, or isolation, of

Running a Railway

the tilt equipment on any vehicle on the train, the train will not be permitted to operate at EPS.

RESCUE LOCOMOTIVES (Thunderbirds)

Several TOCs lease or own 'Thunderbird' rescue diesel locomotives. These are always equipped with electric train supply (ETS) so as to be able to independently supply the coaches. They are capable, at 95/100 mph of hauling a defective train to destination. Relevant TOCs will have drivers trained to work these locomotives and they will either be permanently manned during traffic hours 'hot standby', or only manned by a spare driver when required. The former is far more effective but is of course costly. Be sure to give the use of these locomotives your attention, not least as they will often be used for unusual moves, perhaps after having been instructed to pass a signal at danger onto a failure. Drivers manning them need to be specially briefed on not just the coupling/ uncoupling processes and attachment of ETS cables, but the safe operation of the locomotive under degraded conditions.

The cost of having a Thunderbird locomotive on hot standby can be considerable. Although it provides the 'ultimate' insurance policy against a failure, the benefit needs to be balanced against the cost. Network Rail does have the authority to commandeer locomotives from other operators to clear the line if required. If failures are infrequent this may be a more cost effective option for a TOC to consider.

Where they are provided on a regular basis it is good practise to diagram Thunderbird locomotives to work last trains as it provides Train Crew and fitters with regular hands on experience.

Tips

Reliability

Train reliability can always be improved, work closely with fleet colleagues and ensure that continuous improvement is a constant aim.

If you have not already got one, establish a fleet helpline and then make sure it is used. Calling an engineering expert is always better than guessing.

Know your rolling stock well. Ignorance will exacerbate delays from failures.

6.15 Train Characteristics

Trains are becoming increasingly sophisticated and simple get out of trouble solutions are not as easy as they once were. The following last resort tips for operations managers therefore carry a BIG health warning.

DMUs
Serious failures are usually unsophisticated but expensive in delay - 'cut & run' is often the best approach. Emergency Bypass Switch/Traction Interlock Switch - terminate as a passenger train and clear off to the depot/clear the running line. If the train fails it sometimes helps to get the driver to shut it down, remove their key then reinsert their key and start the train back up.

EMUs
Again, if the train fails get the driver to shut it down, remove his/her key then reinsert his/her key and start the train back up.

HSTs
Summer preparations and contingency plans are crucial.

Know where and when HST sets are forbidden to operate OEO and challenge any suggestion of routine operation in OEO mode.

Loco Hauled
Short term/short notice loco hire can be a weak area - ensure controllers are aware of the specification and how to discharge it, especially in relation to power, ETS and crew knowledge requirements.

Controllers need to be aware of, and act upon, tell-tale signs of an ailing loco. It is better to arrange a loco change, or terminate short than risk a total failure in a remote location.

Ensure Drivers always contact the Fleet Helpline before attempting to rectify any fault.

6.16 Infrastructure and Operations Interface

BACKGROUND

Close working between operators and infrastructure maintainers and engineers is vital at all levels. This has always been the case but became easy to overlook when Network Rail centralised its organisational structure along functional lines. The devolved organisational structure introduced in 2011 in which operations, maintenance and asset management (engineering) functions come together in one Network Operations function at Route level, under a Route Managing Director, recognises this fact. This brings these three vital activities together for the first time in a number of years.

Close working is vital to most aspects of delivery and this has now been cemented within Network Rail by the fact that aspects of engineering access – the development of the plan from about a year out through to management of possessions on the day - now falls to General Managers. One of the biggest problem areas, getting the balance right between running the operational railway and providing sufficient quality access for maintenance and renewal, is now managed entirely within Network Operations. However it is still essential that good relationships are established and maintained between operators and engineer at all levels. Shared objectives and common processes are also vital.

Infrastructure delay minutes are often a large component of overall delay on a rail network and many of the root causes are not technical, they are process, people or interface based.

ORGANISATION

Within Network Rail maintenance is currently undertaken by 40 Delivery Units across Great Britain. Within each Delivery Unit there are Depots (or sub depots) which manage work on a geographical basis. Depots resource & manage maintenance and the response to incidents as well as the planning of work. Due to the nature of the work, maintenance teams are usually organised for both day and night work on a 24/7 basis.

Infrastructure maintenance requirements are primarily governed by technical standards which are written centrally within Network Rail. Each Delivery Unit and Depot is responsible for compliance.

At Route level Network Rail's maintenance teams are responsible for:
- Prioritising and undertaking maintenance work;

6.16 Infrastructure and Operations Interface

- Inspecting and maintaining infrastructure according to standards;
- Responding to infrastructure failures.

At Route level Network Rail's Asset Management Teams are responsible for signalling, track, electrification and plant (including signalling power supply), buildings, structures (bridges, tunnels etc.) and geotechnics (such as drainage, earthworks and embankments). They work in discipline specific teams to:

- Create asset management plans that include all maintenance, renewal and investment activity. They also monitor these plans to confirm they deliver the regulatory output targets.
- Prioritise and manage the investment workbank and sponsor some renewal or enhancement schemes.
- Manage compliance with company asset policies and standards.
- Manage the specification of acceptance criteria for engineering works including design approval, acceptance of equipment, hand back to maintenance.
- Act as engineering authority for engineering deliverables associated with renewal and enhancement activities.
- Provide specialist technical and engineering support to maintenance and operations teams, including, where required, consideration and sign off for derogations to standards, for example, a minor deferment of a 1A Track defect.

ISSUES

Infrastructure/Operations interfaces start with good planning and lead through to close cooperation on real time delivery. This does not only apply to liaison within Network Rail as there are a number of issues where regular dialogue between the relevant Network Rail infrastructure maintainer and TOC/FOC operators and rolling stock/fleet engineers can be really beneficial (e.g. wheel-rail and pantograph-OLE contact system interfaces).

Normal maintenance activities should not affect train running but there will be times when failures or events occur and close working in real time is required. For maintenance teams to rectify faults, staff will need to be conveyed to site, diagnose the problem and in many cases be given sufficient access time to replace or repair the fault. In some cases, rectification estimates may prove difficult to provide until the diagnosis element has been completed. Often this work can be undertaken at quieter times (outside of peak hours or at service close) but sensible dialogue is needed between all parties for this to occur.

Over the past 10 years, Network Rail has made significant progress in terms of train borne examination and detection systems. Track Recording Units (TRUs) are operated to identify track faults. These vehicles along with ultrasonic testing

Running a Railway

vehicles travel the network and use a variety of monitoring equipment to detect faults real time and send data to the maintenance Delivery Units.

Other trains are used to monitor overhead line assets and the Network Rail Measurement Train provides a comprehensive assessment of the condition of the infrastructure. Some service trains are fitted with OHLE/Track monitoring capabilities but this information tends to supplement the core NR arrangements.

The data provided allows maintenance teams to identify faults early in order to minimise train delays and performance or safety risks. Network Rail intends to bring in further train borne detection systems such as pattern recognition technology with the aim of reducing the number of track based inspection staff. The monitoring trains that are used in this way are vital and failure to run (or even diversion) can cause significant problems as substituting manual inspection at short notice will not always be possible.

Planning

Close Infrastructure/Operations cooperation should help address the following requirements/issues:-

- Regular line blockage access e.g. for patrolling. This should provide the access required with train service impact eliminated or minimised.
- Response team management: There is potential for overlap in the duties of signalling response teams and Mobile Operations Managers activities undertaken and base locations should be reviewed together.
- Working jointly on performance improvement measures. A shared view on operational criticality is vital in determining where limited cash is best spent.
- Understanding operational and performance risks: for example spares holdings may be absolutely critical for some assets (usually the non-standard or out-of manufacture components) – the maintainer will understand how difficult it may be to resource in the event of a failure and maintainer and operator will be able to jointly work on the response plan and operational criticality. The engineer will be able to identify opportunities for derogations and will develop the renewal plan.
- Maintainability and operability.
- Renewal plan – owned by the Route Asset Manager but informed (and partially delivered by the maintainer) with a key role for operators in agreeing plans, working on delivery and contingency plans.

It is important that operators understand the interfaces between engineering functions. For example points contain signalling, track and plant elements (e.g. point machines, ironwork, and point heating); track circuits contain track and signalling elements and reliability may be affected by electrification equipment.

6.16 Infrastructure and Operations Interface

Real Time Delivery

Close cooperation and interworking is particularly important in Control Offices
Key points are:-

- Work closely with your maintenance colleagues and ensure this relationship is visible to your team.
- Engender a spirit of cooperation at all levels. Good relationships must run (and be seen to run) from the Directors right through Signallers and Technicians.
- There should be routine liaison between operators and maintainers/engineers. Effective exchanges of information between these people will identify causes of failures, opportunities to avoid failures and opportunities to recover more quickly from failures.
- The term 'Operations Control' is a misnomer – Control Offices manage operations and maintenance activities. Take a close interest in the infrastructure maintenance elements of Control work such as the quality of information recorded in fault management systems. Ensure you have a robust system for recording faults and restrictions
- Monitor day to day delivery. Identify key asset failure types and routinely monitor the level of repeat failures. This is a good underlying measure of reliability.
- Ensure Control is aware of infrastructure restrictions and suitable contingencies for these. Challenge if the numbers of such restrictions exceed targeted levels.
- Remote condition monitoring equipment - make sure that maximum benefit is obtained from the information both in real time and as a source of information for performance improvement.
- Take some time to have a good look at the infrastructure that you depend on (with a member of the maintenance team) and take on board the key maintenance issues/troublesome components that the engineer will point out to you.
- Implement 'Share with Pride' initiatives from other depots.
- Co-ordination of on-site response, agreement on delivery of key roles such as Asset Recovery Manager, Rail Incident Officer etc. are vital areas where close cooperation is essential.
- Response to incidents can involve technicians/engineers from a range of disciplines, e.g. signalling, permanent way, telecommunications, electrification and plant. Signalling response is usually undertaken by 24/7 maintenance teams but remember that other disciplines often use on-call teams.
- Manage the creative tension between the engineer's desire to get to the bottom of a failure and fix it first time and the operator's desire to get trains moving quickly, perhaps with a partial fix.

Running a Railway

- Ensure communications protocols and command structure requirements during incident management are understood and correctly followed.

For RESPONSIBILITIES - Level 1 – Local Operations Manager, see list in 6.14

For RESPONSIBILITIES - Level 2 – Operations Manager/Director responsible for delivery, see list in 6.14

Tips

The Infrastructure/Operations interface is often not given adequate management focus.

Maintenance and Asset Management are key suppliers to operations. Manage the interface accordingly.

Engineering is not all about widgets - good operations to infrastructure integration is worth several PPM percentage points and will repay close attention.

Good relations with the wider engineering and maintenance teams are important. Good personal chemistry works wonders.

Key an eye on the level of repeat failures.

Watch for the emergence of functional silos and barriers - break them down.

Ensure processes are owned - particularly at interfaces. Do not allow the buck to be passed backwards and forwards under any circumstances.

6.17 Track Issues

BACKGROUND

The Permanent Way (or PWay) should be the most reliable component of NR's infrastructure, regardless of whether it is plain line or S&C (switches and crossings).

Track design, maintenance and renewal is a well-established engineering

6.16 Infrastructure/Operations Interface

discipline throughout the world and operators should be able to expect PWay based delays and problems to be almost minimal.

However there are a number of important aspects that all operators should understand because if track issues do arise they can have significant impact on performance and costs.

ISSUES

Track performance will depend on a number of issues but it does not necessarily follow that older installations need be unreliable.

Key points to consider regarding reliability are:-
- The integrity of the sub-structure (i.e. the underlying soil, embankments and cuttings).
- The integrity of the formation (i.e. the ballast, membranes and drainage).
- The integrity of the sleeper, fastenings and rail.
- The effectiveness of the patrolling (inspection arrangements by foot and track recording train).
- The timeliness and completeness of routine maintenance.
- The timeliness of planned renewals and non-routine maintenance.
- The frequency and type of traffic using the infrastructure (heavy freight trains often create the need for more maintenance activity than lightweight passenger traffic).

Provided these aspects are addressed, the incidence of track based problems should be minimal. However this has not always been the case in Great Britain and the following section aims to set historic track reliability in context.

HISTORICAL PERSPECTIVE

There is empirical evidence that BR track renewals declined in the late 80s early 90s during an economic recession as a result of certain sectors of the industry taking a 'maintenance holiday'. This postponement of renewals (mainly on secondary lines) was rooted in a belief that track was being over-maintained.

This thinking carried forward into Railtrack and renewal levels dropped even further. It is also evident that Railtrack did not have an adequate grip on the activities of its Infrastructure Maintainers (IMCs) that resulted in the condition of the track not being accurately assessed or managed. The lack of data/records is a legacy (although in many cases now minimal) that is still causing problems today. For example the unavailability of de-stressing records can result in 'heat

Running a Railway

speed' restrictions being applied during relatively hot weather.

This spiral of decline culminated in the Hatfield train derailment in October 2000 which was caused by poor track condition (Gauge Corner Cracking or Rolling Contact Fatigue).

Following this watershed event, Railtrack and then Network Rail ramped up track renewal and took maintenance activities back in-house. The current improved condition of the track is a direct result of these policies.

CURRENT PROBLEMS

Track problems remain an issue in several parts of the network. Track condition also has a significant impact on certain elements of the signalling system (e.g. Track Circuit reliability). Temporary Speed Restrictions (TSRs) have a major impact on PPM and can significantly impact on timetable resilience.

Current problems that should be strongly managed are:-

- TSRs – these must not exceed ROTR/Engineering allowance and the aim should be zero non-planned TSRs (see also the element covering TSRs and ESRs).

- Emergency Speed Restrictions (ESRs) – can be an indication of inadequate inspection/maintenance (see also the element covering TSRs and ESRs).

- Rolling Contact Fatigue (RCF) – can be caused at the contact point between the wheel and rail. Such damage to the rail head will require either grinding or replacement of the rail to prevent further damage/deterioration. Previously known as Gauge Corner Cracking (GCC) after the Hatfield accident in 2000.

- Side wear – this is the phenomenon of wear to the rail caused by the lateral and horizontal forces of the bogies on the rail edge. Heavy side wear can cause gauge profile problems and in extreme cases could pose a derailment risk.

- Heat issues – generally caused by poor or disturbed ballast shoulders/formation, inadequate de-stressing (or poor/missing de-stressing records). Can also occur in jointed track which can have insufficient expansion gaps available.

Other apparently less serious issues such as wet track beds (poor drainage through the ballast/clay pumping up) and poor ride quality can indicate deterioration in track maintenance. However they are usually associated with the age of the asset, the maintenance opportunities or other issues such as poor embankments or historical drainage problems.

The default position on track is zero delays and particularly no unplanned TSRs,

6.17 Track Issues

or ESRs. Certain routes have achieved the latter objective through a strong managerial focus on preventative maintenance, good forward planning and a shared NR/TOC commitment to eradicate track based delays. It can be done.

Setting aside the historical issues, Train Operators must work with NR to ensure track based delays become a thing of the past.

NR and TOC/FOC operators should have a list of TSRs and ESRs on their desks each week for review and understand why each one is in place. Challenge for removal dates and action, but be aware that adequate access will be required to remedy the defect. Argue for differential speeds where appropriate. TSR numbers have been declining steadily over the past few years through such pressure, as well as good access and better maintenance.

If ESRs are necessary ensure boards are put out immediately and make sure they are secured so they do not fall over. 'Stop and Caution' arrangements should be avoided wherever possible as they will almost certainly cause more delay than the actual speed restriction.

Low speeds after renewals through planned TSRs are not inevitable. Dynamic track stabilisers were present on the network in the early 1990s in order to minimise this aspect, however in recent years renewal sites have typically been handed back at much higher speeds such as 50 or 80 mph.

Tips

The level of delays caused by track related problems in Great Britain has been an issue and your input will assist in causing delay minutes to be reduced.

Condition Of Track (COT) speed restrictions and unplanned TSRs should be the exception not the rule.

Ride quality should be good - it is monitored on a periodic basis by Network Rail against agreed targets by the ORR.

Track based delays are not inevitable or acceptable.

Running a Railway

6.18 Temporary Speed Restrictions and Emergency Speed Restrictions

BACKGROUND

Temporary and Emergency restrictions of speed (TSRs and ESRs) became much more commonplace during the 1980s and 1990s. Since 2008 there has been a large improvement as a result of specific attention to this issue.

The rules governing the application of TSRs/ESRs can be found in the Rule Book Section Module SP - Speeds. The following section addresses some of the key points relating to speed restrictions and their impact on performance.

ISSUES

TSRs are a significant cause of underlying delay. Even when they do not attract a large amount of delay minutes in Trust Delay Systems they can eat into margins with sub-threshold delays and the impact of any other disruptive event then becomes amplified.

Operators in both NR and TOCs/FOCs need to understand how restrictions impact their services and exert pressure on NR engineers to have them removed. Make sure you have current details of all TSRs affecting your patch on your desk at least weekly.

The main points to remember are:-
- Some TSRs are unavoidable but too many could indicate poor forward planning, or an underlying problem on that route, such as a change in traction, age of infrastructure or lack of maintenance due to access.
- Condition of track (COT) TSRs generally indicate poor maintenance/inadequate renewals.
- ESRs can be an indication of poor maintenance but may also be applied to mitigate a specific short term risk (e.g. management of heat related issues).

Note – Heat related speeds at all but the very highest temperatures can be avoided, but you may find that a substantial volume of work is required to achieve this. They usually occur because rail has not been de-stressed, or ballast shoulders have not been maintained correctly.
- TSRs and ESRs will expose previously hidden delays – this is because engineering allowances act as an unofficial performance allowance and TSRs/ESRs have first take - as they are invariably entered as planned delays.
- Watch differential speed TSRs. Whilst the restriction of speed for passenger

6.18 Temporary Speed Restrictions and Emergency Speed Restrictions

trains might be minimal, freight trains can cause havoc when very low differential TSRs/ESRs are applied.
- Operators should be wary about conversion of TSRs to Permanent Speed Restrictions (PSRs). Such conversions should be evaluated by stringent cost-benefit analysis and must be accompanied by an appropriate Network Change notification. They should be subject to serious consideration and discussion.
- ESRs can be a performance nightmare, particularly over long distances or on high speed routes as well as being a safety risk for operators and staff erecting warning equipment.
- TSRs/ESRs should be vigorously pursued by operators and early removal sought. Try to keep the engineering allowance preserved for unexpected issues (and as a performance cushion).
- Train Operators should stop-watch check the actual effect on their trains of TSRs.
- If an ESR has to be imposed make sure this is done promptly in full accordance with the Rules & Regulations. This will normally involve the ESR being 'designed' to determine the location of warning equipment based on the speed, braking distance of traffic and location line side equipment.
- Significant additional delays will occur if the relevant commencement or termination boards are not in place quickly. Similarly boards that have 'blown over' in strong winds or emergency indicators that have run out of battery power will have a similar adverse impact. The delay impact of managing the erection of boards, or of caution for boards that have fallen over can be far greater than the delay caused by the speed restriction itself. Make sure this is managed in the most effective way possible.
- In most cases speed restrictions are designed by specialist staff. This specialist design should be checked in the event of any problems or challenges. You may wish to consider the designs being provided to Control as a matter of course.
- Blanket Speed Restrictions - Sometimes it is necessary to impose a speed restriction over a widespread area (often because of weather conditions). Track equipment will not be provided in these cases and drivers will not be stopped and advised by the signaller. Notification of such speeds is managed through Control arrangements.

Tips

Operators must challenge TSRs and ESRs as much as possible. Keep asking - Why? And When?

Watch for over-long or over-restrictive speeds.

Running a Railway

Make sure ESRs are appropriately signed and late notices cases suitably updated in the required timescales (two hours maximum). Stopping and cautioning each train can cause huge delay and destroy the timetable.

Make sure that TSRs are promptly removed when the need for them has disappeared and the speed is spated (see Rule Book).

Remember – keeping TSRs and ESRs under tight control will help preserve the timetable engineering allowance so it can provide a performance cushion for unexpected issues.

6.19 Level Crossing Characteristics

INTRODUCTION

A level crossing exists where a railway line intersects a road or path at grade. Level crossings date back to the origins of the railway when the first rail roads were built to transport coal and aggregates. Road traffic and train speeds were low, therefore it was not considered necessary to provide bridges to separate road or path from rail. Although there have been technical advances in level crossing safety and operations, many crossings types remain unchanged from 150 years ago. The road rail interface risks now bear little resemblance to those of the 1850s and grade separation or closure is now favoured when optioneering safety enhancements.

Within the railway industry, crossings are categorised according to the level of protection they provide to the rail or road interface, rail passengers, rail staff and public users. Crossings comprise of a number of components including lights, barriers, decking, alarms, interlocking, approach locking and telephones. The following parts of this Section highlight the main points of each type and provide guidance on the issues involved in crossing management.

TYPES OF LEVEL CROSSINGS

Controlled
Controlled crossings are manually operated by a signaller or crossing keeper. In all of these level crossing types, users are physically protected from approaching trains by barriers or gates. Road traffic lights and audible alarms will also be provided at specific crossing types. These are known as protected level crossings. Interlocking is provided in all but a small number of cases meaning that it is not possible to clear the protecting signals unless the barriers have been lowered or to raise the barriers once the signals have been cleared. Included in this type are:

- **Manually Controlled Gates (MCG)**

The traditional type of level crossing utilises gates which are either operated by the signaller or crossing keeper manually pushing the gates or through winding a large wheel. The gates are usually locked and integrated into the signalling system. Where provided at a road, there may also be pedestrian wicket gates provided and these may not be interlocked even where the road gates are.

Running a Railway

- **Manually Controlled Barriers, Local and Remote (MCB, MCB CCTV)**
This type of crossing is operated by the signaller or crossing keeper who initiates the road traffic lights, lowers the barriers and confirms the crossing is clear prior to the clearing of signals for a train movement over the crossing. The signaller may be immediately adjacent to the crossing, a short distance away with a clear view of the roadway or remote from the crossing but with CCTV monitoring. The system may require the signaller to initiate the raising of the barriers or this may be done automatically. Auto lower is sometimes provided as well but there is always a requirement for the signaller to physically check that the level crossing is clear before clearing signals because there is no exit route from the crossing once the full barriers are lowered. These are the only types of road crossing that can be used where the linespeed is greater than 100mph.

Automatic

Automatic crossings do not require any manual activation. The sequence is activated by the 'strike in' of an approaching train usually a mechanical treadle plus activation of a certain track circuit. Included in this type are:

- **Automatic Half Barriers (AHB)**

Automatic Half Barrier crossings were introduced by British Rail in 1961 to reduce operating costs by reducing the number of manned level crossings. Their introduction made it possible to keep open routes which would otherwise have been uneconomical. Where the line speed is high but the road usage is not too high an automatic half barrier may be appropriate. This consists of an automatic system to detect the passage of a train which initiates road traffic lights before lowering barriers across the entry carriageway.

AHBs also reduce delays to road traffic by decreasing the amount of time the barriers are down for each approaching train. This reduction in delays to road traffic is made possible because the operation of the level crossing equipment is not interlocked with the protecting signals for the crossing. With traditional gated crossings it is necessary to close the gates to road traffic in sufficient time to give the train a green aspect at the protecting signal. Because AHBs work independently of the signals it is possible for road traffic to proceed over the crossing while the protecting signal shows a proceed aspect.

The crossing sequence is activated by the approaching train occupying a track circuit in rear of the crossing. In most circumstances this track circuit is backed up with a treadle which protects against the possibility of a train not activating the track circuit. To provide additional protection the AHB equipment is designed to fail 'right side'. This means that if there is a failure of the crossing equipment the barriers will lower and the road lights will begin to flash. The controlling signalbox is provided with equipment to monitor the status of the crossing equipment so that the signaller can take appropriate action if the equipment fails.

Running a Railway

There is a legal requirement on any user to telephone and request permission to take large, low or slow moving vehicles or animals over the crossing. Because it is not possible for the signaller to observe that the crossing is unobstructed there are restrictions on where AHBs may be located:

- The linespeed must be 100mph or less.
- There must be a maximum of two running lines.
- The road layout must allow vehicles to pass each other easily.
- There must be no bumps in the road which could allow lead to a vehicle to becoming grounded on the crossing.
- The road layout and traffic conditions should minimise the possibility of traffic blocking back and building up over the crossing.

- **Automatic Barrier Crossing Locally Monitored (ABCL)**

ABCL crossings are monitored by the driver and not by the signaller. They are protected by signals that are interlocked with the crossing equipment and half barriers are provided. However, it is important not to confuse an ABCL crossing with an AHB crossing simply because the barriers look the same to the road user. The operation of the two crossing types and the instructions that apply to them are very different. A significant difference between AHBs and ABCLs is the way in which the barriers fail. At an AHB where the protecting signal is not interlocked with the crossing the barriers are designed to fail lowered. At an ABCL the barriers will not always fail in the lowered position, but a signal is provided to indicate that the barriers have failed to operate. For AHB the only monitoring is a failure alarm to the signaller, whilst the ABCL has a flashing white light displayed to the train driver to indicate the crossing is working.

6.19 Level Crossing Characteristics

The flashing drivers red or white light is a signal interlocked with the crossing equipment. When the barriers are raised and the road lights are extinguished a red light will flash to indicate to the driver that it is not safe to pass over the crossing. When the road lights operate and the barriers start to lower, the flashing light will change to white indicating to the driver that the equipment at the crossing is working correctly and it is safe to pass over the crossing. At some installations the driver will need to operate a plunger to initiate the crossing sequence for example where the crossing is at a station.

Because it is the driver who monitors that the crossing has operated correctly it is vital that the driver can see the crossing early enough to be able to stop his train without passing over the crossing if that should become necessary. For this reason the line speed over ABCL crossings is normally low never more than 55mph and it is vitally important that the rail approaches to ABCL crossings are kept clear of vegetation so that the driver can observe the crossing. This also explains why trains must not be propelled over ABCL or AOCL crossings without special permission.

- **Automatic Open Crossing, Local and Remote (AOCL/R)**

For low line speeds and usage, an open crossing protected solely by road traffic lights has been used. The crossing is initiated automatically by an approaching train. For the locally monitored variant the driver receives a confirmatory white light to indicate that the crossing is operational. For the AOCR variant a failure alarm is provided to the signaller. The only example of this type of crossing is at Rosarie in Scotland. AOCL crossings were first introduced in 1963.

- **Miniature Warning Lights (MWL)**

For bridleways, crossings only used by authorised persons and some footpaths, information is conveyed to the user by means of red and green lights. Such crossings are activated by the approach of a train and there is no signal protection. There is no indication to drivers that the crossing lights are working correctly.

Running a Railway

Passive
Some level crossing types require users to take action in order to decide whether it is safe to cross; these types of crossings are referred to as passive. This category can be divided into those which can be used by vehicles such as to access a property or for agricultural uses and those which are footpaths or bridleways.

- **User Worked Crossing (UWC)**

This type of crossing is provided for private vehicular access and relies on the road user opening the gates, checking that no trains are approaching, crossing the line and closing the gates. Where sighting is restricted or where animals may regularly be herded across then a telephone may be provided enabling the user to get permission from the signaller.

Historically private user-worked vehicular crossings are provided in two different situations:
- Where the railway crosses an existing private road, which provides access to private dwellings the crossing is known as an 'occupation' crossing as the crossing serves a location that is occupied.
- Where the railway would otherwise have stopped access from a parcel of land then a new route to this land was created over the railway by means of an 'accommodation' crossing; for example, where it may be necessary for the landowner to gain access from one field to another. In this case the railway is accommodating the landowner's requirements.

The distinction between the two types is only a legal one and makes no difference in the way the crossings are operated.

6.19 Level Crossing Characteristics

- **Open Crossing (OC)**

This is similar to a UWC except that there are no gates and it is up to the road user to stop, look, listen and then cross the line.

- **Footpath or Bridleway (FP)**

The burden is on the user to decide when it is safe to cross.

INSPECTION AND RISK ASSESSMENT

Network Rail's All Level Crossing Risk Model has been used since 2007 to enable risk comparison for all types of level crossing using a consistent methodology. Information is gathered from site by Mobile Operations Managers or other staff and input into the model by staff trained to use the tool. The result is a risk assessment score for each crossing consisting of 2 parts:

- Letter score between A to M (where A is highest risk).
- Number score ranging from 1 to 13 (where 1 is highest risk).

The letter part of the result represents individual risk and the number, collective risk.

The tool assesses risk to crossing users, train staff and passengers. Risk scores generated by this system enable further action and improvements to be targeted at the highest risk crossings.

Network Rail also has teams of Level Crossing Inspectors who periodically visit level crossings within their areas to check that all required arrangements are in place at the crossing. They will check things such as crossing signage, adequacy of crossing surface and approach visibility.

Historically level crossings have been managed by a number of disciplines working together with some operational overview. This divided responsibility has made investment strategies and the co-ordination of safety improvements harder to organise. Inspections have tended to be discipline led with Off Track, Signalling, Telecoms, Track and Operations all having a role. These issues are now recognised and some positive steps have recently been taken to improve the approach.

ISSUES

Overall, train accident risk has fallen by two-thirds during the last ten years. This has been driven by a large reduction in the risk from SPADs owing to TPWS installation. The RSSB produces the Train Accident Precursor Indicator Model (PIM) which measures the risk, per million train miles, of a train

Running a Railway

accident – i.e. collision, derailment, fire or striking a road vehicle on a level crossing. Currently the largest risk from the PIM is public behaviour at level crossings. The lower coloured section on the graph below shows the risk from road-rail interface activities. This is dominated by the risk from public behaviour at level crossings, but it also includes small contributions from failures, irregular working and non-rail vehicles on the line at other locations that lead to derailments. You can see that as SPAD risk has declined, Level Crossing risk which has remained fairly static has formed a greater part of the overall risk picture.

Precursor Indicator Model showing road-rail interface risk vs. total system risk

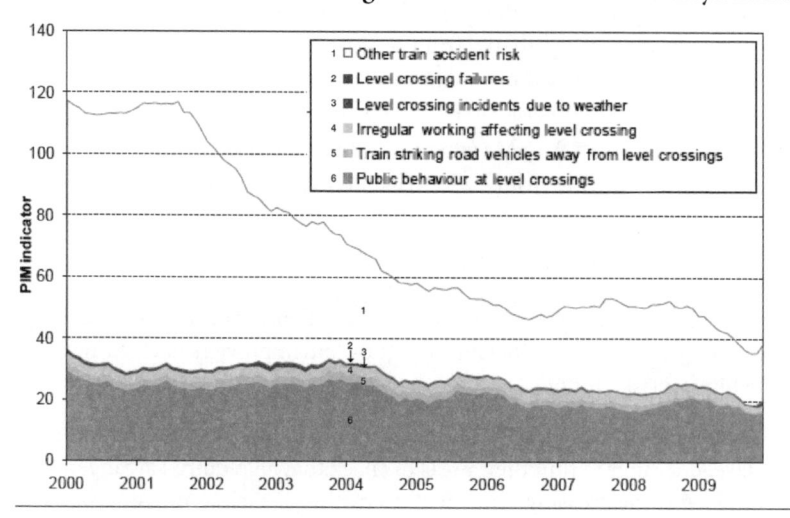

Historic fatality counts at level crossings

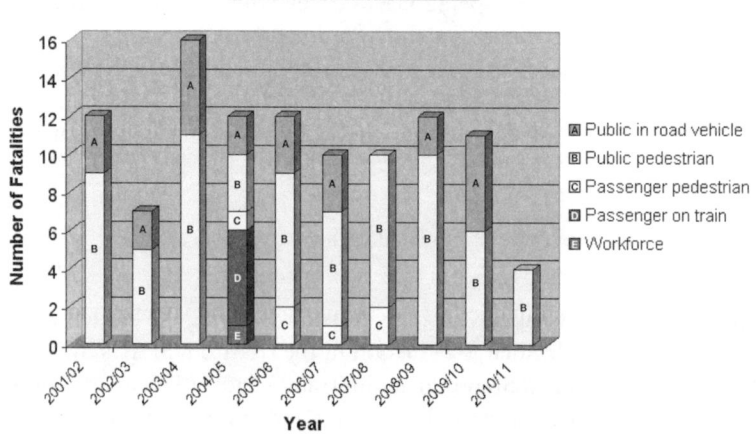

6.19 Level Crossing Characteristics

The overall safety record in terms of fatal accidents in Great Britain is good compared to other countries with large volumes of level crossings. There are more collisions with vehicles than with pedestrians but fewer fatalities. This is mainly because a collision with a pedestrian is almost always fatal whereas the majority of collisions between road vehicles and trains do not result in loss of life. However, the potential for a major multi fatality injury involving train crew and passengers is far greater when road vehicles collide with trains.

The table below illustrates the top 10 incident types contributing to overall level crossing risk, and the percentage contribution they make to the overall safety risk at level crossings:

Precursors	% of LC Risk
1. Pedestrian/cyclist ignores lights / barriers/ yodel alarm or nips in front of train - (Violations)	23.9%
2. Pedestrian (Member of Public/ passenger) fails to stop, look and listen properly (includes 2nd train coming) - (Error)	22.5%
3. Pedestrian distracted/ forced by dog	12.3%
4. Risk to both pedestrians and road Vehicles from poor sighting	11.8%
5. Slips, trips and falls by pedestrians, cyclists and motorcyclists (not violation)	4.3%
6. Road vehicle/ motorcyclist fails to use phone at User Worked Crossing (Telephone) to check line is clear	3.6%
7. Road vehicle or motorcyclist ignores lights/ barriers - includes risk to Member of Public from Level Crossing equipment being struck- includes motorcyclist fall - (Violations)	3.1%
8. Risk from late braking of Road vehicle, Road Traffic Accident	2.8%
9. Road vehicle driver fails to observe level crossing	2.4%
10. Risk from Misuse or error due to gates left open	2.2%

Both Local Authorities and Highways Authorities form an integral part of the management of level crossings. Many of the risks at level crossings are derived from the road approach and therefore there is a joint management responsibility.

They are involved with issues connected with:
- Risk controls on road approaches to level crossings.
- Impact of nearby planning decisions with planning authorities.
- Obligations under the Road Safety Act.
- Closure of crossings and diversion of traffic flows.

Running a Railway

- Improvement of safety performance by road-based controls and the effect of crossings on road traffic delay and congestion.

Users that are key stakeholders also have a significant influence over the way level crossings are managed. Examples include: The Ramblers Association, DPTAC (Disabled Persons Transport Advisory Committee) and the National Farmers Union.

INCIDENTS

Incidents at level crossings are almost always complex because level crossings, by their nature, involve a complex interface between road and rail; operator, user and equipment. The primary objective in any investigation will be to understand how these interfaces worked at the time of the incident. Evidence gathering, on site and in the controlling signalbox will be most important and witness testimony must be gathered quickly before memories start to fade. Where allegations are made against equipment the testing procedures will be lengthy and disruptive so it is all the more important that exact details of the allegation are obtained such as which side of the crossing did the user approach from, exactly which light cluster, right or left was not working etc.

For serious events such as collisions between rail and road traffic independent testing of the level crossing is likely to be required unless it can be established beyond doubt that the level crossing equipment is not at fault. This arrangement is required so that the teams responsible for maintaining the crossing are not also responsible for testing it.

Tips

The point where a road crosses the railway is a point of significantly increased risk to the railway. Treat level crossings with the respect they deserve.

Make sure you understand the high risk level crossings in your area. Do the risk assessments match up with the reported incidents? Is there a new trend developing? Are you sure that the methods of working are being followed by staff and users?

Take every opportunity to close a level crossing. It will improve performance and safety of the railway.

6.20 Electrification Systems

BACKGROUND

Electrical traction power supply is an important area that involves the key interface between the fixed power supply infrastructure (OLE or 3rd rail) and train based collection systems (pantographs or shoes).

Because of this interface between the trains and the infrastructure equipment getting to the root cause of any failure mode can be complicated. This is always best achieved through discussion between the two sets of engineers, train fleet and OLE, using detailed component analysis.

All electrified systems are monitored and supervised by Electrical Control Rooms – ECRs and the Electrical Control Room Operator (ECRO) is a key individual in any incident where the electrical traction supply system is involved.

Consequently, close cooperation and interworking within Network Rail and between NR and Train Operators is vital when electrical traction power supply problems occur.

Also failures can be catastrophic and may cause significant delays, it is therefore vital that Operators understand what can be done to minimise the impact.

25 kV OLE
Description of the System

The AC electrification traction supply system, forms part of the railway infrastructure that is owned and operated by Network Rail. This classic 25 kV overhead line catenary system is supplied by feeder stations and controlled by switching stations and track sectioning cabins. The 25 kV nominal supply voltage may vary, under normal conditions, over the range 16.5 kV to 27.5 kV when operating with modern rolling stock. Power is supplied via the pantograph and is fed to the main transformer(s) on the train, it is rectified (conversion of alternating current, which periodically reverses direction, to direct current, which flows in only one direction) and then inverted (electrical current converted from direct current to alternating current) to provide power to motors installed either on the vehicle body or within bogies where they may be partly supported by the wheelsets. This has to be done because modern AC trains operate with 3 phase AC motors but the OLE is a single phase supply and it is easier to convert the single phase AC to 3 phase AC if it is first converted to DC and then inverted to 3 phase AC.

AC motors are a relatively new concept when compared with DC motors. The technology has moved on very quickly as electronic systems have progressed

Running a Railway

and there are now two main types of AC motors, synchronous which are used on TGVs and asynchronous which are more modern, robust and cheaper. The main things to consider when designing train motors is having a motor with a high starting torque to commence moving and then using electronic systems to control the motor speed. Those two points, high torque and simple speed control are natural characteristics of DC motors but not AC motors and so the AC motor technology developed at a slower pace.

Schematic of Electric Locomotive Parts:

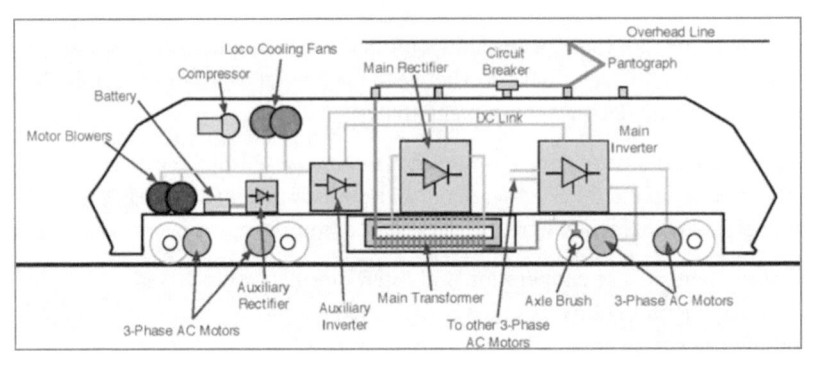

The AC supply to overhead line in Britain can be of either the classic or auto-transformer system.

The AC classic booster transformer system comprises, in very basic terms, a feeder station that distributes power to the locomotives by means of a pantograph on the roof of a train. The current is then returned to the feeder station through the wheels and via the traction return network. Booster transformers are installed roughly every 3.2km. The return conductors are connected to the rails midpoint between booster transformer locations. They are almost at rail potential and carry the largest part of the return current. Essentially booster transformers inductively cancel the current at the position of the load i.e. the current is drained from the rails and earth and distributed into the return conductor back to the feeder station. The system is designed to minimise unacceptable interference and high rail currents.

The more robust power delivery of an AC autotransformer system, or 2 x 25 kV system, consists of a single winding centre-tapped transformer, one end of which is connected to the overhead traction catenary system and the other to the autotransformer feeder conductor, with the centre tapping linked to the traction return system. This system operates on a principle of balancing voltages rather than currents, thus minimising the volt drop across the rail impedance between adjacent autotransformers. Effectively, the voltage at which the power is supplied to the overhead line is doubled for the long distances between substations.

6.20 Electrification Systems

On both type of systems separately fed sections of OLE are kept electrically separate by use of a neutral section in which a non-conductive section of insulation is inserted into the equipment. For operational purposes, these sections are then divided further into sub-sections by manual or automatically operated switches.

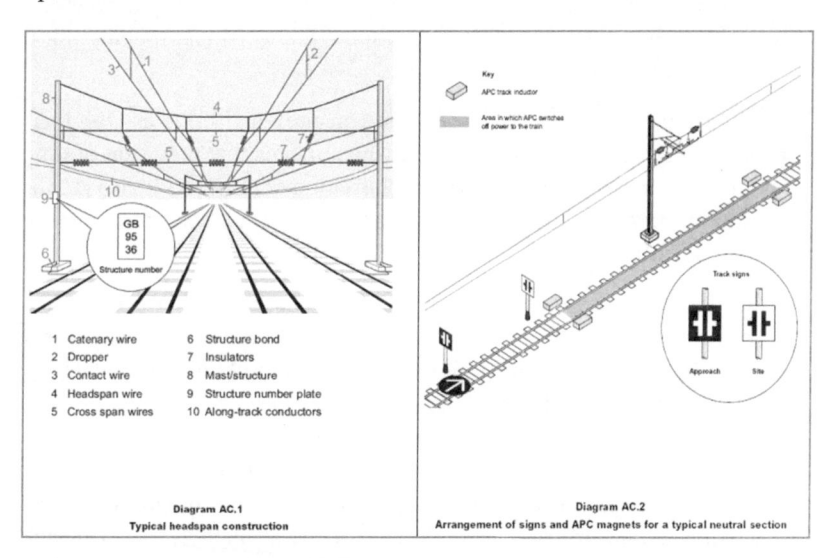

Diagram AC.1 — Typical headspan construction

1. Catenary wire
2. Dropper
3. Contact wire
4. Headspan wire
5. Cross span wires
6. Structure bond
7. Insulators
8. Mast/structure
9. Structure number plate
10. Along-track conductors

Diagram AC.2 — Arrangement of signs and APC magnets for a typical neutral section

- Details of UK electricity transmission and supply are shown at the end of this Section in Appendix 1 on pg 235.
- Details of the symbols used in Isolation Diagrams are shown at the end of this Section in Appendix 2 on pg 236.

Issues

This traction current supply system is relatively robust although a number of routes have inherent problems, for example, large parts of the Great Eastern Mainline has old equipment with no auto-tensioning, which is now being replaced.

Partial failure problems are relatively uncommon – broken or detached droppers are the most usual and can normally be dealt with without significant impact on train performance.

However some OLE faults that sound innocuous, for example, dirty ceramic beads can sometimes lead to major failures. Always treat reported faults with caution and respect.

Train operators should remember to watch for precursors such as increase in chipped carbons.

Running a Railway

The train end of this system is relatively reliable – the design of a pantograph is inherently less complex than the OLE system. Chipped carbons and broken pantograph chains are usually the main train based problems. Generally major problems have their root cause in the OLE.

Whilst major failures are rare they are usually catastrophic. If you receive a report of the "wires down" you should assume the worst and mobilise for a long period of disruption.

It is important to quickly provide adequate on site supervision as OLE incidents are complex and resource hungry which means that provision of time estimates can often take a while. Early mobilisation of resources is also vital as rectification work will almost always require significant labour, components, plant and machinery.

Overhead line damage is almost always seriously disruptive, however caused. Even minor damage, such as a failed insulator, or detached dropper/s below contact, will usually require an isolation, and mechanical rail equipment such as road rail vehicle, or lifting platform to repair. Some items of damaged OLE may not be found until high level access for inspection is available and this could lengthen the time to carry out repairs. This could impact on train service over a longer period, cause infrastructure to be out of use until repaired and possibly greater restrictions on infrastructure availability whilst repairs are carried out, for example, speed restrictions, line blockages, isolations on adjacent lines to protect staff safety.

Recent advances in the field of 'drop or lower pan and coast' will help to reduce delay where the OLE remains unusable but physically clear of the loading gauge. Always investigate if this is possible.

Failing this the practicalities of using diesel hauled traction to haul electric services over the affected line or opening the affected line to diesel hauled traffic only should be considered if appropriate. Another consideration is that it may be desirable that the OLE is made safe and fit for the passage of diesels and then reenergised to keep electrical feeds to other sections adjacent or beyond the affected one to keep electric trains running on these lines and so minimise delay.

Other worthwhile points to remember are:
- A de-wired train will usually be immobilised and trapped for several hours, so make early plans to evacuate any passengers on board – particularly during hot weather. Check TOC contingency plans cover this situation.
- Better still, get a 'Thunderbird' diesel, if available which has Electric Train Supply – ETS -capability) coupled to the train as soon as you can if this is

6.20 Electrification Systems

possible. Loss of power to on board systems such as air conditioning, lighting, toilets, internal doors will lead to rapid degradation of on board conditions, and decisions concerning passengers on the affected train, and any others trapped in the unpowered section, will be needed quickly particularly in cold or hot weather. Conditions can very rapidly become uncomfortable and even dangerous for anybody travelling with breathing difficulties. Evacuation then becomes urgent.

- Beware of over optimistic assumptions about deployment, availability of rescue and recovery resources and repair timescales.
- Emergency isolations and circuit breaker activations cause loss of the traction current over a wide area. Limiting the isolation to just the affected area as quickly as possible is an essential precursor to operating any form of train service on the route, and is a critical NR response. Some motorised switching to shorten the length of the affected area can usually be carried out by the ECR remotely but to achieve the minimum isolated section, staff will probably have to manually operate switches by the lineside. Often this takes a long time so mobilise resources to this straight away.
- On multiple tracks the time taken to repair will depend on the particular construction of the OLE, for example, headspan or 'goal-post' types.
- When OLE damage occurs, a key concern will always be to contain or limit it as much as possible. As a result:
  - Continued operation of electric traction through the damaged section will often be initially declined, even when damage appears minor.
  - If a damaged pantograph is suspected, the affected traction unit needs to be identified and removed from service quickly, consider if it can move under its own power at slow speed or coast if on a gradient or whether another locomotive or unit is required.
  - Diesel traction through the affected area will only be permitted if no physical part of the OLE is foul of any moving trains.
- If the damage has occurred during high winds, repairs will not commence until the wind has abated and it is safe for repair crews to work at height.
- As a minimum, repair crews working from on-track plant such as road rail vehicles RRVs or equipment such as ladders or zip up scaffold will require a severe speed restriction on adjacent roads at the site of repairs. This may also require some or all of these roads to be either Blocked To Electric Trains (BTET) or to all trains.
- The time taken to give up the isolation, test the integrity of the repair and clear, staff, on track plant repair vehicles and / or equipment usually adds 45-60 minutes to any estimate of completion of repairs and should always be factored into assumptions regarding resumption of timetabled operation.
- Trains that have been stranded without power for a long period will have

Running a Railway

lost all air in the brake system. Remember that it can take up to one and a half hours to pump up the supply in a 12-car EMU once power is restored. If these trains did not have their pantographs lowered at the start of the incident then they may have no battery power either.
- OLE wires coming down can cause damage to signalling equipment such as track circuits. Check this factor at the start of the incident, not at the end – particularly if a trapped train could be masking indications.

DC 3RD RAIL SYSTEM
Description of the System
The system has conductor rails mounted on the sleepers in addition to the two running rails and at a nominal voltage of 650V/750V d.c. Electricity is supplied by the Electricity Distribution Network Operators (DNOs) at between 11,000V and 66,000V alternating current (AC) 3-phase to switching stations or substations. From the switching stations, electrical supplies are taken to substations alongside the electrified line by means of insulated cables generally buried in the ground, laid in troughing or supported by hangers.

At the substation, transformers and rectifiers reduce the voltage, convert the supply from alternating current to direct current (DC), fed through circuit breakers, ground level insulated cables and isolation switches to the conductor rails.

Current is collected from the conductor rails by collector shoes on each train. After passing through the electrical equipment on the train, the current is returned to the substations through the axles and wheels and one or both of the running rails. The latter are connected to the substations by insulated cables.

At some locations an additional rail is used to provide an adequate current return circuit. This 4th rail is normally mounted on the sleepers between the running rails and bonded to the traction current return rail(s). London Underground electrification is on the 4th rail principle.

Substations, track paralleling huts and switching stations
Substations and, in some cases, track paralleling huts and switching stations are situated at intervals alongside the electrified lines. Substations contain equipment for transforming and rectifying alternating current to direct current as well as equipment to supply direct current to the conductor rail system and allow sectioning and paralleling of the conductor rails. Track paralleling huts only contain direct current equipment, arranged to connect together electrically a number of sections of conductor rail to support the load on the system and to provide sectioning of the conductor rail. Switching stations contain equipment to supply alternating current to sub-stations. All the switchgear in these buildings is remotely controlled from the electrical control room concerned.

Conductor rail arrangements

The conductor rail is supported on insulators mounted on the sleepers outside the running rails. The distance between the centre line of the conductor rail and the running edge of the nearest rail is 406mm (1ft 4ins). The height of the top of the conductor rail is 75mm (3ins) above running rail level. Gaps are provided in the conductor rail at points and crossings, at some train stop or signal positions, at track crossings, for example, foot or badger crossings, and at other locations for sectioning purposes. Where a gap is provided (for purposes other than sectioning) the conductor rails on each side of the gap are connected by an insulated jumper cable. Ramps are provided at the recommencement of the conductor rail to facilitate the smooth passage of the collector shoes.

Sectioning

The conductor rail equipment for each running line is kept electrically separate from that of other lines and also divided into sections by means of switchgear at sub-stations and track paralleling huts.

Each section is divided into sub-sections by isolating switches which are sometimes known as hook switches. These can be manually operated but may be motorised for remote operation. The switches are either located adjacent to, or mounted directly on, the conductor rail and suitably connected by insulated cable. In consequence, a sub-section of conductor rail can be isolated in case of a fault or for maintenance purposes whilst the electricity supply on other sections and sub-sections is maintained.

- Details of UK electricity transmission and supply are shown at the end of this Section in Appendix 1 on pg 235.
- Details of the symbols used in Isolation Diagrams are shown at the end of this Section in Appendix 2 on pg 236.

Issues

The 3rd rail is colloquially known as the 'juice rail', with electric trains travelling 'on the juice'. Such phrases will be heard in an operating environment. Do not use them in formal or safety messages.

The 3rd rail infrastructure is relatively simple and robust but the interface between the conductor rail and the train shoes is inherently more prone to problems than a catenary or pantograph arrangement.

Displaced conductor rails are relatively common and can often be as a result of routine track maintenance such as high ballast or tamping upsetting alignment. Similarly shoes can be poorly aligned and can displace conductor rails although this is rare. Equally, loss of shoes and on occasions a whole shoe beam through heavy impact with an obstruction or a misaligned conductor rail will

Running a Railway

disable the train and cause a short circuit. As a minimum, the train will need to be rescued and an examination of the third rail infrastructure initiated to identify damage – a potentially lengthy and time consuming pair of processes. If obstructions coming into contact with third rail and running rails damage to the running rails can be the result – sometimes significant.

In complex switch and crossing areas short trains can become gapped where none of the shoes on the train are in contact with the third rail. Rolling clear of the gapped locations can be a solution. Alternatively the unit may need to be assisted clear. These incidents can be very disruptive.

Flashovers across the train shoes and related equipment whilst rarer are more common than pantograph faults. Watch for the robustness of insulation on rolling stock "H" frames which hold the current collector shoes on DC trains.

Any failure of the 3rd Rail electrification infrastructure must be regarded as serious, with probably lengthy disruption to services resulting. Failures may include:-
- Displacement of the 3rd Rail.
- Misalignment of the 3rd Rail which is usually after engineering works.
- Failure of insulation such as pots broken, blown or displaced.
- Short circuit.
- Supply failure.
- Cable failure.

Apart from failure of a shoe fuse, which drivers are trained to change or replace, failure of train borne collection equipment will disable the train, requiring the unit to be recovered:-
- Loss of collection shoe(s).
- Loss of a shoe beam.

LOW POWER

With either system low amps can cause problems. Some sections are known problem areas, for example, the nominally 25kV overheads at Alexandra Palace, Royston, Cambridge and Newark are locations where voltages may drop as low as 15kV, whilst other problems are more transitory such as intermediate feeder out of use. This is an area to watch as low amps can severely elongate Sectional Running Times (SRTs) – particularly on 3rd rail systems. Similarly, where power draw by traction units reaches a critical level, the available power for every train will be limited, affecting acceleration, pulling away from a stand, and attaining or holding line speed.

Such issues are very familiar to drivers, but are invisible to the delay attribution process where delays are either sub threshold, attributed to station dwell, or simply described as time lost in running. Ask the relevant questions if an area of electrified railway does not appear to be performing as it should.

ELECTRICAL CONTROL ROOM (ECR)

Each ECR is continuously staffed under the supervision of Electrical Control Room Operators (known as ECROs) who are responsible for the operation of the traction and signalling power supply system to ensure adequate security of supply is maintained consistent with operating & safety instructions and procedures. To achieve this they carry out the following tasks:-

- Take emergency actions in response to incidents involving the traction supply system.
- Co-ordinate procedures for planned and emergency isolations of plant and equipment with the minimum of disruption to services.
- Validating, issuing & cancelling isolation documentation for track isolations associated with prearranged engineering works.
- Switch H.V. feeder cables with due regard to system loading under both normal and abnormal conditions.
- Arrange track feeding with due regard to system loading under both normal and abnormal conditions.
- Operate the ECR supervisory control system.
- Review method statements for work on, or commissioning of electrification equipment, for operational compliance.

It is vital that ECROs are involved in the decision making processes during serious incidents. Their input can be crucial, particularly when undertaking prioritised incident planning and determining options for service recovery including associated time estimates.

Running a Railway

Tips

OLE
Dewirements should be relatively rare on a well-designed and maintained Overhead Contact System but the root cause/s can be difficult to establish.

Third Rail
Third rail is also relatively reliable and most tension will again surround the causes of failure and the train or infrastructure interface.

Remember in all incidents involving electrical supply problems the key requirements are good estimates for restoration, the structured use of prioritised planning and sound decisions regarding trapped trains.

6.20 Electrification Systems

Appendix 1: UK Electricity Transmission and Distribution

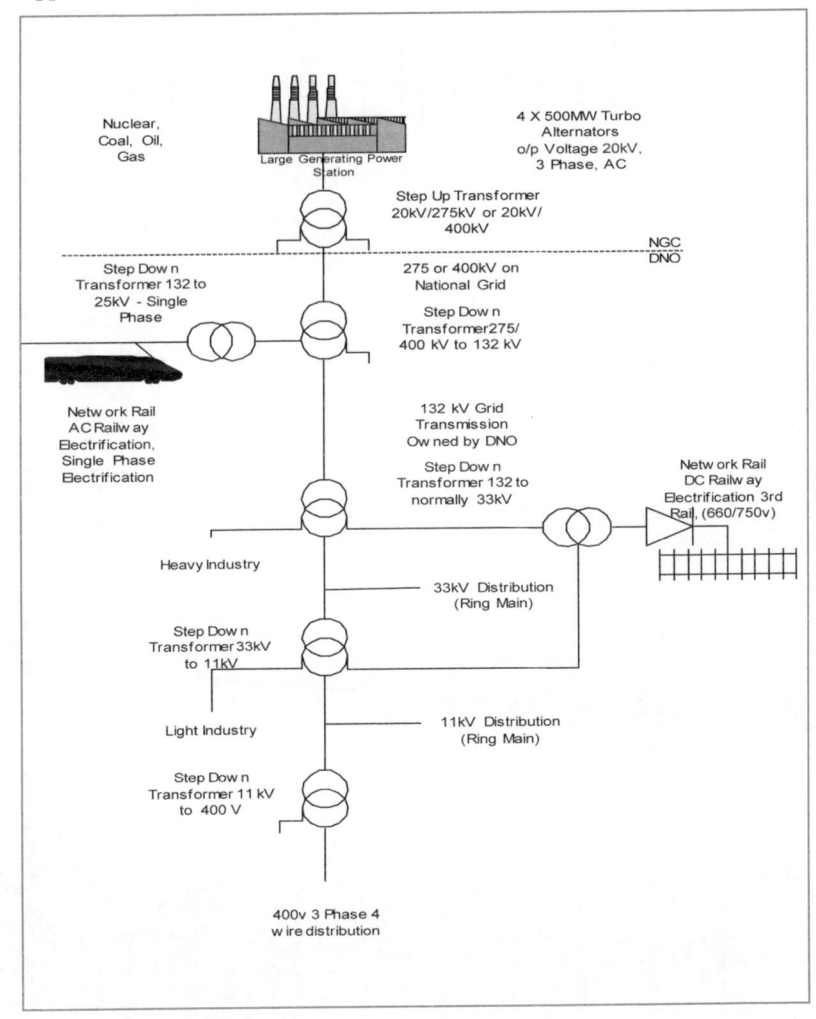

Large Generating Power Station
- Nuclear, Coal, Oil, Gas
- 4 X 500MW Turbo Alternators o/p Voltage 20kV, 3 Phase, AC

Step Up Transformer 20kV/275kV or 20kV/400kV

NGC / DNO

275 or 400kV on National Grid

Step Down Transformer 275/400 kV to 132 kV

Step Down Transformer 132 to 25kV - Single Phase → Network Rail AC Railway Electrification, Single Phase Electrification

132 kV Grid Transmission Owned by DNO

Step Down Transformer 132 to normally 33kV

Network Rail DC Railway Electrification 3rd Rail, (660/750v)

33kV Distribution (Ring Main) → Heavy Industry

Step Down Transformer 33kV to 11kV

11kV Distribution (Ring Main) → Light Industry

Step Down Transformer 11 kV to 400 V

400v 3 Phase 4 wire distribution

Institution of Railway Operators

Running a Railway

Appendix 2: Isolation Diagram Symbols

Key to Isolation Diagram symbols

Slips	Trap points	Signal box	Ground frame	Auto signal / Controlled signal	Shunting signals	Limit Of Shunt signal (LOS)	Flag	Stop Board / Section Gap Board / Station platform

Earth	Mile marker	Kilometre marker	Structure number	Structure number indicating incorrectly sited equipment	Limit of proximity of electricity supply industry overhead power lines		Depot	Tunnel

Booster transformer	2 position OHL switch	3 position OHL switch	Earthing switches	Double 2 position OHL switch	Double 3 position OHL switch with earth position	Double 2 position OHL switch with connecting jumper	ALT or A - Alternate feed / NO or N.O. - Normally Open / M - Motorised	Fuse	Auxiliary transformer	Isolating transformer

Electrified line / Dual electrified line / Non-electrified line	Section ID	Neutral sections	Section insulator	Overlap	Jumper between parallel roads	Cable / Bare Feeder / Sealing End	Busbar	Normally open circuit breaker / Normally closed circuit breaker	Voltage transformer

NOTE: The symbols shown are the symbols relevant to the East Anglia Region Isolation Diagrams. Reference should be made to EHQ/SP/SO30 for further information.

Operators' Handbook

6.21 Signal Engineering Issues

BACKGROUND

Signal maintenance in the rail industry is a huge subject but this Section concentrates on the issues and implications for Operators which emerge from signal maintenance activity.

FAULTS & FAILURE MANAGEMENT

NR created the Incident Controller role to provide a single point of contact and reference when incidents occur on the controlled infrastructure. The concept originated in the time when infrastructure maintenance was brought "back in house" and Fault Controls run by the former infrastructure maintenance companies were combined with Network Rail Operations Controls. Many of the incidents they deal with will be instances of equipment failure, and the Incident Controller is responsible for progressing the failure to a conclusion and liaising closely with other Controllers in the office who are endeavouring to operate the railway around the failure.

In dealing with Signalling equipment failures, the Incident Controller has five primary responsibilities:-
- To receive reports of failures and defects, and record details.
- To prioritise repairs.
- To direct staff and resources to the failure.
- To monitor progress of the repair or defect restoration.
- Maintain strong links with the rest of the NR Operational Control in respect of priorities, progress on repairs, estimates for normal working etc.

Incident Controllers are not multi-discipline engineers, and are unlikely to be technically trained.

RESPONSE TEAMS

Signalling response teams provide the basic repair and restoration resource for a wide range of signal equipment. Much of their work will not be intrusive to the operational railway.

Most teams comprise a minimum of three personnel to allow the team to perform its own lookout duties for work on the track, and the team cannot function as well without three staff. Productivity is an important issue for the

Running a Railway

management of these teams and as such they will often be used to undertake maintenance work in their "down time".

Getting the balance right between planned maintenance activity and ability to drop everything to attend a failure is clearly important and the answer is likely to be different for different teams. Understanding this dynamic for your own area is important as it will help you to balance your resources correctly.

The interface between track and signalling is a vital one and it is likely to be the case that some faults which manifest themselves as a signalling problem require a track solution. In these cases, Signalling Response teams will almost always require Pway attendance for full rectification (points failure requiring lifting and packing of sleepers or track circuit failure requiring pads and nylons replacing for example). Point Care Teams with dual competence are used to improve regular maintenance activity by addressing all aspects in one visit but this is less easy to apply in immediate fault response activity.

FAULT TYPES

As stated earlier, many signal equipment failures, and the repair activity which goes with them, are not intrusive to the operational railway – routine route setting difficulties, indication failures, train describer defects etc. – are generally dealt with as running repairs inside the Signalling Centre, and the signal technicians will be well known to signallers.

However, the faults that do affect the operational railway can be disruptive although they are often capable of mitigation with a degree of forethought and planning.

Wrong Side Failures
Wrong Side Failures occur when equipment fails in a state which reduces the protection normally provided by the infrastructure and therefore increases the risk of an incident. Wrong side failures can be protected or unprotected: a protected failure is one in which another piece of equipment provides an acceptable level of protection. A blank signal for which the signal in rear reverts to red is an example of a protected WSF; a set of points showing out of correspondence (no detection) but with the protecting signal showing a proceed aspect is an example of an unprotected WSF. This is not just a signal engineering term – broken rails or an earth works failures are examples from other disciplines.

Infrastructure faults and incidents are recorded in Network Rail's Fault Management System (FMS) and are investigated so that the fundamental cause can be identified. A detailed risk assessment is undertaken which enables the relative ranking of failures from all disciplines so that appropriate action can be taken. Signalling Wrong Side Failures are recorded in the Signalling Incident System (SINCS) and records may only be closed once adequately investigated and resolved.

Signal Failure

In very modern signalling LED and fibre-optic cable technology is replacing less reliable lamps. Non-LED signal heads are fitted with two filaments, and the most rudimentary of signal failures is the failure of the first filament. This does not affect the operation of the lamp. The failure will be invisible to everyone other than the signaller and in some cases the signalbox technician, who will receive an indication on the signalling panel. Technicians routinely replace these lamps before the second filament fails.

Disruptive signal failures generally manifest themselves as a 'reversion to red', which will require trains to be 'talked by' the failure until rectified. In the case of a double filament lamp failure affecting the red aspect, trains will be 'talked by' the previous signal as well because it will be held at danger by the blank aspect ahead. Whilst such routine failures can be very disruptive – a lot of trains affected for a small amount of delay – the disruption generally only lasts as long as it takes to get a signal response team to site, as repair work can normally be carried out promptly and without blockage of the line.

The more disruptive signal failures are those deemed to be wrong side failures (WSF) – actual or potential, where an incorrect sequence is alleged. This is usually by a Driver, for example, red after a green, or single yellow after a green in four aspect signalling. Similarly, where an incident such as a SPAD has occurred and there is an allegation concerning the signalling, the installation will be treated as if a WSF has taken place. Clear and exact information on what the reporter of the fault claims to have seen is vital as it will guide the testing regime. The degree of certainty in the report is also important – "I think I may have seen …" is very different to "I definitely saw …". This all needs to be reported to the technicians undertaking the testing so that they can gauge the level of response required.

In such circumstances, a testing plan drafted in accordance with Signal Maintenance & Testing Handbook (SMTH) will have to be prepared, approved and exhaustive tests carried out.

In all situations where a WSF has occurred, or is alleged to have occurred, the signalling will need to be 'signed back into use' when the test plan has been discharged, even if no fault has been identified.

Running a Railway

The provision of forward facing CCTV on trains considerably assists the validation or otherwise of claims of wrong signalling sequences but it is essential that evidence be provided as swiftly as possible to aid diagnosis.

Track Circuit Failure (TCF)

A failed track circuit has much the same operational impact as a routine signal failure – the signal in rear is held at danger, and trains have to be 'talked by'. However, the response team generally has to attend at trackside to assess components which is more likely to require line blockages.

Track circuit failures can expose interface problems between Signal and PWay functions. Many TCFs result from poor PWay conditions or maintenance – block joint insulation, ballast condition, drainage, or insulation between track fastenings, and such TCFs take at least twice as long to resolve – usually because the signalling team turn up, investigate, cannot resolve the problem and require a PWay team. The most frustrating failures are those which "blip" intermittently on a regular basis – the root cause can be extremely difficult to track down, particularly if the track circuit concerned consists of multiple parts (a track circuit shown as one on the signaller's panel may in fact consist of a number of separate parts) and is lengthy.

Wrong side track circuit failures are rare – track circuit showing clear when occupied – some failures of this type reported by Signallers are actually minor indication failures on the Panel. However, where such failures can and do occur is in autumn leaf fall conditions where severe contamination of rail and/or wheel treads with leaf mulch can render trains 'invisible' to the signalling system. Similarly rusty rails after engineering work and lines in loops and branches that have not been used for a while can cause such failures.

In such cases, there will be potentially draconian implications, involving restrictive specially authorised operating arrangements for a prolonged period of time. Thankfully such events are now increasingly rare – partly the result of better infrastructure management in the run up to and during autumn, and partly through the fitment of on-train and track equipment (Track Circuit Actuators and TCAIDs) to boost the electrical 'shunt' through the wheels and axles of the most vulnerable rolling stock.

Use of data loggers can help to identify problematic track circuits, either by narrowing down the particular area of the problem or by remotely identifying when short circuit values are becoming inadequate.

6.21 Signal Engineering Issues

Good track circuit maintenance is essential for running a right time railway and the Good Practice Guide below provides some information on the sorts of things that technicians will look for

TRACK CIRCUIT GOOD PRACTICE

Track Circuit Pins – Knocking in and tightening up
Damage on L plate making sure it's secure
Testing jumpers with a current clamp

Checking all bonds are in place
Check bonds are doubled up

Aster unit on its stand and not lying on the ballast
Staff looking for trends on track and circuit cards

Checking for signs of cable damage
Manage Rail in '4 Foot'

Thermal Imaging checks on fuses
Install new Clip or temperary Wiget

Check all T pieces are in good order
Do they need to be repaired
Is IBJ in good order?

Axle Counter Failure

Whilst axle counter technology has been in use within the railway for many years, axle counters have tended to be deployed in locations where track circuits have proved less reliable, such as damp or humid conditions in tunnels, or underground. More recent development of the technology has seen its application more widely in the industry, and axle counters are now preferred over track circuits in resignalling schemes such as the southern end of the West Coast Main Line.

From a train running point of view, there is little difference between track circuits and axle counters – the operational impact of failure is broadly the same, and the same team of technicians will be called to either type of failure. Axle Counters do have the advantage that reset procedures to clear faults can be used in some circumstances.

Points Failure

Points (or S&C, switches and crossings) are complex pieces of kit which are managed by both track and signalling engineers. The discipline-specific inspection regimes for track and signalling do not align and therefore some areas have instituted joint point teams which can address both track and signalling issues, inspecting point work holistically.

Running a Railway

Clearly points offer operational flexibility but this comes at a price of higher maintenance requirements and need for access. Failure of Points is almost invariably in the top five causes of delay so you must consider the trade-off between flexibility and failure-rates when assessing remodelling plans.

There are various types of point operating equipment (POE) from mechanical points, manually operated by the signaller using rodding and cranks to physically move the point blades to electric motor operated and hydraulically operated points. Each type will have its strengths and weaknesses and the best way for you to understand the issues and impacts on your railway is to build your relationship with your maintenance and engineering colleagues.

Clamp Lock

1. Point number
2. Back drive assembly & supplementary detection.
3. General Clamplock installation
4. Stretcher Bar

Clamp Lock Microswitch

1. Kick strap
2. Micro switch
3. Drive lock slide extension

6.21 Signal Engineering Issues

M63 Points Machine   **HW Machine**

AWS/TPWS Failure

This is another area where an interface can generate significant problems, this time between track equipment such as magnets and inductors and train borne receivers and display equipment. Once again, wrong side failures or alleged wrong side failures: bell vice horn or no warning vice horn are the most disruptive, requiring both on train and track equipment to be extensively tested which can lead to a long time lag before resolution, if indeed one is ever determined.

Signalling Power Failure

These are invariably a massively disruptive event when they occur and this has become more common as cable theft has increased. Causes vary:

- Failure of the incoming supply from the electricity generating company.
- Power surge which can be sometimes caused by lightning causing a circuit breaker trip on the 650v signalling supply. This can be rectified by changing the fuse, but may result in failure of other, sensitive signalling components.
- Cable theft.
- More serious failures may come about through cable failure – rodent damage, cut accidentally by machinery, fire or vandalism.

Identifying the cause can take an age to find in miles of cable routes, let alone repair. Cable theft has in recent years become a very significant issue for the industry.

The effect is always the same – instant disablement of the signalling system; signalling panel indications all showing 'occupied'; all lineside signals to red or blacked out; all trains 'invisible' on the system. Safe passage of trains out of the affected area can itself be hugely time consuming, and no trains will be able to enter the affected area until the problem is rectified, or in the case of longer term failures, alternative signalling arrangements are established – usually temporary block working (TBW).

Running a Railway

Many locations have standby power supplies, for example, generators and UPS (Uninterruptible Power Supplies) to combat this, although these can develop faults too – the downside is they can fail to cut in. Ensure standby supplies are regularly tested and that fuel levels are checked as a matter of routine –such emergency supplies can prevent a performance disaster. UPS is designed to prevent changes of aspect on signals which would otherwise occur when a power supply changes from Main to Standby or vice versa. More and more installations are being fitted with remotely monitored Earth Leakage Detection units often known as "Bender Units". These can identify when a cable has an earth fault but will not usually be able to identify earth faults between separate cores within the same cable.

Bender Unit

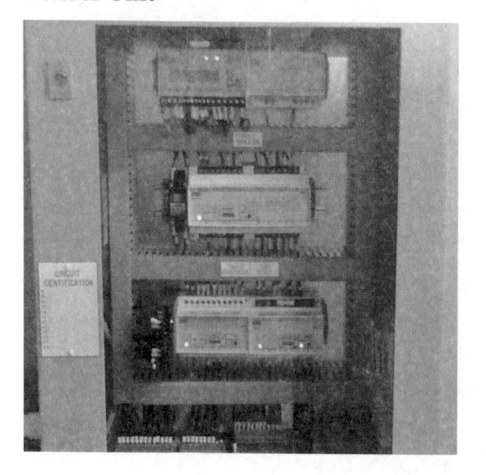

The power supply system is "owned" by electrification and plant teams rather than Signal Engineers and it is important that these staff are called out to manage failures. Bear in mind that there is an interface to manage between signalling and plant teams.

See also Major Signalling Failures (Section 7.12)

Communications Links

As signalling equipment has become centralised into Power Boxes, Signalling Centres and IECCs (Integrated Electronic Control Centres – a solid state signalling system) there has been a requirement for the equipment in the signal control centre to communicate with interlockings which are remote to that centre. Time Division Multiplexer (TDM) or other telecoms links may be provided to perform this function.

In some TDM-type installations an override facility is provided for the signaller so that in the event of a failure, straight routes can be set to work automatically with other routes becoming unavailable. When this happens, the signaller can disregard panel indications as these will not correspond with what is happening outside. Make sure that your signallers are aware of the detailed instructions for working in override sometimes called "Through Routes" or "Selective Auto" and are confident in understanding how it works in practice. Particularly if they have not used the system for some time, its operation can be unnerving – the time taken to set can be longer than expected and the fact that panel signal, TC and points indications can be ignored goes completely against the grain for signallers.

Other installations may be provided with remote panels which have the disadvantage that they require staff to operate but do mean that full flexibility can be maintained with the remote panel staff working to the signaller's instructions. The signaller retains responsibility at all times and remains in the lead for communicating with drivers as communication equipment and train describers are not provided.

More modern signal centres will be provided with diverse telecoms links so that there is always a secondary route available if one leg fails. This provides permanent flexibility but it is possible for corruption on one leg to result in corruption on the other, shutting both comms links down! PTERTS equipment (Production Telegram Error Rate Test Set) can be used to monitor links to identify when errors levels are reaching critical levels. Technicians can monitor for this, call out response staff and may shut down a problematic link to avoid cross-contamination.

PTERTS Equipment

Running a Railway

Panel Failures

Signalling installations consist of many individual sub-systems. At the most basic level there is the control system which the signaller uses to interface with the signalling interlocking which may be in the signalbox or in a remote location many miles away. "Panel Failures" would more accurately be described as the failure of some or all of this control system – it may be as simple as buttons or indications on a panel, a screen in an IECC or the failure of the computer system which 'drives' the Signaller's system in an IECC or wiring which controls the panel. Just as causes are varied so can be the effects!

What may appear to be minor panel faults can be extremely frustrating for signallers and can result in significant difficulties in carrying out their duties. For example, a panel track circuit indicator light failure may not be considered a big problem, but if every indicator for a particular track circuit failed you would be faced with Wrong Side Failure accusations. A WSTCF could go unnoticed because signallers have become used to indication failures and believe this is what they have witnessed.

Good housekeeping of panel and signalbox equipment is a sign of good attention to detail for both signallers and engineers and can be a significant morale game-changer.

Train Describer Faults

Faults and failures on the signalling centre train describer can have two discrete impacts; firstly, the loss of train descriptions means the signaller has no knowledge of train identity – for routing, platforming, regulation etc. – and may need to stop trains to ascertain identity. Secondly, the train describer is often the source of TRUST information, which may be lost or corrupted and may cause customer information systems on stations to fail. Train describer failure should always be treated as a high priority for repair and rectification.

Cab Radio Failure

National Radio Network (NRN), Cab Secure Radio (CSR) failures are usually localised to a single base station and the odd 'black spot', these are rarely operationally disruptive. However, if a more widespread failure affects Cab Secure Radio, which is critical to operations on Driver Only Operated (DOO) routes, this can be highly disruptive. This can be compounded by an inconsistent NR approach to such problems and differing responses by TOC Drivers. Train Operators must ensure that robust contingency plans are agreed with NR and in place to prevent this. At its most extreme, service suspension may be the only solution, as DOO TOCs do not now have the capability to deploy Guards to operate the route in conventional form.

6.21 Signal Engineering Issues

These forms of radio communication are being replaced by GSM-R as this handbook is being prepared. It is anticipated that reliability and coverage will be significantly better than existing systems and on this basis proposals are in place to substantially reduce the number of Signal Post Telephones that will be required in future.

With both systems – NRN and cab secure radio, the interface between NR's fixed infrastructure and the on-train equipment can be problematic, although the existence of a problem wider than a single train is easy to identify!

Radio reliability and availability is an area way outside the 'comfort zone' of most operations managers. Make sure that radio signal and reliability testing is undertaken, follow up reports of 'black spots' thoroughly with engineers (remembering that neither NRN nor CSR are systems designed to provide 100% coverage), and read into the issues so that you have some competence to ask the pertinent questions. Understand how long repairs will take if the system fails and factor this information (with a margin) into estimates if the worst should happen. This will all stand you in good stead for any major problem, should you ever have to face one.

The current introduction of GSM-R to replace the older radio systems is a rare opportunity to really get to understand the way the technology works and to harness its benefits. Early indications are that GSM-R has genuinely contributed significantly to performance improvement in the areas where it has been initially rolled-out through the improvement in the speed and quality of communication.

Tips

A key issue is prioritisation – the balance of priority between fixing the equipment and running a service – a temporary repair to get traffic moving with a later possession to fully repair the defect may be the right overall solution.

However, you need to understand the implications of this option – what is the reduced flexibility, what is the likelihood of second failure, what are the implications of a later fix (lost work etc.).

If you are experiencing repeat failures, engage with the engineers and visit site so that you can see for yourself and demonstrate how important the problems are to you: staff at the "sharp end" may not realise the impact that they are having on the train service.

Operators must ensure that technical priorities support delivery of the required performance targets.

Running a Railway

6.22 Signalling Operations

BACKGROUND

Signalling Operations is almost totally an NR activity (TOCs/FOCs do operate some small panels in depots and yards), and it is crucial to the delivery of good train service performance.

Signalling operations cover the routine signaller focused activity of operating and monitoring the signalling system, managing equipment failures and mitigating the impact.

This element provides an overview and describes how visits to signalling locations should be approached.

THE SIGNALLER'S TASK

Signalling is still primarily the task of operating equipment designed to keep trains a safe distance from one another. The task of operating the equipment is carried out by Signallers based in a variety of different types of signalling locations, from basic mechanical lever frame signal boxes, through to more modern panel boxes using relay interlocking, right up to today's modern Integrated Electronic Control Centres using computer-based interlocking technology.

The prime objective of signalling is to enable train movements whilst maintaining a safe distance between trains, whether during normal working where the integrity of the signalling system maintains this safe distance, or during degraded working where emergency rules and regulations are implemented by the signaller to maintain the safe distances. This is where the skill of the signaller comes into its own. Or as an experienced signaller will often describe it "that's when you earn your money"!

Whatever type of location or equipment, the role of the signaller remains crucial for the safe operation of the railway, and relies on the signaller being vigilant, well prepared and professional at all times.

KEY ISSUES

Training
Initial signaller training now combines many different types of learning, incorporating classroom and computer based theory, practical learning on

simulators and in actual signalling locations, and knowledge testing. Following successful initial training, on the job training in his/her signalling locations allows the signaller to become accustomed to the geographic nature of their location, how the equipment works, and all the information relevant to that specific signal box. This overall training package equips the signaller with the tools to enable them to carry out their duties.

Knowledge and Information

The knowledge required to operate a signal box professionally and safely comes in many forms. Experience in the location can help, but as part of the signal box training process, a manager should always look to place a trainee with a more experienced member of staff, who will support and develop the individual during the training process. The personal experiences of a more experienced signaller that are informally related during this time, can help a trainee be able to recognise situations that inexperience can initially overlook, and as result act more quickly to prevent situations becoming worse.

A signal box training plan provided by a line manager will breakdown the timescales, equipment associated with the location, any specific local features and information applicable, and will require the trainee signaller to document on a daily basis their progress against the plan. Good quality, location-specific training plans are an essential means of making sure local conditions and requirements are consistently understood and applied by all signallers working that location. Relying on anecdotal experiences alone is rarely a successful training approach!

Subtle things can make all the difference between being a good, and an average signaller. Having a good understanding of the infrastructure in the signalling area they control such as line speeds and directions of travel, locations of bridges and level crossings and signals in relation to equipment such as crossings and junctions. Knowing the nature of vehicular roads leading to level crossings, or the type of locations serving user worked crossings is also invaluable. Having a good understanding of how their location interfaces with adjacent signalling locations is a huge advantage, because if a signaller understands the impact of an incident on a location next to them, then their ability to manage any incident improves. Also understanding the requirements of another signaller can help promote teamwork, which is vital to ensure the railway works well during normal and more importantly degraded working.

A professional signaller is required to obtain information from a vast array of sources, and in obtaining that information ensure it is current, relevant, and applicable to their signal box. Communication skills are essential – the ability to process these sources of information, understand the information being

Running a Railway

provided, ask the right questions, establish facts and potential options is just as important as following communication protocols.

Signal Box instructions

These supplement the general rule book regulations, and highlight specific requirements in relation to the location and its equipment. A good knowledge of these instructions is vital to work that location safely and effectively.

Train running information

This can be obtained from a variety of sources. TRUST is a computer based system that provides information on train identities, schedules, and real time running information, and assists a signaller in both regulating decisions and what the train consists of (i.e. type of traffic units and wagons). Most signal boxes have this system.

Signallers also use "simplifiers" which provide a guide to regulating decisions at key locations which may not be so easily discernible from the WTT.

For terminus stations and larger through stations where trains may terminate, station working books are a form of simplifier which provide information on platform workings, which inward trains for which outward bound trains and so on. These may often appear "as if by magic" but it is worth finding out how they are produced and who does them – they are vital and your signallers are likely to be lost without them!

The Weekly Operating Notice (WON)

Published weekly as the title suggests and contains details of a variety of issues:
Section A: Temporary Speed Restrictions. Good signallers will want to know about these as they may impact upon regulating decisions.
Section B: Details of forthcoming engineering works.
Section C: amendments and alterations to the infrastructure.
Section D: amendments to operating publications such as rules and local instructions as well as miscellaneous information.

The Periodical Operating Notice (PON)

A Bi-Monthly publication which contains all the current amendments to rules and regulations and certain miscellaneous information.

The Sectional Appendix

This is essentially a map of the railway detailing track diagrams, line speeds, location of signal boxes and crossings, route restrictions for traction types and so on. It also contains local and general instructions relevant to the Route concerned.

Location Specific Information

Other information that the signaller may need to be aware of and understand relating to their particular location could include:

- Bridge Strike Instructions - detailing dispensations for bridges within their area of control.
- Route setting cards or lists - for the operation of points during degraded working when the integrity of the interlocking is temporarily unavailable.
- Isolation Instructions and diagrams for use in electrified areas - they provide information to signallers on how to adequately protect areas blocked to electric traction for engineering work or incident protection.
- Maximum length of platforms sidings or loops.
- Location of tunnels.
- Telephone numbers for all the people and locations a signaller may need to contact on a daily basis.
- Station working documents and simplifiers detail the order in which trains should be signalled into or out of stations or over converging or diverging junctions.

Preparation and professionalism

The signaller has a key role in ensuring a safe and reliable railway therefore it is vital that any signaller approaches their job being fully prepared;

- By ensuring that they are fully rested before work.
- If they have any personal or health issues that may affect their ability to do their job, then they must speak to their line manager to make them aware of the issues they face.
- They allow sufficient time for their journey to work.
- They have enough food and drink to keep themselves refreshed during their turn of duty.
- When handing over with a colleague they receive and understand all the information necessary to carry out their duties at a level of detail that leaves nothing to assumption.

In such an important role signallers should aspire to be as professional as possible, this is partly down to the leadership they receive, but also down to a sense of personal pride in the job they are doing. Signallers are after all the guardians of safety, and are expected to take the lead in most situations they face. Good communication skills are an absolute must, as a lack of understanding during communications will almost certainly affect the safety of the railway.

Any signaller, no matter what their experience, should always accept the fact that they can learn something new every day. Even if that experience is obtained

Running a Railway

by mistakes (minor ones hopefully) that they, or others, may make. When faced with any incident it is important that a signaller remains calm, assesses the situation, and acts decisively. The old signaller's adage "before jumping in stand back and put the kettle on", was always aimed at directing less experienced signallers to take stock, think about the situation they were faced with, and review all the details before acting in haste. It is as relevant now as it was a hundred years ago, and not just to inexperienced signallers.

SIGNAL CENTRE/BOX VISITS

Signal box (both people and premises) visits are the responsibility of NR Operations Managers but all Operators should have an appreciation of signalling through the relevant Rules and Regulations competence requirements. Additionally, good liaison between NR and TOC/FOC will involve joint visits to various key locations and facilities.

The signaller is the frontline guardian of safety and the first line controller of all railway operations. The signal box, workstation or panel is their "office" and the work activities carried out there have an enormous impact on the railway.

Authorised visitors must switch off their mobile telephone.

The local manager is responsible for the line management of the signallers and is normally occupationally competent for the management of operational activities at the signalling location you are visiting.

Network Rail specifies that each safety of the line visit by a line manager to an individual employee shall never be less than 30 minutes long. Where practicable more than one employee at the same location can be visited together, for example, in a multi-staffed signalling centre.

Always:-
- Read the visitors' brief (where provided) and sign the visitors' book.
- Greet those present and introduce yourself. If there is a box or shift manager, make your way to their desk first.
- Observe the operation of the signalling.
- Ask some straight forward questions (if appropriate) - an example could be the decision points for regulation approaching a converging junction and other relevant performance issues.
- Listen out for any safety critical conversations.
- Look out for outstanding faults.

6.22 Signalling Operations

- Ask signallers what issues they have with a TOC or FOC's service or operation – you may find that working relationships are better at the front line level than even you experience but this may not always be the case.
- Be wary of getting too engrossed in conversation – you do not want to be the source of distraction that results in delays, or worse.

You will be made very welcome, however, if the signaller asks you to leave due to operational incidents or it becomes evident that an incident is taking up a signaller's attention and you can offer no assistance - leave. Do not become a distraction.

Note any good working practices. If you observe good practice - say so there and then.

Positive indicators in a signalling location are:
- Well presented and courteous signallers.
- No unauthorised electrical equipment present, for example, mobile phones.
- The signallers give prompt attention to telephone calls, and use specified railway communication protocols consistently.
- Signalling equipment is operated in due time to avoid delay to trains.
- There is a properly completed Train Register Book(TRB) or occurrence book and other forms.
- There is a tidy and quiet and orderly working environment.

Tips

The general internal appearance of a signal box and the appearance and behaviour of the staff are good indications of how effective the location is. This is equally true of Control Offices and train crew signing on points.

Knowing what good signal operations looks like is essential for all Operators.

TOCs/FOCs should spend peaks in signal boxes and keep observing the operation. This would need NR's permission.

Let the Control Office know where you are and everyone else will then know you are taking a keen interest in real time delivery.

Time in signal boxes, like driving cabs, is time well spent. It will increase your expertise and enhance your reputation.

Running a Railway

6.23 Train Regulation

BACKGROUND

The industry is increasingly measured in terms of PPM (including CaSL) and the Government expects TOCs and Network Rail to collectively deliver continuous improvement in this area.

PPM is an absolute measure – a train is either inside the applicable PPM threshold (Time to 4 minutes 59 seconds or Time to 9 minutes 59 seconds), or it fails to achieve PPM. A train is also a PPM failure if it is cancelled in full, part cancelled (either terminates short or starts forward) or fails to call at one or more booked stations.

The applicable measure was dependent on British Rail Sector divisions and therefore there are some anomalies. Generally commuter and short distance interurban are measured on Time to 5 minutes (4'59') and long distance services are measured on Time to 10 minutes (9'59').

Cancellation and Significant Lateness (CaSL) is a new performance measure that was introduced from the start of Control Period 4 in April 2009. It is a subset of PPM and is designed to target a reduction in total cancellations plus trains arriving at final destination over 30 minutes late. The starting point for the measure was taken as the actual result in March 2008. Standard sector targets have been set for TOCs and NR to achieve jointly by March 2014.

The more recent drive to measure railway performance in terms of right time arrivals has added another layer of complexity.

Initially the privatised rail industry based train regulation on the concept of minimising overall delay. Regulation for PPM varies this concept and the following section highlights the key issues.

ISSUES

Controllers and signallers must take account of PPM thresholds when making regulating decisions. It is no longer acceptable just to minimise overall delay where this is inconsistent with maximising the number of services achieving PPM. Where Automatic Route Setting (ARS) is in use particular care must be taken to ensure that the regulation decisions maximise PPM as ARS has never been programmed to understand PPM. Indeed the algorithms used by ARS assume that minimisation of overall delay is the end goal. Signallers therefore need to intervene when there are really important PPM regulating decisions

6.23 Train Regulation

but their capacity to do this in the large areas of control usually associated with ARS may be somewhat limited.

However a balance must be struck and Train Operators should work closely with their NR counterparts to ensure signallers understand that regulating decisions must now consider all the PPM implications as well as the need to minimise delay.

It is important to make sure that signallers understand that they have the authority to make routine regulating decisions. Such decisions are often made under pressure and the result is not always perfect but signallers must feel that they can make decisions in good faith without the risk of being criticised for trying to get it right. Similarly controllers must understand that they have the power to direct signallers where a key regulating decision must be taken (although in reality this is often a source of friction).

When a late running train cannot meet its PPM target, priority may be better given to other services that can. Reducing the lateness at destination of an InterCity train from 20 minutes to 15 minutes at the expense of three local services not achieving PPM might not be acceptable. Equally, delaying three local services so that they each arrive four minutes late to allow an InterCity service to recover from 15 late to nine late probably is desirable.

Long distance services can pose particular difficulties. A loss of path early in the journey can be difficult to recover and can result in further delays en route. For long distance services it is appropriate to decide what positive interventions can be made to recover right time running during the journey. The PPM Intervention Policies used for long distance operators exemplify this.

A fundamental industry issue is that effective regulation is currently hindered by the nature of the train classification system. About 20,000 trains per day are class 1 and 2 services. The remaining 3,000 trains per day are spread across the other 8 train classes. Traditionally class 1 trains were obviously express services but this is no longer the case and it is much more difficult for signallers to use the train headcode to determine train speed and sectional running times. Many attempts have been made to make better use of the train classifications but this is an area where achieving an industry consensus appears almost impossible. Change is also made more difficult by the number of systems and planning rules involved.

Train Operators must therefore face the practical issues involved and work with NR to provide helpful examples and guidance.

Running a Railway

Key actions for operators should include:-
- Train Operators should agree clear guidance with Network Rail and this must be made available to signallers.
- Monitoring of movements when in signalboxes and controls – ask questions if you see doubtful moves. Similarly monitor when you are travelling.
- Make sure that signallers and controllers take early action to control the spread of delay. A good early regulating decision can prevent significant knock on delay.
- Check that the Train Regulation Policy documents are available in signal boxes - certain trains will be obvious 'peak killers' and will need specific instructions on how to be regulated if things go wrong.
- Ensuring that best use is made of the recovery time and public differential built into the timetable.

Tips

Above all make clear your requirements - signallers and controllers will often have difficult decisions to make in a very short space of time.

Accept that train regulation is not entirely mechanistic - signallers will need to exert judgement and will sometimes make mistakes. It is important that signallers feel empowered to take regulating decisions: the alternative is a lack of action. On the other hand controllers must have the authority to direct (not just ask) where required.

Do not fudge the issues. Managing for PPM is sometimes at odds with the minimisation of overall delay.

Other relevant/useful documents:-
– Train Regulation Policies Railway Operational Code Section from the Network Rail website (www.networkrail.co.uk)

6.24 Signaller Management

INTRODUCTION

The role of the signallers' line manager has been called many things over the years, Inspectors, Movements Managers, Production or Performance Managers, Signalling or Signaller Managers, Local Operations Managers to name a few going back through the years.

Whatever the job title, managing signallers is a job that requires a multi skilled manager and operator. It is also a role that can vary considerably based on the geography of the location and the type of train operations taking place.

There is no pre-requisite to have been a signaller for many years. It can help, but can also be a hindrance in equal measure. Leading people is a privilege and your actions can have a profound effect on an individual, team, and organisation. The standards you display are often the standards you get back, so leading by example, being role model in terms of behaviour, and attitude, is at the heart of any manager's role.

KEY ISSUES

Operational understanding
Whatever a manager's experience, the need to understand the operational practices relating to the role of a signaller in a management area is vital. This can be learned by gaining a good understanding of the area, equipment, instructions and regulations. This can only be achieved by rolling your sleeves up and spending time with your team in the signalling locations. Passing competent for the location is an appropriate objective and in many cases it is essential.

This serves two purposes; it shows your willingness to learn about the challenges the team faces on a daily basis, but it will also enable you to gain an excellent operational understanding of your area. The more knowledge you gain, the better your understanding of the bigger picture, and how you can overcome, or deal with, operational incidents. Your credibility amongst the people you lead will also improve. As the manager you should strive to understand the operation better than anyone else

Competence
The role of the manager in the competence management of signallers is vital, both for individuals and the industry as a whole. Generally a competence process follows a recurring cycle over a set period of time, involving a variety

Running a Railway

of assessment methods such as:
- Computer based simulation.
- Knowledge testing (questions and answers).
- Observational assessment.
- Self-assessment by the signaller.

It is important to remember that people have different styles of learning. For example some staff are uncomfortable using computer based assessment processes, and they may require a fair degree of support in this task. Others become particularly nervous whilst being observed. The role of the assessor is to recognise how to get the best from each person, and then to develop that individual to their full potential whilst ensuring that they are fully aware of their strengths and weaknesses.

A process for documenting the results, including any development needed, will be detailed in processes covering the administering of the competence process. They are also a record of how a signaller has developed and grown into the role over time, and as such should carefully recorded and maintained. Much of it is now maintained electronically, and therefore archived for significant periods of time.

Processes and Practices

To some extent bureaucracy is an unavoidable consequence of managing a safety critical industry, although clearly it should not prevent the manager from actually managing. There is no easy way to deal with this, other than hard work and organisation, it comes with the territory of being a manager in any organisation.

But there are other things that fall within this category, that a manager needs to be aware of that are little more subtle, and not something that is conventionally available for a manager to learn.

For example the principles of rostering of staff in a given area or location can be contained within a national agreement, with an additional local variation, agreed years ago with the trade union. Unless a manager gets to grips with all the agreements, staff may be quick to exploit a lack of knowledge in this area. This could lead to an increased cost to cover locations, as more overtime is needed to cover turns of duty. As a line manager for signallers, you own the financial budget so you need to understand how this is constructed.

There are ways to exploit any rostering system, and it is important that a manager knows what they are, and ensures they have an overview of what is going on. There is a financial implication to this, but there could be a safety one also. Signallers may think that swapping shifts with a colleague, for example, swapping their late turn for an early to attend something without taking an annual leave day does not matter if they are both in agreement. However, if that means someone attending work with a lack of proper rest, then there may well be a safety implication to their actions.

Managers who lead teams of operational response staff, as well as signallers, always have a dilemma in that these individuals are often out of sight for much of the time, rather than in plain view at a location. A manager should be aware of what these teams and individuals do on a daily basis.

Using railway vehicles for non-railway use such as giving lifts to friend or family members for example may appear to be minor violations. But if they were to be involved in an accident then the passenger is not insured, and it would be argued that vehicle was not being used for business purposes. Frequent visits to signal boxes outside normal working hours will ensure that you keep in touch with what is going on and will earn the respect of your staff.

Investigations

Investigating mistakes or errors at work, in the form of local or formal investigations requires you to establish the facts of an incident. It is important to remember in this instance your primarily role is to get to the bottom of why an incident happened so that you can prevent it happening again. Additionally this may help to ensure the person involved recognises what they need to address to improve, and latterly how the wider signaller community can benefit by understanding how an incident occurred and why, and thus prevent a re-occurrence.

Delays

A key area of signaller management is managing regulating performance. No signaller likes to have a delay attributed to them (these are designated as 0 codes) and even less so when they see the reactionary delay which can arise. "0 Code" management is all about detail, spotting trends and trying to eliminate them. This is because this key performance indicator usually consists of relatively large numbers of incidents with small minutes. It should be possible to follow up every delay with the individual concerned – you should expect good signallers to identify what they did wrong and have worked out what they would do differently next time. Look for trends in the delays that occur:

- Same signallers?
- Same location?
- Same trains?

You may identify underlying issues which need resolution.

Running a Railway

It is important to remember that "0 Codes" are only one aspect of your signallers' regulating performance. A key aspect of the signaller's role is regulating to mitigate the effect of any incident. How successfully they perform this task will have a huge impact on overall performance but it also brings with it the opportunity for "management by hindsight" in which numerous "experts" provide you with opinion on what your team should have done differently!

It is vital that you review regulating performance post-event so that the team learns lessons and the signallers involved in the incident benefit from being involved in the review rather than simply being subjected to unwanted feedback. There is always an element of judgement-call in this area so set yourself up a standard process so that your signallers can be involved and know what to expect.

Because this is an area of individual performance, if handled incorrectly you can do more harm than good. Do not use that as a reason for not tackling the issues.

FINALLY

Leading signallers is undeniably challenging, the workload, the flexibility required, and the operational and people skills needed. However as with most key operational roles the rewards can be immense - meeting and beating targets, working as a team and being recognised for a consistent professional approach. All these aspects make a difficult job worthwhile.

Tips

Get to know your signalling areas of control and pass competent to work the panels and boxes.

Know your people and adopt a clear straight-forward approach to managing.

Signallers do have a difficult job when disruption occurs – ensure your contingency plans are realistic.

Good regulation is a skill that has to be developed – encourage your signallers and recognise the positives.

6.25 Signal Box Visits

BACKGROUND

Signal box visits are an important means of providing assurance and exercising due diligence as part of the safety management process.

Network Rail has documented processes for managing this aspect of signaller management as it is vital for;
- Managing staff competence.
- Checking that safe working procedures are being followed.
- Understanding local issues that may need resolution.
- Keeping in touch with staff on a regular basis.

Over and above this, signal box visits can be a very effective way of understanding the dynamics of your railway and many of the current operational issues. You will get the Signallers' views of what is wrong and what could be better.

Only undertake a signal box visit if you are fully authorised to do so or when invited.

ISSUES

The golden rule of the visit is to be aware of the signaller's task and the operating environment and not be afraid of commenting on issues such as regulating or panel displays. It is not the place to have a cosy unstructured chat at the expense of vigilance and concentration. When undertaking an ad hoc visit always:-
- Introduce yourself and show your identification when requested.
- Request entry and explain the reason for the visit. The signaller will usually be delighted to have company but remember the courtesy of asking, not assuming.
- Be sensitive to the signaller's preferences – it is his cabin – if he does not want to chat that is his prerogative (but silence never usually lasts long).
- Adhere absolutely to signal box protocols such as turning off mobile phones, do not obstruct equipment and indications.
- Be attuned to the signaller's task – there are ways of commenting on issues without appearing too overbearing. Make a point of saying that you will temporarily cease the conversation when the signaller needs to undertake specific activities such as take a call, react to a problem or concentrate on a particular activity such as observing a CCTV crossing to check that it is clear before clearing signals.

Running a Railway

- Be mindful of topics that could distract the signaller and steer clear.
- Listen to what the signaller says – over time regular visits can be a very rich source of information concerning a range of issues including industrial relations. The old adage about "two ears and one mouth" is very appropriate here.
- Always be prepared to help out when things go wrong subject to your own competence or if necessary take charge.
- Do not be afraid to deal currently with interface issues with other companies or functions that arise during your visit. Unresolved equipment defects, interaction with shunters or drivers – can often be quickly tackled with a single, appropriate phone call.
- Tackle any issues with the signaller's performance at the time – you do not need to be a Signalling Inspector to spot poor technique, or infringements of rules and regulations. Provide details to their Local Operations Manager and check follow-up.
- Be courteous – polite and professional – always obey prevailing instructions to the letter.
- Always thank the signaller when you leave.
- If you have promised to follow up on something for the signaller, do so and do so promptly. A personalised response to him – even if you have not been able to fix his problem - within a couple of days, will earn huge respect and goodwill. Do not forget to brief or advise his immediate manager of your actions.

Remember that the dynamics in a single-manned location are completely different to those of a Signalling Centre.

Tips

You will really get to know your signallers by undertaking routine ad hoc visits and the amount of information you will pick up is amazing. Signal boxes can be a bit like confessionals - people tend to talk.

Never let discussions cause distraction, and always be aware of the operating environment. Engaging a signaller in animated discussion when they are dealing with a problem or task that requires concentration is foolish.

Signalbox visits will pay dividends but remember the signallers will also be checking your behaviour and, whilst it might not be apparent, listening to everything you say.

6.26 Train Driving Operations

BACKGROUND

Apart from a few specific automatic examples train driving is a core part of running the railway. As such, getting train driving right is absolutely crucial for a safe and punctual railway operation.

It is the importance of the activity of train driving which has been responsible for the aura of elitism around driving. The significant amount of learning required to achieve competence (and within Great Britain also perhaps the deliberate activities of ASLE&F) have also contributed to this view. Train driving is certainly a highly responsible and skilled job. However, the fundamentals of driving are relatively simple; obeying the signals displayed, complying with speed restrictions and stopping at the booked stations are the fundamentals. In fact, successful train driving is largely a product of particular personal behaviours which reduce the risk of a distraction or a mistake rather than just years of accumulated technical knowledge and experience.

A normal driving shift is between six and twelve hours per day. Unless the driver is 'spare' or 'as required' his activities for the day will be very closely specified in his diagram. This will include a specific amount of time for signing on duty, reading relevant notices, walking to the train and preparing it if necessary. Journeys over the day will be specified along with personal needs breaks (PNBs) in line with the agreed diagramming arrangements.

Inevitably drivers spend much of their time at work alone. However, meaningful contact with drivers is very important. Managers must ensure that they have a good working relationship with their staff and that they understand the issues facing drivers on a daily basis. Equally, time spent with a driver is an opportunity to check and improve competence and pass on advice and good practice.

KEY ISSUES

A Typical Day for a Driver
A TOC driver's activities are closely specified in the diagram he is working that day. An example diagram follows. Freight driver's activities will vary slightly from the example discussed here, but the broad principles are the same.

Running a Railway

```
Diagram              Activity  Train Working  Arr       Dep       WTT    StopCode  Route    Unit    DOO
LTP    BE   43
       DVR           PASS      B Stort                  21.47     2S67                      79
On     21.37                   Cheshunt       22.16
Off    06.19         MOB       Cheshunt       (22.23)   22.31     2D67   4001      Sbury    108
Hrs    8:42                    Liv St         23.09     23.30     2U96   0403               108
                               Enfield T      00.02     00+15     5U51                      108
Days FSX                       London Fd      00+33     00+40     5T53                      108
From 12/12/2011      BRTS      ChngfdCES      01+02
To   19/07/2012      TAXI      Chingford                01.30
                               Ilf EMUD       01.50
                     PU        Ilf EMUD                 (04+42)   5H00                      31\32
                     PNB
                     UP        Ilf EMUD                 04+42     5H00                      31\32
                               Liv St         05+03     05.28     2H00   0807      Lea V    32\31
                               B Stort        06.14     (06.14)
                     RELD      by CA 33       at 06.14

                     Taxi also conveys BE.45 BE.46
```

The example shows a diagram worked by a Bishop's Stortford Driver. This is Bishop's Stortford diagram 43. This diagram only applies on Mondays to Thursdays (FSX = excluding Friday and Saturday). This diagram is part of the Long Term Plan (LTP).

The driver signs on at 2137hrs and signs off at 0619hrs, a total diagram length of 8 hours and 42minutes.

The driver's first activity will be to sign on for duty, collecting his schedule card and reading any late notices that are displayed in the late notice case. These will be safety related items that he must know before driving his train. Examples include emergency speed restrictions. This activity is not shown specifically on the diagram, but a time allowance is made for it. The driver is then booked to travel as a passenger on 2S67 arriving at Cheshunt at 2216hrs. The driver is then required to mobilise the train for 2D67 (MOB). This means he will liven up the cab and make it ready for service. In this case there is no need to formally prepare the unit by thoroughly checking all the train safety systems. This will have been done by another driver earlier in the day.

The stop code information shows the code that the driver must enter into the train passenger information system to create the correct on train announcements. This code is unique to the particular stopping pattern for the 2231 service from Cheshunt to Liverpool Street.

The information in the unit column tells the driver the train formation. The numbers 108 relate to the unit diagram for the train he is driving. This tells the driver that he has a train formed of one 315 unit. His train is therefore four cars in length. Longer trains would be shown with multiple unit diagrams against the train e.g. 31/32 lower down the diagram represents a 2 unit train of eight cars.

After arriving at Liverpool Street the driver makes a further journey to Enfield. He then takes the train empty to Chingford sidings via London Fields. The class 5 train reporting number (5U51/5T53) denotes the train as a set of empty coaches. At Chingford the train is secured or berthed (BRTS).

The driver is then required to take a taxi to Ilford EMU depot. He is required to carry out duties there, but because the train service has stopped for the night a taxi is the only viable means of transport. At the diagramming stage the train planners will have tried to identify a way of avoiding the use of a taxi by diagramming differently, but in this case there is no alternative although they have ensured that the taxi conveys three drivers to reduce cost. Note that the driver is reminded of this so that he does not allow the taxi to depart without his colleagues on board!

At Ilford depot the driver is required to prepare an eight car train for service. This involves a thorough check of the safety systems on the train e.g. AWS, DRA, TIS, doors, DSD, PA. Preparation checks are normally undertaken in depots and sidings where the driver can walk round the train easily, although some preparation checks are carried out in station platforms. Preparation is normally carried out once per day on each unit.

After preparing the train the driver has a personal needs break (PNB). Facilities will be provided at Ilford depot to allow him to do this such as toilets and basic cooking facilities. These facilities are normally agreed between management and union representatives. Note that the driver is diagrammed to prepare the unit for service before taking his PNB even though the unit is not required for service immediately. This is a sensible bit of diagramming which allows time for fleet staff to fix any faults that the driver identifies on the unit before it needs to depart.

The driver takes the prepared units (UP reminds him that the units are already prepared) as empty coaches to Liverpool Street (5H00) and then drives the 0528 service from Liverpool Street to Cambridge (2H00). He is relieved by another driver (Cambridge 33 diagram) at Bishop's Stortford where his diagram finishes.

The driver will be provided with further information about the journeys that he drives on his schedule card. This includes the information shown on his diagram with the addition of the station stops he is required to make on the journeys. In some cases schedule cards are provided for the long term timetable as a book which is issued to drivers twice per year. However in many cases schedule cards are now produced daily to reflect short term changes in the timetable. The driver will collect the relevant card when he signs on duty.

It will be seen that the driver's activities are closely defined by the diagram he is working that day. Within each of the journeys he undertakes he will need to respond correctly to the signals displayed, comply with speed restrictions, ensure he stops at the right stations in the right location on the platform and keep to time throughout the journey. The need to be both accurate and timely

Running a Railway

characterise the driver's role.

Selection

Selection of Train Drivers is one of the few roles within the industry that is co-ordinated by a Rail Industry Standard. RIS-3751-TOM specifies a number of physical attributes and mental abilities (e.g. concentration, communication, trainability) that must be tested for when recruiting a new driver. Testing includes a mixture of criteria based interviews and psychometric tests.

Selection tests are designed to ensure that only candidates who have the necessary attributes to be a successful driver will pass on to the training stage. The expenditure involved in testing reflects the fact that there is even more significant cost in training. Minimising the drop-out rate during training is important for cost reasons.

Training

Driver training has traditionally followed this format:
1. Basic introduction to the railway and the role of the Driver including PTS.
2. Actual experience in a driving cab in service trains.
3. Rules and regulations.
4. Principles of route learning.
5. Traction training.
6. Hands on experience with a trainer.
7. Hands on experience with an instructor rotating round rostered turns of duty.
8. Final assessment of competence once sufficient experienced has been gained.
9. Additional route learning as required.

Part 4 covers the principles of route learning. Drivers must have an understanding of the route over which they are driving so that they are able to handle the train appropriately. Drivers are firstly trained to understand what knowledge needs to be gained, what hazards exist and what information is available to assist with learning. The actual route learning takes place as part of section 6, 7 and 9.

The accumulation of experience in part 8 is normally over a core route which covers a significant part of the roster that the driver will eventually work, but is not too complex for a newly qualified driver to get to grips with.

Train Operators are beginning to move away from the traditional training format and are beginning to develop more bespoke courses that meet the specific requirements of the company. In many cases simulators are now integrated into the training programme from the start. Where drivers initially qualify only to work in depot areas courses are modified accordingly.

The time taken to train a mainline qualified train driver can vary from between

6 months and 18 months depending on the complexity of routes required.

RSSB produce a Good Practice Guide to Train Driver Training which is available on the RSSB website www.rssb.co.uk.

Competence Assessment

Drivers are subject to robust competence assessment processes. Competence assessment provides assurance of a consistent performance against required standards.

An important aspect of train driver assessment is to provide assurance that the driver is performing at the required standard when unsupervised. Although the bulk of assessments are usually carried out through driving cab assessments frequent use is made of on-board and remote data recorder information and unannounced assessments. Driver and signaller communication is an important aspect that can be monitored using voice data recordings. For customer service related activities unannounced monitoring is particularly important. For example compliance with announcing standards can only really be measured in an unannounced way on trains in service. Make sure you consider how to get the most out of this form of assessment.

Increasingly simulators are being used to provide additional training and assessment on out of course situations.

Competence cycles are generally two or three years long.

Arrangements for dealing with sub-standard competence are normally more formalised than other operational roles. Traditionally operational incidents which were the responsibility of the driver such as SPADs or station overruns resulted in points being added to the driver's licence. Any points on the licence became expired after a certain period of time. A given number of points could result in the driver being removed from driving duties. Additional assessment activities were normally invoked when a driver's risk profile increased.

In recent years there has been a move away from a points based competence development system. Modern Competence Development Programmes (CDP) or Driver's Competence Development programmes (DCD) focus on identifying development required to regain competence after an operational incident. Both driver and manager must sign up to a programme of competence development activities and assessment. The length of a development plan will be based on the seriousness of the incident and the previous history of the driver. Where it is no longer possible to identify development activities to restore competence then there are formal arrangements to remove the driver from driving duties. In some TOCs this involves union representatives sitting on a panel with managers to decide whether removal is justified.

Running a Railway

What Does Good Look Like?

All Train Operators make a statement of what they expect from drivers through a Professional Driving Policy document. Although related, this is not the same as a competence standard. Early versions of these documents focussed largely on 'defensive driving'. This is a style of driving involving:

- Earlier braking for caution aspects and red signals.
- Slower approach to station stops.
- Stopping further away from red signals.

Professional Driving Policies are now much more developed and now usually include the following as a minimum:

The standards of professionalism expected from drivers e.g.:

- Being adequately prepared for duty. Managing home life to provide the right basis for good performance at work: getting adequate rest, eating well, allowing time to get to work punctually.
- Preparing for the shift and the journey. Allowing time to complete preparation duties and not rushing. Being fully aware of information like stopping patterns prior to each journey.
- Maintaining a tidy working environment including the driving cab. Compliance with the company mobile phone policy.
- Wearing full uniform.
- Considering the needs of the customer.
- Taking responsibility for personal development. Keeping up to date with rules and regulations and remaining competent.

Good practice techniques to avoid errors and operational incidents e.g.:

- Defensive driving principles e.g. 20mph 200yds from the signal and stop 20yds from the signal (20 x 20 Rule).
- Verbalising signal aspects (Press and Call).
- Risk Triggered Commentary Driving. This technique helps to focus attention during times of significant distraction.
- Highlighting station stops on schedule cards.

Guidance on how to carry out instructions in the Rule Book e.g.:

- How and where to apply the Driver's Reminder Appliance (DRA).
- How to undertake the role of the Route Conductor.

There is a significant range in the level of performance amongst drivers. Many drivers do have operational incidents, and some drivers fail to retain their licence. However, there are drivers who have incident free driving careers and there are many who have been driving for more than 15 years without any incident. Experienced, incident free drivers normally say that the secret of their success is that they are always prepared and they never allow themselves to be rushed.

Management of Train Driving Operations

Some Train Operators have separated the line management and competence assessment activities of train driving management. Other TOCs have kept the two activities together in a single role, often titled a Driver Manager. Where the roles are combined, managing the competence assessment system will frequently take up a significant portion of a manager's time.

However, in common with many operational roles it is important to make sure you take time to build up a good working relationship with your drivers. A relationship based entirely around competence assessment is unlikely to be truly productive. Take every opportunity to spend time with drivers in their working environment: at depots, but particularly in driving cabs. You will learn all sort of useful information about how the railway is operating.

Many depots are now unsupervised and drivers sign on remotely. In some ways this is a positive development as it has made drivers take responsibility for their own work activities at the depot. On the other hand it has reduced the amount of routine supervisory contact time.

Time spent with drivers is an important chance to understand personal issues relevant to the driver. Where there is a significant issue at home that might prevent a driver from being adequately prepared for duty or could cause a significant distraction it is important that the line manager helps the driver to manage the risk. Companies have formal care and support arrangements for staff. The risk posed by a distracted driver make these arrangements even more important. In some cases this may result in temporary removal from driving.

Fatalities are a particular occupational hazard for train drivers. Drivers react in different ways to the experience, but clear advice is that early support aides a quick return to work. Although some drivers do take many weeks off work following a fatality, long periods off work are not considered good for long term recovery from such incidents. Make sure you support drivers involved in such incidents and use company counselling facilities where necessary.

Managers can also influence the safety and performance of Train Driving Operations through careful management of diagrammed work, rosters and links (see the separate Section for more details). This is always a balancing act between providing sufficient resource so that the diagrams and rosters deliver high performance without waste. Poorly diagrammed work and poorly

Running a Railway

designed rosters are also a potential source of fatigue which can result in poor operational safety.

Train driving is a crucial part of the railway operation.

Tips

The management of train driving operations requires very robust management processes. The key to success comes from application of professional behaviours rather than in depth technical knowledge.

Management of distraction and never rushing are paramount attributes for a manager.

Spend as much time talking to drivers as you can. It will help you to understand their issues and it will give you a chance to increase their engagement and understanding.

6.27 Train Crew Management

BACKGROUND

In theory managing train crew should not be any different to managing any other groups of staff, but in practice there are a number of aspects, which make train crew – and particularly Driver Management – a specialist role.

- Train crew depots have large concentrations of staff, working for much of the time in largely solitary conditions.
- The workforce is highly unionised.
- Drivers do regard themselves as something of an elite, partly because of the length of training, the specialist requirements of the role, and the culture and history associated with 'the footplate'.
- Working arrangements (diagrams, rosters and links) are very structured and relatively inflexible in the short term.
- Terms and conditions are both prescriptive and complex.
- The work performed by train crew is safety critical and standards of discipline in application are exacting.
- The amount of exposure that individuals get to management is very small – therefore a mess room culture can develop which is often hostile and resistant to management influence at a collective, if not an individual, level.

6.27 Train Crew Management

A major part of traincrew management is about the management of links and rosters. Refer to the Section in section 5.3 for more information on this subject.

MANAGING A TRAIN CREW DEPOT

One of the challenges is to bring personalised management and supervision to a very impersonal working environment.

You do not have to have been a driver, but you do need to appreciate the concerns and the situations that drivers experience, and demonstrate a willingness to engage with the staff both individually and collectively. You need empathy.

Being seen to tackle issues and concerns – not necessarily those that are raised by staff representatives – is important. Equally important is to be honest with staff over what can and cannot be done. Similarly, promising and not delivering should be avoided at all costs if you value your credibility.

Humility is a much undervalued virtue in all fields of management and it is particularly useful when dealing with train crews. Humility should not be regarded as a sign of weakness – there is no inconsistency or conflict between firm and fair management, and humility. Similarly, common courtesy is always important and can have a surprisingly high value with these and all groups of staff; "May I ride with you?"; "May I accompany your ticket check?" Please and Thank You will work wonders.

Devote time and energy to the relationship with train crew supervisors and managers. They are your day to day eyes and ears, are usually recruited from the train crew ranks because of the need for specialist knowledge and often have the greatest difficulty in crossing the divide between staff and management behaviours and attitudes. Helping these individuals make the transition is really important, will help to avoid them 'staying or going native' (in the vernacular 'drivers in suits'), and will have a positively beneficial impact on standards, managerial communication and the quality of the managerial message handed down to crews. Many are first class managers – some others will need your assistance and that of their peers. However your best driver may not make your best manager – the skills are very different.

Generally, the quantum of supervision applied to train crew is now greater than it has ever been. This has had a beneficial impact on standards and discipline at a time when substantial numbers of new recruits have been flowing into the train crew grades.

Industrial Relations are a critical issue with train crew however well managers think they interact with staff representatives. The representatives are almost

Running a Railway

always experienced hands with a far more detailed working knowledge of the agreements, terms and conditions than management. Very often that knowledge will be extensive as the individuals may have had a key part to play in negotiating them. Every train crew council or local committee will have one or two articulate, forthright, very experienced and charismatic representatives who are key personalities in the depot, and have well honed and practised negotiation skills. Trade Unions, such as ASLE&F have developed extremely high quality training courses for representatives in recent years, delivered in university facilities, and which are almost always better than the training offered to managers!

Keeping good records of meetings is the best way of reclaiming some of the initiative in dealing with staff representatives. Well documented agreements and good record keeping will help you defend your position in the future.

Consequently, managing this interface is particularly challenging, especially for newly appointed, young or inexperienced operations managers. Putting into practice the guidance in this section, and consistently applying the Golden Rules set out in the Tips section, will go a long way towards establishing such a manager with the representatives. Respect will be earned and credibility established.

Above all avoid macho management – 'show who's the boss' is an extremely risky line to take, and is not for the inexperienced manager. It always has consequences, one of which is usually abject failure.

If you have an issue you want to press or pursue with a degree of vigour, be sure of your ground, do your homework, and determine your tactics in advance. Be clear about what you want to achieve, and what your minimum/default position is – therefore, have a Plan B, and probably also a Plan C. Never be afraid to adjourn a difficult meeting to get counsel from colleagues, peers or your superiors.

When a result is achieved, try and ensure that the staff side has the ability to sell the outcome – or at least defend the result – amongst the workforce.

Control costs through careful management of availability, utilisation, spare cover and overtime or RD working (RDW). Never get into a position where a reliance on RDW and overtime has resulted in a roster being filled on an ad-hoc manual basis. This is sometimes referred to as 'black ink time'. Such a failure to agree will see crews advised by their representatives to attend and work to their link time rather than the actual rostered time. This has the potential to cause massive disruption as intended, until the staff side have an offer that they feel befits their demands.

Beware the culture developing whereby there is an expectation that being

6.27 Train Crew Management

'spare' means the spare staff do not do any work or staff are spare to allow their colleagues an early finishing time, once set precedents cannot be unset. You are the manager and should act as such.

Finally train crew industrial relations is an area where mentoring of junior and inexperienced managers is vital. When such staff are appointed, always consider how best to provide such support.

Tips

The Golden Rules of effective train crew management are:-
- Engage with individuals in their place of work, as much as possible - on trains, in mess rooms, in the Depot Office. The guidance in the Handbook on cab riding will be useful in this respect.
- Build a strong relationship with staff representatives, but do not lose sight of managerial objectives.
- Involve staff representatives in issues that concern them, for example, discipline and grievance procedures concerning one of their colleagues. A quiet word with a representative concerning the conduct of driver or guard can often reap better rewards than hauling them into the office. It helps build the trusting relationship you need with your staff representatives and gives both credibility and humility to your management style.
- Be wary of any staff side proposal offered up as a benefit to the company or to management - it rarely, if ever, will be.
- Never agree to anything for which you do not fully understand the consequences or implications. Be very wary of anything that you cannot quantify in detail If in doubt, seek guidance or counsel.
- Keep immaculate records of discussion with staff representatives. Make sure any agreement is correctly documented and the records are kept safe. Best practice is to have minutes in an electronic form that can be searched. You can even have old paper versions scanned so that they are searchable.
- Enforce standards firmly, fairly and consistently.
- Maintain managerial control of the roster, its links and any changes to them.
- Maintain managerial control of traction and route learning and refreshing.
- Maintain full complements of staff through effective long term manpower planning.

Running a Railway

- Control costs through careful management of availability, utilisation, spare cover and overtime or RD working (RDW).
- Use your Train Crew Supervisors - but do not overload them - they are a vital tool in train crew management.

6.28 Cab Rides

BACKGROUND

Cab rides are an important component of Train Operator safety management and due diligence arrangements. Specifications for riding with drivers as part of the driver management and competence assessment arrangements will be detailed in the Safety Management System (or equivalent).

Over and above this, cab rides can be a very effective way of understanding the dynamics of your railway and many of the current operational issues. You will get the drivers' views of what is wrong and gain a valuable insight into a range of issues.

Cab pass requirements governing access to cabs are generally covered by a company standard in each Train Operator's safety arrangements.

Only undertake a cab ride if you are fully authorised to do so.

ISSUES

The golden rule of cab rides is to be aware of the driving task and the operating environment and not be afraid of commenting on issues such as restrictive signal aspects. It is not the place to have a cosy unstructured chat at the expense of vigilance and concentration. When undertaking an ad-hoc cab ride always:-

6.28 Cab Rides

- Introduce yourself and show your cab pass in plenty of time before train departure when possible.
- Request entry and explain reason for ride. Check that the driver is not categorised as High Risk. A driver will usually be pleased to have company but remember the protocol of asking, not assuming.
- Be sensitive to the driver's preferences – it is his cab – if he does not want to chat that is his prerogative but silence never usually lasts long.
- Adhere absolutely to cab protocols e.g. turn off mobile phone – have correct attire such as High Visibility Vest (HVV).
- Be attuned to the driving task – there are ways of commenting on issues such as restrictive signal aspects without appearing too overbearing. Make a point of saying that you will temporarily cease the conversation when the driver is running under restrictive signal aspects, braking for a speed restriction or station call.
- Be mindful of contentious topics that could distract the driver and steer clear.
- Listen to what the driver says – over time regular cab rides can be a very rich source of information concerning a range of issues including industrial relations. The old adage about "you have two ears, two eyes and one mouth – use them in those proportions" is very appropriate here.
- Always be prepared to help out or if necessary take charge when things go wrong subject to your own competence.
- Deal promptly with issues involving other companies or functions that arise during your cab ride. Unresolved defects on the unit or loco, regulating issues with NR etc. – things that irritate drivers immensely – can often be quickly defused with a single, appropriate phone call although not whilst in the cab.
- Tackle any issues with the driver's performance at the time – you do not need to be a Driver Instructor to spot poor technique, or infringements of rules and regulations. Provide subsequent details to their Driver Manager and check for follow-up.
- Be courteous, polite and professional – always obey prevailing instructions to the letter. Like asking unauthorised people in the cab such as the guard to leave. Follow such transgressions up.
- Always thank the driver when you leave.
- If you have promised to follow up on something for the driver, do so and do so promptly. A personalised response to him or her – even if you have not been able to fix their problem - within a couple of days, will earn huge respect and goodwill. Do not forget to brief or advise his immediate manager of your actions.

Running a Railway

Tips

You will really get to know your drivers by undertaking routine ad hoc cab rides and the amount of information you will pick up is amazing. Driving cabs can be a bit like confessionals - people tend to talk.

If you live on the patch and commute via your company's services (always a good thing), then your journeys to and from work can result in you getting to know a high proportion of your drivers at a particular depot or group of depots. And you get to really know the infrastructure you are travelling over too.

Never let discussions cause distraction, and always be aware of the operating environment. Engaging a driver in animated discussion when approaching a station stop, a restrictive signal aspect or buffer stops is foolish.

Ad hoc cab rides will pay dividends and broaden your understanding of the railway.

6.29 TOC Short Term Planning

This section covers the management of short term aspects of planning – timetabling, short term diagramming, daily and weekly rosters, and manipulation of resources to fit the various short term planning scenarios and requirements.

Resource Planning usually applies to units or train sets and train crews. However the principles can and should be applied to any finite TOC resource that is critical to Train Service Delivery.

ISSUES

The key principles involved are:-
- Have a clear commercial remit for the plan to be written.
- Understand clearly what resources are available.
- Ensure that clear agreed definitions are in place for all critical activities such as what constitutes an available unit – available at any location, available at the right place.

6.29 TOC Short Term Planning

- Agree fundamental requirements and unacceptable practices such as repetitive sub-standard turn rounds which are not separately codified in ROTP.
- Produce mitigation plans which list and address any 'rule breaks.'
- Ensure suppliers physically sign-off agreed plans. Ownership is all.
- Consult all affected and involved delivery personnel and review feedback.
- Monitor production of next level plans – ECS timings, platform plans etc.
- Test and even simulate more complex aspects of the plan in advance, for example, intense platform working at terminus locations.
- Monitor against the plan requirements.
- Apply 'Plan-Do-Review' principles and fine-tune the plans in a structured way as part of the continuous improvement process.

Short term plans are most frequently written to deal with engineering work or restricted access to the infrastructure. They can also be required to deal with short term unavailability of rolling stock or traincrew resources.

Obtaining a clear remit for the plan is critically important. Identifying likely demand for services can be difficult unless the plan has been operated in similar circumstances before. What effect will the engineering work or the need to use replacement buses have on passenger demand? With restricted access to the infrastructure or reliance on buses there may be little opportunity to correct under capacity on the day. On the other hand provision of too much capacity is wasteful. A good database of load monitoring data from previous short term plans can be invaluable.

Where a greater degree of flexibility and innovation by NR would improve short term plans for both customers and TOC resource utilisation, press hard for it. Opening up diversionary routes, utilising single line working or changing the times of engineering possessions can be win-win opportunities. An extra platform at the location where trains terminate can make a big difference. Devote time to reviewing such plans with your planners – the benefits will always pay back.

Use some standard rules of thumb to determine if the available resources and plans are adequate. Particularly watch arrangements where no contractual safety nets are available, for example, where staff are not contractually required to work on Sundays or where significant numbers of extra diagrams are required. Pay particular attention to the transition between timetables to ensure all aspects are covered such as from Bank Holiday back to normal weekday. Do not leave it to the Control to amend a poor trainplan – Control is there to deal with the unexpected, not to rescue an inadequate plan.

Short term plans and resource manipulation are often wasteful and inefficient. By definition, deconstructing efficient long term deployment plans will almost

Running a Railway

always produce a less optimal result. Consider the overall cost of decisions. Booking taxis to move traincrew around quickly might save diagrams, but if drivers revert to spare when their diagram is cancelled it might be better to plan more diagrams without taxis. Similarly when carrying out short term diagramming it may be better to plan sub-optimal diagrams if these fit better with the existing roster.

The efficiency of short term plans can also be limited by the time and resources available to carry out the planning. At times it is desirable to plan a bespoke timetable for each day of the week. However this will place significant pressure on the train planners and may make the end plan very complex. A simpler, but less optimised solution might be more appropriate.

Where replacement road transport is being used ensure that this aspect of the plan gets sufficient attention. Decisions on resources and timings should not be left to chance. The point of interchange between train and bus requires particular attention. Bus connections can be a source of anxiety for customers and unless managed can import significant delays.

Do not forget to tune depot and station rosters to accommodate variable weekend plans. Saturday, Sunday and Bank Holiday resources are expensive and can often be rationalised on the back of a reduced train service, both to save money and release resources to cover other commitments, such as supervision of rail replacement services.

Short term plans can invalidate contingency plans that are used for normal operation. Part of the short term planning process should be to consider how to deal with unexpected events. The possibility of engineering overruns must always be taken seriously. Consider the following:

- Can additional infrastructure be made available if required?
- In the case of an engineering overrun what infrastructure could be handed back?
- Do you have sufficient spare resources as part of the plan?
- What would happen if access to a key location was lost, for example, a train or bus interchange location or a terminus location?

Always review the success of short term plans. There are always useful lessons for the next plan.

Good resource planning and management starts with an achievable plan that balances commercial requirements with a realistic level of resource availability

Strike the right balance – don't plan to fail (a common theme in this Handbook).

Remember the 'Five Ps' – Proper Planning Prevents Poor Performance.

Tips

Planning on the basis of 100% unit availability or 2% driver sickness is patently absurd and will have obvious consequences.

If plans are rarely met, then the plan or the plan management is lacking.

Setting out some short term planning criteria and targets - not just delay minutes budget - is good practice. This will concentrate minds, and help minimise over provision which is expensive and under provision of resources which is a performance risk.

Carefully planning critical resources will ensure that any resource constraints are identified at an early stage and the likelihood of post-implementation trauma is reduced.

Remember - if you squeeze resources too hard performance will suffer and might even collapse.

6.30 Station Operations

INTRODUCTION

Stations are the 'shop window' both for the delivery of quality customer service and efficient operation of the railway. As a result of this dual role it is critical that key stations are managed effectively. Failure to do so can mean a combination of customer dissatisfaction and poor performance. On the other hand station operations are sometimes incorrectly perceived as less important than activities such as train driving or signalling. This can be a very costly mistake.

Station management is a diverse activity, but almost all of the elements have at least some implication for operations. This Section focuses on the elements most relevant to operations and therefore does not cover issues such as managing retail tenants.

Running a Railway

ISSUES

Train Despatch

The area where the station manager can have greatest impact on operational safety and performance is train despatch. Stationary trains can easily become a magnet for delays. The platform/train interface presents many opportunities for mishaps and customer accidents.

See the following Section for more detail on managing train despatch. However, the basics are:

- Make sure the method statement for despatch is appropriate for the task.
- Although the method statement must cover the risks adequately, simplicity will make it easier to implement effectively and consistently.
- Make sure the method statement is fully understood by all involved.
- Place sufficient attention on observing despatch in action. Watch staff behaviour around the platform as well as the actual process of despatch.
- Have clear rules to aid prompt departure. Make sure the train is announced clearly in advance, but consider removing CIS information before departure to prevent late runners delaying an on time departure. Make sure doors are closed in sufficient time for wheels to be moving on '00' (the exact time = zero seconds). Where necessary barrier platforms in sufficient time for the despatch process to be completed on time. Be prepared to explain to later running customers why this is necessary.
- Right time departures and station dwell time should be routinely measured by KPIs and reviewed regularly.

Platforming Arrangements – Long and Short Term Planning (LTP/STP)

In routine operation the quality of platforming arrangements will be an important influence on performance. This is particularly the case at larger terminus stations, but will also be true for locations where capacity is limited and the infrastructure is being stretched.

As with many station operation issues the best solution is often a compromise between operational requirements and customer service requirements. The ideal operational plan may not deliver the best product for the customer. Keeping a particular service group such as an airport service on dedicated platforms will make it simple for customers to understand, but can place awkward constraints on the platform graph.

Platforming arrangements are often decided towards the end of the timetabling process. Consequently it can often be difficult to make changes once problems are identified. Where additional services are being operated there may be a requirement for extra despatch staff and unless this is understood early enough there may not be time to recruit and train the additional staff. Station Managers should ensure that they engage early with timetable planners, make clear exactly what their requirements are and understand implications of timetable changes for their station.

Platforming arrangements for short term plans must take into account the possibility of crowding within the station. For example, more intensive use of particular platforms may put additional pressure on staircases etc. It is always important to get involved the short term planning process to ensure that station needs are taken into account. This is even more important where the work involved is on the station infrastructure itself as this may affect the operation of the station as well as the platforming. Passenger flow and crowding is discussed in more detail below.

Disruption Management
During disruption station operations will always come under increased pressure. Where key routes have become blocked and train services are not operating the pressure can become intense.

Having a clear plan for the overall management of the disrupted event is vital. Station managers must understand the plan and their role in it. Where there are pre prepared contingency plans it is important that these cover activities at key stations. The station manager must take the lead in tailoring the plan for his area of control. Specific issues to consider are:

- What alternative services will be running? Is this clearly understood by staff?
- How will trains be cleaned and catering replenished at terminal stations. Splash & Dash is a colloquial term for a quick turn round clean and departure preparation.
- How will any replacement bus services operate? Where will they run to? Where will they depart from? Who will control departures? Is information on the route available to hand to bus drivers who do not know the route?
- What are the additional staffing requirements for the plan?
- If the station is a 'hub station' for disruption management how will the 'satellite stations' be kept informed?
- How will the revised service be advertised to customers? Can it be displayed on CIS easily? What announcements will be made? Are posters required?
- How will information be communicated to 'meeters and greeters'?
- How will crowding be managed safely?
- Are the alternatives for customers clearly understood? For example, where tickets are being accepted on other operators' routes do staff have directions to give to customers to advise them on how to get to the relevant station or bus stop?
- Are contingency plans aligned with stations on alternative routes? If your plan involves sending customers to a nearby station will they be ready and

Running a Railway

able to accept the additional customers?

Passenger Flows/Crowding

Passenger accidents at stations are a very significant proportion of the total accident risk to passengers on the railway network. The following graph shows that 36.3 fatalities and weighted injuries a year are caused by slips, trips and falls and accidents at the platform or train interface. This is out of a total risk to passengers of 54.3 FWI per year.

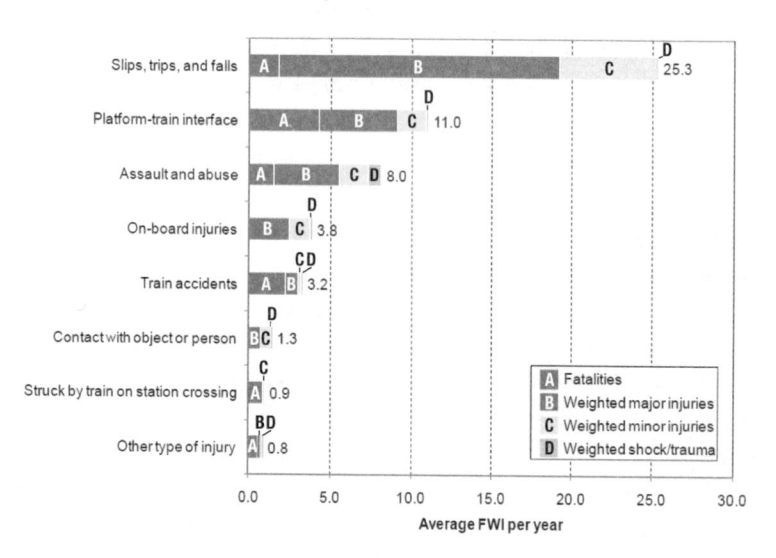

Category	Values
Slips, trips, and falls	A, B, C, D 25.3
Platform-train interface	A, B, C, D 11.0
Assault and abuse	A, B, C D 8.0
On-board injuries	B, C, D 3.8
Train accidents	A, B, C, D 3.2
Contact with object or person	B, C, D 1.3
Struck by train on station crossing	A, C 0.9
Other type of injury	A, B, D 0.8

Legend:
- A Fatalities
- B Weighted major injuries
- C Weighted minor injuries
- D Weighted shock/trauma

Average FWI per year

This proportion of risk deserves adequate attention from station managers. Despatch arrangements must be adequate to control the platform train interface risk. Stations must have specific targeted plans to reduce the risk of slips, trips and falls.

Crowding is a common issue at stations. It can be source of customer frustration for example where there are significant delays in getting through ticket barriers after exiting the train. At the more extreme end crowding can be a serious, potentially life threatening, safety issue. Although rare in the context of transport operations, station managers must consider the possibility of customers being crushed due to the uncontrolled movement of people. Increased instance of slips, trips and falls is a more likely outcome. A specific risk in stations is the possibility of customers being accidentally pushed from platform edges.

Make sure you understand the likely pinch points within the station environment and have clear actions to be taken to control the flow. Plans must be co-ordinated with the emergency services and other agencies to avoid well

6.30 Station Operations

intended acts having unintended consequences. Communication across the station and with other key contacts such as Signallers and Control must be adequate and reliable. Major event planning must be given adequate attention and resources.

Adequate station facilities are vital: stairs and escalators can be accident 'hot spots' so make sure they are in good condition and well maintained.

The materials used in platform and concourse surfaces can have a significant impact on accident likelihood: polished stone or tiles can look great but can become extremely slippery if wet.

Cleaning arrangements and practices are important and changing approach can have a significant impact. Response to liquid spills or water ingress when it rains must be planned.

Security & Emergency Management

Security management is a key activity for station managers and because stations are effectively public areas this is far more difficult to manage than at most other operational locations. The principles are covered in the Security Issues Section of this Handbook but the vigilance of staff, whether or not they are specifically undertaking security duties, is crucial. Appropriate reaction to any perceived threat is also important.

Clear plans are required to deal with the possible emergency scenarios at the station. This includes evacuations of the station for fire or bomb threat. These must be co-ordinated with other parties at the station, for example, Network Rail, BTP, TOCs, commercial tenants. In common with other emergency plans these should be exercised at sufficient frequency to ensure that staff know what to do in an emergency. Incidents should be reviewed and lessons learned included in future revisions of the plan.

A Station Incident Officer will be appointed to take command of emergency incidents at a station. This person will report to the Rail Incident Office (RIO) as part of the overall railway command structure.

Customer Information

Stations are key centres for the provision of information to customers. Despite the growth of modern technology as a means of providing information, stations still have an important role. Indeed the quality of information at stations has come under increased scrutiny since customers now consider the consistency of information between the different sources.

Information during routine operation is important, but customers place far greater emphasis on information during disruption. When things go wrong it

Running a Railway

is important to provide customers with advice on what has happened, what the alternatives are and when the issue will be resolved. However, it is at stations where the crucial information is provided to customers about specific departures. In particular the destination, stopping pattern and departing platform for each service. Despite the importance of information about the overall incident it is the quality of specific train information that will finally satisfy or annoy the customer!

During serious disruption it is important to focus on providing clear information about each departure in sufficient time for boarding. If automatic announcement systems are unable to do this then switch them off and provide manual announcements. Focus on useful information and do not get bogged down with frequent apologies that do not add anything to the quality of information. Make sure that communications with the Signallers and Control are adequate to ensure that services are known with certainty in enough time to announce and board the train.

It is also important to provide appropriate information for 'meeters and greeters'.

Once the incident has finished it may be appropriate to provide suitable explanations and apologies for the incident using the CIS or posters.

Seasonal Preparation

The most significant seasonal issue faced at stations is the increased slip, trip, fall risk in the winter. Sufficient stocks of anti-ice treatment must be available at the start of the season. There is always a balance to be drawn between wasting money holding too much stock and having enough available to cope with a prolonged cold spell. However, when there is a longer spell of cold weather further supplies will be very difficult to obtain. Clearing of snow from platforms is also a key activity.

In summer there may be a need to hold emergency water supplies for instances of stranded trains in hot weather. Higher fire risk also increases the importance of keeping station areas free from accumulations of litter.

Ticket Sales Issues

Whilst not a prime operational issue Ticket Office queuing times and the use of Ticket Vending Machines to improve the effectiveness of station operations is an important aspect of station operations.

Tips

The quality of train despatch will largely influence the safety and performance of the station. Place sufficient emphasis on it.

Do not get caught out by timetable changes that impact on station working. Engage with train planners so that they know your needs and issues.

Customer information in disruption must be a high priority, but make sure you are providing meaningful information and advice not just apologies for what has happened.

There is more to stations than operations: your station plays a key role in the local community and retail opportunities must be properly managed.

Remember that slick station operations are fundamental to good train service performance.

6.31 Train Despatch

BACKGROUND

The effective despatch of trains punctually and safely from stations and depots is a key component of good train service delivery. This role is generally the responsibility of TOCs.

Written procedures that capture the industry safety requirements, and local circumstances on each platform, with each variant of rolling stock, are essential.

The need for almost constant monitoring and supervision cannot be over emphasised. Keeping actual dwell times to plan requires a slick, ordered, safe and thoroughly professional approach. It is a classic example of the Operators task.

Running a Railway

ISSUES

This is a maximum impact task that should always be spot-on. However, it will only be so if:-

- Despatch Method Statements are fully and properly codified using the Risk Assessment process. This will take account of individual station layouts, platforms, staffing arrangements, technical equipment such as Train Ready To Start (TRTS), Close Doors (CD), Right Away (RA) and rolling stock variations and position of the guard.
- Staff are trained, assessed as competent and re-assessed periodically.
- Staff act professionally in carrying out the dispatch process.
  - They are smart and alert at all times.
  - They are ready to dispatch in good time.
  - They follow the method statement.
  - They act with sufficient urgency and care.
- Any changes to procedures or physical characteristics of stations, trains or staffing are codified promptly.
- Staff are regularly supervised and monitored, both formally using competence assessment processes and informally.

Seconds really do matter – a campaign such as 'Go on double - O' where wheels must be turning as the clock clicks over the minute and sensibly carried out dwell time reviews can pay real dividends.

- Remember the careful use of the traditional 'Acme Thunderer' whistle is still the best way to save those few extra seconds. Passengers do board more quickly with sufficient encouragement.

However as well as punctuality, safe despatch is essential. Do not let keenness to despatch result in an attempt to do so against a red signal. There should be no whistles with the signal still red – this can be a serious SPAD risk). Encouraging passengers to run for trains can also be counter-productive as it is a significant cause of slip, trip and fall injuries.

Driver-only dispatch must be of the same high standard as manned dispatch. Make sure that drivers also understand the need to depart exactly on time, closing the doors before booked departure time. Driver-only dispatch must also be carried out safely and this must be given sufficient attention in competence assessments.

Station operations and dispatch can be seen as a less glamorous and important aspect of running a railway than, say, train driving. However, dispatch activities are a considerable cause of delay and are also one of the highest risk aspects of the railway operation. It is vitally important that they are given sufficient

6.31 Train Despatch

attention. Unannounced monitoring of dispatch is an important way of identifying bad practice and raising standards.

The detailed requirements for the specified three levels are contained in the following section.

LEVEL 1 (Person undertaking Train Despatch)

Plan
- Competent in the codified despatch procedures as applied to all stock and at all platform faces. Understand signalling arrangements in relation to despatch.
- Understand role of the guard and other on train staff in relation to despatch.
- Know the connectional policy.
- Understand the reasons why it is important to start the despatch process in sufficient time to ensure wheels turning on 00.
- Knowledge of monitoring arrangements and reporting for late departures.

Do
- Ensure that the despatch process and reporting arrangements are understood and followed.
- Make sure you are on the platform in good time and in the correct place.
- Follow the Method Statement correctly.
- Act professionally with care and efficiency.
- Monitor delays and causes.

Review
- Monitor train despatch in real time and follow up problems immediately.
- Notify any persistent problems with achieving the plan.

LEVEL 2 (Local Manager of Stations)

Plan
- Ensure that a robust process is in place and adequate competent staff are available to discharge the requirements.
- Intimately understand the process.
- Knowledge and understanding of dwell times, station allowances, station contingency arrangements, connectional policy, disabled travel arrangements, policy in respect of degraded modes of operation, for example, due to platform staff shortages), train regulation issues etc.
- Knowledge of delay attribution arrangements.

Institution of Railway Operators

Running a Railway

Do
- Monitor delays and causes.
- Manage by walking about and spot check. Have the confidence to challenge non-compliance or sloppy working real time.

Review
- Owner of station specific KPIs.
- Owner of an established check and assurance and competence management programme.
- Capable of progressing changes when necessary.

LEVEL 3 (More senior Operations Manager)

Plan
- Determine who will despatch trains, whenever possible get train staff to do it (self despatch).
- Ensure that station despatch is as safe as possible and delays are as low as possible with due regard to efficiency of operation.
- Ensure adequate monitoring and management of ALL trains that call at the station you are responsible for not just your own TOC services.
- Ensure league tables of station despatch results are in daily use.

Do
- Personally observe and follow up train despatch effectiveness at every opportunity.
- Manage by walking about, workplace inspections, routine and regular spot checks, safety tours, dialogue and discussions with despatch staff.

Review
- Review key KPIs.
- Review relevant analysis at appropriate frequencies.
- Arrange benchmarking between stations and between TOCs.
- Ensure that arrangements exist to identify, evaluate and adopt if appropriate industry good practice.

Tips

A key measure of any TOC's operational robustness is the effectiveness of its train despatch arrangements.

Because train despatch is so very visible it provides a good indicator of how effective the operations team are in delivering good performance and safe management at the train and platform interface. Dispatchers that look and act professionally are probably on top of the task.

Train despatch is easily checked and is a classic example where poor or sloppy practice should be challenged at the time.

All operations managers should be capable of despatching trains and understand the importance of prompt departures.

Remember - Whistles work wonders!

6.32 Energy Management on Heavy Rail

BACKGROUND

A heading such as this in an operations handbook would have appeared out of place just a few years ago but the transformation in society's and corporate expectations in this regard, and a realisation of the significant financial economies to be made to the cost of running trains has made energy management an increasingly core issue for Operators.

ISSUES

Today's Operator has a fundamental new role. That of influencing driver techniques and harnessing appropriate decision-making support systems to ensure that the minimum possible amount of energy is used, whilst maintaining the punctuality of the timetable and not distracting drivers from their safety tasks.

Key energy saving points are:
- Energy efficiency is partly about good allocation of resources. Trains that are longer or heavier than they need to be are a waste of energy. Getting formations right and minimising unnecessary mileage such as ECS moves can significantly reduce energy consumption. The train operator will get a saving on track access costs too.
- Significant savings can be obtained through the use of regenerative braking. Instead of using friction to slow the train the traction package is used to generate electricity as it slows the train. This electricity is then returned to the distribution system where is can be used by other trains in the section or returned to the grid. Where regenerative braking is being used it is important

Running a Railway

to check that the right discount has been applied to the bill received from Network Rail.
- Sufficient attention must be given to the budgeted and actual energy use. Like all costs if it is measured then it can be managed. Measuring diesel usage is relatively easy. Modern diesel trains have flow monitoring equipment. Measuring electric traction use has traditionally been more difficult. Until recently trains have not carried their own meters and TOC bills for electric current for traction (known as EC4T – Electric Current for Traction) were based on predicted use in each of the feeder station areas with an annual wash up to cover any difference in the bill from the supplier. Increasingly electric trains are being fitted with electricity meters to allow more accurate billing of the actual amount used. Direct metering has the additional benefit of being more predictable than the traditional estimate and wash up method.
- Setting energy budgets is sensible practice. Target your reduction in energy use per unit mile (a measure of how efficient each unit is being operated) and per passenger kilometre (a measure of how efficiently you are delivering your overall product). Budgets should be devolved to the lowest level where managers can influence energy use. This should include each traincrew depot where it is possible to link a particular group of drivers to a particular billing area.

Driving technique can play a significant part in reducing energy usage. The challenge is to raise driver awareness without affecting safety or performance. This has been very successfully done in many TOCs with ten percent or greater savings.

Characteristics of such savings have been:-
- Engaging positively with drivers so as to properly introduce this new dimension to their task.
- Using drivers' union representatives and driver managers to input to the production of 'fuel efficient standard drives' over specific routes so as to be able to provide a baseline of fuel use for specific types of train.
- Again using the experts, identify the best driving style to minimise consumption. For electric trains the most efficient method is to use full power when accelerating, but maximise the amount of coasting. On diesel trains use of low power steps is important.
- The identification as part of route knowledge of the areas where coasting or the taking of less than full power is beneficial. Providing coasting signs as a reminder is useful.
- The assessment of the risk to performance and the risk of distraction from concentration on signals and speed restrictions etc. of the new issue. This can result in 'rules' such as 'continue to take power rather than coasting if running late'. TOCs have found that coasting has not had a detrimental effect on performance.

6.32 Energy Management

- In practice drivers have tended to warmly welcome such initiatives and an element of competition between drivers for the most fuel efficient drive over specific routes can result with an informal league table perhaps emerging.
- Various ways of displaying the relevant guidance (i.e. not mandatory) information to drivers are in use but they basically consist of an easy to read screen display to the side of the drivers desk. These are known as Driver Advisory Systems (DAS).
- Some modern DMUs can be configured such that an engine shuts down once the train has been stationary for a few minutes and may need to be started up again by the driver. All engines will shut down after a longer time. The old feature of leaving DMUs running for hours not now being seen as acceptable. In advanced cases GPS will be used to cut an engine out automatically when the train has crested a summit.

Additionally calculations can quite easily be made of the fuel cost and thus the carbon cost of, say, accelerating away from TSRs. An Operator may likewise be interested to note the cost of signal stops and of a less-than-uniform linespeed profile.

The domestic load from trains can be considerable. It is important to ensure that as many of the train systems are shut down as possible when the train is not in use.

You should also remember the energy use in domestic buildings. Traction energy is a significant cost, but heating, lighting and water supply in the depot also contribute to overall energy use and cost.

All in all the issue of fuel efficiency has only been a core operations requirement for a few years. A good train operator will be working closely with his Fleet and driver colleagues to exploit to the maximum the technology that is fitted or could be fitted to his rolling stock, whether diesel or electric.

He or she will also work closely with Network Rail colleagues to alert them to the fuel and carbon issues stemming from the characteristics of and their stewardship of the infrastructure.

Tips

Using less energy makes sound economic sense and is also good for your company's profile.

This is a new area – exploit the opportunities to reduce energy consumption and go green.

6.33 Risk Management

BACKGROUND

Operators are required to manage risk in almost all aspects of train service delivery. In order to achieve the best all round solution it will always be necessary to assess safety risks in a structured and systematic way.

The formal assessment of routine risks in a safety context using the ALARP (As Low As Reasonably Practicable) principles are covered in Safety Certificate & Authorisation documents and Company Safety Management Systems. This includes the use of Risk Assessment Models to provide a suitable framework and methodology

However Operators will frequently need to informally assess risks when making day to day operating decisions, both real time dynamic risk assessment and in the context of planned performance improvements and/or changes to working practices planned risk assessment. This Section addresses these aspects.

KEY PRINCIPLES

The formal assessment of major industry risk is undertaken using standardised processes contained in Safety Certificate & Authorisation documents and in internal standards. Health and safety legislation requires employers to undertake suitable and sufficient risk assessments of the risks the health and safety of employees whilst at work and other people who may be affected by the activities of an organisation.

The basis of British health and safety law is the Health and Safety at Work Act 1974. The Act sets out the general duties which employers have towards employees and members of the public, and employees have to themselves and to each other. These duties are qualified in the Act by the principle of 'so far as is reasonably practicable'. In other words, an employer does not have to take measures to avoid or reduce the risk if they are technically impossible or if the time, trouble or cost of the measures would be grossly disproportionate to the risk.

What the law requires here is what good management and common sense would lead employers to do anyway: that is, to look at what the risks are and take sensible measures to tackle them.

The Management of Health and Safety at Work Regulations 1999 (the Management Regulations) generally make more explicit what employers are required to do to manage health and safety under the Health and Safety at Work Act. Like the Act, they apply to every work activity. The main requirement on employers is to carry out a risk assessment. Employers with five or more employees need to record the significant findings of the risk assessment. The risk assessment should be straightforward in a simple workplace such as a typical office. It should only be complicated if it deals with serious hazards.

RISK ASSESSMENT

A risk assessment is an important step in protecting your workers and your business, as well as complying with the law. It helps you focus on the risks that really matter in your workplace – the ones with the potential to cause harm. In many instances, straightforward measures can readily control risks, for example, ensuring spillages are cleaned up promptly so people do not slip or cupboard drawers kept closed to ensure people do not trip.

There are five steps in risk assessment:
1. Identify the hazards.
2. Decide who might be harmed and how.
3. Evaluate the risks and decide on precautions (or mitigations).
4. Record your findings and implement them.
5. Review your assessment and update if necessary.

It is not always reasonable or practicable to completely eliminate risk - all that is required, is that you mitigate or remove sufficient risk so that the residual risk is as low as reasonably practicable. The concept of "reasonably practicable" involves weighing a risk against the trouble, time and money needed to control it. Therefore ALARP describes the level to which we expect to see workplace risks controlled.

Deciding whether a risk is ALARP can be challenging because it requires the assessor to exercise judgement. In the great majority of cases, we can decide by referring to existing 'good practice' that has been established by a process of discussion with stakeholders to achieve a consensus about what is ALARP. For high risk hazards, complex or novel situations, we build on good practice, using more formal decision making techniques, including cost-benefit analysis, to inform our judgement.

There are several potential risk treatments available to eliminate or reduce risks. These are risk retention, risk sharing (insurance), risk reduction, for example, outsourcing a risk such as asbestos management to a specialist contractor), hazard prevention (mitigation) and risk avoidance. For some risks you may need to use more than one risk treatment.

Running a Railway

When assessing any situation, you will need to identify all the risks and list the mitigation or potential mitigation. It is good practice for a group of people to take part in the risk assessment process to get a balanced view on the level of risk and potential mitigation measures. This is particularity relevant when the activity you are risk assessing involves more than one function or organisation.

Always look at day to day operating risk in the round. Stopping the railways for long periods, particularly if trains are stranded between stations as a consequence, will generate major risks such as passengers disembarking, with possible injuries as a result. Consequently all the risks, including the often large secondary risk areas, must always be considered. Think about the whole picture. You may need to assess the relative merits of a number of options by undertaking a comparative assessment. The question in these cases is not so much 'Is this a safe system?' but 'Which of these options is safest'?

Risk assessments should be reviewed on a regular basis, particularly following:
- an accident.
- ill health.
- near miss or dangerous occurrence.
- changes to equipment, plant or processes.
- changes in legislation.
- results of monitoring or audit.
- advice or action by the Enforcing Authority or insurance company.
- new information becoming available.

When implementing risk control measures there are often costs involved. In these circumstances it will be necessary to undertake a Cost Benefit Analysis. Your Safety Team will be able to provide guidance on undertaking this sort of analysis.

Dynamic risk-based decision making is particularly relevant when dealing with incidents that involve the emergency services including fatalities and lineside fires. Dynamic risk assessment is defined as the continuous assessment of risk in the rapidly changing circumstances of an operational incident, in order to implement the control measures necessary to ensure an acceptable level of safety is maintained. Being able to argue a case based on risk management principles is likely to be more persuasive because emergency services, particularly the Fire Brigade, should understand the principles of risk-based management.

More information on general risk management can be found on the HSE website at http://www.hse.gov.uk/risk/index.htm and the ALARP principle at http://www.hse.gov.uk/risk/theory/alarpglance.htm

Finally remember that at a lower level, risk management is frequently common sense. We routinely and unthinkingly apply risk assessments and management techniques in our personal lives such as crossing the road.

Do not see risk management techniques as black arts – they are a structured approach to assessing the merits of alternative courses of action.

Tips

Day to day application of risk assessment techniques is the common sense application of structured decision-making to operational situations.

It is a legal requirement to assess the risks of tasks and activities that are carried out by companies. However, risk assessment is not only a legal obligation, it is a useful tool to help Railway Operators to come to the right decision in a structured way.

Other relevant/useful documents:-
- Company Safety Certificate and Authorisation documents.
- Company Safety Management Manual.
- RSSB Guidance 'Taking Safe Decisions'.
- HSE Website.

6.34 Security Issues

BACKGROUND

Security and the threat of terrorist action is an issue that comes and goes although recent developments indicate that a higher level of vigilance will now need to become the norm.

The Department for Transport Security Directorate (TRANSEC) is responsible for enforcing counter terrorist measures on the rail industry in mainland Britain. To ensure effective levels of workable security it is essential that operators form good working relationships with the British Transport Police and TRANSEC. Similarly, regular staff training and briefing will help manage threats effectively and with minimum levels of disruption. Mandatory requirements and industry guidance is set out in the Railways Act 1993 – Instructions for

Running a Railway

Operators and owners of railway stations & Instructions for Operators of passenger trains.

It is important to consider security at key operational locations as well as in public areas such as Stations. For example:
- Signalling Centres.
- Electrical Control Rooms.
- Depots.
- Control Rooms.
- Remote Interlocking Rooms.

KEY ISSUES

Effective security will be greatly assisted by maintaining a tidy operating environment, professional, vigilant staff and good customer service.

Similarly, good liaison arrangements with BTP, NR and TOCs including joint protocols that are essential to routine operations will provide a solid foundation for effective security.

'Target Hardening' techniques (making a target more secure and less vulnerable) are important and the cost-benefit for adopting various measures will vary significantly dependent on the operational significance of the location, for example, compare an Absolute Block signalbox controlling 7 miles of railway to a Signal Control Centre with a 50 mile span of control to a major London terminus with a huge throughput of people.

Each location should have an individual security or emergency plan which sets out the specific operational arrangements at that location

The additional layer of security and terrorist precautions will need to be agreed between Train Operators, Network Rail, British Transport Police and other specialist agencies such as TRANSEC.

FOUNDATIONS

The foundations for good security include attention to the following key areas:-

Joint protocol with BTP
Agreement on pro-active and reactive policing arrangements that cover all potential problem issues and locations. These arrangements will explicitly cover deterrent and preventative measures aimed at reducing the likelihood of all types of crime and disorder. They will also include liaison arrangements for

dealing with disruptive events such as suicides and various levels of security readiness including actual terrorist incidents.

Internal NR and TOC procedures

Clear codified arrangements for ensuring that security is given appropriate attention at all times. These procedures should cover basic good housekeeping concerning railway premises and address escalating levels of terrorist threat and actual terrorist events through integrated staff training, briefing and support.

Each organisation will have a formally security cleared "nominated security contact" who is charged with disseminating communications from TRANSEC and providing details of security incidents to TRANSEC. Each TOC is required to develop a security plan for its stations and is required to establish a security committee for each Category A & B station, including train operators using the station, Network Rail, BTP and other businesses present on the station. This is where good practice and anti-terrorist measures can be discussed.

Station Security arrangements

When reviewing security arrangement it is important to consider the following:-

- The issue of photo identification passes for staff based at Category A or B stations.
- Controlled access arrangements for non-public areas.
- Vehicle access in controlled areas of a station.
- Arrangements for the management of waste such as locking bulk waste bins.
- Arrangements for screening and searching left luggage and lost property.
- Management of post boxes and bicycles on stations.
- Arrangements for conducting station searches.
- Provision of security awareness messages to passengers.
- The need for a formal written Station Security Program that records roles and responsibilities for staff carrying out security functions and action to be taken on discovering a suspicious article or behaviour.

Engineering arrangements

These will include items such as:-

- CCTV (covert or overt coverage, recording and monitoring).
- Fencing and security cordons.
- Engineered exclusion areas around operational locations.
- New building construction measures.

Staff training, briefing and motivation

Security aspects must be incorporated in all relevant training including induction courses. This must form part of any competence management arrangements and cover the balance between responding to suspicious events (e.g. an unattended bag) and maintaining an appropriate level of service.

Training should cover the following:-

- Awareness of security threats.
- Layouts and organisation of the area they are working in.
- Recognition of suspicious articles.
- Operation of any luggage screening equipment.
- Action to be taken on discovering a suspicious article or behaviour.

Ensure the HOT routine is understood and applied to all suspicious items. Are they:-

- **H**idden?
- **O**bviously suspicious?
- **T**ypical of environment?

Routine inspections are a key defence against terrorist action. Visibility of staff deters, and thorough checking of risk locations maximises the chance to prevent a successful attack. However maintaining vigilance after numerous negative checks can be difficult.

Make sure security checks are thoroughly audited and use unannounced exercises to retain alertness.

Regular briefing and visible support

This is essential during periods of increased threat and actual security or terrorist incidents. This aspect is vital in order to achieve adequate levels of safety.

Regular liaison

Routine liaison with the BTP at nominated levels is absolutely essential. Whilst the meetings might only deal with routine non-critical issues most of the time, it is imperative that managers know their BTP counterparts. Similarly the nominated TRANSEC security contacts in each TOC and NR must maintain an appropriate level of regular liaison with TRANSEC. These contacts will considerably ease any difficulties during actual incidents and security alerts.

Escalation arrangements

Influence will often need to be exerted at the highest levels. Furthermore, any security situation on railway premises which is in the hands of civil Police will be an order of magnitude more difficult to handle and control. Therefore it is essential that the escalation arrangements within NR and BTP are in place and regularly reviewed as a matter of normal management routine.

Tips

Major security alerts tend to escalate very quickly and it is often difficult on the day to exert any influence on the way that the BTP and security services choose to manage the risk.

Good regular liaison between all levels of the TOC, NR and BTP are essential as are key relationships between TOC and NR, and between the TOC and NR and TRANSEC

Ensure escalation arrangements are agreed and documented - ad hoc liaison has no place during security alerts.

6.35 Trespass, Vandalism and Disorder

BACKGROUND

Trespass, Vandalism and Disorder is an increasing problem in Britain throughout society. The scale of the problem on the railways reflects this worsening position. Not only does vandalism including graffiti and disorder cost significant sums of money, both direct and indirect, but it is also a rising cause of delay. A look at your trend on TRUST 402, 503 and 701F coded delays over the last two years will confirm this.

This is a countrywide problem and Operations Managers must take steps to address both the symptoms and any causes within their direct control. Society is generally becoming less respectful of property or 'officialdom' and rising unemployment amongst the young is exacerbating the problem.

ISSUES

In many rail organisations, strategies and plans to combat vandalism and disorder are not yet well developed. Whilst this is a difficult area to tackle and manage, all companies need to be determined to approach this in a focused systematic way.

Proactive as well as reactive measures must be considered. Pro-active examples include education and risk assessment of lineside fencing and T&V sites; reactive examples include lineside patrols and access gate checks.

Running a Railway

It is also important that response to trespass incidents is not over cautious but is clearly specified and followed. Considerable delays can be caused by searching for or reacting to trespassers that have long since disappeared. Stopping the railway completely is rarely justified. Even cautioning may only be necessary for child trespassers or trespassers who appear to be of unsound mind.

LEVEL 1 – Local Manager

Plan
- Ensure that you are aware of the TOC's strategy and that the requirements are incorporated in all relevant routines and tasks.
- Ensure the aims and requirements of the strategy are properly briefed and understood.
- Target hot spots for action.
- Identify vulnerable points.

Do
- Liaise with BTP and other relevant agencies at a working level.
- Regularly raise TV&D issues during routine visits and walkabouts.
- Work with your teams to reduce TV&D problems and associated delays.
- Undertake risk assessment of key locations.
- Identify and implement mitigation measures.
- Undertake security patrols.

Review
- Feed back issues for action that require new plans and fresh initiatives.
- Ensure TV&D issues are root cause investigated.
- Check that plans remain appropriate and relevant.
- Identify and consider new issues and trends from analysis and information.
- Identify hot spots.

LEVEL 2 – Operations Manager

Plan
- Develop a TOC route strategy for addressing V&D in conjunction with TOC and NR colleagues.
- Ensure adequate tactical plans are developed by all departments that hold safety responsibilities and/or performance budgets.

6.35 Trespass, Vandalism and Disorder

- Target resources to deal with hot spots.
- Plan regular liaison with the BTP at all necessary levels.

Do

- Actively raise V&D as an issue.
- Ensure staff know this is a key area of concern.
- Carry out extensive staff briefing to demonstrate level of action within the company.
- Support staff affected by V&D.
- Adopt a zero tolerance approach.
- Create business cases to gain authority for mitigation measures identified.
- Collect intelligence to allow individuals to be excluded through ASBOs where repeated offences occur.

Review

- Check that V&D is reviewed at all appropriate forum.
- Seek out good practice from all other parts of the railway and all other relevant industries.
- Identify hot spots – locations, train services, times of day or week etc.
- Monitor the scale of increase of V&D delays rather than the absolute numbers.

Tips

Visit problem areas and visit at problem times such as school finishing times or late evenings.

Manage the problem in a structured way but do not let it become a crusade.

The effect on staff can be very serious - ensure that staff see what is being done, and engage with staff to identify appropriate responses. Local staff will know the local issues, access points and trouble spots.

Muster all available resources - local authorities, councils and interested groups such as Travelsafe can help.

Make sure BTP liaison is first class. Proactive, targeted, preventative policing can pay real dividends.

This is a rising problem - meet it sensibly but firmly.

Running a Railway

6.36 Signals Passed At Danger

BACKGROUND

The signalling system is provided to maintain a safe separation between trains. The term Signal Passed At Danger (SPAD) is used to describe an event where a train proceeds past a signal at danger without the required authority.

Without adequate mitigations in place SPADs present a significant safety risk. Following a SPAD trains can collide at high speeds. Some of the most serious rail accidents in British railway history have been caused by signals being passed at danger, the most serious example was Quintinshill in 1915 (226 killed - the worst accident in British railway history). Since privatisation two of the most serious rail accidents, Southall (6 killed, 150 injured) and Ladbroke Grove (31 killed, 523 injured) were the result of signals being passed at danger.

Because of the high risks posed by SPADs and the increased likelihood (due to rising traffic volumes) the industry has devoted significant effort and resources to mitigation. In terms of equipment this principally includes The Automatic Warning System (AWS), the Train Protection Warning System (TPWS) and Drivers Reminder Appliance (DRA). Other important measures include improved driver recruitment processes, increased driver and driver management training, improved SPAD investigations and an increased awareness of the risk posed by different infrastructure configurations.

All these issues are covered in the following Sections.

AWS and DRA

The Automatic Warning System (AWS) was progressively fitted to the network from 1956 to provide drivers with an audible and visual warning of signals displaying caution and danger aspects. However, AWS will only apply the brakes where the driver fails to acknowledge the warning. If the driver fails to take appropriate action after cancelling the AWS warning then a SPAD can still occur.

AWS is also ineffective in the case of SPADs where the Driver starts the train while standing at a red signal because the train will already be in advance of the relevant track based AWS equipment. These SPADs are known as Start Against Signal (SAS) SPADs. The Driver's Reminder Appliance is fitted to trains to help remind the driver of the signal aspect in these circumstances. A Start On Yellow (SOY) SPAD is a similar occurrence where a train starts (normally from a station) with a single yellow aspect, but the next signal is passed at danger.

SPAD Indicators

High risk locations are sometimes fitted with SPAD indicators to alert the driver when a SPAD has occurred. SPAD indicators are three aspect signals which are normally unlit. If a SPAD occurs the indicator shows two flashing and one steady red aspect. SPAD indicators are being fitted less frequently now that TPWS has been installed across the network.

TPWS

The big breakthrough in SPAD mitigation was the introduction of TPWS from 1998. This was so successful that by 2003 it had been fitted to all mainline signals that prevent a conflicting move (automatic signals are not generally fitted).

TPWS was implemented in the UK as an interim measure to reduce the consequences of SPADs, pending implementation of full protection through systems that monitor driver performance continuously. In the reports into the Ladbroke Grove accident it was envisaged that this higher level of protection would be delivered by the roll out of ERTMS (European Rail Traffic Management System) within ten years. However in the intervening period it has become clear that the roll out of ERTMS will take considerably longer and hence TPWS will be the primary means of mitigating SPAD risk for a period significantly beyond that originally envisaged.

TPWS consists of track mounted loops (antennae) and train mounted receivers. Loops are fitted adjacent to stop signals. When the signal shows a danger aspect the loops are energised. The receiver on the train detects the radio frequency transmitted from the loop and applies the brakes if the train passes over the loops. Loops adjacent to stop signals are known as Train Stop System (TSS).

Loops are also fitted on the approach to stop signals, known as Over Speed Sensors (OSS). In this case there are two loops placed a distance apart. When the signal ahead shows a danger aspect the loops are energised. The first loop triggers a timer on the train. If the timer has not counted down by the time the train reaches the second loop then the train is travelling too fast and the brakes will be applied. Loops are fitted so that an approaching train will normally be stopped within the overlap of the signal. In high risk locations, particularly where the possible approach speed is high a further set of loops may be fitted at a greater distance from the signal. These additional loops are known as TPWS+.

SPAD Alarms

Many signal boxes are fitted with SPAD alarms to alert the signaller to the

Running a Railway

possibility of a SPAD. They work by monitoring the operation of the signalling system and alerting the signaller to a set of circumstances that "look like" a SPAD. It is not possible to monitor every signal nor is it possible to rule out other causes but these alarms are specifically designed to alert the signaller quickly to the location of an event so that signallers monitoring large areas can react quickly.

ISSUES

Following Ladbroke Grove the Railway Safety Regulations, 1999 required the industry to fit a system to stop trains that pass signals at danger or approach stop signals too fast (see http://www.legislation.gov.uk/uksi/1999/2244/made). On most of the mainline railway this is achieved by the Train Protection and Warning System (TPWS).

SPADs are categorised as follows:

Category	Description (Notes: No degree of severity or importance is implied within or between these categories).
A	A1 – When a SPAD has occurred and, according to available evidence, a stop aspect, indication or end of in-cab signalled movement authority was displayed or given correctly and in sufficient time for the train to be stopped safely at it.
	A2 – When a SPAD has occurred and, according to available evidence, the stop aspect, indication or end of in-cab signalled movement authority concerned was not displayed or given correctly, but was preceded by the correct aspects or indications.
	A3 – When a SPAD has occurred and, according to available evidence, verbal and/or visual permission to pass a signal at danger was given by a handsignaller or other authorised person without the authority of the signaller.
	A4 – When a SPAD has occurred and, according to available evidence, a stop aspect, indication or end of in-cab signalled movement authority was displayed or given correctly and in sufficient time for the train to be stopped safely at it, but the train driver was unable to stop his train owing to circumstances beyond his control (for example, poor rail head adhesion, train braking equipment failure or malfunction etc.).

6.36 Signals Passed At Danger

B	B1 – When a SPAD has occurred because a stop aspect, indication or end of in-cab signalled movement authority, that previously showed a proceed indication, was displayed because of infrastructure failure (for example, signalling or level crossing equipment has failed or malfunctioned).
	B2 – When a SPAD has occurred because a stop aspect, indication or end of in-cab signalled movement authority, that previously showed a proceed indication, was displayed because it was returned to danger or displayed in error.
C	C – When a SPAD has occurred because a stop aspect, indication or end of in-cab signalled movement authority was not displayed in sufficient time for the train to be stopped safely at the signal, indication or end of in-cab signalled movement authority as it had been returned to danger automatically or in an emergency in accordance with GE/RT8000 Rule Book.
D	D – When a SPAD has occurred because vehicles without any traction unit attached, or a train which is unattended, had run away past the signal at danger or without an in-cab movement authority.

Clearly the most significant risks are posed by category A and category D SPADs. When these occur it is important that the correct processes are followed to deal with the incident. A thorough investigation must also take place to understand the causes of the incident (see the Sections on accident investigation and root cause analysis for more information). The signaller is required to ask the driver specific questions following a category A SPAD. When undertaken correctly this can provide valuable evidence for the investigation.

Apparent category A SPADs are classic "think worst case" incidents. There may be occasions when a driver reports that he/she has "SPAD-ed" but this does not indicate as such on the signalling system, or where the signaller's indications lead them to believe that a SPAD has occurred but this is denied by the driver. In such cases managers must be sensitive to the parties involved but the incident must be dealt with as if a SPAD has occurred. It is far better to down grade later than to regret that key investigatory steps have not been taken.

Since 2001 category A SPADs have also been subject to a risk ranking made up of the following components:
- An initial collision potential assessment: could the train have collided with another train before reaching the next stop signal? - Yes/No?
- An accident vulnerability ranking. A weighting of the probability and seriousness of an accident as a result of the SPAD. - From A (most serious) to K (least serious).
- The risk ranking score. - An overall risk score from 0 to 28.

Running a Railway

An example risk ranking would be 'No J 12'.

Although less serious it is important that the instances of category B SPADs are kept as low as possible. Category B SPADs can cause considerable anxiety for drivers and are a performance risk. Although category B SPADs cannot normally result in two trains colliding because of the interlocking, frequent instances of category B SPADs can undermine confidence in the integrity of the signalling system.

Reliable statistics for SPADs are available since 1985 and since 1996 there has been a statistically significant reduction in the overall numbers of SPADs. There were 688 in 1996/7, 436 in 2001/02 and 307 in 2010. Since the fitment of TPWS there has been a steady reduction in the number of SPADs and even more crucially, a significant reduction in the risk from SPADs. SPAD risk now represents a relatively small proportion of the overall risk to the railway, although the possibility of a high magnitude and high profile accident due to a SPAD means that they continue to justify considerable management attention.

However since 2009 SPAD numbers have started to rise very slightly. The reason for this increase is not clear, although increasing network congestion and an over reliance on TPWS by drivers may be a contributing factor.

SPADs and SPAD Risk 2001 - 2010

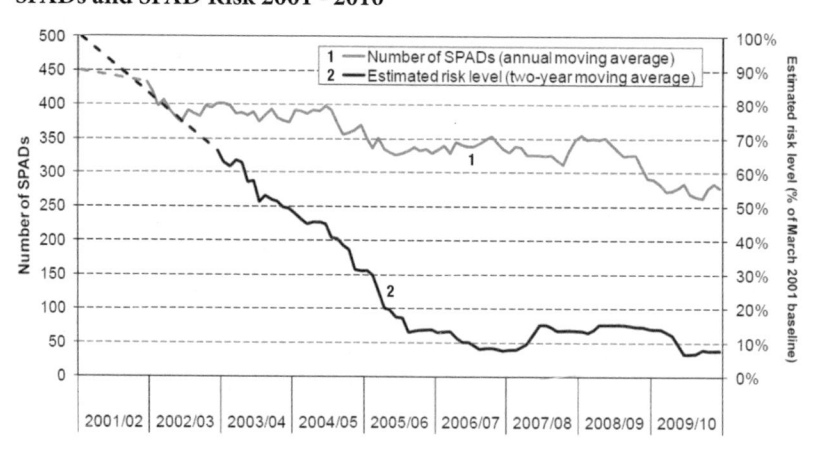

Source: RSSB Annual Safety Performance Report 2009/10

CAUSES AND PREVENTION

SPAD causes are complex but they are generally categorised by human factor causes as shown in the table below.

Infrastructure clearly plays an important role in determining the likelihood of a SPAD. Although standards for the sighting and visibility of signals are strict, certain signals have a higher likelihood of a SPAD than others. Management of 'multi SPAD' signals is vital to minimise SPAD risk. Multi SPAD signals are classified as signals which have been passed at danger at least 3 times in the past 5 years. Following the Ladbroke Grove accident considerable attention was paid to reducing the risk from the top twenty two most passed signals on the network and the risk from multi SPAD signals has reduced as a result.

Infrastructure also influences the seriousness of SPAD consequences. Fitment of train control systems like TPWS has obvious benefits, but design of the infrastructure is also important. Track layouts that reduce the likelihood of a collision following a SPAD are clearly desirable from a risk perspective, but can be more expensive to install and maintain. The series of accidents at single lead junctions in the 1980s and 1990s (Belgrove 1989, Newton 1992) demonstrates this point.

It is also self-evident that SPADs can only occur if the signal being approached is at danger. Congested and low performance railways will always be more vulnerable to a SPAD and signaller performance plays an important role in minimising the opportunity for a SPAD to occur. Good regulation and attention to detail will reduce the number of red signals displayed.

Signaller performance can also be crucial in mitigating the consequences of a SPAD. Use of train radio messages and prompt movement of points can sometimes prevent a SPAD turning into a collision.

However it is ultimately the driver's responsibility to stop at a red signal and the table below shows a breakdown of all SPAD causes between January 1998 and October 2011 categorised by human factors.

Running a Railway

SPAD Causes January 1998- October 2011

Description of Cause	Number of SPADs	% of SPADs
Failure to react to caution signal	1178	21.36%
Failure to check signal aspect	972	17.62%
Failure to locate signal	497	9.01%
Viewed wrong signal	362	6.56%
Violation of rules/instructions	304	5.51%
Anticipation of signal clearance	232	4.21%
Not monitoring for a signal	224	4.06%
Misjudge train behaviour	209	3.79%
Viewed correct signal, misread aspect	166	3.01%
Misjudge environment conditions	142	2.57%
Ambiguous/incomplete information given	103	1.87%
Ignorance of rules/instructions	83	1.50%
Wrong information given	76	1.38%
Correct information given but misunderstood	64	1.16%
Misread previous signal	33	0.60%
Information not given or N/A	870	15.78%
TOTAL	**5515**	

Source: OPSWEB

An RSSB research project in 2004 attempted to identify areas of priority for SPAD management. Driver individual factors were identified as the highest priority. The schematic below illustrates the issues involved and the prioritisation advice at the time.

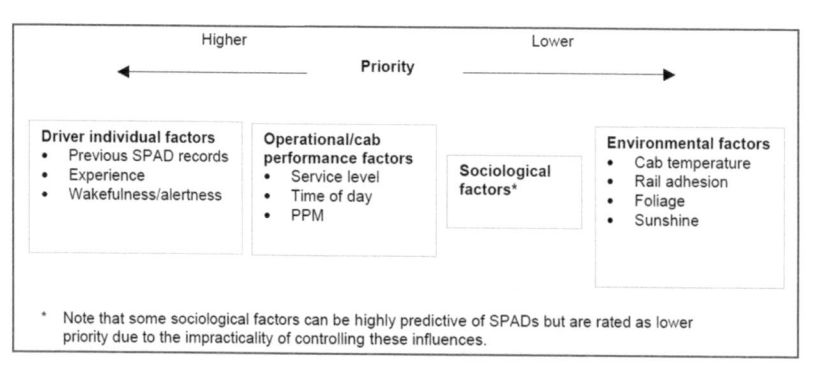

```
              Higher                                    Lower
                        ◄──────── Priority ────────►

  ┌─────────────────────┬─────────────────────┬─────────────────────────┐
  │ Driver individual   │ Operational/cab     │                         │
  │ factors             │ performance factors │ Environmental factors   │
  │ • Previous SPAD     │ • Service level     │ • Cab temperature       │
  │   records           │ • Time of day       │ • Rail adhesion         │
  │ • Experience        │ • PPM               │ • Foliage               │
  │ • Wakefulness/      │                     │ • Sunshine              │
  │   alertness         │                     │                         │
  └─────────────────────┴─────────────────────┴─────────────────────────┘
                              Sociological
                              factors*

  * Note that some sociological factors can be highly predictive of SPADs but are rated as lower
    priority due to the impracticality of controlling these influences.
```

Source: Prioritisation of SPAD risk factors - further analysis of May/Summer peak in SPAD occurrences, RSSB 2004

An effective SPAD mitigation programme will emphasise:
- Managing drivers with existing operational incident records.
- Achieving the highest levels of competence and compliance through use of the competence assessment system.
- Identifying emerging issues with individual drivers at work or at home.

Further information on SPAD causes and good practice for preventing SPADs can be found on the OPSWEB pages (www.opsweb.co.uk).

Tips

Never forget the potential that SPADs have to cause a major accident – however, do not let SPADs take your attention from other issues that now present a higher risk, for example, level crossings.

Human factors play a significant role in causing SPADs. Engage effectively with your drivers and signallers in order to keep the numbers as low as possible.

Ensure you and your team are aware of emerging issues or changed circumstances (either infrastructure, rules based or at an individual level).

SPADs are a very obvious and ever present risk – give this issue the attention it deserves.

6.37 Cable Theft

INTRODUCTION

At the height of the problem cable theft was costing the UK rail industry £18m per annum in Schedule 8 payments and replacement costs and accounting for 350,000 minutes of delay per annum. The London North Eastern route alone experienced an average of around 20 thefts per week.

Though this has reduced significantly in 2012/13 theft of cable is still a significant contributor to external delay. Theft can involve signalling, power supply, telecoms and overhead line cables. However, redundant track, earthing strips and even pandrol clips have been targeted by thieves in their quest for metal.

Running a Railway

Copper prices have increased and are expected to continue to do so as the appetite from the Far East for this essential industrial element shows little sign of abating. However, an increase in the number of arrests and sentence durations being given to those who are caught has recently reduced the number of thefts. Some high-profile deaths (caused for instance by sawing through return conductors or structure bonds – see Section on Electrification) may also have made thieves more wary.

This is an area where early efforts were piece-meal but more recently the rail industry has agreed an overriding strategic objective underpinned by supporting objectives for individual organisations within the industry.

The overriding strategic objective for the industry recently was to eliminate the impact of cable theft on the network by the end of Control Period 4.

The underpinning objectives being at that time:-

- **Network Rail**

  To eliminate cable theft and its impact on train performance, on Britain's railways to levels that are as low as reasonably practicable.

- **BTP**

  To support and act on agreed priorities in efforts to eliminate the impact of cable theft on Britain's railways.

- **TOCs**

  To support the industry's strategy in tackling cable theft acting on tactical plans in close co-operation with Network Rail.

ISSUES

The industry approach focuses on four main areas:
- Education - raising the awareness of the issue and lobbying for changes and stiffening of law around this issue.
- Engineering - finding effective and innovative ways of making railway cable less attractive or harder to steal.
- Enablement - offering operational methods of deterring or preventing, and better responding to incidents of cable theft.
- Enforcement - looking at ways to use the law to stifle demand and act as a deterrent to all involved in cable theft and its onward sale.

A structured, coordinated approach needs to be adopted in order to be successful, as piecemeal tactical initiatives will not be successful. This is an area ripe for sharing good practice and lessons learnt as it is not within the traditional skill set of operators, and good practice is continually evolving.

6.37 Cable Theft

Make sure you engage with security experts to develop your action plans. Included below is an extract from Network Rail's Cable Theft Toolkit. It contains some useful ideas for potential activities and Network Rail contacts should be able to access the latest versions of this toolkit or have similar 'shopping lists' available.

Cable Theft incidents often result in significant loss of signalling throughout an extended area. See also the Sections on Working in Degraded Mode and Major Signalling Failures in Section 7 of this Handbook.

Tips

Assess the impact of cable theft in your patch to work out if this is an issue which can be dealt with as part of the day job or if it is significant enough to require the specific focus of dedicated resource.

Develop good working relationships with BTP and local civil police.

Share ideas with other companies that may be experiencing similar problems – Local Electricity suppliers or BT for example.

Tackle the issues vigorously including publicity - remember that changes to legislation have now become a reality with a new Scrap Metal Dealers Act becoming law in 2013. However, ongoing work with magistrates to continue to hand out sensible sentences is vital.

EXTRACTS FROM THE NETWORK RAIL CABLE THEFT TOOLKIT.

Education

Asset
Media & Communications.

Description
Pro active communications internally and externally.

Deployment (How, where, when, by who etc)
- Media relations manager as gatekeeper, includes rewards for information, posters, media campaign targeting hot spot areas.
- Work with BTP to publicise and highlight local arrests and convictions, publish CCTV images (with BTP approval) and support TOCs with direct passenger communications raising awareness and vigilance.

Running a Railway

Evaluation & Feedback (How successful? Ease of implementation, installation and operation?)
- Concern that if the message is not put out correctly this can encourage an increase in cable theft raising awareness of Network Rail as a target so needs to be used with caution.
- Wide success engaging media with extensive coverage in targeted regions.

Asset
Railway cable theft "campaign".

Description
Development of "brand" for theft of metal specific to the railway to support direct rail staff and passenger communications as well as stakeholder lobbying.

Deployment (How, where, when, by who etc)
Posters, leaflets:
- Scrap yard dealers.
- TOC train, station crew and other rail staff.
- Local community or generic.
- Lineside signage – "CCTV in this area" or similar, deterrent and reinforce message to lineside staff.
- Information packs.

Evaluation & Feedback (How successful? Ease of implementation, installation and operation?)
- Brand awareness of campaign materials.
- Increase in reports to police from public or informants.
- Increased staff engagement and support for mitigation measures.

Engineering & Technology

Asset
CCTV Cameras.

Description
- A discreet CCTV system that can record imagery either still pictures or film in all light conditions, sufficient for evidential requirements.
- Covert CCTV cameras so that the thieves are unaware of their presence while they gather evidence.
- Overt CCTV cameras clearly visible to act as a deterrent.

Deployment (How, where, when, by who etc)
- Installed at hot spots, movement activated - provide an alert and automatically send photographs to Control Rooms. A number of these systems are deployed in existing problem areas.
- May require supplementary lighting.
- Consider power supply and repair of damage. Also, if covert, how these will be deployed covertly and frequency of battery change required.

Evaluation & Feedback (How successful? Ease of implementation, installation and operation?)
Success is limited by the level of detail that is required to assist the CPS in securing a conviction. The rule of thumb is that an offenders face needs to cover at least one third of the screen and to be clearly lit.

Asset
Install cable tremblers at hot spots (or provision of kits to enable use when hot spots emerge).

Description
Physically attached to cable on movement sends an alert to control - generally used in conjunction with cameras - but range is wider than tremblers can be used over 2KM.

Deployment (How, where, when, by who etc)
- A number of these systems are deployed in existing 'cable theft problem areas'
- Each trembler will require 12-monthly battery replacement.

Evaluation & Feedback (How successful? Ease of implementation, installation and operation?)
- Tremblers can be difficult to locate for battery replacement.
- The potential for false positives is high, for example activated by vermin and rolling stock.

Asset
Provide fixed CCTV at project sites

Description
High quality CCTV - including infrared provided at major works sites.

Running a Railway

Asset

Cable Burial

Description

Scratch Burial (up to 1 foot) or cover the cables with a ballast drop. Deep Burial usually involves replacing the cabling and the use of turning chambers to a depth of 3-5 feet.

Deployment (How, where, when, by who etc)

Deep Burial is very effective but also very expensive, time consuming and resource heavy.

Evaluation & Feedback (How successful? Ease of implementation, installation and operation?)

- The practice has been trialled on the Durham Coast project and has been marginally effective in preventing the cables from being stolen. Thieves have dug slit trenches to locate the buried cables to steal them.
- Continue to bury new cables in ducts in known cable theft areas. Only apply retrospective if cable theft is frequent and causing significant delays and cost.

Asset

Fencing Enhancements.

Description

The installation of welded palisade fencing etc.

Deployment (How, where, when, by who etc)

Ensure that the fencing at hot spots is welded palisade and not just bolted palisade. Identify incursion point and ensure that fencing at the location is fit for purpose and in a good state of repair.

Evaluation & Feedback (How successful? Ease of implementation, installation and operation?)

- Fencing is already in place so additional work would be enhancement to the existing where the fencing is in good order. High security fencing will stop all but the determined criminal.
- However, fencing can also be a theft target.

6.37 Cable Theft

Asset
Specialist Cable 'TrakDNA'

Description
This product contains a unique identifying code on microdots placed within the sheathing. Microdots are specific to locations enabling traceability of cable back to a specific site location.

Deployment (How, where, when, by who etc)
Deployment in new cable installations. First projects are now starting to use. Marginal cost increase above ordinary cable.

Evaluation & Feedback (How successful? Ease of implementation, installation and operation?)
Early indications look positive, coupled with deterrent signage.

Asset
Steel banding on Troughing Routes.

Description
To permanently secure all cables in an existing to the concrete trough. One tensioned, stainless steel band is secured around the troughs upright wall and the cables are bundled and secured to the first band with a second stainless steel band.

Evaluation & Feedback (How successful? Ease of implementation, installation and operation?)
- Time-consuming and noisy to remove so deters thieves. Cheap to install and keeps the cables in place and prevents service disruptions and associated costs. Can be modified to counter the theft threat by quickly and cheaply adding extra bands as desired.
- Trialled on LNW, LNE and Wales and being rolled out nationally.

Running a Railway

Asset
MULTIduct.

Description
Bury 'MULTIduct' multiple duct bank system with plastic chambers.

Deployment (How, where, when, by who etc)
A cost-effective alternative to burying cables in ducts that is being trialled in Rochdale.

Evaluation & Feedback (How successful? Ease of implementation, installation and operation?)
- Only usable for new cables because the associated cost of lengthening existing cables would be prohibitive. Expected to be lower cost and provide greater theft resilience than separate buried pipes.
- Trial in progress in Rochdale.

Asset
Aluminium conductor.

Description
The scrap value of aluminium is one third that of copper and is significantly lighter so a thief would need to harvest more to achieve the same weight.

Deployment (How, where, when, by who etc)
- Deploy aluminium electrical cables in appropriate locations.
- Aluminium conductors are not suitable for telecoms or signalling cables.

Evaluation & Feedback (How successful? Ease of implementation, installation and operation?)
This technology is already in use in electrical cables but unfavourable electrical parameters restrict its use in S&T cables.

6.37 Cable Theft

Enablement

Asset

Provide cable theft - response kits.

Description

Cable jointing kits or testing equipment and specialist personnel.

Asset

Single Point of Contact for Cable Theft.

Description

Single senior appointment to lead on all aspects of Route cable theft strategy and programmes.

Deployment (How, where, when, by who etc)

Lead contact with BTP and have regular liaison meetings or discussions.

Evaluation & Feedback (How successful? Ease of implementation, installation and operation?)

- Develops clear leadership and develops expertise.
- Shares good practice and undertakes stakeholder liaison.

Asset

Route-level cable theft groups.

Deployment (How, where, when, by who etc)

Meeting with key stakeholders in each Route to discuss tactics and response.

Asset

Identify Route-based 'hot-spots'.

Description

Collate data from cable theft incidents to identify locations where serious and repeated theft occurs.

Asset

Contingency & response plans.

Description

Use of resources to reduce response times.

Running a Railway

Enforcement Quadrant

Asset
Provide security patrols either mobile or on foot.

Description
Security personnel deployed to provide deterrence, reporting and intelligence in support of BTP.

Deployment (How, where, when, by who etc)
Agree Route or Area-level remit to ensure that Route issues are identified and addressed by contractor.

Evaluation & Feedback (How successful? Ease of implementation, installation and operation?)
An expensive solution but can be effective - some being done with 'in house resource'.

Asset
Use of Air Support Units (ASUs).

Description
Use of either Network Rail's helicopter resource or buying time from Police ASUs to provide surveillance in support of BTP operations.

Evaluation & Feedback (How successful? Ease of implementation, installation and operation?)
This is an expensive asset therefore tasking must be intelligence led and in support of specific operations.

Asset
DNA Tagging of cabling.
Deployment of DNA Tagging warning signage.

Description
Smart Water, RedWeb or SelectaDNA is painted on assets and provides a "DNA" type code that makes stolen assets traceable.

Evaluation & Feedback (How successful? Ease of implementation, installation and operation?)
Deterrence factor high with good perceived reputation for conviction amongst the criminal fraternity but limitations exist in using evidence gleaned for identification of offenders and subsequent prosecution.

6.37 Cable Theft

Asset
Deploy 'Q' trains.

Description
Use of either a train or cab riding to assist with surveillance or apprehension of criminals.

Asset
Provide security patrols either mobile or on foot.

Description
Security personnel deployed to provide deterrence, reporting and intelligence in support of BTP.

Deployment (How, where, when, by who etc)
Agree Route or Area-level remit to ensure that route issues are identified and addressed by contractor.

Evaluation & Feedback (How successful? Ease of implementation, installation and operation?)
An expensive solution but can be effective - some being done with 'in-house resource'.

Asset
Camera Technology.

Description
Fixed, mobile and covert cameras.

Deployment (How, where, when, by who etc)
Route and BTP to task to locations.

Evaluation & Feedback (How successful? Ease of implementation, installation and operation?)
Most effective when supported by automated response or patrols.

Section 7: Running a railway during disruption

7.1	Disruption Management.	321
7.2	Prioritised Planning	323
7.3	Estimates for Resuming Normal Working.	332
7.4	Restricted Track Access	337
7.5	Service Recovery	339
7.6	Passenger Information During Disruption (PIDD).	345
7.7	Major Incident and Accident Management	352
7.8	Working in Degraded Mode - including Single Line Working/ Pilot Working/Temporary Block Working.	354
7.9	Possession Overruns.	361
7.10	Failed Trains	363
7.11	Major Track and Civil Engineering Issues - including Bridge Strikes	366
7.12	Major Signalling Failures	376
7.13	Fatalities.	379
7.14	Operational Irregularities	383

7.1 Disruption Management

BACKGROUND

Management of disruption should be a seamless extension of real time performance management. Provided properly integrated arrangements are in place, a full suite of contingency plans is available and escalation and on call arrangements codified, then the management of disruption should occur in a structured framework.

The main impediments to effective disruption management are poor information (see the section 7.3 for Estimates for Resuming Normal Working) and an absence of effective leadership. Operations managers must recognise when it is necessary to take charge and how this can best be achieved.

This section addresses the general principles and the section 7.2 addresses managing around a major incident or accident.

More detailed, important advice is contained in the Section covering Prioritised Planning.

KEY CONSIDERATIONS

The main points to consider when managing disruption or supervising/reviewing the management of disruption are:-
- Establish good communications links between NR and TOCs/FOCs.
- Gather all available information.
- Assess the position considering any gaps in information.
- Break the problem down into the key parts.
- Refer to contingency plans and previous outcomes.
- Reach a clear understanding regarding who is in charge of what.
- Act quickly, to contain initial disruption as much as possible.
- Summon appropriate response staff – call out too many, not too few; and too quickly, not too late.
- Ensure Customer Service/handling arrangements have been mobilised.
- If the incident merits TOC attendance on site, appoint a TOLO (Train Operations Liaison Officer).
- Verify the key parts of the problem(s) to be resolved and prioritise.
- Determine and promulgate the plan of action.
- Review at specified frequencies or as more and better information becomes available.

Running a railway during disruption

- Modify action as necessary.
- Restore normal working using service recovery arrangements.
- Review the incident and action taken.
- Provide feedback to those involved.

Note – A suitable checklist should be provided as part of your company's Standing Orders covering Managing Service Disruption

ISSUES

Most incidents/events have a clear lead organisation for example; train failures are TOC, point failures are NR; although Network Rail is always responsible for overall co-ordination of service management. However, sometimes the impact is so large that management of the failure becomes a subsidiary technical issue compared with the management effort required to manage the ensuing disruption (e.g. a signalling blackout). In such situations there must be clear agreement between and within organisations about who is managing what aspect of the incident.

Incidents that escalate dramatically often do so because of managerial involvement either being too late or not enough or tragically both. Train failures too often fall into this category. Also beware of apparently benign events that gradually escalate and turn into serious incidents that are not adequately managed. Assuming that events will follow the best case scenario is a common failing. Provided adequate escalation arrangements have been built into on-call arrangements and these cover working hours as well as out-of-hours the problem should not arise. However, it frequently does.

If you are part of a general oncall list and you are advised of an incident or event by pager or email, and you read the message and then carry on doing what you were doing – think…

Has everyone else done the same? If I am not responding, who should be?

A quick phone call to Control by the appropriate line manager is easy to make and it can prevent the emergence of an awfully embarrassing situation. Some incidents can quickly spiral out of control and the rail industry does manage to do this to itself fairly regularly.

Ensure that contingency plans are in place, particularly for predictable/known events (e.g. adverse weather) and structured planning in advance helps speedy decision making on the day and removes the need for detailed negotiation in the heat of battle.

Disruption management needs consistent plan-do-review application. Get stuck into the fire-fighting by all means: it is absolutely necessary and highly instinctive but ensure you keep a broad perspective and that the review element of Plan-Do-Review is enacted on every appropriate occasion. Operators may get a buzz from fire-fighting whilst planning is harder to find the time for – however it will be worthwhile in the longer term.

Remember that disruption will rarely be managed perfectly – that is why post event review is vitally important. It is probably the most critical activity in the process.

Tips

The more frequently disruption occurs the easier it is to manage. However, as we become better at running the railway to plan, the more important a structured approach to disruption management becomes.

Make sure that NR and TOC Passenger Information During Disruption arrangements are robust, understood and strictly followed.

Always make sure that the needs of passengers and customers are fully considered - they are fundamentally not a 'bolt on'.

Ensure Control Offices are strengthened during serious disruption but avoid everyone phoning Control.

Make sure your escalation protocols are clear and strictly followed by control.

Ensure that there is always adequate on call cover. It is a real sin to not be immediately contactable and available if you are on call.

Always split the issue into the key parts and prioritise the actions – this will ensure an optimal outcome.

7.2 Prioritised Planning

BACKGROUND

This section provides a step-by-step guide to structured incident management based on proven problem-solving techniques. The intention is to provide

Running a railway during disruption

a structured approach to incident management for use throughout the rail industry and not to create additional extra workload for those involved in incident management.

A key principle is the prioritisation of activities and objectives so that the needs of passengers and other customers are properly balanced with service normalisation and infrastructure restoration requirements. This is achieved by adopting a systematic approach to planning and prioritisation.

Control Office Managers should specify how these principles will be implemented in their control office in consultation with managers responsible for site staff. A common approach should be shared by each organisation present in the control office and this must take account of key control contacts which are not co-located.

Communication of the Prioritised Plan is essential although the audience and level of detail will vary from incident to incident. Control Managers should specify how the Prioritised Plans produced by their control office are to be recorded, published and communicated as well as how messaging from the control office is to incorporate detail from these plans. It is important to be clear in the control guidelines produced that prioritised planning does not relate to infrastructure activities alone but must include other activities (such as train service management, degraded working methods and stranded trains/passengers for example).

Prioritised Planning is not something that can be taken for granted. It needs to be actively managed and encouraged within the Control and wider railway. Thought must be given to emphasising prioritised planning skills as part of your recruitment, training and assessment processes.

STEP BY STEP GUIDE

STEP 1 - Gather Information

When an incident occurs the first need is to:
- Assemble facts we already know or have.
- Identify information we need.
- Interpret and sift the information.
- Start to identify the skills and resources we will need.

At this stage it is vital that details are recorded because potentially a huge amount of information will be received very quickly in the control office. This will come from a variety of different sources and be received by different members of the team.

Recording the information will help you:
- Clarify what is actually happening.
- Share knowledge between different members of the team.
- Identify gaps, conflicting information, problems and opportunities.
- Identify what needs to be done.
- Supply accurate information for post-incident reviews.

Accordingly it is vital that information is recorded in a format that can be easily shared amongst the whole team dealing with the problem (and this may include team members outside of the control office). This does not need to be high-tech and should take the most convenient suitable form. Examples include white boards and shared logs.

STEP 2 - Scope the Incident and Break into Key Parts

The important principle when breaking an incident into key parts is to take a strategic view and try to write down the four or five component elements (it is unusual for there to be many more). Try to use problem-solving statements to help identify the key parts rather than simply defining technical tasks (this will aid understanding of relative importance and clarify the thinking behind element prioritisation).

Good quality questioning techniques will enable each aspect of the problem to be identified and understood. It will also help to keep an open mind so that specific issues, which may impact later, are not overlooked. It is important to understand that this is an ongoing process.

All incidents will consist of a number of distinct aspects and consequences, for example;
- A failed train.
- delaying passengers on that train.
- causing a line blockage disrupting other services/customers.
- at a level crossing delaying road traffic.

Initial information will be sparse (e.g. "all trains at a stand" and little else) but as questions continue to be posed and answered, greater understanding will be made possible. Good questions are;
- What are we trying to achieve in dealing with this problem?
- What will success look like when we have finished?

Running a railway during disruption

An example illustrating this is shown below.

TASK/PROBLEM SOLVING STATEMENT	AIM
Repair the damaged Overhead Line (OHL) equipment on the fast lines.	To enable a full service to operate from start of service tomorrow.
Rescue the failed train or detrain passengers	Minimise the delay and discomfort to these passengers and prevent the incident escalating through uncontrolled passenger action (e.g. unauthorised detraining).
Restore operation on the slow lines	To enable a contingent service to operate for the evening peak.

STEP 3 - Prioritise

It is vital that the clear priorities are assigned as soon as possible. These may change over time but prioritisation will enable everyone involved to clearly understand the things that are most important. It is important because one task may conflict with another, or even be reliant upon delivery of another. Using the above example, priorities may well be as follows:

PRIORITY	TASK	WHY
1.	Rescue the failed train or detrain passengers	Because of heat build up on the train as air-conditioning is non-operational
2.	Restore operation on the slow lines	Because the full evening peak service can operate over two lines
3.	Repair the damaged OHL equipment on the fast lines.	Because repairs will require the down slow to be blocked and the work can be done overnight instead.

In this example it is possible that dealing with priority one first may divert some resource away from priorities two and three (e.g. the Mobile Operations Manager). Also priorities two and three may conflict in the way that they impact upon the working practices adopted by engineers on site.

It is important to note that prioritisation is not the same as a milestone plan (which is just a sequence of events). In the example above priority 1 is to rescue the passengers because of the potential discomfort that could build up quickly. Priority 2 is to run a service on the slow lines. A clear decision has been taken not to repair the fast lines because the strategy is to run trains on the remaining infrastructure.

7.2 Prioritised Planning

Where resources are required for two or more tasks they should be allocated according to the priorities.

STEP 4 - Assess & Question

Assessing and questioning will continue throughout the incident cycle; the existence of Step 4 does not mean that it stops after this phase. Step 4 will;
- Determine a decision on the course of action for the next stages of incident management.
- Rule in/out certain options.
- Enable decision-making with the fullest available information (as it is unlikely to be possible to go back and change without impacting on the whole recovery process).
- Sense-checking the combined information.
- Task specific individuals with specific actions to clarify existing information and/or obtain further information.

In essence the quality of assessments made at this stage and the quality of questioning and the answers received will determine the quality of the plan. If assumptions are not identified and tested at this stage it is possible that fundamental flaws will not be dealt with.

This step is still very early in the incident cycle and the full picture will still be emerging. Once the problem has been broken into key parts and prioritised, subsequent information gathering and the processes used to obtain this further information can be structured according to the priorities given.

Clear timescales should be allotted to immediate actions so the plan can be promptly finalised and tracked. This is vitally important, as whilst most plans will involve the control office and site staff, they are likely to include other staff at different locations: for example staff in signalling centres or Electrical Control Room operators. Actions should be given to the person most likely to be able to carry them out effectively and promptly. All requests should be recorded.

At the end of this phase there should be a clear plan to bring stability to the situation although some aspects of the plan may still contain gaps and therefore need further structured information gathering. It may not yet be possible to accurately estimate completion timescales but you should know "what" the problem is and have plans to tackle it;

Running a railway during disruption

PRIORITY 3	ACTIONS	KNOWN	REQUIRED
Repair the damaged OHL equipment on the fast lines	Staff to assess damage and understand requirements for repair have been mobilised to attend site	It is a long job, affecting at least the next 2 Peaks, ETA on site 10 minutes	Detail of damage and what is required to repair
	Person in charge (an Asset Recovery Manager) identified and appointed	ETA on site 40 minutes	Options for recovery which get the slow lines open quickly
	Personnel and equipment being organised	Named person at depot arranging	Immediate mobilisation of longer lead-time equipment
	Owner within Control has been appointed and advised to ARM	Incident Controller	Liaison with all parties, contact adjacent depots for support

In other words, the full picture will be emerging and the next steps will be understood.

It is vital to remember:-

- To identify and test assumptions (and preliminary estimates) at this stage: questioning is about checking that the plan which is being formulated will actually work!
- That the plan will not be fully formed and it is better to be decisive and roughly right within an acceptable timescale than precisely wrong some hours later.

STEP 5 - Circulate Draft Plan & Refine

The purpose of this stage is to;
- Refine.
- Validate.
- Check the basic plan.
- Create a sense of common ownership amongst those who are to work on it and deliver it.

In the early stages this may involve a control office arranging a time-out to briefly discuss the problem, the priorities and current actions to resolve it, along with an overview of the objective. It is important to check that the agreed

7.2 Prioritised Planning

action plan can deliver the objectives in accordance with the priorities adopted.

Undertaking this stage will act as an important sense-check. Problems and potential showstoppers may be identified here. It is vitally important to question any problem to check whether there is another way of addressing it.

Using the example in Step 3;

	PRIORITY 2	**PRIORITY 3**
Emerging Problem	Allowing trains to run on the slow lines …	… means that we cannot repair the damaged OHL equipment on the fast lines in time for the start of service the following day
Why		Because machines will need 10 hours to complete the work and we need the slow lines blocked to get machines to the site of work

This illustrates the kind of conflicting priorities that frequently have to be resolved in such situations. There is no right answer but the trade-off will need to be between a short slow line block (to allow machines access to the fast lines) and the risk of an overrunning possession the following morning. This must be a negotiated balanced solution.

To successfully refine the plan it is vital that:
- All relevant parties are involved in the discussion.
- The discussion is both time-bound and structured.
- The discussion has clear leadership to avoid the risk of debate with no agreed solution/plan.
- The plan is circulated to engage with those who may be able to help validate or test it (on-call managers) and to provide information to those impacted by the problem (customers).
- The intended plan is verified by the appropriate on-call/line manager. This is particularly important for non-routine and complex incidents.

It is all too easy to miss the input of those who are not based in the control office; in the dewirement example used above, the Electrical Control Room operators are key parties and should be fully involved.

STEP 6 - Delegate Responsibility & Issue the Plan

Once a fit for purpose plan is formulated, responsibilities for delivery should be allocated. Do not simply give all on site actions to the Rail Incident Officer, just because a Gold-Silver-Bronze command structure has been implemented. The command structure is not designed to constrain or inhibit the appropriate response to an incident. Different controllers may take ownership of individual elements of the plan and prioritised individual steps for everyone involved should be set out in a time-line.

Circulating a prioritised plan with clear responsibilities and reporting milestones will ensure everyone involved knows what is planned and who is tasked with delivering the different parts.

STEP 7 - Reporting Progress

Once the plan is issued each step can be measured and any change in plan (e.g. a timescale slipping) can be reviewed in the context of the whole plan to establish the potential impact.

It is vital that those reporting understand their role in delivering the overall objective. They will need to understand which issues are mission-critical and need to be flagged. Often people can fail to pass on a piece of information that later proves to be critical because it did not seem important at the time.

For example, the lack of a suitable access point close to the scene of the dewirement may not seem vital whilst dealing with the first priorities of the stranded train and restoring operation on the slow lines but if it subsequently transpires that this fact results in an extension of the rectification time into an additional peak period, it may be that different decisions would have been taken at the very start of the incident to avoid this problem.

The simple rule is to report anything that has the potential to upset delivery of the plan.

Use of a template to report progress in pager messages can be useful.

STEP 8 - Review & Refine the Plan as Necessary

Once there is a plan in place it should be subject to consistent ongoing review. Logically, suitable review points can be agreed and these may result in structured conferences or internal reviews. The importance of a structure to the communications plan cannot be emphasised enough. Planned update timescales from site, planned communication with customers and planned reviews

7.2 Prioritised Planning

based around key milestones which provide an opportunity to react effectively to any problems that are identified during the review.

Reviews and conferences require clear, structured management. They can quickly become talking-shops, which achieve little other than take up precious time. Consider carefully your attendees and structure your agenda, be clear about agreed actions and owners.

STEP 9 - Service Recovery & Restoration

The plan does not finish at restoration of the infrastructure. The plan aims will be to provide our customers with the service that we promised in the first place. The plan must extend through to restoration of normal train services both in respect of the basic train plan and in customers' perception.

For example, the OLE may be repaired, passengers may be experiencing the twenty minute train service that they expect but unit and crew resource is completely off plan. Loosing grip on the detail at this stage may result in deterioration later.

See section 7.5 on Service Recovery.

OTHER CONSIDERATIONS

The ability to manage incidents according to prioritised planning principles must be a key competence of Control staff and also those involved with incident management on the ground. However you cannot take for granted that staff will be able to work in this way automatically. Considerable effort is needed in training, incident review and competence assessment to achieve the standard required. Because prioritised planning is so important for Control staff it should also be included as skill that is considered when recruiting Control staff.

Tips

Planning is iterative therefore assessing, reviewing, refining and revising will be needed in some part whenever something changes

This process is a tool – not an end in itself

The degree to which structured planning is applied should be dependent on the scale and impact of the incident

Running a railway during disruption

Remember the objective is not rigid adherence to a process but the best possible outcome in the quickest possible time

Do not forget – this is a prioritised planning example. It is vital that the regular provision of good information to staff and passengers and robust customer service arrangements flow from the decision making process.

7.3 Estimates for Resuming Normal Working

BACKGROUND

It is a fact that most people involved in fault rectification are too optimistic and often do not consider the individual steps required to rectify the problem and how long those steps will take. Consequently lengthy disruption is usually bedevilled by poor estimates, "another twenty minutes guv", and poor decision-making. The reality is that one frequently leads to the other. People who are 'do-ers' by nature often do not want to stop to plan but this is absolutely essential and will result in more accurate, well-informed time estimates. That is why the previous Section 7.2 on "Prioritised Planning" is so important.

The risks entailed in getting estimates wildly wrong are enormous. If the estimate is too optimistic, decisions taken to restore, or ramp up, the train service may lead to far greater disruption, for longer than should be the case. Critically our customers often make their individual travel decisions based on the estimates provided. Poor estimates can make the decisions they reach very sub-optimal (much to their annoyance!)

Once an estimate has been over-shot it is highly unlikely that the next estimate will be any better. An inaccurate plan is unlikely to be replaced with a better one when people are under even more pressure. That is why one poor estimate is often replaced with another, then another … and then none at all!

If the estimate is too pessimistic, the lost opportunity to use the repaired infrastructure more fully earlier may provoke criticism. In reality, there is no 'right side failure' here, and much to be gained from giving the best and most accurate estimate at whatever stage the job has reached, and for fully and properly assessing the risks.

Finally, bear in mind that there is a difference between estimates for resolving the problem and estimates for resuming normal services; relax once the

7.3 Estimates for Resuming Normal Working

problem is fixed and the impact will continue for longer than it should.

Good estimates are the single most important issue in managing service disruption and providing good information to customers.

WHAT DOES 'ESTIMATE' MEAN?

This may seem a daft question but clarity is needed because different information will be possible at different stages of an incident and a request for an estimate may be understood as one thing when another was meant.

There is no real common meaning defined within standards but the following can be used as a guide.

Initial Estimate

A time estimate for how long disruption will last is one of the key pieces of information required by our customers. As soon as we first tell them that their travel plans are disrupted, they will rightly expect to be told by how much and for how long! Traditionally the railway has been awful at providing this information but the need to get much better is now recognised.

As soon as the incident has commenced, an initial estimate must be provided. This will be very heavily caveated because it will be based on limited facts, previous experience and a healthy dose of pessimism – it is by necessity little more than a 'guesstimate'.

More robust contingent 'guesstimates' can be created for controllers in advance by analysing timescales for common types of incident at key locations to draw up some standard times. Asking control and response staff to evaluate such estimates for reasonableness will improve their value and obtain more buy-in.

Initial estimates are unlikely to need much input from site staff – they may not even have arrived on site when you need to provide one! Accuracy may not be all-important – initially it may be sufficient to know whether you are aiming at rectification for the morning peak, the evening peak or tomorrow. However, site staff should be expected to provide an initial estimate based on their immediate findings but bear in mind that this will be highly subjective.

Interim Estimate

You may not be able to provide an estimate for rectification or for normal service resumption because it is simply impossible to say. This may be because an investigation is required to find the actual fault e.g. a major signalling failure caused by a suspected cable fault that will require cable testing to identify the location of the problem before technicians can work out what they need to

Running a railway during disruption

do to rectify it. It may be because the problem appears to be complex and you simply have insufficient information to make the call.

In these cases it is best to proceed on a worst case scenario. What if the technicians find the cable fault in the last piece of cable that gets tested and it requires a new cable to be run out and spliced in? You will however be able to provide estimates for interim milestones and these may be sufficient to help you and your customers make decisions e.g. 'Technicians expected on site to begin investigations in 45 minutes' or 'It may take as long as 2 hours to locate the problem'.

Firm Estimate

Once you have a detailed plan of activities required to resolve the problem it should be possible to put times to each step and work out how long the job will take. This will be a detailed estimate and can be expected to have a high level of accuracy. However you may have to wait a while to get it and there is a balance to be struck between "calling it" and waiting for the last minuscule detail. The 80-20 rule applies!

Targets

There is no harm in pushing for better timescales and setting targets but be careful that people do not tell you what they think you want to hear because this is likely to backfire. Challenge should be phrased along the lines of, "You've given me an estimate of 1700, what would you need to do to get that back to 1530?"

Milestones

A firm estimate for long jobs is always more credible if it is backed up with a number of key milestones which have their own estimates for completion. Tracking against milestones allows an assessment of whether the firm estimate is still achievable or whether progress is slipping.

ISSUES

The Prioritised Planning Section 7.2 addresses the issues to be considered when determining the strategy for resolving a disruptive incident. Estimates can affect the strategy: if a decision is being made about whether to prioritise running on two lines or repairing so that all four can be used, then the estimate for repair will clearly be important.

7.3 Estimates for Resuming Normal Working

Remembering the following will help produce robust estimates:

What is the experience of previous incidents of this type?
- Is there an established estimate that can be used?

What information is known and what is not known?
- What are the best and worse cases depending on this information?
- How long will it be before this information is available?
- How are you going to obtain this information?

What is the estimate dependent on?
- Are there critical resources that are needed to achieve the estimate?
- How certain are you that these resources will be provided and on time?
- Are their any remaining unknowns?
- How will the estimate be affected by environmental conditions?
- Are the estimates to get the required staff to the site appropriate?
- Has the estimate been checked for compatibility against other activities taking place?

Has the estimate been checked?
- Does the estimate make sense? You can't walk a mile and examine overhead line on foot in five minutes for example.
- Was the estimate produced by someone under pressure to deliver on site?
- Is there an independent person there to take a dispassionate view?
- Is there a milestone plan? For more complex tasks is there a full project plan with resources allocated and dependencies checked?

Has anything been missed?
- Does the estimate include time taken to remove equipment from site and hand back possessions and isolations?
- Does the estimate include time for the first trains to pass through the section at caution if this is required?
- Does the estimate include time taken to rescue any units trapped in the possession. It can take a considerable amount of time to build up air.
- Does the estimate include a contingency buffer or not? Should it?
- Are the assumptions used to create the estimate correct? E.g. lines to be blocked, extent of possession, caution to be applied to adjacent lines etc

Note: Any solution that loses additional running lines, even on a temporary basis, will require careful consideration, particularly during peak operating times.

Running a railway during disruption

Making a decision on the best information is crucial. This will require knowledge of the infrastructure configuration and knowledge of the critical technical issues (but be aware that 80% of the problems are caused by 20% of the issues so do not hold out for 100% certainty). Ensure information comes from as close to the problem as possible but beware over burdening key people at the site. Conversely do not rely on hearsay as this usually exaggerates any situation.

Ensure you develop a rough milestone plan and re-visit this periodically during the incident to refine it as necessary.

Forging a good relationship with key infrastructure and fleet managers is essential. Similarly, ensuring those managers understand the operating requirements and imperatives will pay dividends.

An Engineering Supervisor in a possession, or a Fault Team Leader working on a track circuit failure will have pressing concerns with the work, and be less inclined (and have much less incentive) to give or discuss estimates for resumption. Appointing an Asset Recovery Manager (ARM) will improve the quality of estimates and communication from site considerably.

Having a manager there to deal with this aspect of the incident leaving the frontline engineers to fix the problem is best practice. For TOC incidents such as train failures, deploying a TOLO in addition to the fleet engineer can provide the same facility. For complex incidents such a dewirements both TOC and NR resources for communication will be invaluable.

In all cases consider the skills of the individual on site charged with creating the time estimate. Often it will be a senior operator or maintainer within NR who can be reasonably assumed to have good knowledge of the job, the routines needed to complete it, and the time this will take. However do check on this, the first responder may be an inexperienced individual who happened to be closest to the incident. In such circumstances the provision of more experienced support may be sensible.

More detailed information on Prioritised Planning is contained in the relevant Section 7.2, but the key steps are:-
- Understand the problem.
- Understand the options and their impact.
- Evaluate and assess the potential outcomes.
- Determine the optimal solution.
- Communicate the decision.
- Review regularly.

Beware misplaced optimism and estimates that fly in the face of previous outcomes. Once an estimate is approved, ensure that the information is quickly communicated to key people and, most importantly, the passengers.

Tips

Be clear about what you ask for and what you are getting: Initial Estimate or Guesstimate, Interim Estimate or Firm Estimate

There is no reason why some sort of estimate cannot be provided.

Challenge estimates to increase your level of confidence.

Remember - wanting something to happen does not make it happen. Always apply common sense to the estimates you are given.

7.4 Restricted Track Access

BACKGROUND

This term is used to describe a temporary reduction in line capacity due to an incident or unplanned event.

When line capacity is reduced the available number of paths is reduced. As a consequence operators will have to operate reduced services or in some cases completely cancel services. This section describes the arrangements that should be deployed to best manage any restriction of access.

There are clear duties on Network Rail and on TOCs contained in the Railway Operational Code. Essentially this requires Network Rail to plan for reasonably foreseeable circumstances and to pre-agree train service plans with TOCs for those circumstances. In the event of disruption Network Rail has the overall responsibility for implementing these plans in agreement with the affected operators but also has the power to implement plans where consensus cannot be reached.

ISSUES

NR will have contingency plans covering Restricted Access. These should

Running a railway during disruption

be agreed in advance by all train operators involved and be reviewed at each timetable change or when other circumstances change for example, a change in service patterns, traffic flows etc.

These NR plans should be supported by a range of TOC/FOC train services contingency plans that must match and support the specified levels of access.

Relevant TOC/FOC plans must be:-
- Based on the range of reduced access possibilities detailed in NR plans.
- Capable of being resourced.
- Robust and resilient.
- Capable of delivering an appropriate level of service.
- Underwritten by customer service plans.

Restricted Access plans are a key feature of contingency plans and such plans must be appropriate, robust and fully agreed.

Issues to consider when producing or reviewing Restricted Access contingency plans are:-
- Use of Temporary Block Working.
- Use of Single Line Working.
- Coasting to avoid damaged but physically clear OHLE.
- Flighting (several consecutive trains in the same direction).
- Coupling trains together in order to share paths through the restricted area.
- Introducing an amended timetable possibly omitting intermediate stops.

The main problems with Restricted Access plans occur when there is a failure to implement the relevant plans or a deviation from the plans. Insist that the agreed plans are implemented and escalate the problem as far as necessary to get resolution at the time.

Recently it has become possible to hold validated contingency timetables within Network Rail's integrated timetable planning system (ITPS). This makes it considerably easier to implement a restricted access plan on a day A for day B basis since the timetable will flow to downstream systems such as CIS (Customer Information Screens), ARS (Automatic Route Setting) and TRUST (Train Running System Tops). Currently only a limited number of plans have been developed to this level of detail, the majority are designed to deal with significant reductions in network capacity due to severe snow.

Tips

Always plan for this eventuality in advance and on the day implement the relevant plans. Better to have any disagreements and resolve them at the planning stage rather than on the day.

Make sure that TOC plans are appropriate. Mis-matches between agreed diversionary route requirements and Driver route knowledge requirements are a real risk.

Finally do not necessarily accept restricted access as a given.
- Is there an alternative e.g. diesel hauled trains, temporary block working?
- Have all possibilities been explored?

But remember - do not be over ambitious with use of the available capacity.

7.5 Service Recovery

BACKGROUND

Service Recovery is a general term which describes the operational process by which train services are returned to timetabled working following disruption. This may be achieved by a variety of means, including curtailing of late running services, omitting station call, running fast, cancellation and stepping up or stepping down of rolling stock and crews.

However most TOCs have a train service reliability target established in the franchise agreement, and this imposes a ceiling on the number of full and part cancellations allowable in any four week period before contractual obligations with Government are threatened. Potentially this creates a tension between good operational practises that are in customers' interests and a TOCs' contractual obligations.

However the Government does recognise that actions taken to restore timetabled operation following disruption are generally in the best overall interests of customers, and is prepared to discount full and part cancellations resulting from the application of service recovery principles. Cancellations for which dispensation has been given by the Department for Transport (DfT) will be excluded from the TOC contractual reliability targets.

Running a railway during disruption

As a result, a set of relevant arrangements have been codified in an industry Approved Code of Practice (ACOP), Service Recovery which details the formal actions, arrangements and procedures which must be applied, and the records which must be kept, to allow a successful claim by a TOC for dispensation for cancellations to be made to the DfT.

Essentially therefore the ACOP is a means of trying to avoid contractual arrangements on one party (TOCs) getting in the way of good customer focused operational decision making for all parties (TOCs, FOCs and Network Rail). Recovering the service is therefore made easier by removing the conflict generated by differing objectives.

Service Recovery is therefore a term which has two meanings:
- The operational processes for recovering the service to normal running after a disruptive incident.
- The arrangements agreed with the DfT to allow cancellations caused by service recovery to be excluded from TOC franchise service reliability targets.

OPERATIONAL PROCESSES AND PRINCIPLES

A fast return to the normal timetable is important following disruption. However, whilst speed of recovery is important so are customer service requirements. It is therefore vital that the process of recovery does not unduly damage the service being operated in the meantime. A balance needs to be struck between rapid and effective recovery and not leaving customers stranded as a result of the recovery process!

When developing operational processes for service recovery the following principles should be considered:-
- Have a plan for the most frequently occurring types of disruption. This might include incidents at a particular time of day or where particular groups of lines are blocked. Recovery in the late afternoon in time for the evening peak is a good example. Your customers will appreciate consistency.
- Act quickly. The effort required to recover the service is usually smaller if the service alterations are made quickly.
- Prevent bow waves of services. It does not make sense to allow large numbers of services to approach key turn round points. Prevent services from starting where you can and turn services progressively along the route.
- The easiest service recovery actions can be to prevent services from entering the network in the first place. Services that start from carriage sidings prior to the evening peak are an example.
- Identify opportunities to start journeys at right time with the right crew.

Once you have achieved this then the remainder of the traincrew and unit diagrams have a good chance of running to time as well.
- Consider how much time can be regained through turnround at destination. There may be little point in terminating a train that is 10 minutes late short of destination if it normally has a 20 minute turnround.
- Provide additional resources at key locations to help with communication and command and control. Having an authoritative manager on site can mean that the decisions made by the Control are implemented more quickly.
- Have a plan for special stop orders to cover for cancellations. These plans should define those services that should stop and those services that must not.
- Make sure you understand traincrew and catering staff implications of service recovery decisions. Cancelling a train that is due to carry a number of drivers travelling passenger to form other services might cause more problems that it is worth!
- Know what the acceptable limits of service recovery are. At times it will be necessary to run trains to provide sufficient capacity. Try to have these conversations in advance rather than in the heat of the recovery process.
- Do not forget fleet maintenance issues and the required balance of rolling stock for the following day. Service recovery can backfire if units cannot be maintained and especially fuelled, or there is not the right amount of stock in key locations to form the morning service.

A particular tactic sometimes employed as part of service recovery is the use of emergency headcodes. This involves cancelling off the original services and operating an alternative with a revised headcode. Care is needed here. In some cases emergency headcodes are an obvious solution: for example when implementing an unplanned shuttle service in a branch line, or to identify trains that are running with significantly altered stops as part of the recovery process.

In other cases it is a tactic that is used simply to reduce the delay minutes of an incident without having any effect on the service to the customer. It can also introduce problems such as difficulties in matching traincrew diagrams and CIS databases with the revised timetable, and increasing the likelihood of wrong routings by Signallers. It is an approach that should be used only when absolutely necessary and with great care.

DfT SERVICE RECOVERY AGREEMENT

General Provisions

The principal DfT requirements relating to Service Recovery are shown below. These are only a summary of the requirements and Managers should familiarise

Running a railway during disruption

themselves with the full provisions of the ACOP, and any supplementary guidance which may be issued from time to time.

Service Recovery is the process by which normal timetabled operation is restored, or an agreed degraded timetable is implemented following a disruptive event which blocks or restricts access to the infrastructure. The purpose of service recovery is to;

- Expedite recovery and return to the normal timetable as quickly as possible
- Minimise overall disruption to all customers by providing a more balanced, integrated service.
- Minimise overall delay.
- Apply contingency arrangements in a consistent manner.
- Allow dispensation to be secured from DfT for eligible franchised TOC cancellations.

The Network Rail Route Control Manager (RCM) will initiate the service recovery process by calling a conference of all affected parties following notification of a disruptive event

The time of this first conference is deemed to be the time at which the service recovery arrangements have been initiated, after which cancellations may be eligible for dispensation by DfT, subject to the TOC making a satisfactory claim – the Service Recovery Commencement Time (SRCT) will be formally logged by both TOC and NR, and will be supporting evidence in any claim to DfT.

In practice there will be at least three phases to any disruptive incident:-

- An initial phase immediately following the incident when delay and disruption occurs in an uncontrolled manner.
- A second phase following the service recovery conference, when the contingency plans are implemented, and an orderly revised or reduced service is implemented whilst the disruptive event is still taking place.
- A third phase when the disruptive event is resolved or contained at which point a full recovery to normal working can be initiated.

The transition points between phases are absolutely crucial. These are the risk areas where service management can be lost, particularly in transition from contingency to normal operation.

Subject to having applied the contingency plans in a suitable manner, cancellations which occur in all phases following SRCT are eligible for dispensation.

Both the TOC and NR Duty Managers should keep a full record of events as they develop in the Control Log. These records will be required to support any claim for dispensation from DfT.

7.5 Service Recovery

The NR RCM will be responsible for monitoring progress at the incident site, and for liaison with any staff on site, such as the Rail Incident Officer (RIO). He/she may call conferences from time to time to review operations, the effectiveness of contingency plans, and progress towards restoration of normal working. At the point at which NR advise a 'Firm' estimate for restoration, the TOC should plan for an orderly return to full service and normal working.

The incident will be formally closed with the closure of the TRUST Incident Number (TIN). A review of the event, and the recovery process, should be undertaken between the TOC and NR Controls at a suitable time soon after the incident is resolved.

For 'Force Majeure' events (those which extend beyond 12 hours and for which an emergency timetable is implemented and uploaded to TSDB), the requirement to seek dispensation for cancellations will not apply as different contractual arrangements can be invoked. However, the operational and customer service requirement to run an optimal contingency service in conjunction with NR continues to apply at all times, and it is expected that the operational provisions within service recovery will be routinely applied to incident management and contingency in all circumstances.

Summary of Service Recovery 2009 Revision

The service recovery provisions contained in the form of a Code of Practice have existed in the industry since 1999, and have been updated and reiterated on a number of occasions. The most significant recent alterations cover the definition of Eligible Cancellations, and the use of the term 'capacity' to describe seats to plan;

Eligible Cancellations : Where these have been occasioned within a legitimate service recovery event which meets the criteria outlined in the ACOP e.g. the cancellations have occurred between the start of the incident (the SRCT) and the closure of the TRUST Incident Number (TIN) - they are deemed to include:-
- Full cancellations.
- Part cancellations (start forward or terminate short).
- Missed stops or other deviations from scheduled calling points.
- Diversions from booked route.

In general, services affected directly by train failure, or cancelled en route for lack of a relief train crew, are deemed to be 'culprit' trains and are not eligible. This applies not just to the primary service affected, but cancellation of any other working of that train in diagram.

Running a railway during disruption

There is, however, an important exclusion to this policy. The DfT is keen to ensure that the 'culprit' train provisions are not overly onerous on TOCs or lead potentially to perverse behaviour. Such reaction is felt to be possible in two specific scenarios. Branch line failures, where a single train failure could lead to a large number of cancellations; and low frequency, long distance services.

In both scenarios, TOCs may mitigate the impact of such cancellations on the Franchise Agreement Reliability Regime (Schedule 7) through deployment of a pre-agreed contingency plan. The plan must, by definition, be customer focused, and must significantly mitigate customer impact from the service suspension. Generally speaking, on branch lines this is likely to be some form of road substitute, for an agreed period of time, after which the planned train service would need to be reinstated.

On long distance services, the contingency plan might include special stop orders on closely following fast trains, or diversion of one or more services from an alternative route, although any impact on customers on these trains must be minimised.

In both of the above scenarios, the TOC must firstly pre-agree its contingency plan with NR, in accordance with the Railway Operational Code, then with the relevant Franchise Manager at the DfT.

Capacity Shortfalls - In certain circumstances, dispensation under service recovery may be granted post-event to TOCs for train service capacity shortfalls, where, due to circumstances during the Service Recovery incident, it was not possible to log all instances of train service capacity shortfall. This will be particularly relevant for instances of train service capacity shortfall that do not cause delay or cancellation and consequently no TRUST Delay Incident (TDI) for service recovery exists, or where the volume of services being below capacity due to a disruptive event, overwhelms the TOC Control's capability to maintain the desired log in real time. The Network Rail Route Control is required to keep records of such circumstances should the TOC need evidence to support its claim. Full details are shown in the current Service Recovery ACOP.

GENERAL ISSUES

The processes and procedures for managing service recovery are both well established and thoroughly tested within the industry. Consequently there are no grounds, or justification for failure to implement customer focused arrangements that adhere to both the letter and the spirit of the Code of Practice.

Reasons (excuses) sometimes given for not adhering are:-
- "Contingency plans not right for the circumstances".
- "NR/TOC wanted to do it differently".
- "Didn't have time to discuss the arrangements with NR/other TOCs".
- "Didn't need to claim dispensation for the cancellations/failures to call – TOC threshold not in danger of being exceeded".
- "Didn't have time to log all the details".

None of these are valid reasons – each one of them would, if true, constitute a primary failing in the Control Office and should be addressed robustly.

Issues between a TOC and NR, or other TOCs, must be flushed out at an early stage – an operator demonstrating a firm commitment to disciplined application will often be enough to force other, more wayward, organisations into line.

Tips

Control Managers and Controllers need support and challenge to stay disciplined in the application of Service Recovery.

Applying structured service recovery arrangements is not just about TOC contractual dispensation - it is first & foremost a sound operational tool.

Effective Service Recovery is totally dependent on the application of proven procedures - use them, they are a key to good customer-focused train service delivery.

7.6 Passenger Information During Disruption (PIDD)

INTRODUCTION

The need for timely, correct and consistent passenger information is at its highest during disruption, particularly serious disruption. However this is when the provision of such information is most difficult and all passenger train operators should therefore have robust arrangements that can cope with all foreseeable circumstances. It is essential to include all the relevant people and processes within the TOC, Network Rail and other key organisations, such as National Rail Enquiries.

Running a railway during disruption

This Section outlines the generic issues and must be read in conjunction with the Section covering Passenger Information in Section 6.

The Sections covering Prioritised Planning and Estimates for Resuming Normal Working are also fundamental to the advice provided in this Section.

BACKGROUND

There has been an increased focus on providing better passenger information during disruption since 2008 and in 2012 the ORR made certain aspects of information provision a licence conditions for TOCs.

This is not a new issue but it is one which the industry is increasingly coming to grips with. PIDD is one of the few challenges that span the entire operational railway, from incident response staff to those on the front line at stations and those in call-centres. It also involves many different companies and organisations

It is therefore important that operators make sure the arrangements they rely on are robust and remain fit for purpose at all times.

Detailed information on current industry requirements are contained in a code of practice issued by ATOC. This document is not legally binding but it does cover all relevant activities and has been in place since 2009.

It is vital that organisational boundaries do not become obstacles to delivery. Train operators will rely heavily on NR to provide significant input into the arrangements that are essential to information provision. They will also invariably rely on other companies' station operators to provide information to their customers at some stations, other companies' controllers may provide certain information and even internally it is possible that PIDD responsibilities will be split between departments (e.g. Retail / Customer Service and operations).

PRINCIPLES

Passenger Focus has identified six key elements in how passengers in disruption want the situation to be handled and these are:
- Treat me with respect.
- Recognise my plight.
- Help me avoid the problem in the first place.
- You got me into this, help get me out.
- Act joined up.
- I am 'always' delayed, do something about it!

7.6 Passenger Information During Disruption (PIDD)

The key aims of robust PIDD arrangements must be to ensure that:-
- All staff know what they need to do to deliver good quality passenger information.
- Systems are aligned and configured to deliver 'One Version of The Truth'.
- The best current information is regularly provided to all staff and customers.
- Network-wide processes are consistently applied and measured & reviewed.

The arrangements must cover all the following activities:-
- Site Actions.
- Control Operations Actions.
- Management Engagement/Involvement (Real time).
- Control Information Actions.
- Core information requirements.
- NRCC Information Actions (National Rail Enquiries).
- Station Information.
- On Train Information.
- Internet and telephone Information.
- SMS/Email/Social Media alerts.

These are illustrated in the following schematic that illustrates how the provision of good information to passengers depends on all activities being properly aligned and integrated; and then delivered by trained, competent people.

Running a railway during disruption

Key PIDD Outputs

Incident Management

Site
- Initial assessment provided
- Clear understanding of problem/issues
- Correct operational and technical resources mobilised/engaged
- Provision of robust estimates in line with emerging Plans
- Provision of updates against plan milestones

Control Ops
- Early Holding Message to all points
- Problem broken into key parts & actions prioritised
- Mobilisation and co-ordination of on site resources
- Escalation to appropriate (On Call) managers
- Prioritised Plan disseminated
- Implementation of Ops Contingency Plans
- Estimates of resumption of services

Information Formulation & Dissemination

Management Involvement
- Engagement of appropriate (On Call) managers
- Actions & tactics validated
- Estimates common sensed and Prioritised Plan verified
- Clear separation of Operations and Customer Service responsibilities
- Implementation of supporting Service Disruption arrangements

TOC Control Info
- Provision of regular Core Messages
- Information on operational tactics
- Respond to station staff enquiries
- Respond to traincrew enquiries
- Supervise CIS/PA systems

NRCC Info
- Input of regular summary messages to NRE systems
- Liaise with TOC/FOC/NR controls
- Input changes to NRTD (Darwin)
- Monitor impact of incident
- Enhance predictive forecasts as necessary

Customer Information Provision

Station Info
- Mobilisation for enhanced customer support
- Liaison with Hub Station/or Control
- Supervise CIS/PA systems
- Supplementary CIS/PA announcements
- Displaying Special Notices etc.
- Response to individual passenger enquiries

On Train Info
- Regular liaison with signaller/Control as necessary
- Regular liaison between Driver & Guard and Guard & OBS/CATs
- Good quality regular PA announcements in accordance with defined script/specification
- Visual information via On Board PIS system
- Enhanced levels of support (Customer Info & Care)
- Responding to emerging customer special needs

Internet Info
- Regularly updated information
- Disruption information overtly available/flagged
- Information that is consistent with other sources
- Linked to choices/alternatives where possible

Phone Info
- Regularly updated information
- Disruption information offered when affecting chosen journey
- Information that is consistent with other sources
- Linked to choices/alternatives where possible

Section 7

348 Operators' Handbook

7.6 Passenger Information During Disruption (PIDD)

ISSUES

Each Passenger Train Operator must pre-define service disruption thresholds above which their PIDD arrangements will always be applied. A threshold may cover the entire operating area (e.g. TOC) or be route specific. Thresholds must take account of industry passenger feedback and research. They must also be set such as to avoid inconsistencies between operators using the same routes and recognise that almost 40% of passenger journeys involve more than one TOCs services.

This will enable Passenger Train Operators and associated Network Rail Route(s) to trigger their enhanced information arrangements at an appropriate point and provide staff (and third parties such as NRE- National Rail Enquiries) with the confidence that regular information will be available for passing on to passengers. It will also enable Passenger Train Operators to introduce any additional predetermined operational/ customer service arrangements that are associated with their management of Major Delays/Disruption.

This enhanced level of mobilisation/information provision is generally designated Customer Service Level 2 (CSL2).

Current good practice links CSL2 to simple pre-defined service status phases (often colour coded like London Underground).

This is shown in diagram form below:-

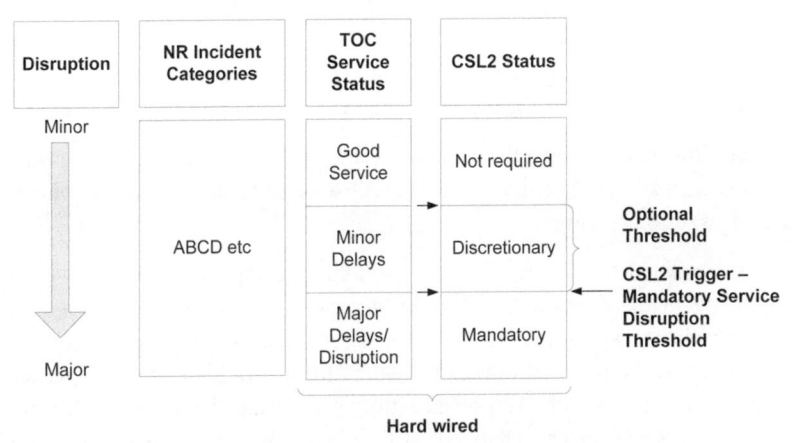

Disruption	NR Incident Categories	TOC Service Status	CSL2 Status	
Minor ↓ Major	ABCD etc	Good Service	Not required	
		Minor Delays	Discretionary	Optional Threshold
		Major Delays/ Disruption	Mandatory	CSL2 Trigger – Mandatory Service Disruption Threshold

Hard wired

Running a railway during disruption

Whenever disruption occurs an initial (holding) message should be issued.

When disruption exceeds a TOC threshold the designated staff in control offices will normally be required to:-
- Issue notification that CSL2 has been put in place.
- Appoint a Lead Operations Controller and a Lead Information Controller.
- Send Core Messages at intervals not exceeding 20 minutes.
- Prepare a prioritised plan.
- Engage the appropriate TOCs and Network Rail resources and managers.
- Consider activation of other TOCs and Network Rail arrangements, which may be pre-defined, according to the emerging circumstances (e.g. Hub Stations).

During long-term disruption, once the train service is stable (even if a reduced timetable) and customer service needs are in steady state, there is less need for Core Messages at 20 minute intervals. Under such circumstances, CSL2 may be withdrawn.

The key test for withdrawal of CSL2 is that normal customer service arrangements can be applied.

The site and control operations activities are an essential foundation for good information. The effectiveness of these will be heavily dependent on the application of the principles contained in the Section covering Prioritised Planning.

Control information activities rely on a clear control operations focal point for providing information on the current plan and progress against the plan. The person central to this is often designated a Lead Operations Controller.

Note: Information Controllers can get seriously overloaded if they are bombarded with all the information that flows back and forth with control offices during a serious incident.

Consideration of the structure of workload for Information Controllers needs to be taken. On top of structured information provision they are often responsible for co-ordinating customer service aspects such as arranging alternative road transport and liaison with other transport providers for ticket acceptance issues. They may also be responsible for maintaining the accuracy of train running information (cancellations, part-cancellations etc) in passenger-facing information systems.

Therefore, Information Control resources will often need to be strengthened during serious disruption. Use of "hub" stations can assist here since it reduces the number of people in direct contact with the Information Controller and delegates some of the communication workload to the hub station staff.

7.6 Passenger Information During Disruption (PIDD)

Line Managers and On Call Managers must be properly engaged in any incident, but oversight of PIDD arrangements must be a key part of a nominated manager's responsibilities.

Information Controllers will generally use IT systems to issue core messages. Systems such as Tyrell I/O have much of the current PIDD good practice built in but be wary of slavishly following a template as this can result in 'mechanistic' or impersonal information being issued.

An initial holding message and subsequent core messages are the absolute essence of good PIDD arrangements. Guidance covering this aspect is contained in the ATOC PIDD Code of Practice.

The National Rail Communications Centre (NRCC) operated by National Rail Enquiries has a critical role in providing Passenger Information to a wide audience and Train Operators must ensure their arrangements are integrated with NRE. This is best achieved by a Service Level Agreement setting out the obligations of each party. TOC operators should meet with NRE staff on a regular basis to discuss information requirements.

Customer Service arrangements that will apply during serious disruption can be sensibly linked to PIDD arrangements.

Frontline staff on stations, on trains etc. must have the confidence that good consistent information will be provided at the agreed frequencies.

Scripts provided to station staff and on-train personnel such as Guards, must include PIDD arrangements and be linked to the Core Messages that will be issued whenever CSL2 is declared.

A common weakness in communication arrangements is provision of information to drivers of Driver Only Operated (DOO) services. Station staff can provide information at station stops, but the most effective form of update is the radio general call from the signalling centre. Arrangements must be put in place to support Signallers in making these calls frequently during even minor service disruption. Customers expect updates from drivers after only a few minutes of delay. General calls are often only started when there is major disruption.

PIDD focused review arrangements must be established if PIDD provision is to be given an appropriate priority. Operators should consider if including PIDD in standard SPIRs (Serious Performance Incident Reviews) will give passenger information adequate attention.

Running a railway during disruption

Finally, remember that a good Core Message must contain 3 key pieces of information:-

The Problem – What has occurred?
The Impact on services – What impact will this have on passenger journeys (including time estimates)?
The Advice – What passengers should do?

Tips

Pre-defined PIDD arrangements covering all activities are the only way to provide timely, correct and consistent information during major delays/disruption.

Establish integrated arrangements that cover all activities from site, through control and right up to the passenger.

People need training properly (briefing will not be enough).

Always issue an initial (holding) message whenever disruption occurs.

Declare CSL2 whenever your threshold is breached and send Core Messages at sub 20 minute intervals

Ensure post incident review arrangements give passenger information and customer service proper attention

Without good Core Messages your PIDD arrangements will fail. Make sure you give your people the skills to master the art of writing regular concise messages.

7.7 Major Incident and Accident Management

BACKGROUND

Arrangements for managing incident/accident sites are well established and codified in the various rules and company instructions. Network Rail's Emergency Plan (NR/L2/OCS/250) contains detailed guidance on the responsibilities for every rail incident role that could possibly be involved in a major incident. However be aware that many of these roles will almost never be appointed as the document is written from a worst-case perspective.

7.7 Major Incident and Accident Management

This section looks beyond the actual incident/accident site and considers the wider requirements of train service delivery as part of effective incident/accident management. This Section should be read in conjunction with the Sections 7.1 and 7.2 covering Disruption Management and Prioritised Planning.

ISSUES

It is essential that incident/accident sites are properly resourced and that all specified requirements contained in emergency and contingency plans are provided. However, the Operations team must ensure that the wider railway (beyond the accident/incident) is properly managed. To achieve this:-

- Always remember the needs of your passengers/customers.
- Always follow the guidance in the element of this Handbook covering Disruption Management and Prioritised Planning.
- Avoid everyone going to site, but do appoint a Rail Incident Commander, a Rail Incident Officer (RIO) and a Train Operations Liaison Officer (TOLO) for the duration of the incident. These roles will almost certainly need support at the site of the incident; the type of support will depend upon the incident characteristics and scale. Where there is a station involved remember the need for a Station Incident Officer (SIO).
- Appoint lead managers (and supporting team if necessary) to manage the incident off site in order to allow Control to run the remaining railway.
- Strengthen the Control as necessary.
- Follow the guidance in the TOC Standing Orders covering Major Service Disruption and PIDD.
- Send TOC resources to manage real time train crew rostering changes - particularly at busy turnround points for example London Termini.
- Plan ahead to ensure all essential posts and functions are covered for the expected duration of the incident.
- Understand the specific requirements of Strategic and Tactical leadership along with functional delivery and ensure that clear appointments are made into these roles. This Gold-Silver-Bronze command structure is designed to aid clear communication of accountability and responsibility, including with external organisations.
- Establish conference call/progress meetings with all relevant parties.
- Establish links with support functions – customer service staff, stations, alternative transport providers etc.
- Establish communications & information links to senior managers and Directors including the PR team.
- Quickly mobilise train planning resources as necessary to produce a modified

Running a railway during disruption

timetable and diagrams.
- Communicate these control & command arrangements throughout your company and to other interested parties, i.e. Network Rail, TOCs/FOCs etc.
- Ensure comprehensive logs are kept. This includes the ongoing activities once the railway has been repaired and the normal service resumed. Continued logging of interaction with affected customers and investigating authorities can be important, particularly if legal proceedings or insurance claims result from the incident.
- Jointly review outcomes and learn the lessons using table top exercises.

Tips

The main tip is to reinforce the advice of avoiding everyone rushing off to site - this is just not necessary and could well be counter-productive.

Operators excel during a mishap - but at such a time the rest of the railway will need a higher level of 'tender loving care' than normal, possibly for a duration extending well beyond the shift, or even the day of the incident.

Ensure the balance between managing the incident and managing the resulting railway is appropriate.

7.8 Working in Degraded Mode - Including Single Line Working/Pilot Working/Temporary Block Working

BACKGROUND

Introducing, operating and withdrawing alternative methods of working when normal arrangements cannot be applied, is an important part of the operator's role. Responsibility for the infrastructure aspects normally falls to Network Rail operators but TOC operators will have a role in deciding how the method of working will impact upon their arrangements and are likely to be responsible for infrastructure aspects within depots etc.

Such arrangements are often called "working in degraded mode" because the normal safeguards provided by equipment and systems have been removed, either completely or in part. Implementing degraded modes of working in

7.8 Working in Degraded Mode

an emergency involves a high level of skill, knowledge and co-ordination. For Temporary Block Working (TBW), Single Line Working (SLW) and Pilot Working in particular the need to co ordinate multiple activities in a pressurised situation is crucial.

Some methods of operation are covered in more detail below:-
- Single line working.
- Working of single lines by Pilotman.
- Temporary Block working.

Single line working and Pilot working arrangements are fully covered by the Rule Book in Modules P1 and P2 and supplemented in the relevant Sectional Appendices/Signal Box Special Instructions. Temporary Block Working is covered in further depth by the Rule Book in Module T1B.

Other situations may require methods of working to be adapted using various aspects of Rule Book procedures dependent on the circumstances. Remember that the Rule Book is not designed to tell you why train movements cannot happen, but to tell you how they can be made safely. It is a rare situation which requires that all train movements must be stopped. However you will need to carefully risk assess each situation to determine how you can enable train movements to take place, and to what level.

ISSUES

General

Do not underestimate the risks that result from working in degraded mode, even when alternatives seem simple – equipment and interlocking safeguards are provided for a reason. Such arrangements can apply in planned and in emergency situations but the important issues, even in emergency situations are:-
- Plan activities as much as possible.
- Depart from normal operating practice as little as possible.
- Amend the level of service to a level suitable for the circumstances.
- Appoint a named individual to take charge of the arrangements.
- Identify the number and competencies of staff required in accordance with rules and regulations e.g. hand signaller, pilotman, clipping up points etc.
- In emergency situations, agree a planned time for commencement of operations and then identify the first train planned through the SLW or TBW, based on this time estimate. This can be used by all to target delivery.

Running a railway during disruption

The Person in Charge (PIC) has many responsibilities and is therefore a vital role. The following is a list of considerations for the PIC when setting up degraded mode operation. It is not exhaustive and all PICs must be familiar with rules and procedural requirements.
- Staff welfare and relief arrangements: toilets, food, meal breaks, relief.
- Safe system of work:
  - Moving trains within the affected area out prior to TBW/SLW.
  - Arrangements for producing forms.
  - Arrangements for clipping up points.
  - Does the TBW involve a section of non-Track Circuit Block?
  - Start and finish points e.g. does the method of working include a shunt movement which will add complexity and delay.
  - Availability of hand signallers.
  - Sighting and ease of stopping: e.g. can the area of TBW be extended to start/terminate at a station which will be safer for the staff involved, provide welfare opportunities and may improve performance.
  - Track safety requirements;
  - Maximum/minimum staff numbers e.g. can you implement with reduced numbers then increase to improve the arrangements.
- Communications, mobile phones and available battery power.
- Workload and experience of Signallers involved/other staff involved.
- How robust is the train service?
- Arrangements if the method of working extends beyond 24 hours.
- Arrangements for checking the method of working.

Single Line Working

A method of working for multiple track lines where trains in either direction travel over a single line. It is used when one line is blocked due to engineering work or an obstruction.

Some lines equipped with more modern signalling systems are fitted with bi-directional signalling. This enables trains to run in the wrong direction under signal control, although this is sometimes installed with minimal functionality and no AWS (Simplified Bi-Directional Signalling – known as SIMBIDS). This avoids introducing manual SLW and speeds up the implementation of contingent operation during a line blockage. Technically, single line working refers to the situation when such signalling systems do not exist and a pilotman must be provided to manage the passage of trains over the single line.

Use routine joint NR and TOC/FOC contingency plan review meetings to agree what can be achieved. Robust preparations for the deliverability of SLW plans will include resources, training, implementation plans and briefing of the

7.8 Working in Degraded Mode

specific arrangements. Make sure that train per hour capacity available during such working has been pre-determined and properly allocated.

Ensure contingency plans recognise the opportunities for combining trains or flighting trains (successive trains in the same direction). Remember that all trains in the wrong direction will run at no more than 50 mph and will be considerably slower over points and where crossings are on local control. There are a number of tips for making SLW as efficient as possible. These include:

- Implementing the arrangements as efficiently as possible. Examples include; continuing to run trains in the right direction until the very last minute possible and allocating resources efficiently (i.e. the person arriving earliest should be sent to the furthest location required).
- Authorisation to split the section with an intermediate handsignaller to allow greater through-put.
- Authorisation for not placing an attendant at a CCTV crossing.
- Use of a location with a main aspect signal to return to the right line to remove the requirement for a hand signaller.
- Where ever possible use crossovers which avoid shunts to get on or off the single line.
- Accepting trains up to a handsignaller displaying a red handsignal at the end of the section where necessary.
- Consider closing little used stations within the temporary block working section to increase overall throughput. Replacement transport can be provided from nearby stations.

Make sure you understand how junctions at either end of the single line can be worked to keep normal traffic flowing and be clear about intermediate junctions which it will not be possible to operate. The rules in this area are often poorly understood particularly in absolute block locations.

Over recent years introduction of SLW under emergency arrangements has been far rarer than was previously the case as resources tend to be fewer. The expertise that does exist tends to be gained during pre-planned SLW as a result of engineering possessions. Consequently when SLW is introduced in an emergency situation it may not be managed optimally. The solution is effective robust contingency plans, underpinned by effective practice and management attention on the day.

Ensure contingency plans that call for SLW are underpinned by training, including table top exercises.

Make sure that all instances of SLW being used are reviewed to identify lessons learnt. Similarly, keep an eye on incidents where SLW would have been

Running a railway during disruption

appropriate and ensure this aspect is covered in the appropriate investigations.

SLW is a vital tool in the operator's armoury.

Working of Single Lines by Pilotman

Working of single lines by pilotman following a track circuit failure, or to/from a point of obstruction, is more common than SLW. Unlike SLW, it should be possible to operate many single line sections with a pilotman (other than those with particularly tight re-occupation times) and avoid any significant additional delay once the arrangements are up and running. There are a number of alternatives to the use of a pilotman which can be explored to manage services more efficiently. These will need to be risk assessed, documented and pre-published:

- Modified Working, effective when a pilotman is not immediately available but not for longer term.
- Working in one direction only, either pre-determined or signallers' decision on the day.
- Physical observation that the single line is clear.
- Shutting a single train into a single line branch line.
- Exceptions allowed for in the Rule Book.

Ensure you understand where these methods of working can occur and how they will be implemented. Be clear about the rare circumstances when service suspension may be the better option.

Temporary Block Working

Temporary Block Working (TBW) enables trains in track circuit block areas to pass two or more consecutive signals at danger at a time by using handsignallers at the start and end of the affected area and issuing tickets to each train which passes through. In this way trains can be run through areas of multiple signal failures or planned disconnections.

As cable theft has increasingly caused major signalling failures in many areas, experience in implementing TBW has increased but remember:-.

- Capacity will always be substantially reduced.
- Trains in the affected area will need to be cleared from the section prior to commencement of TBW.
- Resource mobilisation for TBW and therefore implementation timescales are almost always lengthy, particularly if multiple sets of points need to be clipped up.
- Junctions cannot be worked in the TBW section.

Ticket working will be very slow therefore it is usually necessary to work out the theoretical throughput and reduce it by 30%. Remember that all trains will run at no more than 50 mph. Long queues waiting to pass through the

7.8 Working in Degraded Mode

section should be avoided. The exception may be during commuting peaks when lengthy delays might be acceptable in order to provide capacity and there is no viable alternative routing for passengers. The afternoon peak will be a particular challenge – the day's commuters have been taken to work and need to be taken home. A morning peak major failure may result in many passengers abandoning their trip to work and reducing pressure on the railway.

Tips to improve efficiency of TBW include:-
- Allocating staff efficiently. Send the first person to arrive to the furthest location for example.
- It may help to prepare one line at a time if resources are limited. Better to have TBW implemented on one line than to be half way through making the arrangements on both lines.
- Try to arrange for ticket handover locations to coincide with stations. This will reduce the number of stops each train needs to make.
- Consider closing little used stations within the temporary block working section to increase overall throughput. Replacement transport can be provided from nearby stations.
- Splitting the TBW section. This will only help over long sections because of the significant amount of time needed to handover and receive tickets.

When the signalling is restored there will be an expectation of a rapid return to normal working. Remember that points will have been clipped, operating staff are on the ground and service restoration will need to be particularly well controlled and systematic. See also 7.12 the section on Major Signalling Failures.

Bespoke Methods of Operation

Occasionally a specific situation or problem will require a more unusual method of working to be set up – maybe during stage works for a project commissioning or a failure mode which extends for some time. Issues to consider are;-
- Use standard Rule Book methodologies where ever possible - they will be more familiar to staff and stepping outside standard principles is likely to require formal derogations.
- The longer a degraded mode of operation continues the more likely errors or violations are to occur, it maybe tempting for staff to try and find a short-cut – consider how you will monitor operational standards in the risk assessment you do.
- Keep it as simple as possible and make sure unambiguous formal instructions are issued and properly briefed and understood.
- Remember that engineered equipment safeguards such as signalling interlocking are safer than procedural or skill-based measures so maintain as

Running a railway during disruption

much of this type of security as possible and keep timescales without it as short as possible.
- Remember that your staff will have varying levels of skill, experience and confidence – do not base your method of working on the capabilities of your very best people.

Tips

Making a quick decision to implement SLW, TBW or similar is vital – resources can always be stood down but being slow off the mark will only extend already lengthy timescales.

Do not over-commit – there is nothing more demoralising than pulling all the stops out to get TBW in only to see delays spiral because a poor train service has been implemented.

Make a personal commitment to go and watch the operation of the railway at a time when planned or unplanned degraded mode operations are taking place.

Make sure any non-planned SLW takes account of the time that will be taken for the first train to pass through the section.

Ensure that you assess front line staff for SLW/TBW competence and, where available, use simulators to test such scenarios in a simulated environment.

Before you sign off an instruction pause to think: "is this scenario one which could and should be undertaken with the security of the equipment interlocking"

SLW is easier to talk about than it is to introduce and operate - help reverse this trend.

7.9 Possession Overruns

BACKGROUND

The robust management of possessions has always been a key issue for railway operators, primarily because the consequences of overrunning possessions are often extremely damaging.

It is also a fact that possessions are dangerous places to work, essentially because normal train control arrangements are usually replaced by bespoke arrangements that are prone to human error.

They can also be extremely busy places, with a large quantity and variety of plant in use at any one time. The consequence is that work in possessions is responsible for a large number of railway incidents and accidents.

Possessions will have different characteristics dependent on whether they have been taken to address short term problems and failures or undertake engineering work that has been planned in advance using the Engineering Planning processes.

ISSUES

Every possession will be risk assessed by NR to determine the probability of overruns. Higher yet 'acceptable' risk possessions should be specially monitored by NR Control. This methodology should be used to drive the need for any temporary contingency plans.

TOCs should have routine arrangements with NR for reviewing possession plans where the risk of disruption is high.

Preparation of NR contingency plans for high-risk possessions should include break points, arrangements for scaling back work if required, and arrangements for shortening possessions to handback the maximum infrastructure in the case of an overrun.

TOCs must demand that NR risk assess possessions and TOC operators must understand the overrun probability limits that are being used.

Whilst this is primarily an issue for Network Rail, the consequences of an overrun usually impact the TOC. It is therefore essential that Train Operators understand how critical possessions are being managed and if possible become actively involved in the real time review processes.

Running a railway during disruption

NR routinely undertake possession checks and although these are predominantly safety focused, TOC operations managers should arrange to accompany their NR colleagues at regular intervals.

Gaining this insight will then enable managers to identify the critical issues for real time review arrangements. It will also ensure that critical maintenance/renewal activities become part of the routine performance management agenda.

POSSESSION OVERRUNS

Overrunning possessions should be very rare. Unfortunately this is not yet the case. The solution is not necessarily for NR to include large amounts of recovery time in the possession plan, thus extending the duration TOCs cannot run trains. In recent years NR has become more and more sophisticated at ensuring that the 'stageworks' (sequence of tasks) within a possession will deliver an on-time handback to traffic.

Depending on the scale of the work involved, the key requirements are:-
- An overall possession plan.
- Project management arrangements.
- Detailed work plans including specialist plant requirements.
- Resource plans for key personnel.
- Method statements for key tasks.
- Contingency plans for plant failures etc.
- Identified milestones.
- NR progress check arrangements.
- Pre-planned abort points.
- Defined reporting arrangements.
- A structured real time review process which, for critical possessions would-include the TOC.

Post event reviews should be routine and covered by formal Plan-Do-Review assessment.

Ensure that NR provides TOC Controls with regular update on progress within possessions.

Provided adequately thought through arrangements are in place the potential for overruns should be reduced. However, when things do go wrong it is essential that the early warning systems are fully effective.

If information is not forthcoming in accordance with defined reporting milestones, or a key work milestone is missed, do not hesitate to escalate your concern to an appropriate level. Persistent possession overruns are not an occupational hazard, they should be rare events.

Similarly ensure that your control office has a procedure for monitoring low risk routine possessions and dealing with the occasional surprise overrun.

If operators take a view that possessions are a separate, technical activity overruns will continue at a high level.

Get involved, possessions are as integral to train service delivery as routine train maintenance.

Tips

This is a key area where close collaboration with your colleagues will pay real dividends. It is also highly likely that your technical or engineering colleagues will welcome the support you can give.

Possessions can be very dangerous places to work. Rigorous planning and checking will help minimise the risks.

Be aware of the large number of independent sub-contractors that often work in a possession (particularly large ones). Every interface increases the potential for risk both in terms of safety and work completion.

It is essential that all operators within TOCs and FOCs as well as NR become attuned to possessions risks and become competent in assessing the effectiveness of possession management arrangements.

Unfortunately it is still necessary to be prepared to deal with possessions that do overrun. Review your contingency plans to ensure they cover such eventualities.

7.10 Failed Trains

BACKGROUND

For an Operator every failed train is a potential major incident and robust processes must be in place to ensure that such failures are managed effectively and that they do not recur. It is also worth remembering that many of the

Running a railway during disruption

principles contained in this section will also be relevant if a train is trapped by a catastrophic infrastructure failure.

Fleet Engineers categorise any individual fleet delay greater than three minutes as a casualty. A cancellation due to fleet causes is also categorised as a casualty. It is this metric that is generally used to measure train reliability (MTIN = Miles per Technical Incident).

Unfortunately a failed train can sit still on the running line between four minutes and four hours – the MTIN measure does not differentiate between the length of delay.

ISSUES

When a fleet failure is identified the following issues need to be considered:

Fixing the failure

Is this something that the Driver can fix alone?

Make sure that support is available to the Driver though a fleet helpline. Make sure that the Driver is using it. Many modern fleets have remote condition monitoring which means that the Fleet helpline staff may know what the problem is before the Driver does. They may also be able to give him direct instructions on what to do about it

Will additional resources be needed on site to help e.g. a Fitter? How long will that take?

Can the failure be fixed within the limits of the cut and run policy? Would assisting the train to clear the line be a better option?

Clearing the line

If the train cannot be fixed, can it be moved under contingency arrangements? What does the contingency plan say about where the train should terminate in these circumstances?

Is assistance required? If so what traction is compatible?

Will adapter couplings be necessary to assist the failure? Would it be easier to bring a compatible unit in from the front rather than assisting with an incompatible unit from the rear? NR hold a database of unit compatibilities, make sure it is checked

Can the available traction be used to push the failure to a less disruptive location e.g. passenger service pushing a freight train into a nearby loop?

What are the immediate customer care arrangements?

Does the train have electrical power for lighting, heating and air conditioning? If the train is sealed without windows what arrangements need to be put in

place to prevent the train from overheating?
What are the communication arrangements with the traincrew?
Is it clear how many customers are affected?
What arrangements are in place to keep passengers informed and comfortable?
Is there a risk that passengers might self evacuate from the train? What action can be taken to prevent this?
What arrangements need to be made for evacuation?

What lessons can be learned for the future?
Make sure the incident is thoroughly reviewed and lessons learned.
Make sure an adequate fleet investigation has taken place into the cause.
Pass on lessons to those involved.

Under most circumstances the aim is to clear the running line as soon as possible and look after passengers. Precise objectives are dependent on line usage and location. On intensively used suburban lines a five minute failure will have a significant impact. On a lightly used branch line there may be much more time available to rectify the failure before the incident impacts other services.

Expected passenger behaviour will also guide response action and the presence of particular hazards such as third rail electrification will shape the required response.

Remember train failures should be infrequent but they can escalate into very large incidents.

Tips

Make sure that initial fault diagnosis and rectification arrangements are slick and quick.

Ensure that confirmed train failures trigger an immediate response at all appropriate levels.

Mobilise and then stand down if necessary.

Remember that most Drivers never experience a failure from one year to the next and so their fault-finding expertise is likely to be low.

Also reflect that the train is a far more complex piece of kit than it used to be albeit with driver-aiding fault-finding diagnostics. The days of using a hammer or well-placed kick to solve a problem are largely over.

Never accept a No Fault Found / No Defect Found as the conclusion for a train failure. Get to the root cause - trains are machines.

7.11 Major Track and Civil Engineering Issues - including Bridge Strikes

INTRODUCTION

The permanent way (or PWay) should be the most reliable component of railway infrastructure, regardless of whether it is plain line or S&C (switches and crossings). Track design, maintenance and renewal is a well-established engineering discipline throughout the world and operators should be able to expect PWay based delays and problems to be almost minimal.

However when track defects do occur they can have a drastic impact on train service delivery. This Section outlines the most common types of failures and describes how NR manages preventative monitoring and actual track and civil engineering failures.

This Section also outlines the issues relating to the prevention and management of bridge strikes.

ISSUES

Categorisation of Rail Defects

An extremely important aspect of managing the track asset is the inspection of rail. This is carried out by a strictly managed regime of visual examination of the surface area and ultrasonic testing to identify internal defects.

Network Rail Track Standards require that the ultrasonic testing of rails is carried out to all running lines at a set frequency determined by the Track Category. This takes into consideration the speed of the line and the equivalent mean gross tonnage per annum using it. The testing is required to identify internal defects within the rail at head, web or foot, as early as possible so that their repair or removal can be appropriately managed such that the risk from cracked or broken rails is reduced to a level that is as low as reasonable practicable.

Ultrasonic testing can be carried out either by using manually operated pedestrian equipment or, where approved, by train borne equipment carried by one of the Ultrasonic Test Units (UTUs). The initial prioritised findings reported from a UTU have to be verified by pedestrian testing within a prescribed period and the findings acted upon accordingly.

7.11 Major Track and Civil Engineering Issues - including Bridge Strikes

If ultrasonic rail testing confirms the presence of a rail defect(s) then Network Rail Track Standards specify the required action to be taken by applying a Minimum Action Code (MAC). The most onerous of these MACs is the 1A rail defect. The '1' signifies that a 20mph ESR must be imposed and emergency clamped fishplates fitted where possible. The 'A' requires that the defect is removed with 36 hours.

This means that the defect should be removed no later than the second night after the defect was found e.g. a defect found at 08.00 on Day 1 shall be removed on the night of Day 2 at the latest. Removal of the defect beyond this timescale is not permitted and the line will be blocked unless dispensated by the responsible Route Asset Manager (Track) and any mitigation applied. There are also 1B rail defects which are to be treated similarly to 1As but the removal timescale is 7 days.

The application of the 20mph ESR by the erection of the necessary speed board equipment must be carried out no later than two hours after the discovery of the defect. However there are three exceptions to this when a 20mph ESR must be imposed immediately by stopping and cautioning:

- on a high cant deficiency curve i.e. where the cant exceeds 150mm.
- where there is a visible crack and where the rail is not fully supported (i.e. there is voiding or a slurry spot.
- where track components are not fully effective etc.

Responding to the findings of Track Recording Vehicles (TRVs)

Network Rail operate a growing fleet of track specific specialist train borne examination vehicles that can monitor, measure and record a variety of different parameters including structural clearances, ultrasonic examination of the rail integrity, track geometry and in the future, the routine inspection of general track components to replace the basic visual inspections currently undertaken by Patrollers. The advantage of these trains is that they record the actual condition of the track as it is under load (i.e. dynamically) whereas manual visual inspections can only look for tell tales signs of what the track is doing when under load as every length of track cannot realistically be monitored from the lineside to the same standard.

The most frequently seen of these examination vehicles are the trains colloquially known as TRVs which measure and record track geometry including:

- vertical and longitudinal alignment (top and line).
- twist.
- cross-levels (cant).
- cyclic-top (a combination of top faults).
- dip angles.

Running a railway during disruption

It can also record data sufficient to determine the track quality which is assessed to be defined quality bands. The main TRVs are the New Measurement Train (known as the NMT which is formed from two HST power cars and associated Mk3 trailer vehicles) Track Recording Coach (or TRC) usually loco hauled either top and tailed or with a single loco and DVT) and the Track Recording Unit (or TRU formed from a two car Class150 derived DMU). A further vehicle – the Track Inspection Coach (or TIC – loco hauled) can sometime be used to deputise for an unavailable vehicle.

New Measurement Train (NMT) Track Recording Unit (TRU)

Discrete geometry faults in particular, if left undetected, can be a risk to the continuing safe passage of trains and can also lead to the premature and catastrophic failure of key track components thereby increasing the risk of derailment or the track geometry fault itself may be sufficient to lead to reports of poor riding and in extreme cases a derailment. Network Rail Track Standards define these geometry faults in three categories; Immediate Action - Intervention limit faults (previously known as L2 defects or exceedances) and Alert Limit faults (previously known a L1 defects).

Immediate Action faults require action to be taken to reduce the risk of derailment to an acceptable level. For example; by closing the line, reducing the speed of trains, the prompt correction of the fault or a combination of these. The most significant of this type of faults are twists (e.g. where the variation in cross level/cant over 3m exceeds the required limits). Where the variation exceeds 33.3mm (or 1:90 gradient) then the line must be blocked immediately. This is carried out by the Train Captain on the TRV who reports the fault to the responsible Integrated Control Centre within 60 minutes of discovery. They must then notify local staff within 30 minutes of receiving them.

The only response to twist faults of this magnitude, once confirmed, is to carry out rectification work by lifting and packing the track. At the time this may be a 'rough pack' to temporarily resolve the situation and to enable the running of trains to recommence but more substantive works may be required when it can be properly planned and resourced.

Other twist faults of a lesser magnitude may also detected but the requirement for immediate action may vary between 36 hours and 14 days.

7.11 Major Track and Civil Engineering Issues - including Bridge Strikes

Another Immediate Action fault which will require the immediate closure of the line is due to wide gauge (e.g. 1472mm or greater on lines with a Permanent Speed Restriction (PSR) of 105mph to 125mph or 1478mm or greater on line with a PSR up to 100mph). Wide gauge is usually caused by the poor condition of the track fastenings or sleepers (or a combination). Rotting wooden sleepers are a likely cause and where movement of a baseplate or chair is usually evident. It is usually possible to affect a temporary repair by fitting insulated temporary gauge tiebars pending more substantive works to the sleeper or fastening system.

A more common Immediate Action fault is cyclic top. Cyclic Top is a series of evenly spaced dips in the track that can be a problem to certain types of rail vehicles at particular speeds. What separates this defect from normal poor top is that it can derail certain types of rail vehicles, even though each top defect may not look that severe. Derailments happen when a vehicle begins to bounce up and down and at the same time starts to roll from side to side. It will also yaw from end to end. The whole process can develop very quickly and is increasingly likely to occur as speeds increase over 30mph. The motion becomes violent enough for one wheel to become very lightly loaded. With the yawing of the vehicle there is everything needed for flange-climb and thus a derailment. Most cyclic top derailments occur on curved track although they can and do happen on straight track. It is the vertical movements of the vehicle, combined with the yawing motion, that cause cyclic top derailments on straight track.

In severe cases the detection of Cyclic Top will require the immediate imposition of a 30mph Emergency Speed Restriction applicable to all freight traffic and correction within 36 hours. However the requirement to impose an ESR can cause unnecessary delays to all rail traffic during the period from the notification of the fault to the erection of speed board equipment. In many cases it is preferable to carry out immediate repair works, which can often be quickly executed to reduce the effects of the immediate problem pending more substantive repairs and sufficient to remove the need for an emergency speed to be imposed. This work might comprise of some localised lifting and packing to remove the poor top that triggers the dynamic vehicle response.

Some less severe Cyclic Top faults may still require the imposition of an ESR but within 36 hours of being reported with a correction period of 14 days.

Rough Track
Track faults associated with poor ride quality are commonly reported as a 'rough ride' or 'bumps'. A 'bump' might be a track fault at a discrete location in amongst otherwise satisfactory track whereas a 'rough ride' might refer to poor

Running a railway during disruption

ride quality over a particular section of track. However there are no specific mandated requirements which state which term should be used.

Generally dynamic track faults are usually found in the form of either a lateral (alignment or 'line') or vertical ('top') fault which can manifest themselves to those travelling on a train as either a 'kick' or a 'bump' respectively. Some alignment faults are also reported as 'kinks'. Great care needs to be taken when reporting such defects and wherever possible the difference between an alignment fault and a more significant track buckle (or distorted rail) should be made.

Being able to differentiate between the types of faults and then effectively communicate this information can be extremely useful for those who have to determine the required action upon receipt of the initial report of an incident. These faults can sometimes be the symptom of a more serious underlying problem but get the terminology wrong and you may "stop the job" when only cautioning of trains at 20 mph was required.

The Rule Book uses self-explanatory terminology such as 'broken, distorted (includes buckles) and damaged' to describe rail related faults but there is no specific definition of what a 'rough ride' or 'bump' actually is: it is down to the perception of the reporter.

From the track maintainer's perspective 'rough rides' or 'bumps' can occur for three main reasons:
- a deliberate act, for example, ballast being placed on the rail or debris on the line etc.
- a sudden catastrophic failure - broken rail/fishplates, track buckle, supporting earthwork failure etc.
- a deterioration of the general asset condition e.g. wet beds, defective or voiding sleepers, dipped/battered rail joints, earthworks issues - embankments particularly running on/off underbridges) etc.

These types of faults can be reported by railway staff during the course of their normal work or by members of the public travelling as customers. It should be noted that sometimes those travelling in the passenger area of a train may experience a different ride quality to that of the driver in their cab. Therefore just because a train driver hasn't reported a problem doesn't necessarily mean that it doesn't exist.

For track related faults (i.e. not specifically rail related), in the first instance the fault will generally be reported to the responsible Signaller by a train driver. The Signaller may allow a train to examine the line but only in accordance with their strict instructions and at a speed not exceeding 20mph. The report of the fault

7.11 Major Track and Civil Engineering Issues - including Bridge Strikes

will also be attended to by competent track maintenance staff that will inspect the track and attempt to identify the problem so that appropriate action can be taken.

Poor Top running onto under-bridge

Poor top due to drying out of supporting embankment

Buckled and Broken Rails

For rail related faults, for example, broken, distorted or damaged rails or where both fishplates have broken on the same rail, the immediate action to be taken by the Signaller is to stop trains over the affected line pending inspection by the relevant competent person.

Railway Group Standards Rule Books define the actions that can be taken once the rail has been examined. The action that can be taken is dictated by:

- The type of break, examples include:
  - a vertical/transverse break.
  - part of the rail head broken away.
  - breaks in lower part of rail.
  - arcing damage.
- Where it occurred, examples include:
  - in an S&C rail which is free to move.
  - in severe Rolling Contact Fatigue.
  - with a gap exceeding 75mm.
- Its position relevant to adjacent track features for example, at or near a weld or joint.

Running a railway during disruption

Permissible immediate actions that can be taken may include either the line remaining blocked or the imposition of a either 5mph or 20mph emergency speed restrictions.

In a circumstance where the line has to remain blocked then the options to be considered may include the replacement of the broken rail sufficient that the line speed may be reinstated without further restrictions being required.

However if there is insufficient time available to do this consideration might be given to installing a temporary rail sufficient to enable the train service to start running. There are a number of specific requirements that need to be satisfied but dependant on these there are options available to enable a length of rail to be temporarily held in place by either an approved clamping system (i.e. 'G' clamps) or back-holed bolted (i.e. where the rail is drilled to enable bolts to be installed in the outer holes of a fishplate) up to a maximum 50mph (if all relevant criteria are satisfied) or up to 90mph if the joint comprises of tight jointed fishplates fully bolted with high tensile bolts. If these options are taken, then it can be permissible for the temporary arrangement to remain in place for usually either 7 or 14 days (depending on the type of joint used) which should provide sufficient time for remedial works to be properly planned etc.

There are a number of reasons why track buckles occur but one of the more common ones is due to a shortage of ballast. If there is inadequate ballast to resist the lateral forces then the track will move bodily when excessive compressive forces occur in the rail as it gets warmer during hot weather. Shortages of ballast can occur as a consequence of maintenance works such as tamping and localised digging out of wet beds etc. Also disturbance of the ballast caused by maintenance work can loosen the ballast and reduce its resistance to buckling. Lines formed from Continuous Welded Rail are designed such that the rails are stressed when installed so that between 21C to 27C (27C to 32C for crimp ended steel sleepers) the rails are stress free (known as Stress Free Temperature or SFT) with no thermal force present (i.e. this is the rail temperature at which the rail is the same length as it would be in an unrestrained state). Sometimes a situation can arise where the SFT is less than required meaning that excessive compressive forces in the rail can quickly build up as temperature rises and (particularly in association with other deficiencies) can lead to a buckle occurring.

A reportable track buckle is a misalignment which renders the line unfit for the passage of trains at line speed and/or necessitates emergency remedial work to a running line under cover of either a temporary restriction of speed or closure of the line. Remedial work may consist of adjusting or cutting rails or slueing the track.

Misalignments that occurs during work whilst under a possession of the line or a misalignment in a siding, do not constitute a reportable buckle.

7.11 Major Track and Civil Engineering Issues - including Bridge Strikes

If a track buckle is discovered the initial requirement is to safeguard traffic by advising the Signaller immediately to block the line. Before any traffic is allowed to pass over the buckled length the track may first need to be slued, preferably outwards on a curve or to an easy curvature on the straight, and a speed restriction imposed pending more substantive remedial works.

Track Buckles

Heat Management

Prior to the onset of hot weather, Track Engineers review the maintenance requirements and carry out any outstanding works required to ensure that the track is in an appropriate state to reasonably withstand the effects of hot weather. Such works may comprise of replenishing and/or re-profiling track ballast, lubricating fishplated joints, carrying out adjustment switch maintenance, re-stressing works, rail adjusting and anchoring (of jointed track) etc.

During periods of hot weather Track Engineers calculate a Critical Rail Temperature (CRT) for all sections of line. The CRT is the rail temperature to which CWR may be allowed to rise before measures to protect traffic shall be taken. The CRT will depend on the stress-free temperature (SFT) of the rail and the quantity and degree of consolidation of the ballast.

Network Rail Track Standards define the CRT for various combinations of track condition and track type etc. at three thresholds CRT (W), CRT (30/60) and CRT (20).

When the rail temperature is expected to exceed the CRT (W) a watchmen shall be placed on site to monitor the length of track concerned. They shall remain on site whether or not speed restrictions are imposed, to take rail temperatures, monitor any known "trigger" points and observe for early indications of movement of the track. They shall continue to do so until the rail temperature falls to, and can be expected to remain for that day, below the CRT (W). The watchman must be able to continuously observe the length of track concerned. Watchmen shall block the line or impose a speed restriction if a buckle occurs and shall be equipped and competent to do so.

Running a railway during disruption

Where the CRT(30/60) or CRT(20) are exceeded then emergency speed restrictions of 30/60 or 20 mph shall be imposed over the affected track and maintained until the rail temperature falls to, and can be expected to remain for the remainder of that day, below these CRTs.

Earthworks and Embankments

These are in many ways the most fundamental assets the railway operates over and whilst they will rarely cause delays, when they do so the results can be catastrophic! In many respects asset management and performance is a direct function of the type of construction methods adopted when the railways were first built by the likes of Brunel and Stephenson.

Asset management is through a series of examinations which Network Rail currently sub-contracts to civil engineering companies. Each asset is 5 chains in length and the examination principally takes into account slope geometry, geology, geomorphology, vegetation type, cess width, drainage, and precursors to failure. The overall score will place the asset in one of three categories these being poor, marginal or serviceable and the condition rating dictates the examination frequency to annual, 5 year or 10 year intervals. Poor assets are evaluated by staff within the Route Asset Management team. The evaluation usually takes the form of a site visit to corroborate the condition rating and decide on a course of action. For example, does the asset need to be renewed or fixed, could we monitor it using installer, inclinometers or piezometers or are we content for annual examinations to continue as a mechanism of managing the risk of asset failure.

As a result of inclement weather the autumn and winter seasons are the time when assets are most susceptible to failure and track maintenance workers are potentially at our busiest dealing with emergencies. Clay embankments can also be susceptible to shrinkage during periods of prolonged dry weather. This is a fairly predictable phenomenon. However it can require considerable tamping efforts to maintain the top and alignment of the track to an acceptable standard.

Bridge Strikes

Bridge strikes on overline or underline structures can cause significant delays and disruption to train services. The railway's management of these incidents has improved significantly over the years with a strong risk-based approach being adopted. The rule of thumb ten years ago was to stop the job and undertake a controlled re-start

7.11 Major Track and Civil Engineering Issues - including Bridge Strikes

after a detailed examination on site. Now, individual structures examination and risk assessment has led to a system of dispensations such that in many cases trains can begin to run again under signaller's instructions dependent on the classification of the bridge and the lines over it.

Staff attending a bridge strike will need to be competent as either a Bridge Strike Nominee (normally an operational member of staff) or as a Bridge Strike Examiner (normally a structures engineer) and anyone who does not hold one of these competences will not be permitted to examine a bridge with a view to authorising movements.

Network Rail has published a Good Practice Guide for Bridge Strike Nominees (NR/GN/CIV/201) which covers this area in detail and provides a lot of good advice.

The disadvantage of the risk-based approach is that the "rules" have become more complex. This down-side is vastly outweighed by the positives but does have implications:

- Make sure you understand the Red, Double Amber, Amber, Green categorisation.
- How do you deal with light vehicles striking bridges (what is a light vehicle and what are the exceptions).
- What do you do with wedged vehicles (for dispensated and non-dispensated structures).
- What are the speeds that you can authorise resumption at.
- What do you do for bridges over waterways.

Consider how you can improve performance in this area:

- When were dispensations last reviewed on your patch; do your structures engineers think they may be able to adopt a less-conservative approach if they re-ran the assessments.
- Can the conspicuity of key bridges be improved.
- Can the cost of bridge protection measures be justified by the performance benefit.
- How can you work with local highways authorities to resolve particular issues.

Tips

The level of delays caused by track related problems in Great Britain should be very low.

Operators should be aware of the catastrophic impact that serious track failures can have (Hatfield and Potters Bar accidents) and watch for any signs of deteriorating track quality.

Take an interest in track quality and fault levels – it is an aspect that can lead to delays and potentially to more serious consequences.

7.12 Major Signalling Failures

BACKGROUND

Major failures of the signalling system have become more common in many areas as cable theft problems have impacted upon railway operations. When they occur, they are amongst the most disruptive events to afflict a railway operation. Signalling 'blackouts' are the most serious form of signal failure and are usually caused by power failures, lightning strikes, cable failure or cable theft . Perversely, partial blackouts are even more difficult to manage than total blackouts.

Most modern signalling centres have dual sourced power supplies, or a separate standby generator but blackouts can still occur when key cables are affected. Be careful of the term 'blackout' as there are a number of scenarios depending upon the specific equipment problem. It may be that the signaller sees a signalling panel with all track circuits showing occupied in the affected section, no train descriptions or even a seemingly normal set of indications but without the ability to control equipment. Drivers may see a forest of red or black signals. Whether signals on the ground are powered is actually a key piece of information to help with diagnosis.

When all signalling functionality has been lost the arrangements in the Rule Book provide alternative signalling processes. Temporary Block Working (TBW – commonly also called 'ticket working') effectively applies Absolute Block working between two nominated points but it is a slow and restrictive method of working. To achieve the best possible results TBW must be properly resourced and well managed. In single line areas Working by Pilotman will be required (see also Sections covering Prioritised Planning and Degraded Mode Working).

ISSUES

The most appropriate course of action during a blackout will be almost entirely dependent on the estimate for resumption of normal working.

7.12 Major Signalling Failures

If the root cause has been quickly diagnosed then forward planning will be relatively easier, i.e. a cable fire on a 48-core cable will mean many hours of no signalling as a new cable is run out, jointed and then each core tested, but a blown 650v fuse may be resolved quickly (provided the root cause is indeed the fuse rather than that being the symptom of an underlying problem).

If the cause is unknown it may be that resumption will occur at an indeterminate time. For example the specific fault may lie in a 5km length of cable and until the fault location is found, an estimate for normal working cannot be determined because the rectification action will not be understood. It is prudent to always assume the worst, and mobilise for a long shut down. However, it should also be possible to provide time estimates for the investigation phase (see Section covering Estimates for Resuming Normal Working).

TOC operations managers need to work closely with NR as once it has been ascertained that the incident will be long (or at least is not definitely short), any trains heading towards the affected area will have to be stopped, and either held awaiting clarification, or terminated. The position of stranded trains will need to be ascertained by signallers and these trains cleared one by one from the affected section(s). This will be slow and laborious, particularly if there are switches and crossings on the routes, which will require to be secured for the passage of trains. A particular issue exists in Visual Display Unit (VDU) controlled signalling centres where a power loss can also result in the Signaller losing his map of the network. Hard copy maps are then required.

This step will not be quick and if Cab Secure Radio (CSR) / National Radio Network (NRN) systems are unavailable, the time taken could be very lengthy. In parallel with the clearance of trains the proposed method of TBW will need to be established and the necessary people briefed and put in position. It is likely that the individuals involved will be those clearing the stranded trains therefore there will probably be a long delay between clearing the sections and establishing ticket working.

Remember to allow plenty of time for the first train to go through the affected section (see Section 7.8 Working in Degraded Mode).

When the signalling is restored there will be an expectation of a rapid return to normal working. Remember that points will have been clipped, operating staff are on the ground and service restoration will need to be particularly well controlled and systematic.

TOCs should help NR review the contingency plans as part of the post incident investigation. Blackouts are thankfully rare therefore the lessons learnt should be carefully identified and acted upon.

Running a railway during disruption

Sometimes this type of failure may be caused by a failure in the communications links between the signal box and the interlocking room that controls the equipment. To overcome problems with such electronic links many interlockings have an override facility (sometimes known as 'Through Routes') which enables the signaller to switch from normal operations to automatic operation of the specified area. Such operation will only be available for a single range of routing options – normally straight up and down and there can be complications at some key pieces of equipment such as level crossings.

The indications a signaller will receive and the processes for undertaking this type of operation all too easily become unfamiliar so make sure that signallers get the opportunity to understand exactly how it works and what it looks and feels like. Ideally they will find an opportunity during a quieter period to go into override but this is not always possible without impacting on some aspect of service delivery.

Make sure you avoid delays and disruption caused because a signaller has mis-interpreted how the override facility should work (e.g. forgotten there is a time delay involved). Where appropriate always check if the Signaller has tried to use the override facility (if provided).

Other emergency facilities sometimes incorporated in signalling systems are 'slave panels' at remote interlocking locations. When required a qualified operator will need to attend and work under the signaller's direction - so make sure you and those around you remain competent. Planned use in quiet periods is good practice.

Tips

The management of blackouts is rarely straightforward - largely because of the loss of vital control systems and the difficulty in clearing affected sections of trains.

Consider all available information and plan carefully.

Heavily sense check that the initial throughput estimate is realistic . If you think it needs reducing then say so. Mobilise the necessary resources within the first 30 minutes of the failure.

Resources can always be stood down but lost time can never be re-gained.

Remember with the protection of the signalling system lost, the railway is being operated in a much less safe way. Be careful.

7.13 Fatalities

INTRODUCTION

This Section covers incidents in which members of the public are struck by trains. These are often, but not exclusively, suicides and there are clear roles for the parties which attend these tragic events. It is vitally important that operators understand the important but conflicting objectives that the key players will have such as Coroner, Police, Railway Operators.

An absolutely essential requirement is that the deceased person is accorded dignity and respect. This consideration must run through all of your dealings with the incident itself.

ROLES

Coroner (In England and Wales)
Determines the cause of death in cases where the death was sudden, unexpected, occurred abroad, was suspicious in any way, or happened while the person was under the control of central authority (e.g., in police custody). The coroner may make recommendations for safety practices that may prevent deaths.

Procurator Fiscal (In Scotland)
Investigates any deaths which appear suspicious or where investigation is mandatory regardless of the suspicion of crime. A Fatal Accident Inquiry will take place before a Sheriff and there is no jury. The Sheriff is required to produce a determination which considers five distinct areas:
- Time and place of the death.
- The cause of death.
- Any precautions which may have avoided the death.
- Any defects in the system of working which may have avoided the death.
- Any other relevant considerations.

Evidence is presented by the Procurator Fiscal in the public interest, and other parties may be represented.

British Transport Police (BTP)
Attend all fatalities on the railway and assess the circumstances to determine whether a death is non-suspicious, unexplained or suspicious, including forensic examination of the scene. A role the BTP use is Police Incident Officer (PIO).

Running a railway during disruption

Ambulance Service
Most ambulance services now have agreed protocols in place permitting them to confirm death without a doctor attending. If the death is being treated as suspicious the Police Incident Officer (PIO) may decide that a doctor is needed.

Undertaker
Most Coroners will now allow a Network Rail approved undertaker to attend site to remove the body. The PIO is responsible for directing when it is permissible to remove the body and, in conjunction with the Coroner's office, where it is to be taken to.

Rail Staff
A RIO will act as lead rail representative on site although a TOLO or similar should attend to look after train crew welfare etc. Will take responsibility for managing the impact of the incident on train services.

ISSUES

There are well established procedures which cover when rail traffic can resume prior to the body being removed from site. Shielding the scene will almost always help if it would otherwise have been visible to passengers.

Police categorise these incidents into three self-explanatory groups:
- Non Suspicious.
- Unexplained.
- Suspicious.

As far as railway staff are concerned there is little difference between Unexplained and Suspicious - a Crime Scene Examiner must attend both to investigate cause. It is worth considering whether there is anything that can be done to help an 'Unexplained' become 'Non Suspicious' (e.g. Are there any witnesses, including the driver, who could speak to the BTP Control?).

It is standard procedure now to get the driver involved patched through to BTP control. The driver is often the only witness to the incident and therefore a valuable source of information that can help clear up exactly what happened through answering some key questions. Incidents are often categorised as non-suspicious on the basis of the driver's evidence alone. It can also be useful for other witnesses to be put in contact with the BTP control to add further detail. Make sure that this practice has been adopted in your area.

Liaison with the police is vital, particularly proactively so that a common understanding can be developed. The BTP are particularly understanding of the needs of the railway and you may find that there are things that you can do to facilitate their work. It is often the case that the civil police will arrive on the scene first and this can be a mixed blessing: whilst their response arrival times may be quicker they are not so familiar with the railway environment and are used to working to their own timescales when external time pressures do not weigh so heavily. Encourage any civil police on site to liaise with the BTP.

Fatality incidents are hugely disruptive largely because they require a complete block of all lines, at least initially. It is important that the RIO emphasises to the police the need to open as many lines as possible as quickly as possible. If two lines of a four track railway can be opened the disruption will be significantly reduced. Agreement not to stop at the affected station may assist with getting lines open. Providing screening with police agreement can also help.

The site will be treated as a scene of crime in all but non suspicious cases. This will require forensic examination and whilst BTP will undertake as much forensic analysis away from site as possible it will always be time consuming. You can do much to assist them, even if it is simply controlling access to the site to avoid contamination of evidence or recording what has been done at the scene and by whom: for example if the ambulance crew have searched the body for some form of ID and then left it neatly placed by the body, this will appear suspicious to the police unless they are told what has happened. Protection of evidence will speed up work times for the Crime Scene Examiner.

Once the site has been handed back from police to the railway, do not forget the clean-up operation. The pressure will be on to re-open asap but failure to adequately clear the site can be extremely distressing for members of the public or even for family members who may wish to visit as part of their grieving process. This can be particularly difficult at night so always consider a follow up site visit post-event to check that an adequate job has been done.

There can be a frustrating delay between handing back of the site and the start of train operations. This is often due to the lengthy chain of communications from site via control rooms to the Signaller. The RIO can assist by getting the PIO to speak direct to the Signaller on the nearest signal post telephone to confirm that the line has reopened.

Fatalities are rarely cleared up in less than 60 minutes and 90 minutes is more the norm. It is important to be honest about expectations in communication with customers but remember announcements should refer to a 'person hit by a train' rather than a fatality.

Being involved with an incident where a person is struck by a train can be very distressing for the Driver and also for staff responding to the incident.

Running a railway during disruption

It is important that they are given sufficient support. However it must be recognised that in some cases a speedy return to normal work may be the best way of recovering from the trauma of the incident. Every individual needs individual support.

WHAT PREVENTATIVE ACTION CAN BE TAKEN?

Clearly these types of incident are largely beyond the control of the rail industry but effective preventative action can still be taken:
- The Samaritans do excellent work in this field. Develop your relationship with them, publicise their services on stations and take advantage of any training they can provide to your front line staff
- Identify and review hot spots
- Review your security measures at stations and vulnerable points. Are areas where the public are not meant to be clearly identifiable, are access restrictions possible, and is CCTV coverage adequate? Research shows that persons intent on committing suicide are reluctant to challenge authority to do so. Clear no entry signs and barriers can be very effective.
- Train front line staff to identify and talk to possible risk individuals.
- Review operational procedures, for example how quickly can CCTV evidence be made available, do staff patrol vulnerable locations.
- Identify local community issues and develop relationships with community groups that may be able to help, for example are there any facilities local to the railway which vulnerable people may use.
- Make sure you have agreed lines of communication with high risk organisations such as local mental health hospitals.

Tips

Develop a close working relationship with the BTP.

Do all you can (proactive and real time) to facilitate speedy work by Crime Scene Examiners.

Get as much of the railway open as quickly as possible.

Do not ignore preventative actions and measures.

Remember whilst some individuals may seem unaffected by fatalities these incidents can be very disturbing so make sure that everyone has support.

7.14 Operational Irregularities

BACKGROUND

Any manager leading a team has an obligation to maintain safety in accordance with the many applicable acts, regulations and approved codes of practice. One of an operator's primary responsibilities will be managing the way your team undertake their duties.

Dealing with operational irregularities (sometimes known as irregular working) within a safety critical operational environment is something that every manager in this field will be faced with at some point in their career. An operational irregularity can be defined as an unauthorised departure from agreed methods of working which results in loss or has the potential for loss.

Company safety management systems will define the processes to be followed in the event of an operational irregularity. However it is difficult to precisely set out in a procedure how to manage the human aspect of this type of incident.

A manager needs to be able to deal professionally with members of staff involved while understanding the implications for those involved and the wider industry. The aim must be to maintain professional integrity, follow all the procedures required, yet retain an empathic touch. A fair and consistent approach, will allow you to deal with this particularly challenging aspect of any manager's role.

An important part of understanding how operational irregularities occur is investigation of the human factors that lie behind the immediate cause. This aspect is covered in the Section on Root Cause Determination in Section 8.10 of this handbook.

EXAMPLES OF OPERATIONAL IRREGULARITIES

It is worth considering the main types of event that can be viewed as an Operational Irregularity.

- **Speeding**
A train is found to be be exceeding the speed limit. This could be either a permanent limit - PSR or a temporary limit – TSR or ESR). This is usually as a result of a speed check using a radar 'gun'. The train will usually be stopped by signals at a manned station and the driver challenged. In extreme circumstances the train will be held until a Traincrew Manager or supervisor can attend.

Running a railway during disruption

- **Signal Passed At Danger (SPAD)**
Where a train passes a signal displaying a danger aspect without authority.
- **TPWS Activation/Intervention**
Where the TPWS system on the train activates because the train is travelling too fast on approach to a signal at danger or a speed restriction. An intervention is defined as the situation where the TPWS applied the brakes before the Driver.
- **Wrong routing of a train**
The signaller has set the route at a diverging junction in the wrong direction from the booked or planned route. This incident is made more serious if the driver accepts the route. Safety risk may be minimal but if the train has gauge or route restrictions the implications can be greater.
- **A change of signalling aspect or Category B SPAD**
The signaller has affected the sequence of aspects a driver will receive, most commonly by returning a lever or switch to danger too early, affecting other signals in the sequence.
- **Points run through**
During emergency or degraded working the signaller sometimes cannot rely on the integrity of the signalling system and is required to manually set points to the correct position for a train movement or may have a Points Operator working to their instructions. Should a set of trailing points not be set in the correct position, the train can 'run through' the points concerned.
- **Train routed into a line blockage**
The signaller having allowed the line to be blocked to train movements with a member of an on track team then allows a train towards, or into that section.
- **Overhead line or Isolation incidents**
Primarily occurs when following a request to block a section of electrified overhead line to electric traction rolling stock, the signaller then signals an electric train toward this section.
- **Two trains in one signal section**
Where two trains occupy one signal section without authority. This is very rare and normally occurs when regulations for degraded working are not implemented correctly.
- **Level Crossing Irregularity**
There are various types of Level Crossing (LC) irregularity.
  - pressing crossing clear on a CCTV LC without properly observing that the crossing is clear, trapping a person or vehicles
  - authorising a user to cross at a user worked crossing with telephones when a train is approaching
  - failure to work correctly with a level crossing attendant at a crossing on local control

7.14 Operational Irregularities

These can all result in a train passing over the crossing without road traffic being protected.

- **Station Overrun**

A driver fails to bring his train to a stand within the length of the station platform. This could be due to misjudging braking or poor rail adhesion. The incident is a station overrun if the driver attempted to stop but could not achieve this in the correct location.

- **Fail to Call**

A driver fails to stop at a station due to forgetting that the train was booked to call. The incident is a fail to call if the driver did not recognise the need to stop at the station.

- **Open Door/door on the catch**

The person responsible for train despatch fails to identify that a door has not been closed properly prior to authorising the train's departure

- **Door opening error**

The person responsible for controlling the doors fails to open the correctly, e.g. opening them on the wrong side of the train or failing to operate selective door operation correctly in a platform that is shorter than the train length.

This is not an exhaustive list and there are many other incidents that could constitute irregular working, and will require an initial investigation by the line manager.

The list above applies to irregular working incidents in the operational sphere, but there are incidents that relate to the maintenance function, possession management and project management, protection being placed incorrectly, train or machine movements in possessions being made incorrectly. The process of responding to, and recording the event, and subsequent actions are broadly the same in each function or company.

MANAGING AN OPERATIONAL IRREGULARITY

Irregular Working events are usually highlighted by the individuals directly involved in the incident, be that a signaller or driver, or a member of an on track team, or station staff. However, there are occasions when an incident is not notified so clearly. In some situations incidents will only become apparent through routine analysis of results from data recorders. A thorough, detailed investigation should take place as soon as an incident has been identified.

The normal process is for individual control organisations to be advised of the circumstances. The control organisation is then responsible for escalating the incident to the relevant manager and furnishing this person with all the

Running a railway during disruption

details of the irregular working event. The requirements for logging of events are covered in section 6.10 Logs – Using Control and Other Logs.

It is at this point that the manager needs to take hold of this type of event quickly and professionally, irrespective of the profile of the incident:
- What actually happened?
- Who was involved?
- Can staff continue working or is relief required?
- Is 'for cause' screening required for any of the staff involved?
- Does the incident point to any fundamental issues with how the railway was being operated?
- What are the train service implications now?
- Does any of this have implication for tomorrow's service?
- Is there any perishable evidence that needs to be secured?

A wrong routing caused by a signaller may not involve any significant delay, and as such, you may think that it would require a lesser response than say a points run through, which will undoubtedly cause significant delay and damage to both the infrastructure and the company's reputation due to train cancellations etc. However, speaking to the individual(s) involved quickly will allow an initial investigation of the incident to occur and this may highlight other issues that are underlying factors, such as personal or performance based issues, sub-standard communications protocols, or failure to adhere to rules and regulations.

Several minor incidents can often be pre-cursors to a major incident occurring, therefore it is vital that each instance of irregular working is investigated quickly and the true picture of what occurred is established, documented and that lessons are learnt.

A line manager commencing the initial investigation is required to establish the facts relating to the incident. This will nearly always start with asking the person(s) involved for their explanation, and this is where your people skills will be required.

Points to remember when interviewing someone involved in an incident are:-
- Conduct the interview as quickly as possible – time always blurs events.
- Ensure that you look after the welfare of the individual when carrying out investigations. Asking whether they are OK goes a long way.
- Act discreetly. The person being interviewed should be taken to somewhere private away from other members of the team.
- Make sure you can sit down face to face with the person involved.
- Explain the reasons for the interview – that it is for the purposes of investigating

an alleged incident only and that as the investigating manager you have a duty to thoroughly investigate all aspects of the incident.
- Explain that you need to make notes as a way of recording the details (ensure the time and date are included on the notes).
- Always start by allowing the individual to give their account of what has happened. Do not ask leading questions or contaminate their evidence with comments you have had from other witnesses.
- Once you have established the basic story then make sure you probe the evidence to test accuracy and completeness.
- Record the thoughts, observations and details of the person being interviewed. Write down as much detail as you can to enable you to have an accurate account.

It is worth remembering that an individual may often feel under pressure and vulnerable when faced with a manager investigating their actions relating to an incident concerning safety. Especially if the outcome could result in some sort of punitive measure being taken against them. It is therefore essential to maintain discretion and professionalism throughout.

Following a review of the person's actions, an investigating manager will almost certainly require other forms of evidence to complete the full picture. These could include voice recording downloads from the incident. The vast majority of signal boxes have all phone calls recorded and these can often be valuable source of information. On-train downloads, other witness statements, and data recording downloads from signalling equipment or train involved can all provide information relating to the initial incident, and allow the investigating manager to make an informed judgement.

The manager must consider requesting that the people involved are tested for evidence of alcohol or drug taking. Again this is a sensitive issue as the person involved may feel that they are being punished by being subjected to this type of action. It is important to ensure that the reasons for testing are fully explained and that it may remove one of the possible causes for an incident occurring.

It is vital to remember that the test is not being performed because you believe that alcohol or drugs were involved (although obviously, if you suspect this you will require screening) but to determine whether the individual's actions or omissions may have a part in the irregular working incident. Most company standards now allow for a member of staff to return for work prior to the results of the test being made available if it is subsequently proved that they could not have had a part to play in causing the incident.

All of the investigating manager's evidence of the incident including completed forms required by the company in the event of irregular working, should be

Running a railway during disruption

forwarded to the company Designated Competent Person (DCP). This person will then decide on whether the incident requires a local or formal investigation, and who should complete this. The basis of this process is primarily the same throughout the industry and the decision on whether a full investigation is needed is based on the risk attached to the incident itself.

Many companies will carry out an initial review of the incident (sometimes known as a 72 hour review) to ensure that all relevant evidence has been obtained, learn early lessons and direct the remainder of the investigation.

An example of how Network Rail assesses the risks of each incident is included at the end of this Section, pg 390. This is a simple risk assessment that guides the DCP in the decision making process.

The ultimate goal of any investigation is to fulfil our obligation of running a safe and reliable railway. This can be achieved by learning lessons from each incident and using the information to prevent similar incidents from happening again. Too often in the past an investigation stopped at the individual level because 'it was caused by the signaller' or 'it was the result of the driver's actions'. This is not good enough and to prevent incidents from happening again it is vital to understand the underlying causes.

LESSONS LEARNT

Over time if the causes of operational incidents are carefully recorded it may be possible to identify trends which can lead to focussed initiatives to improve operational safety.

Local or area wide application
- Will enable other managers to identify with an individual where gaps in their knowledge or performance exist. This will allow action plans to be developed to address these gaps. This could be through additional briefing or training. Where it is found someone has violated the rules intentionally disciplinary action may be considered as a means to rectify behaviour.
- You may discover a widespread misunderstanding of a rule or process that reveals fundamental problems, for example, with a briefing process. Or perhaps the defined procedure is impractical for a number of reasons, resulting in uncontrolled shortcuts being taken.
- The investigation and documenting of incident details will allow operational functions or individual areas and locations to identify potential risks or local trends. Preventative measures to reduce the likelihood of the incident occurring again can then be taken. This may include area wide briefings, new localised instructions, or other forms of communications.

7.14 Operational Irregularities

National application
- All incidents should be uploaded into The Safety Management Information System (SMIS). This is the industry's national safety recording system managed on behalf of the industry by the Rail Safety and Standards Board and is used to record all safety related accidents and incidents.
- Access to good quality safety knowledge and intelligence data is vital in assisting the industry to implement action plans and projects that reduce the number of safety incidents that occur. This can be done through national briefings, rule book changes or changes to standards. It may include different ways of training, or the introduction of a new role or department to drive changes through.

Tips

Improving the safe operation of the railway requires a thorough investigation of all instances of irregular working

Care should be taken to ensure that causes are correctly identified – look for root causes, not just the obvious consequential causes.

Sensitivity will be needed in order to correctly identify any human factors.

Remember – operational irregularities can lead to major accidents.

Running a railway during disruption

Network Rail
Irregular Working Initial Investigation form

Guidance on Irregular Working Risk Ranking

Score on the basis of:
1. Identify worst foreseeable outcome (across the top)
2. Estimate how close this outcome was to happening (down the left)

Enter codes shown in boxes on page 3

Foreseeable outcome / Closeness to happening	No foreseeable safety loss [O]	Injury [L]	Single Fatality [M]	Multiple Fatalities [H]
High chance of happening [D]		Medium risk	Potentially Significant	Potentially Severe
Medium chance of happening [H]		Low risk	Medium/High Risk	Potentially Significant
Low chance of happening [J]		Low risk	Low risk	Medium risk
No foreseeable safety loss [K]	Nil			

Use the following statements to help categorise the specific incident being risk ranked

Foreseeable Outcome — Ranking

Multiple Fatalities includes	• High speed collision (> 40 mph) or • Derailment > 15 mph, train outside the kinematic envelope (potential for roll-over, secondary collision with another train or collision with a line side structure)	[H]
Single Fatality includes	• Multiple major injuries or • Collision (> 15 mph but < 40 mph) • Derailment > 15 mph, train inside the kinematic envelope (low likelihood of roll-over, secondary collision with another train or a collision with a line side structure) • Level crossing collision with road vehicle or pedestrian	[M]
Injury includes	• Low speed collision or derailment (< 15 mph)	[L]
No foreseeable safety loss	• No consequences identified - The design of the railway or controls in place prevented the possibility of consequences arising	[O]

Closeness to happening — Ranking

High chance of happening	• Potential accident only prevented by restricted time window for accident or recovery action	[D]
Medium chance of happening	• Significant escalation of event required before accident could occur	[H]
Low chance of happening	• Potential accident prevented by automatic intervention	[J]
No foreseeable safety loss	• Escalation to accident highly unlikely – The design of the railway or controls in place prevented the possibility of an accident occurring	[K]

August 2011 — Page 4 of 4 — NR2072W

Operators' Handbook

Section 8: **Reviewing**

8.1	Identifying and Adopting Good Practice	392
8.2	Plan-Do -Review and Continuous Improvement	393
8.3	Targets & KPIs	394
8.4	Improvement Tools & Techniques	396
8.5	Meetings Management	397
8.6	Remits and Terms of Reference	400
8.7	Audits and Auditing	401
8.8	Processes	407
8.9	Incident and Accident Investigation	409
8.10	Root Cause Determination	414

Reviewing

8.1 Identifying and Adopting Good Practice

BACKGROUND

The identification and adoption of Good Practice is an important managerial task that is too often neglected due to the pressures of the day job.

Using feedback from audits and reviews provides a solid base but it is also important to look out for other examples by expanding your own understanding and experience of what others do.

DETAILS

Good practice will be present throughout the rail industry, in other industries and in everyday life.

The best approach to this aspect of management is to have an established process for evaluating identified Good Practice within a suitable recognised meeting such as a Performance Forum.

Using this approach enables any manager to propose an example of potential Good Practice and know that it will be properly considered.

Good practice is an essential part of continuous improvement but remember that not all good practice works in every situation. Always apply an appropriate level of structured review.

Tips

Good practice is often very simple and obvious. Striking examples can often be found in everyday life.

Use a structured, pre-defined approach for evaluation. Do not just think of the negatives.

Somebody, somewhere already uses a technique on their railway which may be of use to you.

8.2 Plan-Do-Review and Continuous Improvement

BACKGROUND

Plan-Do-Review (PDR) should form the core framework for everything we do. It is the technique that helps drive continuous improvement in the way we manage any aspect of the business.

DETAILS

Plan-Do-Review is often presented in a number of different guises:-
- Plan Do Check Act (PDCA).
- Quality Improvement Process (QIP).
- Problem Solving Process (PSP).
- EFQM RADAR – Approach, Deployment, Assessment & Refinement.

The fundamental principles are:-
- Plan (work out in advance what you intend to do, how and why you are doing it and how you will measure whether you have been successful).
- Do it (implement the plan).
- Review the results (against the plan).

Then start again.

The fundamental questions when undertaking a review are:-
- Did the output meet the specification? If not
- Was the plan flawed? or
- Was the plan incorrectly enacted?

It is by considering these issues that the plan or the way in which the plan was actioned can, if necessary, be refined for the next cycle.

This is why it is important to introduce measures with expected variance limits for key aspects which are often referred to as Key Performance Indicators - KPIs. They are particularly vital for routine repetitive processes where the review phase does not occur naturally.

In reality many managerial tasks are continuous with no discernible start or finish. Therefore the review phase of PDR can be a formalised "pause for thought", review meeting or audit diaried to enable consideration of a particular aspect of the business.

Reviewing

Thinking of this as a continuous rolling process will help reinforce the connection between PDR and continuous improvement.

Tips

PDR = learning from your mistakes.

Continuous Improvement = continually learning from your mistakes…

… not continuously making mistakes!

There is always the opportunity to improve - a structured approach will maximise the size of the delivered improvement.

8.3 Targets & KPIs

BACKGROUND

Targets and Key Performance Indicators (KPIs) are now an established part of managing any business and a dominant feature of railway operations.

As with any management tool it is important to understand the best way to use them and appreciate some of the common pitfalls that they can bring.

This Section aims to help you set sensible targets and KPIs and work using targets and KPIs in a way that makes critical tasks more focused and structured.

ISSUES

Targets and KPIs are essentially two sides of the same coin.

Targets are usually defined objectives that can be used at company, team or an individual level in order to make delivery against broader business goals more certain.

A KPI is a measure of a key business output (or pulse point). PPM is a good example.

- Targets

A good target is one that is clear and achievable although it often will be challenging.

8.3 Targets & KPIs

A bad target will be non-specific, for example, improve train punctuality by 2% - is this PPM? Is it all routes? Or so stretched as to be impossible. This will almost certainly de-motivate those who are given the target to reduce delays at stations to zero.

The use of benchmarking – comparing your operation or business against similar operations or businesses will aid the identification of challenging but achievable targets

- KPIs

Experts usually advise identifying the five critical measures from your business and developing a KPI for each. In theory this should enable managers to understand how the business is performing on an hourly, daily and weekly basis. However, you also need to look where you are going and be aware of the environment around you.

KPIs are vital but you can never run your business by KPIs alone. Be careful that the KPIs you chose encourage the correct behaviours or at least that you are aware of the behavioural implications. A KPI to simply reduce delay minutes is likely to result in an increased number of train cancellations. Is this acceptable to your operation?

Concentrating solely on lagging indicators should also be avoided. Lagging indicators are measures of outputs from a system such as PPM failures, train cancellations or SPADs. You should also consider leading indicators to satisfy yourself that the underlying processes are working correctly. Leading indicators might include competence assessments carried out, percentage of platforms with the right numbers of dispatch staff etc.

Also remember:-
- Good results can sometimes be achieved in spite of poor underlying compliance.
- KPIs and Targets must be understandable to those expected to use them.

Tips

A small number of well thought out targets and KPIs will help you and your team deliver your business goals.

Targets must be relevant and deliverable – benchmarking can help you set appropriate targets.

KPIs should include just the business critical few.

Make sure you understand what your KPIs will not tell you.

Reviewing

8.4 Improvement Tools & Techniques

BACKGROUND

There are a number of recognised improvement tools and techniques that can help managers deliver continuous improvement. Most of these are focused on solving problems or delivering improvements in a structured, systematic way.

Over the years these management tools have been given various description, for example, Quality Improvement Tools but the techniques are relatively timeless and can be applied to any discipline including Operations.

KEY POINTS

Structured improvement tools & techniques will help you to:-
- Base action on analysis of facts.
- Plan activity to a timeline.
- Provide visibility & obtain buy-in.

Remember - identifying the problem is sometimes easier than applying a solution which will often needs participation and support from many different parts of any number of departments and/or organisations.

Tips

Always use structured arrangements to solve problems and drive improvement but do not end up with paralysis by analysis.

Whilst you may instinctively know the cause of the problem - use suitable problem solving tools to verify (you might be wrong!).

Define tasks with tight remits before you dive into the detail.

Using these techniques within working meetings will help provide focus and purpose.

A full description of the main improvement tools and techniques is contained in the TQMI booklet entitled Problem Solving – Tools and Techniques. Available from www.tqmi.co.uk.

Balance your knowledge and judgement with the results of structured analysis and systematic investigation.

8.5 Meetings Management

BACKGROUND

Meetings should be managed effectively in order that decisions can be reached quickly and information exchanged in order that you can get on with the rest of your day job. Where it is not practical to assemble all attendees together use alternatives such as teleconferencing or discuss an issue via email. In the case of email you need to be clear on the decision you are asking people to make and when you need a response by.

ISSUES

Planning a meeting:
- Only invite those who really need to be there:
  - Those involved with the decision making.
  - Those with specific knowledge to contribute.

Note: With long agendas give people specific times to join the meeting providing relevant information.

- Circulate a draft agenda in advance of the meeting listing:-
  - Meeting location – include map if required.
  - Start and finish time.
  - Meeting objective.
  - Proposed attendees.
  - Topics and suggested times with details of who will lead each discussion item.
  - Background information including relevant documents.
  - Contact details of chairperson in case of emergency.

Preparing for the Meeting
- Read any material provided to you in advance of the meeting – you may be required to make decisions based upon it.
- Make sure you are the right attendee for your organisation and have the right level of authority for the discussion.
- Seek other opinions where this is appropriate.

When to hold a meeting
Research has shown that the best time to hold a meeting is either before lunch or towards the end of the day as this motivates people to focus on the agenda

Reviewing

and prevent the meeting from overrunning. If you are holding meetings over lunch consider any special dietary requirements.

Taking the minutes
If you are chairing the meeting ideally find someone else to take minutes to allow you to concentrate on steering the meeting. Ensure the person taking the minutes understands the subject matter and does not get lost with any jargon used. Be clear about what is required – is it sufficient to record just action points or do you need to record the discussion as well?

Preparing the venue
- Ensure the meeting room is booked and of adequate size and layout.
- Ensue the room is tidy.
- Provide sufficient tables and chairs.
- Ensure equipment is available if needed such as a flip chart or paper and pens.
- Ensure there is enough light and that heating and ventilation is comfortable.
- Ensure there are sufficient power points for laptops and projectors.

Running the meeting
- Start on time – this gives the meeting momentum.
- Introduce everyone if needed and explain the purpose and objective of the meeting.
- For other than regular review meetings describe the agenda and ask attendees to list their expectations of the meeting (make a note of these on a flip chart).
- Summarize the discussion at the end of each item and restate the agreed decision and action point.
- Politely and firmly move the discussion on if a subject has become exhausted.
- Do not allow vocal individuals to dominate the meeting.
- Do not allow individuals to run separate private meetings during the discussion.
- Ask attendees not to use phones during the meeting.

Closing the meeting
- Thank everyone for attending.
- Restate the agreed action points.
- Note who is responsible for them.
- Agree the deadline to complete them.
- Review the meeting expectations to check if they have been achieved.
- Agree date of next meeting if applicable.
- Agree with the minute taker when the minutes will be circulated.

EFFECTIVE MEETINGS

Effective meetings are essential. The following keys to effective meetings are very simple but not followed frequently enough. They are not operations specific and can be applied to any regular meeting – most can also be applied to ad hoc meetings.

The key to effective meetings are:-
- Remits.
- Planning.
- Listening.
- Awareness (i.e. read body language).
- Cabinet responsibility (the meeting's decision overrides any views or discussion and 'positions taken' during the debate before the decision).
- Notes & Actions.

Tips

Do not be afraid to question the purpose of a meeting. Cancel meetings that do not have a clear purpose.

It is really worth developing your skills of meeting management - to allow you extra time within your working week to actually get things done.

Develop these skills and run meetings on time - and to time. You will then have mastered one of the key frustrations of being a manager.

Also remember
- too many attendees make meetings ineffective.
- too many meetings make attendees ineffective.

8.6 Remits and Terms of Reference

BACKGROUND

Clear remits and Terms of Reference are essential when solving problems, setting tasks, delegating responsibilities, creating a forum or meeting and a wide range of other management activities such as investigations and projects.

Given the volume of meetings in the rail industry it is essential to set clear remits. Similarly, when delegating tasks, setting projects or even tackling an issue yourself, a clear written remit will significantly enhance the likelihood of a successful conclusion that delivers the output you require.

ISSUES

The framework shown below can be applied to a wide range of situations that require a systematic approach.

When should a remit be set?

Any request to undertake an activity that is not simply part of "the day job" will benefit from having a remit set. In reality a remit is simply a means of setting out a clear instruction.

TASK	The general description of the need to do something to address an opportunity or concern.
PURPOSE	• Why we are doing the task? In order to… • What it is for? So that… • Who it is for?
END RESULT	What we want to achieve when the task is complete What the finished "article" will look like.. When is it required? What are the other constraints to be met, for example, financial?
SUCCESS CRITERIA	What will indicate that we have been and are being successful? Milestones. How can we assess the fitness for purpose of the results?
INFORMATION	Assembling relevant facts, information and data requirements, support etc.

Tips

Actively using remits to help solve problems and complete tasks is a top ten tip.

Practice writing remits - they are invaluable.

It may be difficult at first but practice with some simple tasks. Tight remits help everyone involved but surprisingly it is not a widely practiced skill.

Work through the framework - concentrate on End Results and Success Criteria.

Use written remits and terms of reference to improve delivered results.

8.7 Audits and Auditing

BACKGROUND

An audit is a highly structured review process, usually using a fixed base of questions, and deriving marks or scores against tightly defined criteria.

Audits are an essential aspect of all management activities. They help check conformance with processes and related behaviours, identify areas for action, examples of good practice, signal what is important and provide measurement.

Like any management tool – the level and type of audits should be appropriate to both the risk and the degree of importance of the aspect in question.

Audits generally fall into 3 categories:
- Internal check (self- assurance and audit and check).
- Internal audit (separate auditor from the same organisation or department).
- External audit (an independent auditor from a separate company).

Audit and check processes should incorporate an element of self-assessment and self-certification; these are important aspects of auditing. Structured routine audit and check will help establish and consolidate crucial processes and arrangements.

Reviewing

Do not just audit processes – there are many examples of good processes poorly or inadequately used. Auditing behaviours is more difficult but it is probably more informative about the effectiveness of your arrangements and the responsible managers. In essence you must check that your defined arrangements are used ('deployed' in auditor terms).

Certain audits should be independent. This does not mean that they must always be conducted by external agencies or consultants. It does mean that those involved need to be impartial and consistent and that they focus on evidence, facts and deriving logical conclusions.

Audit either internal or external, when carried out well, will always be of real benefit to Operators. Deficiencies found early will always be easier to sort than when they continue longer term.

TOC AREAS FOR AUDIT

Typical TOC audit and check requirements are shown in the following table. Remember that your own TOC may have differing requirements.

AREA Internal	FREQUENCY
Safety Management System	Annually
Safety Tours by Functional Directors	12 per annum
Safety of the Line :- - Driver/Conductor Depot Audit - Out of hours visits - Train Despatch checks - Shunting activities - Safety Critical Staff	 Annual Determined by individual TOCs Annually Annually Annually
Performance Management	6 monthly
Incident Management	6 monthly
Train Crew Efficiency	Annually

AREA External	FREQUENCY
Performance 'Best Practice'	Annual
Safety Certificate (ROGS)	Annual

8.7 Audits and Auditing

NR AREAS FOR AUDIT

Network Rail currently uses a self assurance system with independent audit. The self-assurance system is specified in Section 7.02 of the Network Rail Operations Manual and follows this format:

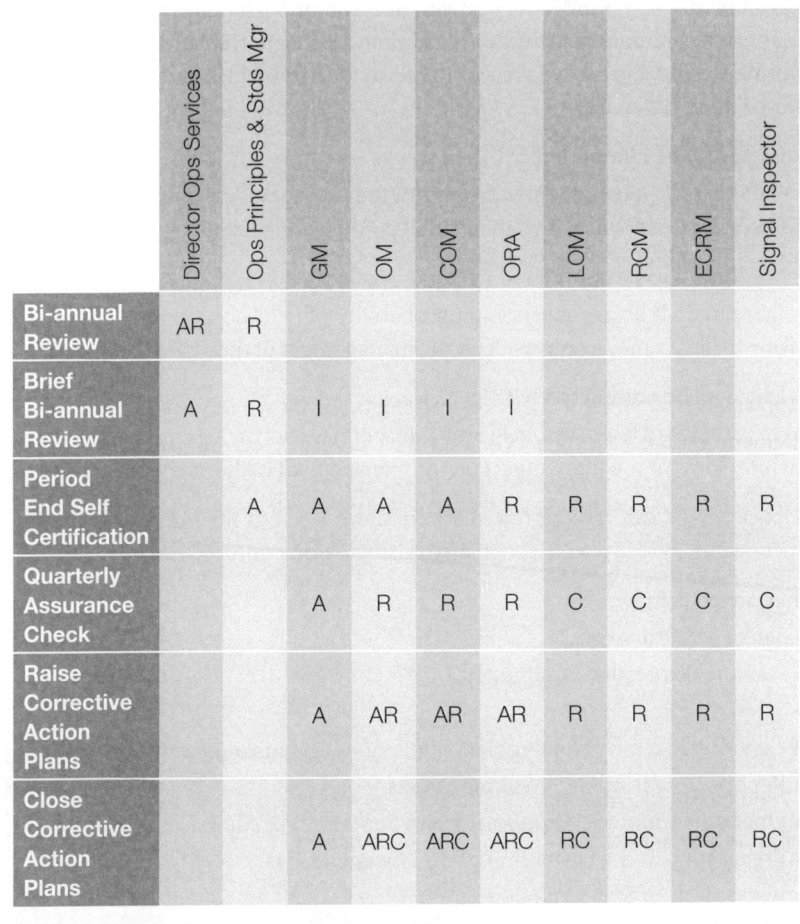

	Director Ops Services	Ops Principles & Stds Mgr	GM	OM	COM	ORA	LOM	RCM	ECRM	Signal Inspector
Bi-annual Review	AR	R								
Brief Bi-annual Review	A	R	I	I	I	I				
Period End Self Certification		A	A	A	A	R	R	R	R	R
Quarterly Assurance Check			A	R	R	R	C	C	C	C
Raise Corrective Action Plans			A	AR	AR	AR	R	R	R	R
Close Corrective Action Plans			A	ARC	ARC	ARC	RC	RC	RC	RC

R – Responsible for carrying out the task.
A – Accountable for seeing that the task is carried out.
C – Consulted and provides input.
I – Informed, no formal need for input.

Network Rail's annual National Core Audit Programme (NCAP) is developed for agreement each year by its Tactical Safety Group (TSG). The NCAP sets out a programme of in-depth audit of processes which can impact on safety – including Health & Safety Management System audits, special topic audits

Reviewing

and cross-functional audits – at a frequency that reflects the significance of a failure of the control. Network Rail's Operations audit programme is based around compliance with its Operations Manual and Managed Stations Manual in which each General Manager's area is audited once every two years.

An audit may result in Non-Conformances (failures to comply with a requirement of a documented procedure, standard or legislation). These are often notified using Corrective Action Requests (CARs) which must be actioned to specified timescales:

- **High – to be completed within 4 weeks**
When there is potentially significant risk to safety, or where there is an absence of necessary control arrangements that could lead to significant risk.

- **Medium – to be completed within 8 weeks**
Where there is an average or high probability of risks occurring and they are likely to have a medium impact on the management of the operational railway.

- **Low – to be completed within 12 weeks**
Where there is a low or unlikely probability of risks occurring and they are likely to have a low or medium impact on the management of the operational railway.

Observations can also be raised where there is room for improvement, but insufficient evidence exists to justify raising a non conformance.

Key areas include:
- Safety Critical Work.
- Personal Protective Equipment.
- Safety Briefings.
- Control of Excessive Working Hours for Persons Undertaking Safety Critical Work.
- Reporting of Irregular Working Events.
- Operator Additional Monitoring and Support Procedure.
- Preparation and Distribution of Emergency Plans.
- Inspections of Staffed Operating Premises.
- Checks of Completed Operational Forms.
- Mandatory and additional Visits to staff at Manned Locations.
- Visits to Employees at Operating Locations by the Signalling Inspectorate.
- Safety Critical Communications.
- Route Lists and Card Check.
- Temporary Block Working.
- Competence Assessment and Monitoring of Operations Employees.
- Fire Safety Arrangements.

Special Topic Audits can also be undertaken into specific areas, usually because the area has a relatively new approach, or because it is an area of particular risk or because it is an area which appears to have some underlying difficulties.

AUDIT PROGRAMME

Introducing a mandatory audit programme is an essential requirement but all managers should also recognise the benefits of commissioning a one-off audit if a critical process or set of arrangements are causing concern. When undertaking such a step it is vitally important to prepare a clear remit, and employ competent auditing resources, whether these are internal or independent personnel.

The purpose of an audit should always be clearly explained to those involved. Management expectations regarding participation, preparation, production of evidence, meetings and interviews with the audit team, and the priority to be accorded to these, should be clear. Explain the participants are able to treat the audit as a learning and improvement opportunity.

AUDIT RESULTS

Audit results will not always be correct therefore managers must ensure that findings and recommendations are fully considered before they are formally accepted.
- Challenge incorrect findings but be prepared to consider audit results with an open mind.
- Once results are accepted, action must be taken.
- Develop action plans to deal with deficiencies and track progress through the routine (Plan Do Review) arrangements.
- Ensure line managers understand what is required and why.
- Make sure all actions are brought to a successful conclusion.
- Finally re-audit at some point to ensure the issues have been properly and permanently resolved.

Because audits can be very useful in highlighting areas that require attention, they can help in obtaining necessary resources and commitment from more senior management. Critical problem areas can then be resolved and organisations can be improved. The more informal mechanisms for achieving the same ends are covered in section 3.6 Management by Walking About.

Reviewing

Tips

- Ensure audits are planned, diarised and delivered.
- Treat audits seriously and let others know you treat them seriously.
- Ensure robust follow up of actions.

The traditional defensive view of audits is that they are designed to catch you out. The reality is different although they do identify shortfalls.

Honesty will always produce the best audit results. A deficiency will usually get a worse score if you try to cover it up. A mature approach treats audit as a means of highlighting improvement opportunities, and helping to set the action agenda in the subject.

Never commission an audit and ignore the findings.

8.8 Processes

BACKGROUND

The three main inputs to most operations are:
- People.
- Plant.
- Processes.

The EFQM model lists five "Enablers" (input activities) as part of the nine key criteria that define any company. One of these Enablers covers processes.

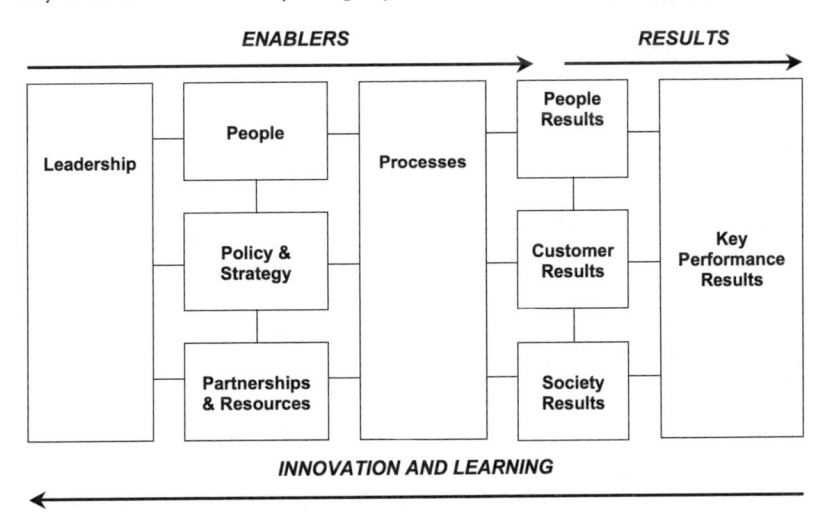

```
          ENABLERS                           RESULTS
──────────────────────────────→   ──────────────────────────────→

                    People
                   Results
         People
Leadership        Processes
                                              Key
         Policy &      Customer          Performance
         Strategy      Results             Results

         Partnerships  Society
         & Resources   Results

              INNOVATION AND LEARNING
←──────────────────────────────────────────────
```

Processes constitute the largest Enablers section within the rail industry. Work by British Rail in the 1990s suggested that 14% of EFQM scoring criteria were directly dependent on processes within the rail industry.

The EFQM model also heavily focuses on the concept of RADAR. This is:-

Results (through)
Approach
Deployment
Assessment (and)
Refinement

Good documented processes are therefore essential but remember without those processes being actively used by well trained people the arrangements will never work!

Reviewing

ISSUES

Whilst processes are an integral part of the overall management arrangements, an industry such as ours is heavily dependent on the people involved in train service delivery undertaking their individual tasks in a prescribed and consistent manner.

The Rule Book codifies a number of key safety requirements and procedures but examples of defined processes are relatively rare. A lack of defined processes increases the risk that tasks will not be undertaken in a consistent manner, this will inevitably generate variations in delivery because the task itself will be completed in a variable way. This will also make interfacing tasks more variable and less well integrated.

For this reason processes that are mission critical should be defined in detail and form part of the training and competence management arrangements. Regular adherence to processes can be boring but delivery of high quality outputs always requires relentless and remorseless attention to detail.

First class railways in the rest of the world frequently have flow-charted processes covering almost all eventualities. Many have timed responses for dealing with routine problems, for example, a bridge bash at location X is known to take 18 minutes to clear.

Identifying and codifying all major train service delivery processes is a mammoth task. Identifying areas of repeat process failure is a good point at which to start. Document these processes and follow the critical path for train service delivery management.

A documented Cut & Run process that is integrated within the Control Office and with the operations and fleet organisations is a good example of a critical process.

Remember - processes by themselves will not deliver good results but an absence of adequately defined processes will make consistent delivery of good results improbable.

Tips

Document your critical processes and use them!

The rail industry has historically loved fire fighting and has prided itself on its ability to meet all emerging situations. This will never produce world-class results and is no substitute for preparation, processes and training.

Without codified processes the railway will be like a football match, a group of players, a set of rules and 90 minutes of action that produces relatively unpredictable results.

What we need is a ballet where every step and every move is choreographed with an entirely predictable result.

8.9 Incident and Accident Investigation

BACKGROUND

Arrangements for formally investigating incidents and accidents that trigger certain thresholds are specified in the Group Standard GO/RT3119, and the associated Guidance Note (GO/GN3519). The standard provides criteria to determine whether a local or formal investigation should be undertaken and also sets out which organisation should normally take the lead in the investigation. Each railway organisation is required to appoint a specific person to manage the investigations process:

- to make sure that incidents are reviewed daily to determine whether an investigation is required,
- to set a remit and agree this with other affected parties,
- to appoint the investigator,
- to review and sign off the report and check progress as it is being produced.

The Rail Accident Investigation Branch of the Department for Transport commenced its work in October 2005. This body now covers many of the responsibilities for the investigation of train accidents formerly held by RSSB. Certain types of accident and incident must be notified to RAIB by Duty Holders and in some cases, particularly involving fatalities, RAIB must carry out an investigation. RAIB investigations are independent of the rail industry and the findings are always published.

Lower level incident or accident investigations are covered by Network Rail and TOC internal company requirements and your company will have internal standards based upon the Group Standard and Guidance Note mentioned above.

Formal accident investigation is a specialist skill for which comprehensive training is recommended. For certain posts, satisfactory completion of such

Reviewing

a course and examination is part of the competence requirement which will be periodically assessed.

The requirements for performance investigations are not so strictly defined within standards, but this does not reduce the importance of a speedy and effective investigation. The techniques involved are very similar.

REQUIREMENTS

All accidents should be subject to some form of investigation. For the smallest incidents a preliminary investigation can be co-ordinated and closed by Control and on-call staff. Preservation of evidence at this stage is vital and will ease any future investigation. More significant incidents may require further informal investigation, for example, through a daily review of the Control logs.

Significant accidents and incidents will be subject to a more formal review. This may be a Local or a Formal Investigation. It is vital to consult others when determining what type of investigation will be undertaken and who will lead it. The standards provide clear guidance but others, internally and externally will have important views and you are likely to need their help and expertise in gathering evidence and evaluating it.

Your organisation is likely to have documented the types of incident that should trigger either a formal or local investigation. Suspected Category A SPADs in particular have a formalised process for determining both the level of investigation and which organisation (TOC or Network Rail) should lead it. This is based on the risk rating for the SPAD and the SPAD history for the particular signal.

Some organisations have adopted the practice of undertaking quick, formal reviews within a short timescale sometimes called a '72 Hour Review'. The objective of this type of review is to:-
• Establish the basic facts.
• Focus the ongoing (possibly formal) investigation.
• Learn any immediate lessons.
• Put in place urgent action to prevent recurrence.

The panel for any investigation should be chaired by a manager with sufficient experience, authority and competence. The panel should include relevant managers including those from other companies where appropriate and should consider evidence from parties involved.

For significant performance incidents it is critical that the TOC and NR have clear processes for carrying out investigations. These are known as Significant

8.9 Incident and Accident Investigation

Performance Incident Reviews (SPIRs). Make sure that arrangements for triggering, carrying out and learning from SPIRs are codified and understood. Also make sure the lessons learnt are implemented.

TECHNIQUES

Incident and accident investigation techniques are frequently taught as part of established learning programmes. The investigation process can be broken down into four key stages:

Evidence Collection

Make sure that all necessary evidence is preserved following the incident. This may require immediate action to prevent information being lost. Examples include OTMR data which may be overwritten after a period of time or 'witness marks' on rails or wheels following a derailment. Witness evidence is perishable too. As time passes, individuals will have a less reliable recollection of events. Make sure an initial interview is conducted quickly.

Good record keeping and suitable sorting of evidence will help the analysis stage. For example, make sure photographs are labelled or clearly named and ensure that clocks are checked on CCTV, OTMR etc before the data is downloaded. Check mobile phone use.

Producing a fishbone diagram is one way of ordering information prior to further analysis. For serious incidents you may need to consider whether independent testing is required. Standards will require this for certain types of incident, for example, accidents at Automatic Level Crossings where equipment failure cannot be immediately ruled out.

Analysis

Analysis is a structured and formal process of examining evidence and determining the causes of an accident from it.

Firstly the sequence of events must be identified. This may be as simple as producing a timeline of the events described by the evidence. Evidence that does not fit logically into the sequence of events or is contradictory should be examined again to establish if it is valid.

The immediate causes of the incident can then be determined. Immediate causes are the unsafe acts or conditions that led to the incident taking place. Examples include failure to use the correct equipment, the failure of a component or excessive speed. Remember that the last of the sequence of events may not be the only cause. Failings earlier in the chain of events may be equally important. When several 'wrong' things line up the inherent safety of the railway system is

Reviewing

weakened and an incident is more likely to occur. This is known as the 'Swiss Cheese Model' of accident causation. See the other relevant/useful documents section of this element for more information pg 413.

Identifying immediate causes is insufficient to prevent an incident happening again. To get rid of weeds you need to dig out the root. If you only remove the foliage the weed will grow back. The next stage of analysis is to identify the underlying causes behind the accident.

Underlying causes are the system, organisational or human factors causes behind the accident. Examples include inadequate procedures, failure to supervise adequately or fatigue. There are usually layers of underlying causes with the most fundamental cause known as the root cause. Techniques such as 'Five Whys' can help in identifying underlying and root causes. See section 8.10 on 'Root Cause Determination'.

Human Factor issues deserve special attention. Engineering causes of accidents are gradually being eliminated as design, manufacture and maintenance processes become more reliable. Increasingly accidents are caused by human failings. Identifying the type of human error will help to identify suitable actions to prevent recurrence. The categorisation shown at the end of the Section should be used.

Often an investigation will identify issues which were relevant to the incident but cannot be considered as part of the causal chain. These can be labelled 'factors for consideration'. It is important that these are identified and followed up as they may be a causal factor in a future incident. An example might be that a track worker hit by a passing train was not wearing the appropriate PPE even though the cause of the accident was failure to block the line correctly.

Risk Control Measures

Identify measures which could prevent the incident for happening again. If these measures should already have been in place it is useful to ask why they did not work.

Were the measures adequate or simply not complied with? New control measures should be included as recommendations from the investigation. Make sure that the recommendations address the causes identified. This includes any human factors issues. Do the recommendations match the category of human failure which was identified (see the next section on Root Cause Determination)?

8.9 Incident and Accident Investigation

Action Planning and Implementation

Recommendations from the investigation should be SMART:
- **Specific** (Clear in their outcome and improvement).
- **Measurable** (Clear understanding of benefit).
- **Achievable** (Within the managers realm of responsibility).
- **Realistic** (A sensible level of response to the deficiency; implementable).
- **Time based** (Clear milestones for delivery of the plan with clear ownership).

Decisions will need to be taken about how recommendations are to be implemented and progress must be adequately tracked.

Tips

Formally investigating events is often useful even if the incident does not trigger any of the specified criteria.

Investigation is purely a structured forum that keeps asking Why? Why? Why? Why? Why? until the root cause is determined. Use this technique formally and informally to get to the correct understanding of any given problem. See next section.

If something doesn't seem right - hold an investigation.

Other relevant/useful documents:-
- RAIB website: http://www.raib.gov.uk
- This includes a number of leaflets on the role and operation of RAIB and a guidance note on application of the Railway Accident Investigation and Reporting Regulations.
- 'Investigating accidents and incidents - a workbook for employers, unions, safety representatives and safety professionals' (HSE Ref. HSG245). A useful workbook for investigations that encourages rigor in analysis, identification of human factors and identification of recommendations. A useful table helps to match underlying causes to immediate causes.
- The following web page provides an overview of James Reason's Swiss Cheese model: (http://en.wikipedia.org/wiki/Swiss_Cheese_model).
- An overview of fishbone diagrams is show here:-(http://en.wikipedia.org/wiki/Ishikawa_diagram).

Reviewing

8.10 Root Cause Determination

BACKGROUND

Determining the root cause of an incident or event including poor performance is a task that is vital to delivering continuous improvements.

The root cause is the most fundamental cause of an accident and normally relates to processes or procedures that are missing, not followed or inadequate. Although the root cause may be distant from the incident in terms of time and space it is important that the root cause is established. Dealing with the root cause will prevent the incident happening again and is likely to prevent other similar incidents too.

ISSUES

It is very easy to mistake a symptom for a cause and therefore "drilling down" to root cause is an essential aspect of operations management. Recognising the root cause is not difficult – the following example illustrates the principles:-

Issue	Time lost in running
1. Why?	Low power
2. Why?	Two traction motors isolated
3. Why?	Train failed previous day *
4. Why?	Fou fou valves failed
5. Why?	Latest batch are unreliable
6. Why?	New sub contractor has not followed correct refurb specification – ROOT CAUSE!!!

* Additionally in this example there was a further line of inquiry beyond Step 3:

It is established that the failure was not entered in the repair book.

8.10 Root Cause Determination

Issue	Why did train enter service with traction motors isolated?
1. Why?	Not entered in repair book
2. Why?	Previous driver forgot
3. Why?	Custom and practice is not to log faults if reported to Control
4. Why?	Discipline is not enforced
5. Why?	It has not been deemed important enough
6. Why?	Drivers want more pay for logging faults therefore the issue has been avoided – ROOT CAUSE!!!

Human Factors

Increasingly the need to understand underlying reasons behind the Human Factor failings that lead to an incident is being recognised as essential for preventing a recurrence. Equipment safeguards, processes and procedures are designed to prevent accidents and incidents but human failings will still occur and these can frequently explain the underlying reasons for an incident. "Human Factors" are simply a categorisation of various types of human failing.

The information below is taken from Network Rail's guidance. Other companies may use slightly different definitions but the principles are exactly the same and should be used by investigators.

Essentially a human factor failure can be either an Error or a Violation (deliberate). Errors can be one of four error types whilst Violations are either routine or situational/exceptional.

All failures are attributed to one or more Incident Factors (ten in total).

More information and guidance on this important aspect can usually be obtained from the Safety Management experts within your company.

Reviewing

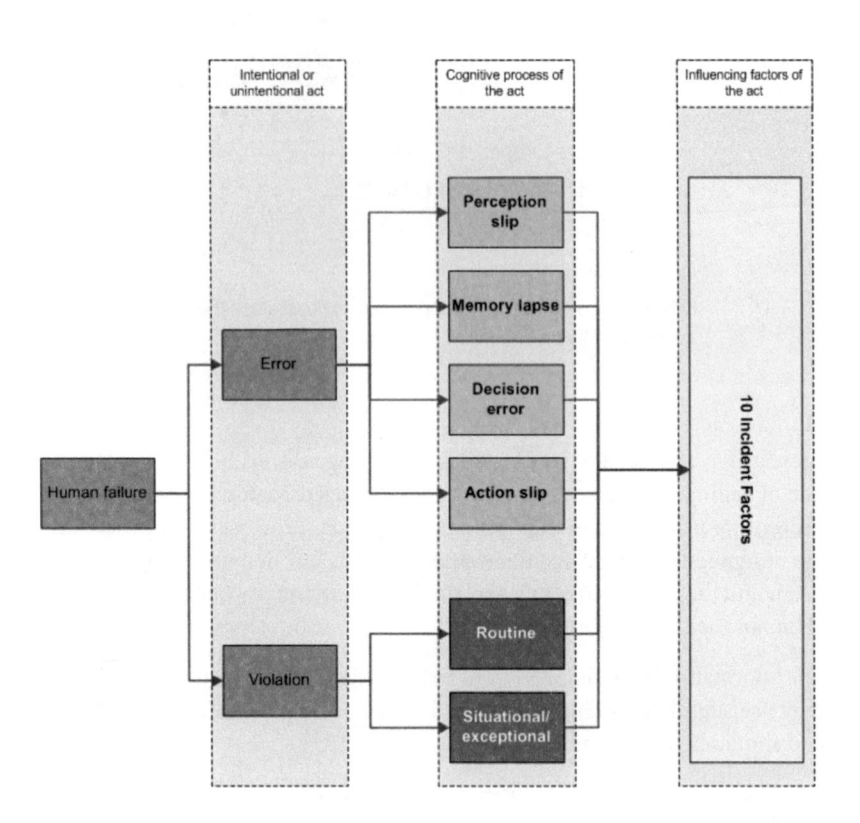

8.10 Root Cause Determination

Error Categories:

Perception slip	Perception slips are errors in visual detection and searching, and listening errors So these error types are to do with if a person mis-saw or mis-heard, or failed to hear or see something.
Memory lapse	Memory lapses are errors concerned with failure of short or long-term memory. So these error types are to do with if the person forgot or mis-recalled information, or forgot to do something.
Decision error	Decision errors are errors in acts or judgement, decisions or strategies. They typically rely on knowledge and information being correctly recalled but wrongly applied. So these types or error are to do with errors in making decisions or deciding on what to do in situations.
Action slip	Action slips are when actions or speech are not performed as planned i.e. unintentionally. Such errors or speech are the execution of correctly formed decisions. So these types of error are to do with a person doing or saying something they did not intend, or being inadvertently incorrect or unclear.

Incident Factors:

Communications
Practices and processes
Information
Equipment
Knowledge, skills and experience
Supervision and Management
Work Environment
Teamwork
Personal
Workload

Reviewing

Tips

Root Cause will be determined by repeatedly asking 'Why'? At first this may seem odd - you will be like a child that questions everything. The technique is known as the 'Five Whys'. In most situations it will be necessary to ask why five times to reach the root cause. In other cases there will be more questions ...

However, persevere and you will soon discover that:

- Many investigations fail to identify the true root cause.
- Performance improvement initiatives often tackle the wrong issues.
- Problem solving is quite complex and what appear to be simple issues may have complex (and sometimes surprising) root causes.

Other relevant/useful documents:-
– An overview of the Five Whys technique is available here: (http://en.wikipedia.org/wiki/5_Whys)

Section 9: **Change management**

9.1	Operating Standards Management	420
9.2	Change Management	422
9.3	Managing a Small Project	426
9.4	Managing the Interface with Major Projects	428

Change management

9.1 Operating Standards Management

BACKGROUND

Industry and Company Standards provide a safe framework in which we can operate. Standards deliberately reduce our freedom to act and describe safe practices that allow us to operate within ALARP principles.

However standards can become too restrictive and curtail judgement. Similarly if too many standards are set it will become more and more difficult to know and apply them. Such situations must be actively managed.

Applying certain standards can also be a bit like applying some laws – open to a degree of interpretation.

ISSUES

The best way to avoid over restrictive standards is to ensure that:
- Consultation on Group Standards (or similar) is handled at the appropriate level in your company.
- The practical operating viewpoint is given during any consultation phase.
- The people that represent your company must understand the issues and not be bureaucratic "box tickers."
- Appropriate internal control is exercised over the way standards are implemented.
- Organisations are represented on relevant Industry forums by practitioners rather than theorists.

Those reviewing and commenting on standards must always consider cost and performance impacts. This has been a weakness of the industry approach in recent years - those implementing standards must formally consider the potential impact on performance and reliability.

Reviewing and challenging standards can be time consuming and bureaucratic. Implementing standards sympathetically is challenging. However a failure to resource these aspects properly can allow restrictive standards to appear. Give this area appropriate attention and encourage your operations colleagues in other companies to do the same.

If such standards do slip through the net or, as is more likely, overly restrictive company standards appear (that are not subject to wider industry consultation) – it is essential that a robust challenge is made.

There are many examples of unnecessarily restrictive standards being implemented but two illustrative cases where a successful post implementation reversal was achieved are shown below. However the effort that was involved in each of the cases to achieve the relaxation was immense. This clearly demonstrates the importance of getting properly engaged before such standards are introduced.

Case 1

Network Rail's West Coast Main Line Tranche 2 (WCML T2) patrolling policy which closed pairs of line on the four-track south end of the route for periods during the day. The policy was introduced during mid-2000 and became a significant performance issue that generated a great deal of friction between NR and the TOCs. After much debate over alternative approaches, revised arrangements were introduced that enable compliance with the required standards without the negative performance impact.

Case 2

Following the Southall rail accident in 1997 standards for dealing with defective on train equipment were tightened up. Whilst this was clearly a necessary response to the causes of the accident, the revised standard produced some unintended consequences. Actions required following certain types of equipment failure were found to be unnecessarily restrictive resulting in increased numbers of train cancellations. In part this was due to the requirements of the standard. In other cases the cause was the way in which the standard was being interpreted by train operators.

As a result clearer guidance was subsequently issued and in a number of areas the standard has been revised allowing greater flexibility of response while retaining a clear overall framework for contingency plans. An example includes work to risk assess the circumstances in which a train can continue in service with a defective Track Circuit Actuator. This has saved significant numbers of cancellations for some operators without importing more risk.

An important question is always whether the measures in a standard are proportionate for the risk they are intended to manage.

The best approach to mounting a winning challenge includes the following:
- Be knowledgeable.
- Gather evidence and facts (most gripes about standards are based on anecdotes).
- Undertake a rudimentary assessment of the impact on your operation.
- Gather allies – industry groups such as ATOC Operations Council, NTF Operators Group etc. can be very useful. Your company will be represented at such meetings.
- Propose alternative control measures.

Change management

- Lobby at a senior level through "one-to-ones" (internally and cross-company).
- Use the established forums such as Train Operations Management Standards Committee (TOMSC).

Provided the issue involved can be shown to have a material performance impact, there is a strong likelihood of industry support and success.

But remember, standards that overtly address safety issues are usually a one-way ratchet. It is very difficult to gain relaxation or dispensation – spotting changes early is the key to success.

Tips

This is an area of anecdote heaven. There are few tangible examples of over restrictive standards within the Group Standards but unfortunately some of these have been very large examples e.g. Defective On-train Equipment.

Maintain good dialogue with Industry colleagues, engage in standards consultations and participate in industry forums.

Make sure that standards are applied in ways that minimise any adverse performance impact.

Always consider the potential performance impact of changes - reversal is always more difficult after introduction.

9.2 Change Management

BACKGROUND

Change is a constant feature of most dynamic industries. Adapting to new business circumstances and requirements is essential.

Consequently the management of change is a vital skill – particularly as major operational change frequently generates high risks e.g. franchise change, organisational change, new rolling stock, replacement signalling, new timetables etc. It is also an aspect of management which mostly lends itself to a structured project approach – Plan-Do-Review.

The rail industry in Great Britain has an established safety validation process that independently reviews specified change that is deemed safety critical. However if change is to be effective the management arrangements usually need to be far broader than this statutory minimum.

Most of us are uncomfortable with change and prefer the status quo. Additionally many reorganisations are not well thought through and give change management a bad name – often deservedly.

However it is a fact that companies that do not change, adapt and periodically reinvigorate the management focus, go stale and often perform badly. It is also clear that poorly managed change can be counter productive.

ISSUES

The world around us is constantly changing. An operations manager's job is actually to instigate and implement appropriate change without upsetting the running railway.

Also it is important to be clear about what needs to be changed and why, and communicating this effectively, honestly and with an appropriate degree of sensitivity to those likely to be affected is a key challenge. This is not the same as 'consulting with the Unions or Company Council', where a large dose of political posturing (on both sides) may well corrupt or dilute the message.

The responsibility for telling people things they need to know and soliciting thoughts and concerns of the affected staff is an individual responsibility of every manager.

You should also be clear about expected outcomes, and over what period these are expected to be achieved.
- How will these be measured?
- How will any unintended effects be managed?
- How will potentially negative impacts be handled?
- By whom?

These kinds of issues are particularly important where change is being promulgated from management senior to you, and where the extent of strategic control by you and your team is limited. Your integrity, honesty and the trust which staff place in you, will be most tested in this situation.

Change management

LEVEL - TACTICAL

Plan
- Convert the strategic aims into a tactical plan and ensure that aims and objectives are transparent.
- Ensure that risks are correctly identified and that appropriate mitigation has been developed.
- Develop an appropriate training structure – supplement with a core brief where necessary.
- Prepare carefully the documentation for formal consultation with local staff representatives and schedule formal meetings.
- Ensure the aims and objectives of any change are fully understood by all involved staff.
- Be clear with staff about what is to change and why.

Do
- Comment on plans, do not be afraid to give your opinion.
- Check the briefing process is being undertaken and provide visible support by selective participation.
- For large schemes raise your profile and lead from the front.
- Ensure the plan is followed and any deviations are notified immediately.
- During the transition take charge of relevant decision making as necessary. This may apply to certain decisions that are normally made at a working level, e.g. in Control Offices.
- Communicate, communicate and communicate.

Review
- Instigate structured reviews for larger schemes capturing feedback in a structured way (use a facilitator if appropriate).
- Monitor the ongoing impact of the scheme – using temporary KPIs if appropriate.
- Are the benefits and outcomes being delivered?
- Are we measuring the appropriate things?
- Actively seek out feedback, record it and determine any necessary action.
- Debrief staff involved and capture learning points.
- Confront any unintended consequences and propose or action mitigation.

9.2 Change Management

LEVEL - STRATEGIC

Plan

- Identify change events or requirements and mobilise appropriate arrangements to manage.
- Identify all those who need to be involved and/or consulted - including stakeholders.
- Devise project plans and time lines and identify resources to manage.
- Be realistic about benefits, outcomes and timescales for achievement.
- Develop a disposition plan i.e. show what happens to retained tasks.
- Ensure accountabilities are clear.
- Hand pick the people to manage the change.
- Document intended or required outcomes and objectives including cost and benefit assessment if appropriate.
- Apply structured Risk Assessment techniques and ensure all proposed mitigation is documented and allocated an owner.
- Develop an appropriate briefing and communication plan incorporating core briefs as appropriate.
- Prepare formal consultation documentation for staff, reps, and schedule formal meetings.
- Develop the review requirements and arrangements.

Do

- Manage the change event through designated Managers.
- Recognise that culture change is often very difficult and protracted.
- Provide visible leadership during large change events.
- Communicate, communicate, and communicate.

Review

- Instigate and lead the review arrangements for larger schemes.
- Commission a formal audit if appropriate.
- Ensure learning points are documented and fed back to the scheme sponsors.
- Have overall objectives including financial been met and delivered?
- Brief the Board and Executive as appropriate.
- Check relevant KPIs for an appropriate post-implementation period.

Change management

Tips

Change must be carefully managed to avoid distraction and disruption to the core operation. However, change management is increasingly part of the day job.

The knack is to embrace change and relish the opportunities it provides whilst ensuring that damaging changes are not made.

You must be honest and up front, and be prepared to confront difficult issues, even when they may be outside your control or for which you do not have an answer. You will be greatly respected for doing so.

Remember if you see change as a threat it will be.

If you see it as an opportunity, it is very likely to be.

Other relevant/useful documents:
Changing Trains. V Stewart and V Chadwick. David and Charles 1987.

9.3 Managing a Small Project

BACKGROUND

Managing a small project is now a core competency for all managers. The scope of small project management covers both external projects for customers and internal projects including organisation and process change. The fundamental guide to successfully delivering a project is to ensure each project you undertake fits with the business strategy. There will often be many projects jostling for scarce resources including finance and people.

Details of the issues involved in Managing Major Project Issues are contained in a section 9.4.

9.3 Managing a Small Project

ISSUES

Use a consistent staged approach to manage projects:-

Action Checklist
- Proposal.
- Identify the idea or need. What needs to be achieved, what is the expected outcome, what needs to be delivered and how will you measure success?
- Appoint the project manager.
- This individual should have a proven record with the required technical and general management skills, be a good communicator, a good motivator and effective in controlling costs.
- Initial investigation.
- Develop a brief overview of the possible requirements and solutions, develop the terms of reference and an initial scale of resources required.
- Detailed investigation.
- Undertake a feasibility study of the options and define the chosen solution. Construct a Work Breakdown Structure Document (WBSD) and break the project down into defined phases for budgeting and monitoring purposes.
- Develop a quality plan. Develop a cost plan. Develop a time plan. Make sure you understand the dependencies between different parts of the project.
- Develop the chosen solution.
- Build the solution and test with scenarios.
- Implementation and closure.
- Put the project into practice and close the project management phase. Review the output to check if outcome has been delivered.

Place sufficient emphasis on the first four bullets above as research has proved that a sound investment in these areas reduces the overall implementation time, risks and cost of the project. Further de-risk the project through the testing stage. Engage stakeholders in the project actively to ensure it delivers what is expected.

Projects are not just about introducing new technology; they normally include culture and process changes – all of which require significant engagement from stakeholders. In formal structured organisations project teams must be capable of working in teams across functional boundaries to deliver the maximum potential of the project.

Ensure a detailed plan is developed to deliver the project and monitor progress against this plan. Identify risks to successful delivery of the project and develop mitigations for these. When monitoring a project, look at what remains to be delivered not just what has been completed to date.

Change management

Tips

Successful projects usually have a strong leader and a very clear set of objectives.

It is relatively easy to analyse why particular projects have gone well, therefore it is staggering how rarely sound project delivery techniques are properly employed.

If you are involved in delivering a small project put plenty of effort into the planning stage. Do not be tempted to move into Action mode too quickly.

9.4 Managing the Interface with Major Projects

BACKGROUND

Major projects are critical to the railway's future business objectives and it is imperative that operators ensure that any revised or new scheme is fit for purpose. The scale and cost of major projects means that operators need to be involved early on in projects that affect the infrastructure or the operation of the railway. Such involvement must be from the design stage through to final delivery, so that when a major project is completed the infrastructure left behind supports delivery of end customer requirements.

It is imperative that design, reviews and final sign off involve all parties. It is critical that the requirements of the end user are met.

Modern standards have developed over time and for good reason. The requirement to apply current standards in major project works sometimes means that the way a layout or location operates today cannot be continued in the future. It is therefore critical that during the project design stage we make sure that we will be able to retain current operational requirements as well as delivering any additional scope that a major project is remitted to provide.

If there are problems with delivering a railway that will support current operational requirements then this must be resolved to the satisfaction of all involved before the scheme is signed off.

It will also be necessary to identify and resolve any future proofing and spare capacity requirements well in advance.

9.4 Managing the Interface with Major Projects

It is vital that operators ensure they have the best scheme attainable and pay attention to how the scheme will be delivered, for example, blockades, restricted access, modified working etc. whilst maintaining an acceptable level of service to end customers. All of these issues will obviously influence the costs of any scheme and in some cases may be significant cost drivers.

There is often a view that we should gold plate the end product of a major project whether it is a new track layout, a station redesign or a resignalling scheme. But there is a fine line between a scheme that is fit for purpose and offers some additional benefits, and designing a scheme that the rail industry cannot afford.

APPROACH TO PROJECT MANAGEMENT

We all have to ensure we attain the best value for money a major project can achieve, but it is essential that all affected operators clearly understand what a scheme allows operationally.

Any issues that arise after a major scheme has been commissioned will generally result in significant additional time and costs to deliver and there is always a risk that high rework costs will make subsequent change prohibitively expensive. In such situations operators could be left to work with a sub-optimal layout.

Most organisations will use a formal process for project management; for example Network Rail uses GRIP (Guide to Railway Investment Projects). This approach is based on best practice within industries that undertake major infrastructure projects and practice recommended by the major professional bodies including the Office of Government Commerce (OGC), the Association of Project Management (APM) and the Chartered Institute of Building (CIOB).

Change management

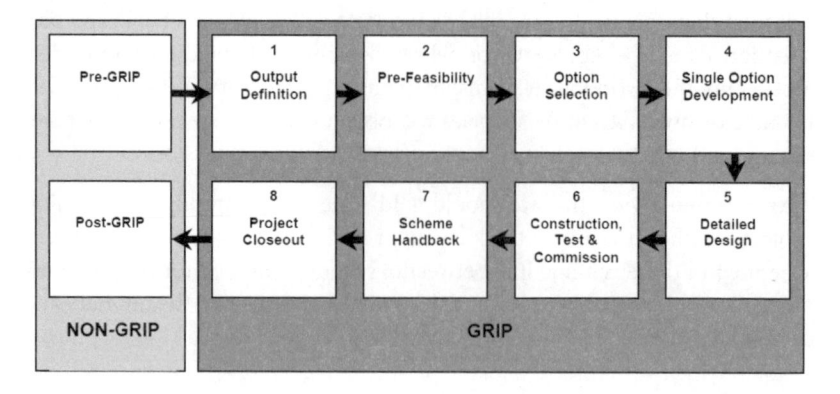

```
Pre-GRIP → 1 Output Definition → 2 Pre-Feasibility → 3 Option Selection → 4 Single Option Development
Post-GRIP ← 8 Project Closeout ← 7 Scheme Handback ← 6 Construction, Test & Commission ← 5 Detailed Design
NON-GRIP | GRIP
```

GRIP is designed to minimise and mitigate the risks associated with delivering projects that enhance or renew the operational railway and consists of eight stages.

Key issues for Operators at each stage are:

Stage 1-3

These stages are about identifying a range of options to deliver the output required by the customer of the project. It is important to have a clear idea of the limitations of the current infrastructure and what Operators would want from a replacement or enhancement. These issues may have been identified over a long period as a result of, for example, performance investigations or timetable aspirations that cannot be delivered with the existing infrastructure. The challenge is to ensure that these issues are clearly communicated at an early stage of the project and understood by the project team.

The things line operators want may be outside of the scope for the project but sometimes such items can be delivered for no extra cost or the cost of delivering as part of a larger scheme may be substantially reduced. The earlier your suggestions are made, the more likely they are to be delivered but there is no guarantee.

Stage 4-5

For operators the next key point is moving from GRIP 3 to GRIP 4 when a single option is selected and then developed for delivery. Operators will need to get closely involved prior to GRIP 4 because after this stage it becomes very difficult to consider any change to the scope of the project. You will need to be careful about what you sign off at this stage because you may be fixing something that cannot be changed afterwards. Project teams are generally keen to involve operators (and if they are not – take the initiative) and will need your sign off on various documents and processes. It is vital that you understand very clearly how your objectives and theirs are at odds and where they align so that you can maximise the benefit to all parties. Involve your teams – Signallers, Drivers, Station staff etc. Front line staff work with infrastructure and systems day-in, day-out so they will have good insight into what will work best.

There will also need to be involvement at this stage to agree the most appropriate operational strategy for delivering the scheme including possession strategy, replacement services and compensation.

Stage 6, 7 and 8

Inevitably during delivery of a major project the infrastructure will have to be handed over to the delivery team to some extent. This can mean the asset is completely unavailable in which case the issue will be managing with the remaining infrastructure. Where the project is delivered while normal operation continues you will need to maintain good performance and safety around the delivery of the project. Maintaining good performance despite the distractions of major project delivery is notoriously challenging.

In all cases operators must be fully involved in the planning for delivery. Staged works need to be tested so that you fully understand what is available on completion of every stage and the risks associated with any reduced availability between stages. Possession plans should be fully scrutinised. There must be robust contingency plans to mitigate possession overruns and difficulties with the new infrastructure which must be jointly prepared between operations teams and project delivery staff.

Finally make sure that snagging items are correctly closed out and that there is a process for dealing with emerging issues with the new infrastructure.

ITEMS TO CONSIDER

- Understand what the project is and what it is aiming to deliver in scope terms. Is it a train fleet introduction, line speed increase, life expired renewals, like for like renewals, enhancements, etc or a combination?
- Does the project cater for today's and tomorrow's planned railway?
- Ensure you understand how the proposed changes will affect the way in which the railway is operated. The new infrastructure may not allow the same methods of working.
- What spare capacity does a scheme offer?
- How will you liaise with the project, for example, will there be a project interface role? If there is who does that role report to?
- Work closely with the project sponsor and project manager so that you build a good working relationship with them and they understand who the key operations representatives are.

Change management

- As early as possible get an operations requirement specification written and agreed. This is a project deliverable and will aid the project and the contractor in understanding exactly what you require.
- Operators need to be involved in projects as early as possible. The earlier you are involved the less chance there is of a scheme being designed that is not acceptable to you when you see it first. This will avoid, at best costly re-design or re-work or at worst having to accept a sub-optimum end product.
- Think about any other projects that may be impacted by or impact on the project you are involved with. Make sure early discussions take place with those parties as soon as is feasible.
- Ensure you involve the end users, for example, signallers and drivers. Whilst many of us who work with projects understand operations we do not operate it every day.
- What is the delivery mechanism for the project and what are its effects on blockade, stages, etc?
- Think about how you would operate the infrastructure under perturbation. This is not about gold plating a project but an early chance to understand the risks such a project brings with it and what it means to the operational railway when the project completes.
- What are the junction controls for signals, for example, flashing aspects and free yellows? You may not understand these terms, make sure you do if a project team starts using them, especially the operational implications.
- Are signalling release points at their optimum?
- What training do operations staff such as signallers, MOMs, and drivers require?
- What are the costs for operators over and above normal business as the project will need to cover these, for example, release of signallers and drivers for training?
- Have all the maintenance and inspection aspects of the scheme been considered and does that fit with the access available?
- Check carefully where ground equipment such as TPWS loops, AWS, etc are being placed in platforms where trains terminate or turn-back. Also consider these where stations have permissive working or attaching and detaching.
- Where speed increases are considered ensure the performance of rolling stock is considered. Many layouts can be designed to optimum speed albeit the trains cannot achieve it for various reasons. Also watch the amount of speed signs being put up in order not to over complicate a layout. Speed zones may be an option.
- Ensure operators have a suitable person on signal and sign sighting committees.

9.4 Managing the Interface with Major Projects

- Scheme plan reviews, prior to sign off, are better done as a group so that all ideas and information are discussed. What is good for you may not be suitable to another party.
- During scheme plan reviews ensure that other documentation such as aspect sequence charts, TPWS effectiveness and control table requirements are considered and reviewed.
- Controls should balance safety, cost and performance requirements, for example, if a junction layout has 'double red' controls ensure you understand whether they are un-conditional (sometimes referred to as 'Hard double reds') or if conditional, what the conditions are so that you protect headways and junction margins.
- Understand what headways and junction margins the scheme is being designed to. Make sure you understand where requirements are not achievable and what their effects are. If using the current values, are these actually achievable in practice.
- Where protection systems such as lockouts are provided, do not over complicate them and make sure maintenance people are involved in the agreement of the areas. Do not make the lockout areas too small, in order to have the optimum choices for use, as this will run the risk there are too many to use and they are not utilised as they should be.
- Despite time pressures, make sure you thoroughly review and understand documents and plans. Once a scheme is designed it is very difficult to go back and fix any omissions or errors.
- Make sure you understand any temporary non compliances and derogations that are being sought for a project. Can you support them?
- Where a project affects operations resources such as additional staff or a reduction in staff, ensure you understand what they are, that they are correct and that you have brought into the detail.
- Is a simulator required or an upgrade of an existing simulator required? Is it being delivered, with the right data in sufficient time to complete the required training?
- Ensure any simulator agreements take account of adding or amending timetable detail into any new or upgraded simulator.

Change management

Tips

Many project operations interface roles work directly for a project. It is therefore vital that all affected line and route operators understand and sign-off all aspects of a project.

The earlier line operators become involved the better the outcome will be for all concerned.

During and after a project the operator will be responsible for meeting customer requirements. Make sure projects deliver fit for purpose outcomes.

Remember – unplanned disruption during projects can be avoided by proper planning and control.

Abbreviations index

A&U return	Availability and Utilisation Return	92
ABCL	Automatic Barrier Crossing Locally Monitored	218
AC	Alternative Current	225-230
ACOP	Approved Code of Practicable	340
AFAIRP	As Far as is Reasonably Practical	53
AHB	Automatic Half Barriers	218
ALARP	As Low as Reasonably Practical	292, 293
AOCL/R	Automatic Open Crossing, Local and Remote	219
APM	Association of Project Management	429
APT	Advanced Passenger Train	201
ARM	Asset Recovery Managers	163
ARS	Automatic Route Setting	254
ASLE&F	Associated Society of Locomotive Engineers and Firemen	272
ATOC	Association of Train Operating Companies	8, 156
AWS	Automatic Warning System	243, 432
BR	British Rail	3, 132
BTET	Blocked to Electric Trains/Traction	229
BTP	British Transport Police	8, 283, 296, 379
CaSL	Cancellation and Significant Lateness	107, 254
CCIL	Control Centre Incident Log	175
CCF	Control Centre of the Future	172
CD	Close Doors	286
CDP	Competence Development Programme	267
Christmas Trees	Trains cannibalised for spares	176
CIOB	Chartered Institute of Building	429
CIS	Customer Information System	281
CL	Class (of train)	142, 197, 264
CON	Container	134
COT	Condition of Track	211, 212
CPPP	Confirmed Period Possession Plan	66
CRT	Critical Rail Temperature	373
CSL2	Customer Service Level 2	148, 349-352
CSR	Cab Secure Radio	246, 377

Abbreviations index

D(x)	From Access Condition Part D of the Network Code. Refers to trains or changes to train times to be in timetables (x) weeks before the timetable change date.	60
DAG	Delay Attribution Guide.	178
DCD	Driver's Competence Development	267
DAS	Driver Advisory Systems	291
DC	Direct Current	225-230
DfT	Department for Transport	3, 57
DMU	Diesel Multiple Unit	6
DNOs	Distribution Network Operators	230
DOO	Driver Only Operation	246
DPTAC	Disabled Persons Transport Advisory Committee	224
DRA	Driver's Reminder Appliance	268
DSD	Driver Safety Device	265
DVT	Driving Van Trailer	199
EAS	Engineering Access Statement	63
ECR	Electrical Control Room	147, 185, 225
ECRO	Electrical Control Room Operator	225
EMU	Electric Multiple Unit	198
EPS	Enhanced Permissible Speed	201
ESR	Emergency Speed Restriction	210
ETS	Electric Train Supply	200
EWS	English, Welsh and Scottish Railway	134
FMS	Fault Management System	163
FOC	Freight Operating Company	3
FP	Footpath or Bridleway	221
GCC	Gauge Corner Cracking	210
GRIP	Guide to Railway Investment Projects	429
GSM-R	Global System for Mobile communications - Railways	247
HAW	Heavy Axle Weight	138
HSE	Health and Safety Executive	154
HST	High Speed Train	6
HVV	High Visibility Vest	275
IECCs	Integrated Electronic Control Centres	244
IFC	Infrastructure Fault Control office	168
IRO	Institution of Railway Operators	192
ITPS	Integrated Timetable Planning System	72, 338

JPIP	Joint Performance Improvement Plan	14
JPR	Joint Performance Review	14
KPI	Key Performance Indicator	259, 394
LC	Level Crossing	215, 411
LOM	Local Operations Manager	184, 186
LOROL	London Overground Rail Operations Ltd.	186
LTP	Long Term Planning	264
MAA	Moving Annual Average	174
MAC	Minimum Action Code	367
MCB	Manually Controlled Barriers	216
MCG	Manually Controlled Gates	215
MOM	Mobile Operations Manager	163
MTIN	Miles per Technical Incident	364
MTU	Motoren-und-Turbinen-Union a German diesel manufacturer	199
MWL	Miniature Warning Lights	219
NCN	Network Change Notice	67
NMT	New Measurement Train	368
NPS	National Passenger Survey	130, 157
NR	Network Rail	4
NRE	National Rail Enquiries	9, 157
NRN	National Radio Network	246, 377
NRCC	National Rail Communication Centre	9
OC	Open Crossing	219
OEO	One Engine Only	199
OGC	Office of Government Commerce	429
OHLE	Overhead Line Equipment	11
OLE	Overhead Line Equipment	150, 225-230
OM	Operations Manager	184, 186
ORR	Office of Rail Regulation	3, 158
OTDR	On-train Data Recording	79
OTMR	On-train Monitoring and Recording	178

Abbreviations index

P2	A system for tracking train services	172
PA	Public Address	171
PDCA	Plan-Do-Check-Act	393
PDR	Plan-Do-Review	393
PIC	Person in Charge	356
PIDD	Passenger Information During Disruption	161, 345
PIM	Precursor Indicator Model	221
PIO	Police Incident Officer	379, 380
PMIP	Performance Management and Improvement Plans	159
PNB	Personal Needs Break	263
POD	Professional Operators Development	22
POE	Point Operating Equipment	242
PON	Periodical Operating Notice	250
PPE	Personal Protection Equipment	412
PPM	Public Performance Measure	107, 394
PSP	Problem Solving Process	393
PSR	Permanent Speed Restriction	57, 369, 383
PT&R	Promotion, Transfer and Redundancy	89
PTE	Passenger Transport Executives	7
PTERTS	Production Telegram Error Rate Test Set	245
P Way	The Permanent Way	208
QIP	Quality Improvement Process	393
Q path	Pre-secured paths suitable for very short-term freight routes	73
RA	Route Availability	137
RA	Right Away	286
RAIB	Rail Accident Investigation Branch	3, 409
RCF	Rolling Contact Fatigue	210
RCM	Route Control Manager (NR)	342
RIO	Rail Incident Officer	343, 380
RMDs	Route Managing Directors	17
ROGs	Railways and Other Guided Transport Systems (Safety) Regulations	15
ROSCO	Rolling Stock Leasing Company	3
ROTD	Rules of the Depot	190
ROTR	Rules of the Route	210
RSSB	Rail Safety and Standards Board	8, 221
RDW	Rest Day Working	96
RUS	Route Utilisation Strategies	77

S&C	Switches and Crossings	208
SIMBIDS	Simplified Bi-Directional Signalling	356
SINCS	Signalling Incident System	239
SIO	Station Incident Officer	184
SLC	Service Level Commitment	57, 71
SLU	Standard Length Units	140
SLW	Single Line Working	12, 354-358
SMS	Safety Management System	274
SPAD	Signal Passed at Danger	30, 302, 395
SPIR	Serious Performance Incident Review	351
SRCT	Service Recovery Commencement Time	342
SRTs	Sectional Running Times	232
SSM	Shift Signalling Manager	185
STP	Short Term Planning	58, 142
SWT	South West Trains	70
T(x)	See TT(x)	
TASS	Tilt and Speed Supervision System	201
TBW	Temporary Block Working	243, 354-360, 376
TCRAG	Timetable Change Risk Assessment Group	69
TDA	Train Delay Attribution	175
TDI	Trust Delay Incident	344
TDM	Time Division Multiplexer	200
TfL	Transport for London	14
TGVs	Train à Grande Vitesse, meaning high-speed train	226
TIC	Track Inspection Coach	368
TIN	Trust Incident Number	343
TIS	Train Information System	265
tph	trains per hour	75
TOC	Train Operating Company	3, 4
TOLO	Train Operations Liaison Officer	184, 380
TOMSC	Train Operations Management Standards Committee	422
TOPS	Total Operations Processing/Planning System	139
TPWS	Train Protection and Warning System	302
TRANSEC	The Department for Transport Security Directorate	295
TRB	Train Register Book	253
TRC	Track Recording Coach	368
TRTS	Train Ready to Start	286
TRU	Track Recording Unit	205, 368
TRUST	Train Running System TOPS	170
TRV	Track Recording Vehicle	368
TS	Transport Scotland	4

Abbreviations index

TSDB	Train Service Data Base	72, 170, 343
TSRs	Temporary Speed Restrictions	67, 81
TT(x)	Timetable. Refers to trains or changes to train times to be in timetables (x) weeks before they are due to run	60
UB	Underbridge	138
UIC	International Union of Railway Organisations	77
UTU	Ultrasonic Test Units	366
UWC	User Worked Crossing	220
VDU	Visual Display Unit	377
VPF	Value of Preventing a Fatality	53
VSTP	Very Short Term Planning	73, 170
WON	Weekly Operating Notices	161
WBSD	Work Breakdown Structure Document	427
WCML	West Coast Main Line	421
WSF	Wrong Side Failures	238
WTT	Working Time Table	61, 72, 250

Index

Abbreviations	435
About this Handbook	ix
Acknowledgements	viii
Attributes and Behaviours	19
Audits and Auditing	401
Cab Rides	274
Cable Theft	309
Capacity and Reliability	74
Change Management	422
Competence	21
Contingency Plans	110
Control Office; Issues and Management	165
Decision Making and Escalation	43
Delay Attribution	177
Delegation	47
Disruption Management	321
Electrification Systems	225
Empowerment	50
Energy Management on Heavy Rail	289
Engineering Allowances	81
Engineering Work Planning Management	114
Estimates for Resuming Normal Working	332
Failed Trains	363
Fatalities	379
Fleet and Operations Interface	189
Freight Perspective	134
How to use this Book	x
Identifying and Adopting Good Practice	392
Improvement Tools & Techniques	396
Incident and Accident Investigation	409
Industry Abbreviations	435
Infrastructure and Operations Interface	204
Leadership	30
Level Crossing Characteristics	215

Index

Logs – Using Control and other Logs. 174
Major Incident and Accident Management 352
Major Signalling Failures. 376
Major Track and Civil Engineering Issues - including Bridge Strikes. . 366
Management by Walking About. 40
Managing a Small Project 426
Managing and Motivating a Team 37
Managing the Interface with Major Projects. 428
Meetings Management. 397
Message from David Franks, IRO. vii
Operating Standards Management 420
Operational Irregularities 383
Organisational Design and Capability 84
Out of Hours Visits. 147
Ownership of Delivery. 35
Passenger Information 156
Passenger Information During Disruption (PIDD). 345
Passenger Perspective 130
Performance Management Real Time 148
Performance Planning with Industry Partners 107
Personal Presentation and Values. 25
Plan-Do-Review and Continuous Improvement 393
Possession Overruns 361
Prioritised Planning 323
Processes 407
Professional Judgement 51
Railway Geography and Infrastructure Configuration 11
Railway Industry Structure 3
Remits and Terms of Reference 400
Resource Planning 87
Restricted Track Access 337
Risk Management. 292
Role of First Line Operations Staff 183
Role of the Operator 2, 146
Root Cause Determination 414
Safe Performance. 29

Safety Management	152
Seasonal Planning and Reviewing	120
Security Issues	295
Service Recovery	339
Signal Engineering Issues	237
Signalbox Visits	261
Signaller Conditions and Rosters	104
Signaller Management	257
Signalling Operations	248
Signals Passed At Danger	302
Simplifiers	182
Station Operations	279
Targets & KPIs	394
Temporary Speed Restrictions and Emergency Speed Restrictions	212
Time Management	26
Timetable Development and Validation	69
Timetable Planning Rules, Engineering Access and Network Change	63
Timetables - Working and Public	72
TOC/FOC and Network Rail Interface	13
TOC Short Term Planning	276
Track Issues	208
Train Characteristics	195
Train Connectional Policies	126
Train Crew Links and Rosters	91
Train Crew Management	271
Train Despatch	285
Train Driving Operations	263
Train Planning	56
Train Regulation	254
Train Service Delivery Systems & Processes – Overview	159
Track Issues	208
Trespass, Vandalism and Disorder	299
Winning	36
Working in Degraded Mode - including Single Line Working/ Pilot Working/Temporary Block Working	354

All to join for...

» Membership
» Area events
» Academic qualifications
» Professional Development
» CPD schemes

www.railwayoperators.co.uk

The Institution of Railway Operators